The Yale Edition of the Complete Works of St. Thomas More

VOLUME 3

PART I

TRANSLATIONS OF LUCIAN

Published by the St. Thomas More Project, Yale University,
under the auspices of Gerard L. Carroll and Joseph B. Murray,
Trustees of the Michael P. Grace, II, Trust

Luciani viri q̃ disertissimi cõpluria opuscula longe festiuissima ab Erasmo Roterodamo & Thoma moro interpretibus optimis in latinorum linguam traducta.hac sequentur serie.

Ex Erasmi interpretatione

Toxaris siue de amicicia Luciani dialogus.
Alexander qui & Pseudomantis eiusdem.
Gallus siue Somnium eiusdem quoq; luciani
Timon seu Misanthropus.
Tyrannicida seu pro tyrannicida eiusdem declamatio.
Cum declamatione Erasmica eidem respondente.
De iis qui mercede conducti degunt dialogus eiusdem.
Et quædam eiusdem alia

Ex Mori traductione.

Tyrannicida Luciani Moro interprete.
Declamatio Mori de eodem.
Cynicus Luciani a Moro versus
Menippus seu Necromantia Luciani eodem interprete.
Philopseudes seu incredulus Luciani ab eodẽ Moro in latinã linguã traductus:

Ex ædibus Ascensianis.

Title page of first edition, 1506, Paris, Josse Badius Ascensius (reduced)

The Complete Works of
ST. THOMAS MORE

VOLUME 3

Part I

Edited by

CRAIG R. THOMPSON

Yale University Press, New Haven and London, 1974

Library of Congress catalog card number: 63–7949
International standard book number: 0–300–01472–4

Designed by Crimilda Pontes
and set in Baskerville type.
Printed in the United States of America by
The Murray Printing Company, Forge Village, Massachusetts.

Published in Great Britain, Europe, and Africa by
Yale University Press, Ltd., London.
Distributed in Latin America by Kaiman & Polon,
Inc., New York City; in Australasia and Southeast
Asia by John Wiley & Sons Australasia Pty. Ltd.,
Sydney; in India by UBS Publishers' Distributors Pvt.,
Ltd., Delhi; in Japan by John Weatherhill, Inc., Tokyo.

To

Isabella McMaster Thompson

PREFACE

IN HIS DEDICATORY LETTER to Thomas Ruthall, More describes these Latin versions of Lucian as the "first fruits" of his Greek studies. His fondness for Greek literature and his consistent concerns as a moralist attracted him to this ancient writer, whose dialogues and declamations he and Erasmus enjoyed translating in 1505–1506. The translations were long admired in the sixteenth century, not without reason; but, except in a photofacsimile edition of his Latin works published in 1963, More's versions have not been reissued since 1689, nor have they ever been edited for the use of biographers, historians, or other students of More's career as a scholarly man of letters, a humanist. It seems appropriate, therefore, that the text of these translations, accompanied by materials for their study, be provided in the Yale Edition.

Readers who may want to consult English translations of Lucian will find in an appendix the Loeb Classical Library versions by A. M. Harmon and M. D. Macleod. The publishers of the Loeb series have kindly allowed these to be reprinted. Anyone interested in the details of More's work as a translator, however, should compare his Latin version with its probable source, the Aldine edition (1503) of Lucian, reproduced photographically in this volume, for there are many (though usually minor) differences between the Aldine text and that of modern editions. The translations of More's letter to Ruthall and his declamation replying to Lucian's *Tyrannicida* are my own.

For photographs of the fine copy of the 1503 Lucian and permission to include them here I must thank the Pierpont Morgan Library. For other photographs and permission to use them, or for photographs and microfilms of editions consulted, I am grateful to the Houghton Library of Harvard University, Yale University Library, Huntington Library, Folger Shakespeare Library, Universitätsbibliothek of Basel, British Museum, and Bodleian Library. I wish to thank for their valued assistance Louis B. Wright, Carey S. Bliss, Curt F. Bühler, Chr. Vischer, Philip A. Knachel, Lloyd W. Daly, and the Guggenheim Memorial Foundation. I am under special

obligation to Professor James Hutton of Cornell University for his patient scrutiny—*castigatio* would be the sixteenth-century term—of an earlier version of this work. As More writes in the conclusion to his letter to Ruthall, "Etsi tam acre tibi iudicium sit, ut quicquid erratum fuerit, nemo penetrantius uideat: is tamen est ingenii tui candor, ut nemo libentius conniueat."

To Professor Richard S. Sylvester, Executive Editor of the Yale Edition, I am indebted not only for valuable advice but for exemplary patience. Thanks are due also to Elizabeth Coffin and Patrick O'Connell for their vigilance in checking typescripts and proofs.

More's name is now in the liturgical calendar of the Church. Although he was not canonized by reason of his scholarship, those whose business is with sixteenth-century texts may hope at any rate that he has supernal patience with their editorial sins, whether of omission or commission.

C. R. T.

University of Pennsylvania
January 1971

CONTENTS

ILLUSTRATIONS

INTRODUCTION

INTRODUCTION

"... et Luciano cum primis est delectatus"

i

OUR ASSUMPTION that Greek literature will be accessible in translation is itself a legacy from Renaissance scholarship. Shakespeare may have had what seemed to Jonson small Latin and less Greek, but in our own time (characterized lately as one of "less Latin and no Greek") it is worth recalling that in the fifteenth and early sixteenth centuries Greek had little effect until Latinized. "While for two or three generations," as E. P. Goldschmidt remarked, "the Greek texts continued to be the close preserve of a restricted circle of linguists, as they are again now, the Latin translations of the Renaissance carried the decisive impact of Hellenic literature to Europe." [1]

Translations of many Greek authors, Lucian among them, could not be made earlier than the fifteenth century, because the manuscripts were not available to the West. During the fifteenth century this situation changed so drastically that manuscripts of many texts, then Latin translations, and finally printed texts and translations of previously unfamiliar ancient authors became the common possession of scholars and men of letters, first in Italy and gradually in other lands as well. To the humanists, this new wealth and the manifold uses made of it were what the "Renaissance," in the older and restricted sense of that term, was about: the recovery, dissemination, study, and cultural consequences of a large body of ancient writings hitherto largely unknown at first hand or little understood.[2] Important writings discovered or recovered included Latin as well as

[1] "Lucian's *Calumnia*," in *Fritz Saxl*, ed D. J. Gordon (London, 1957), p. 229; cited hereafter as "Lucian's *Calumnia*." Full titles of all works cited in this Introduction will be found in the Bibliography, below, pp. 131 f.

[2] Both as a concept and as a phrase descriptive of an epoch, "the Renaissance" signifies far more than advances in scholarship and literature; but in considering sixteenth-century translations of ancient authors it is useful to remind ourselves of the earlier and narrower

Greek texts, to be sure, but since the Greek language and literature were more novel to Western Europe, they were likely to be the more exciting.

Of Greek writers introduced in their own tongue to Italy in the fifteenth century, Lucian of Samosata (ca. 125–90) may not have been the most popular, but by the end of that period he had become something of a favorite, attracting for many good reasons an impressive number of translators and imitators. Undoubtedly assertions of this same kind could be made about the Renaissance reputations of other Greeks; above all of Plato, who contributed more to *Utopia*, and is mentioned more frequently in the text, than any other author ancient or modern. In stature and influence Plato and Plutarch may stand highest in the sixteenth century, but Lucian had a vogue, especially in the first half of the century, when More's and Erasmus' Latin translations helped to make his writings known to a wider audience. If we admire such brilliant Lucianic creations as Erasmus' *Moriae encomium* and *Iulius exclusus*, ponder the probable though less obvious contributions of Lucian to More's *Utopia*, and appreciate the extent of Rabelais' indebtedness to Lucian, we may fairly conclude that this Greek (by language, not by birth) deserves the attention he has received from students of sixteenth-century humanism.

A large part of Lucian's appeal must have been due to the sheer variety of his eighty-two compositions,[1] which embrace dramatic dialogues, rhetorical discourses of different kinds, literary and social criticism, satire, fiction—in *Icaromenippus* and *Vera historia* he wrote the first accounts of voyages to the moon, a type of story we are well acquainted with today—and moral philosophy of an informal but lively sort. One recent treatise on Lucian requires nearly 800 pages to discuss this gifted, prolific writer.[2] He was a professional rhetorician

meaning of "Renaissance" as this term was used by classical scholars and literary historians. Cf. Wallace K. Ferguson, *The Renaissance in Historical Thought* (Boston, 1948).

[1] The authenticity of at least a dozen of them is questioned, however.

[2] J. Bompaire, *Lucien écrivain* (Paris, 1958). This is the most comprehensive analysis of Lucian's literary theory and art. For biography see Jacques Schwartz, *Biographie de Lucien de Samosate* (Brussels, 1965). Of older studies see M. Croiset, *Essai sur la vie et les oeuvres de Lucien* (Paris, 1882); M. Caster, *Lucien et la pensée religieuse de son temps* (Paris, 1937). Francis G. Allinson, *Lucian Satirist and Artist* (New York, 1927) is a brief account for the general reader. Loeb and Teubner are standard editions. The most complete translation is that which accompanies the Loeb text, eight volumes, by A. M. Harmon, K. Kilburn, and M. D. Macleod (London and Cambridge, Mass., 1913–67); cited hereafter as "Loeb Lucian." Very readable, but not complete, is the version by H. W. and F. G.

who as "ghost writer" wrote speeches for clients to use in court and as a performer traveled about through Greece, Italy, and other Mediterranean regions giving public exhibitions of his skill. *Tyrannicida*, which More translated, is a specimen of his rhetorical pieces, and twenty-five others survive.[1] They include panegyrics, witty essays on linguistic usage or stylistic nuances (no wonder the Fowlers were attracted to Lucian), and "introductory remarks" to lectures. He wrote a dozen essays and dialogues on philosophical, social, and moral topics. Although these have the satirical tone and dexterous irony characteristic of his non-rhetorical works, they are at the same time serious critiques of social, artistic, and literary subjects: e.g. *Lexiphanes*, *Hesiod*, and *Quomodo historia conscribenda sit*. *Adversus indoctum* describes an uneducated book-collector, *De iis qui mercede conducti degunt* a dependent scholar in a boorish Roman household. *Hermotimus*, *Nigrinus*, and *Demonax* contrast sincere philosophers with pretentious and hypocritical ones. *Toxaris* is a dialogue on friendship, *De calumnia* an essay on slander, *Anacharsis* a dialogue on athletics, *De saltatione* an essay on the dance. Another set of writings, including *Alexander*, *Mors Peregrini*, *Rhetor*, and *Parasitus* exposes various types of charlatans.

In mid-career, as he explains entertainingly, though possibly with exaggerations, in *Bis accusatus*, Lucian abandoned rhetoric for dialogue. Not only that, but he has been credited with inventing a new literary genre by combining prose dialogue with comedy. The result—light, brief prose conversation, satirical in tone—proved an excellent medium for ironical and critical expression and for his dramatic gifts.

> Dialogue and comedy were not entirely friendly and compatible from the beginning. Dialogue used to sit at home by himself and indeed spend his time in the public walks with a few companions; Comedy gave herself to Dionysus and joined him in the theatre, had fun with him, jested and joked, some-

---

Fowler, *The Works of Lucian of Samosata*, four volumes (Oxford, 1905); cited hereafter as "Fowler Lucian." There is a good translation of representative pieces by Paul Turner (London, 1961).

[1] *Imagines*, *Pro imaginibus*, *Demosthenis encomium*, *Muscae encomium*, *Domus*, *Harmonides*, *Hercules*, *Herodotus*, *Prometheus es in verbis*, *Patriae encomium*, *Scytha*, *Pro lapsu inter salutandum*, *De electro*, *Somnium*, *Iudicium vocalium*, *Dionysus*, *Dipsas*, *Abdicatus*, *Zeuxis*, *Phalaris* I and II, *Hippias*, *Longaevi*, *Halcyon*, *Nero*.

> times stepping in time to the pipe and generally riding on anapaests. Dialogue's companions she mocked as "Heavy-thinkers," "High-talkers," and suchlike. She had one delight—to deride them and drown them in Dionysiac liberties. She showed them now walking on air and mixing with the clouds, now measuring sandals for fleas[1]—her notion of heavenly subtleties, I suppose! Dialogue however took his conversations very seriously, philosophising about nature and virtue. So, in musical terms, there were two octaves between them, from highest to lowest. Nevertheless I have dared to combine them as they are into a harmony, though they are not in the least docile and do not easily tolerate partnership.[2]

His dialogues are of several kinds. Some deal with aspects of everyday life; examples are the conversations of courtesans, *Dialogi meretricii*; or *Philopseudes*, which More translated. Then there is a group of so-called Menippean ones, though the nature and amount of Lucian's debt to Menippean example is disputed.[3] Some of Lucian's best writing belongs to this group: his *Dialogi mortuorum*, *Dialogi deorum*, *Dialogi marini*, *Menippus* (translated by More), *Icaromenippus*, *Iupiter confutatus*, *Cynicus* (translated by More), and *Saturnalia*. Many of these satirize religion or philosophy. A third group, likewise satirical, includes *Cataplus*, a journey to Hades; *Charon*, *Timon*, *Gallus*, *Vitarum auctio*, *Prometheus sive Caucasus*, *Iupiter tragoedus*, *Concilium deorum*, *Navigium*, *Mors Peregrini*, *Fugitivi*, *Bis accusatus*, and *Piscator*.

These categories comprise at least half the works in Lucian's repertoire. Even this listing should suggest his resourcefulness. He is inventive, amusing, trenchant but not profound, ironical but occasionally penetrating, consistently skeptical, tough-minded, "a hard bright intelligence, with no bowels,"[4] a combination not unusual in lexical purists and literary critics. When asked by Philosophy about his calling, he replies: "I am a Syrian, Philosophy, from the banks of the Euphrates. . . . I am a bluff-hater, cheat-hater, liar-hater, vanity-hater, and hate all that sort of scoundrels, who are very

---

[1] In the *Clouds* of Aristophanes, 144–52.

[2] Loeb Lucian, *6*, 425–27.

[3] Barbara P. McCarthy, "Lucian and Menippus," *Yale Classical Studies, 4* (1934), 1–55; Bompaire, *Lucien écrivain*.

[4] Fowler Lucian, *1*, xxix.

numerous, as you know."[1] He is impatient with the delusions and frauds of vulgar religion; as one of his seventeenth-century translators, Ferrand Spence, says, he endeavored to "drive and whoop idolatry out of the world" and to show "all the gods and goddesses to be no better than a company of gypsies."[2]

Lucian first became known to Western readers in the first quarter of the fifteenth century; Guarino da Verona and Giovanni Aurispa were the first, or among the first, to bring manuscripts of his writings from Constantinople to Italy.[3] In the next generation translations circulated, and after 1470 or thereabouts printed versions of Lucian in Latin became available. A volume containing Latin translations of five of his dialogues (and *Palinurus*, a fifteenth-century composition, imitating Lucian, written by Maffeo Vegio) was printed in Rome by G. Lauer, ca. 1470, though Lauer may have issued two dialogues by Lucian in Latin translation even earlier.[4] Twenty-one distinct editions of thirteen different dialogues of Lucian, in Latin and issued earlier than 1500, are reported,[5] and there may have been more. The most popular writings were *Charon*, *Vitarum auctio*, *Vera historia*, and two of the *Dialogi mortuorum*, x and xii. Translators and imitators included such well-known literati as Aurispa, Poggio, Carlo Marsuppini, Pontano, Rinucci Aretino, Francesco Griffolini, and Leon Battista Alberti. Aeneas Sylvius, the future Pope Pius II, tells a story from Lucian's *Menippus* in his *De curialium miseriis*. Matteo Maria Boiardo made a popular dramatic version of Lucian's *Timon*.[6] The

---

[1] Loeb Lucian, *3*, 31.

[2] Quoted by Hardin Craig, "Dryden's Lucian," *Classical Philology*, *16* (1921), 146.

[3] For the manuscripts of Lucian known in the fifteenth century, see R. R. Bolgar, *The Classical Heritage and Its Beneficiaries* (Cambridge, 1954), pp. 480–81; P. O. Kristeller, *Iter Italicum* (London and Leiden, 1963–67), passim.

[4] José Ruysschaert, "A Note on the 'First' Edition of the Latin Translations of Some of Lucian of Samosata's Dialogues," *Journal of the Warburg and Courtauld Institutes*, *16* (1953), 161–62.

[5] E. P. Goldschmidt, "The First Edition of Lucian of Samosata," *Journal of the Warburg and Courtauld Institutes*, *14* (1951), 7–20.

[6] Histories of classical scholarship, biographies of Renaissance humanists, and writings on Italian, French, German, and English literature of the fifteenth and sixteenth centuries give some useful information on the fortunes of Lucian in the Renaissance, but the subject still awaits a full, detailed study. Scholarly investigation began with Richard Förster's paper in *Archiv für Litteraturgeschichte*, *14* (1886), 337–63. Some other works: Adolf Hauffen, "Zur Litteratur der ironischen Enkomien," *Vierteljahrsschrift für Litteraturgeschichte*, *6* (1893), 161–85; J. Rentsch, *Lucianstudien*, Plauen, 1895; Gottfried Niemann, *Die Dialogliteratur der Reformationszeit nach ihrer Enstehung und Entwicklung* (Leipzig, 1905);

description in Lucian's *De calumnia* of a picture by Apelles inspired Botticelli's painting, "La Calumnia."

The *editio princeps* of the Greek text, edited by Janus Lascaris, was published in 1496 (Florence, L. F. de Alopa); the second and more widely distributed edition was that of Aldus Manutius, Venice, 1503. After this date, and partly because of the availability of the Aldine edition—even More's Utopians keep up with Aldine publications [1]—Lucian comes into favor north of the Alps, especially in Germany. A German translation of *Lucius sive asinus* from the Latin of Poggio was made ca. 1477. Few other versions of Lucian by Germans before 1500 are recorded. Rudolph Agricola made Latin versions of *Gallus* and *De calumnia*, Johannes Reuchlin a German version of *Dialogi mortuorum* xii; and Reuchlin is said to have translated *Concilium deorum* into Latin. Later translators include such contemporaries or acquaintances of Erasmus as Pirckheimer, Melanchthon, Ulrich von Hutten, Hans Sachs, and Peter Mosellanus.

ii

The fact that Thomas More made some translations from Greek into Latin is scarcely surprising. But why Lucian, whose name was a synonym for "mocker," "skeptic," "atheist"? Even today some readers familiar with Lucian are perhaps more likely to think of him as an eighteenth-century favorite, congenial to Gibbon, Voltaire, and Hume, than as a fit companion for More. All very well for David Hume to read Lucian on his deathbed [2] and to make jokes about Lucian's Charon—who, said Hume, would refuse his plea to be

P. Schulze, *Lucian in der Literatur und Kunst der Renaissance* (Dessau, 1906); Natale Caccia, *Note su la fortuna di Luciano nel rinascimento* (Milan, s.a.); Albert Bauer, "Der Einfluss Lukians von Samosata auf Ulrich von Hutten," *Philologus*, *75* (1919), 437–62; Rudolph Altrocchi, "The Calumny of Apelles in the Literature of the Quattrocento," *PMLA*, *36* (1921), 454–91; Olga Gewerstock, *Lucian und Hutten* (Berlin, 1924); Martha Heep, *Die Colloquia Familiaria des Erasmus und Lucian* (Halle, 1927); E. P. Goldschmidt, "The First Edition of Lucian"; *The First Cambridge Press in Its European Setting* (Cambridge, 1955), passim; "Lucian's *Calumnia*."

[1] *Utopia*, ed. Edward Surtz and J. H. Hexter, the Yale Edition of the Complete Works of St. Thomas More, vol. 4 (New Haven and London, 1965), 182/3–4. Cited hereafter as "*CW 4*."

[2] See Adam Smith's letter to William Strahan, November 9, 1776, appended to *The Life of David Hume, Esq. Written by Himself* (London, 1777), pp. 47–51.

spared a little longer for the purpose of preparing a new and corrected edition of his *Works*—but why the devout More? Why should he have been attracted to the flippant critic of all religions?

That the man for all seasons had hours for Lucian is undeniable. Yet there is no mystery about this taste if we distinguish sharply enough between what More liked, and what he rejected or ignored, in Lucian. If we read Lucian for ourselves (bearing in mind that his reputation during the Renaissance was due to spurious as well as genuine writings), we have no difficulty in finding the humor, shrewd wit, fancy, and plain common sense More obviously enjoyed. In the second place, if we attend to what More himself tells us, in his prefatory letter, about his translations, and resist the temptation of identifying too facilely the More of 1505–1506 with the More of the final phase,[1] the answers are fairly clear. Had "the king's good servant but God's first" occupied himself toward the end of his life with reading Lucian or the *Greek Anthology* or Lucretius, we would have a good deal to explain. The literary recreations of a rising young lawyer and member of Parliament in the early years of the century seem remote irrelevancies, indeed *Utopia* itself seems in some measure irrelevant, for those to whom More's fascination lies in the conflicts of his last years. If the controversialist assailing Tyndale, and later the writer of spiritual meditations in the Tower, ever thought of Lucian at all, he may have been merely embarrassed by recollection of the book he and Erasmus had produced nearly thirty years earlier. We remember his vehement protestation of 1532:

> I saye therfore in these dayes in whyche men by theyr owne defaute mysseconstre and take harme of the very scrypture of god, vntyll menne better amende, yf any man wolde now translate Moria in to Englyshe, or some workes eyther that I haue my selfe wryten ere this . . . I wolde not onely my derlynges[2] bokes but myne owne also, helpe to burne them both wyth myne owne

[1] "A man who has moved away from and beyond all his friends, who has chosen to abandon all his interests rather than to compromise with what he sees as evil, who has known illness, treachery, the threat of a painful and disgraceful death, and the ultimate solitude of misunderstanding from those he loved most—this is not the same man as the friend of Erasmus and the centre of Holbein's family group" (David Knowles, *The Historian and Character* [Cambridge, 1963], p. 8).

[2] Erasmus'.

> handes, rather then folke sholde (though thorow theyr own faute) take any harme of them. . . .[1]

On this passage Chambers comments: "In speaking of earlier works which he would have burnt, More was, I fancy, thinking not so much of *Utopia* as of some of the *Epigrams*, and of his translations from Lucian—such things, for example, as the epistle to Dr. Ruthall prefixed to the translation of the *Necyomantia*."[2] Chambers' main point here is undoubtedly correct, though we might observe that in his letter to Ruthall, More does at least distinguish between what is good and what should be rejected in the pages of Lucian. By 1532, association with Lucian could be embarrassing. When, in that very year, John Frith, then a prisoner in the Tower, taunted More himself as "another Lucian, neither regarding God nor man," such a libel must have hurt.[3]

Whether his translations caused More later embarrassment or not, Lucian was at one time a literary favorite of his. The translations made in 1505–1506 are part of his literary history and must have a place, if a minor one, in his *Opera omnia*.[4] They have a place also in the history of classical studies in sixteenth-century England. More

---

[1] *The Confutation of Tyndale's Answer*, ed. L. A. Schuster, R. C. Marius, J. P. Lusardi, and R. J. Schoeck, volume 8 of the Yale Edition of More's Complete Works (New Haven, 1973), 179/8–17. Cited hereafter as "*CW 8*."

[2] R. W. Chambers, *The Place of St. Thomas More in English Literature and History* (London, 1937), pp. 49–50. *Cynicus* is printed first among More's translations, and the letter to Ruthall is a preface to three of More's translations, not to that of *Menippus* alone.

[3] *A Mirror or Glass to Know Thyself; The Works of the English Reformers: William Tyndale and John Frith*, ed. Thomas Russell (London, 1831), *3*, 267. "Lucian" and "Lucianist" became common epithets in the literature of controversy. Thus in Elizabethan times we find Gabriel Harvey denouncing Robert Greene as "a contemner of God and man, a desperate Lucianist" (*Renaissance England*, ed. Roy Lamson and Hallett Smith [New York, 1956], p. 442). "Every country hath its Machiavell, every age its Lucian," says Sir Thomas Browne (*Religio Medici*, pt. 1, sect. 20).

Another current example of a name loaded with unfavorable connotations was that of Epicurus, despite some recent (fifteenth-century) attempts at rehabilitation. Erasmus even argues in *Epicureus* that Christians are the "true" Epicureans (cf. Craig R. Thompson, *The Colloquies of Erasmus* [Chicago and London, 1965], pp. 535–51; cited hereafter as "*Colloquies of Erasmus*"). Epicurean philosophy, shorn of some of its most objectionable features, plays a prominent part in *Utopia*, but the words "Epicurus" and "Epicurean" do not occur in the text. See *CW 4*, 160/13–178/18 and commentary, pp. 441–64; also Surtz's *The Praise of Pleasure* (Cambridge, Mass., 1957), pp. 9–43.

[4] The last edition preceding the present one was included in the Frankfort and Leipzig, 1689, *Opera omnia Latina* (republished in facsimile, Frankfort, 1963; see *Archiv für das Studium der neueren Sprachen und Literaturen, 201* [1964–65], 208–10).

appears to have been the first Englishman to translate Lucian into Latin, and his versions were the first by an Englishman to be printed. Except for two letters, these translations and his reply to Lucian's *Tyrannicida* are More's earliest surviving Latin prose compositions. With the improbable exception of his English life of Pico della Mirandola, the first edition of which is undated (1510?), they were the earliest of his prose writings to be published and, save for a few epigrams,[1] his first writings of any kind to appear in print. They were praised and remembered; in More's lifetime, it seems, they were printed more frequently than any other of his writings: at least nine times before the end of 1535 (*Utopia* six times in Latin, once in German, and once in Italian, before 1549).[2] Hindsight assures us that More's literary avocations of 1505–1506—if they were merely that—could have had little to do with what mattered most in his intellectual life and public career after 1515. But the number of printings suggests that whatever we are likely to think of the comparative interest and value of his versions of Lucian when these are contrasted with *Utopia*, the sixteenth century may have thought otherwise.

The evidence at our disposal indicates clearly enough that Thomas More first learned Greek from William Grocin and Thomas Linacre, but probably in London and not, as Stapleton would have it, at Oxford.[3] In the letter to John Holt which Miss Rogers dates ca.

---

[1] Two epigrams to John Holt: see *The Latin Epigrams of Thomas More*, ed. and trans. Leicester Bradner and Charles Arthur Lynch (Chicago, 1953), pp. 238–40 (cited hereafter as "Bradner and Lynch"); Harris Fletcher, "The Earliest (?) Printing of Sir Thomas More's Two Epigrams to John Holt," *Studies in Honor of T. W. Baldwin*, ed. Don Cameron Allen (Urbana, 1958), pp. 53–65. On a third, Bradner and Lynch, p. 189, and *Moreana*, *17* (1968), 21–26.

[2] R. W. Gibson and J. M. Patrick, *St. Thomas More: A Preliminary Bibliography* (New Haven and London, 1961), Nos. 78–83, 85–87, 1–5, 34, 37 (cited hereafter as "Gibson and Patrick"). Inclusion of No. 84 in the Gibson and Patrick bibliography implies that More's translation of *Menippus* was reprinted by Martens, Louvain, in 1522, but this was a reissue of the Greek text, not the translation.

[3] Thomas Stapleton, *Tres Thomae* (Douai, 1588), p. 12, says More was sent to Oxford as a youth "vt Philosophiam audiret, tum etiam vt Latinis Graecam adderet," and that Grocin and Linacre were teaching Greek there. More might well have been at Oxford when Grocin was there, ca. 1493, but we have no evidence that More got any Greek while at Oxford. As for Linacre, he was in Italy until 1499; see P. S. Allen, "Linacre and Latimer in Italy," *English Historical Review*, *18* (1903), 514–17; R. J. Mitchell, "Thomas Linacre in Italy," *ibid.*, *50* (1935), 696–98. On Greek in England in the fifteenth century, R. Weiss, *Humanism in England During the Fifteenth Century* (Oxford, 1957), especially chs. 9–12.

November 1501, More says he has laid Latin studies aside and is pursuing Greek, with Grocin; he speaks as if his progress were slow: "Ita enim sepositis Latinis litteris, Grecas sequor vt illas amittam has non assequar."[1] Writing in 1515 to Dorp, he recalls having heard Linacre lecture on the Greek text of Aristotle's *Meteorologica*,[2] but we do not know the date of those lectures; 1500 or 1501 seems the most likely. If More began Greek earlier than 1501, perhaps his interest in the language was whetted not only by contact with Grocin or Linacre but with Erasmus, who had made his first visit to England in the autumn of 1499. At that date Erasmus himself probably had precious little Greek, but we know he was attracted to it. His statement in the spring of 1500 that he was now concentrating on Greek studies[3] sounds as if he had been working at Greek for some time. He was self-taught,[4] but by 1502 could write Greek fairly well. In 1503 he made translations from Libanius; between 1502 and 1504 he translated Euripides' *Hecuba*; and in 1506, while in England, finished a translation of *Iphigenia in Aulide*.[5] These versions of Euripides were printed in September 1506 (Paris, Badius Ascensius), a few months earlier than his and More's Lucian.

By the autumn of 1501, More was working at Greek, and within a few years had become fairly proficient, for in late 1505 or early 1506 he could translate Lucian competently. At one time or another he translated also, in rivalry with William Lily, many epigrams from

---

Erasmus says (1520) that More studied Latin "a puero," Greek as "iuuenis," and that his teachers were Grocin and Linacre (*Erasmi epistolae*, ed. P. S. Allen et al. [Oxford, 1906–58], *4*, 294.92–93. Cited hereafter as "*EE*" by volume, page, and line). He uses the same term, *iuvenis*, when he refers elsewhere (ibid., *4*, 17.141–42) to More's study of Greek. But the only thing these statements tell us is that More, like everybody else, learned Latin before he learned Greek. *Iuvenis* is too imprecise to permit us to deduce the date of More's introduction to Greek.

In 1518, More did good service to Greek studies by writing, at the king's request, a strong letter denouncing opponents of Greek at Oxford. See *EE*, *3*, 546.183–547.194; text of the letter in *The Correspondence of Sir Thomas More*, ed. Elizabeth Frances Rogers (Princeton, 1947), pp. 112–20 (cited hereafter as "Rogers").

[1] Rogers, 4/12–13.

[2] Ibid., 65/1319–23.

[3] *EE*, *1*, 285.22–24; 288.62–63; 404.34–35.

[4] There was a teacher of Greek, G. Hermonymus, in Paris during Erasmus' residence, but Erasmus is scornful of him; *EE*, *1*, 7.22–24. In the *Compendium vitae*, Erasmus says his father, Gerard, knew Greek as well as Latin ("Graece et Latine pulchre calluit," *EE*, *1*, 48.22), a remarkable statement if accurate. But the authenticity of the *Compendium vitae* is still disputed.

[5] Ibid., *1*, 4.29–31; 5.23–27; cf. 365.6 and n.; 418–20.

the *Greek Anthology*, but these were not published (as *Progymnasmata* and *Epigrammata*) until 1518. It is tempting to think that at least some of these translations were made early, say in 1503 and 1504, but the opinion of their editors is that they must be dated some years later.[1] We are limited to saying that if More did make any translations from the *Anthology* as early as 1503 or 1504, he must then have read a bit of Lucian, since some of the poems he turned into Latin were ascribed to Lucian.

Erasmus paid his second visit to England in 1505, arriving some time between March and the end of the year; we cannot date his arrival more narrowly.[2] By this time he was certainly familiar with Lucian, whom he had known in Latin as early as 1499 when he referred to *Vera historia*.[3] He made an early attempt to translate Lucian's *Tragoedopodagra*, a mock-tragedy on gout, but gave up, "potissimum deterritus epithetis, quibus abundant chori."[4] More meanwhile may have discovered Lucian for himself. He may have had access to the Aldine 1503 edition of Lucian in the year before Erasmus' second visit. Possibly their friend Andreas Ammonius brought a manuscript of Lucian or a copy of the 1503 edition with him when he came to England.[5] There is good reason to think that Ammonius had an interest in Lucian,[6] but we have no proof that this interest existed as early as 1504–1505. Surviving correspondence between Ammonius and Erasmus does not commence until 1511, and none between Ammonius and More seems to exist. Ammonius was in England in 1506, having arrived apparently sometime in, or shortly after, the autumn of 1504.[7] In 1509 he was in the service of Erasmus' friend and patron Lord Mountjoy. He may have been

---

[1] Bradner and Lynch, pp. xi–xiii. Erasmus says that "Epigrammata lusit adolescens admodum ac pleraque puer" (*EE*, *3*, 57.9–10), but here too it is impossible to say exactly which years are meant. Probably he did not have, or did not remember, more precise information.

[2] *EE*, *1*, 414.

[3] Ibid., *1*, 224.27–28.

[4] Ibid., *1*, 6.36–7.6.

[5] I owe this suggestion to Dr. C. Reedijk.

[6] Cf. *EE*, *1*, 492.33. Erasmus sent his translation of Lucian's *Icaromenippus* to him in 1511 (ibid., *1*, 493.1–3).

[7] Ibid., *1*, 455; 545.72–73. Clemente Pizzi, *L'umanista Andrea Ammonio* (Florence, 1956), p. 18, thinks he went to England in the autumn of 1504. This date had been suggested by Allen, *EE*, *1*, 455.

known to More in London as early as 1504 or 1505, but we cannot be sure.

Which of the two friends, Erasmus or More, knew Lucian first, and which of them first suggested the common enterprise of translating some of Lucian's writings into Latin, we simply do not know. Assertions that More probably "discovered" Lucian[1] or that it was he who "had led Erasmus to Lucian"[2] may be correct—but cannot be proved. I think it more probable that Erasmus knew Lucian first. The fact of importance, however, is that in late 1505 or early 1506 they decided to turn some Lucianic writings into Latin. More's efforts and most of Erasmus' were completed by June 1506 (Erasmus' preface to his first translation, *Toxaris*, is dated January 1, 1506; his prefaces to *Timon*, *Gallus*, and *De iis qui mercede conducti degunt* were probably written in June).[3] The results were published in November 1506 at Paris by Badius Ascensius: a volume containing eighteen very brief dialogues and ten longer ones translated by Erasmus, four translated by More; in addition, an original declamation by each man and Erasmus' poem, *De senectute*.[4]

Nothing is known of the manuscripts of More's and Erasmus' translations. Nor does More ever tell us anything about this enterprise except on one occasion, when he dedicates his versions to Thomas Ruthall, Royal Secretary. All our information about the collaboration, except what can be inferred from the volume itself,

---

[1] J. A. K. Thomson, "Erasmus in England," in *England und die Antike* (*Bibliothek Warburg, Vörtrage*, 1930–31), Leipzig, 1932, p. 75. Cited hereafter as "Thomson, Erasmus in England."

[2] Walter Kaiser, *Praisers of Folly* (Cambridge, Mass., 1963), p. 31. Similarly H. A. Mason, *Humanism and Poetry in the Early Tudor Period* (London, 1959), p. 59. Evidently these scholars noticed that Erasmus says in his introduction to his declamation replying to Lucian's *Tyrannicida*, "Latine declamare coepi, idque impulsore Toma Moro" (*EE*, *1*, 422.3). But this sentence tells us only that More had proposed the writing of answers to *Tyrannicida*—Erasmus' word *declamare* is the important term here—and not that More had proposed the enterprise of translating Lucian. Cf. *EE*, *1*, 18.26–28; *4*, 21.254–56.

We should note too that in reviewing his early study of Greek, which was renewed after interruption ("Ad Graecas literas vtcunque puero degustatas iam grandior redii"), and his failure with *Tragoedopodagra*, Erasmus then speaks of his translations of Lucian without mention of More (*EE*, *1*, 7.19–8.13).

[3] *EE*, *1*, 416–17; 423–25; 429–30. Allen (*1*, 429) thinks the preface to *De iis qui mercede conducti degunt* may have been written even later.

[4] On this and subsequent editions of the translations, see below, "The Text." Another project begun, but not finished, during Erasmus' residence in England in 1505–1506 was his translation of the New Testament, finally published in 1516 and 1519.

comes from Erasmus. Even when acknowledging, in 1522, the eloquent dedication by Conrad Goclenius of a translation of Lucian's *Hermotimus*, More says nothing whatever about his own work on the same author.[1]

Three of More's translations (of *Cynicus*, *Menippus*, and *Philopseudes*) are named in his dedicatory letter to Ruthall, which is undated. The fourth, *Tyrannicida*, and the declamation replying to it, are not named in the letter; an omission which may mean they were composed later than the letter. As for the other three, we do not know whether More translated *Cynicus* first, then *Menippus*, then *Philopseudes*. They appear in this order in the 1506 edition (but not on the title page of 1506, which announces *Tyrannicida*, the *declamatio*, *Cynicus*, *Menippus*, *Philopseudes*); the Greek texts did not follow this sequence in the 1496 or 1503 Greek editions. Perhaps *Cynicus* comes first in More's texts because, like some other translators, he began with the shortest and simplest text.

Cynicus is a short dialogue (possibly not by Lucian) in which a Cynic praises to an inquiring friend the moral virtues of the simple, uncomplicated life. The lesson is that *radix malorum cupiditas est* and that, as a much later moralist affirms, a man is rich in proportion to the number of things he can afford to let alone.[2]

Next is *Menippus* or *Necromantia*,[3] a characteristic piece in which Menippus, perplexed by the unedifying behavior of the gods as reported by the poets, consults the philosophers, hoping to learn from them what kind of life is best. Since the philosophers, as usual, disagree, he goes to the underworld with one of the Magi to consult Tiresias. After an adventurous journey, during which they see the shades of the illustrious dead, they come to Tiresias. He tells them: "The life of the common sort is best, and you will act more wisely if you stop speculating about heavenly bodies and discussing final causes and first causes, spit your scorn at those clever syllogisms, and counting all that sort of thing nonsense, make it always your sole

---

[1] Rogers, pp. 267–73.

[2] On a Tudor English translation of *Cynicus*, see below, pp. 140–41.

[3] What does Tyndale mean when he says that in Henry VII's reign Cardinal Morton "had a licence of the pope for fourteen to study necromancy, of which he himself was one; and other I have heard named, which at this time I pass over with silence" (*Practice of Prelates*, ed. Henry Walter, Parker Society edition [Cambridge, 1849], p. 305)? As a youth More had lived in Morton's household.

object to put the present to good use and to hasten on your way, laughing a great deal and taking nothing seriously."[1]

Longest of the pieces translated by More is *Philopseudes*, a satire on man's insuperable credulity, or what Hume calls "the usual propensity of mankind towards the marvelous." This pervasive weakness afflicts not only the naive but even the so-called philosophers. Through the stories told by the skeptical Tychiades, and the self-evident mendacity of his friends, Lucian persuades us that this habit of telling lies can be cured, if at all, only by constant and resolute skepticism: "We have a powerful antidote to such poisons in truth and in sound reason brought to bear everywhere. As long as we make use of this, none of these empty, foolish lies will disturb our peace."[2]

These three translations present no difficulties. More's other contributions to the 1506 volume take longer to describe. At his suggestion—and Erasmus tells us on three separate occasions[3] that this proposal originated with More—he and Erasmus composed replies to Lucian's *Tyrannicida*, which each man had also translated. More wanted to see what he could do in competing with Erasmus in such an exercise: ". . . me voluit antagonistam habere, quo certius periculum faceret ecquid profecisset in hoc genere."[4] These replies are the only extant examples of literary competition between the two friends. For this reason, and secondarily because of the nature of the theme, More's declamation has a certain interest. *Tyrannicida*, it should be added, is a specific kind of rhetorical discourse; and since More's and Erasmus' answers to it are intended as works of that same kind, they must be judged as such.

Lucian's *Tyrannicida* is the speech of a claimant before a court. In a city-state ruled by a tyrant there is, oddly enough, a standing reward for tyrannicide. This claimant had gained access to the tyrant's stronghold, hoping to assassinate him. He failed to find the tyrant but encountered and killed his son, and left his sword in the body. The tyrant discovered his son's body and, overcome with

---

1 Loeb Lucian, *4*, 107–09. On an English translation of *Menippus* in verse, accompanied by More's Latin version, see below, p. 142. In his notes to Augustine, *De civitate Dei*, 2, vii (first printed 1522; I have used the Frankfort and Hamburg edition of 1661, *1*, 156–57), Juan Luis Vives quotes some lines from More's translation of *Menippus* and adds generous praise of More.

2 Loeb Lucian, *3*, 381.

3 *EE*, *1*, 422.1–6; *1*, 18.26–28; *4*, 21.254–56.

4 Ibid., *4*, 21.255–56.

grief, slew himself with that same sword. Subsequently the killer of the son demands the reward for tyrannicide. We are to presume that another citizen has objected to this claim, and the case now goes to a jury.

After reminding the jury of the city's former misery, the claimant relates the particulars of his deed. His argument may be summarized as follows:

> I have rid the state of two tyrants: the father and the son who would have succeeded him. My sword slew the son; grief for his son caused the father to kill himself. Therefore I have not only freed you from tyranny but from the dread of future tyranny as well. Yet it now appears that someone opposes my request for the official reward for tyrannicide. He impudently questions the patriotism of my motives; but in truth his opposition is inspired by grief at the tyrant's death and a desire to avenge it.
>
> The citizens had no hope of deliverance, for the tyrant had a son who was in all but name the real tyrant and who committed atrocious crimes. But I went boldly into the citadel, alone, routed the watch, found the son, and after a hard struggle killed him. Thinking it would be too kind to allow the father to die by any hand but his own, I left my sword behind me. Seeing this when he found the body of his son, he took it and killed himself, just as I intended and foresaw that he would do.
>
> Even if I had not succeeded, I would deserve something for the attempt. But I *did* succeed—and the city is free. My opponent also objects to my claim for reward on the ground that since the law provides reward for one who kills the tyrant, and I did not (he says) kill the tyrant but the son, I have not fulfilled the requirements of the statute. But there is no essential difference between killing him and causing his death. I caused his death by killing his son, and thus I liberated the city. The tyrant's death was not fortuitous; I had planned the whole course of events. I had foreseen that the son's death would be such a grief to his aged father that the father would slay himself then and there. Had grief not killed him, despair would have done so. I brought this about and therefore I deserve the reward.

Lucian's speech is an example of the declamations that formed a standard part of Greek and Roman education: stock speeches on stock subjects, but prized by some for their verbal dexterity and their polish as oratorical or theatrical pieces when delivered by a master of the art. As forms of prose discourse governed by fairly strict conventions, they were acceptable to ancient theories and conditions of education because of their supposed usefulness in preparing for legal or political life and as training for the supreme goal, eloquence. They were common in the classrooms of teachers in the Roman Empire and in the repertoires of itinerant rhetors such as Lucian himself, who wrote many pieces belonging to this genre.

Technically *Tyrannicida* is a *μελέτη* or *declamatio*, specifically the type of *declamatio* called *controversia*. Commonly two kinds of declamations were studied and practiced. The more elementary were the deliberative sort, *suasoriae* (corresponding to *theses* in the older rhetoric), which posed questions the speaker could examine and in which he could reach conclusions or give advice to historical or semi-historical characters: Should Carthage be destroyed? Should the three hundred Spartans remain at Thermopylae? Should Hector's life be spared? *Controversiae* were forensic declamations, to be used, or imagined as used, in civil or criminal suits. They were therefore likely to be more elaborate and more difficult than *suasoriae*, because they had to take into account laws, court procedure, and so on; to what extent they stayed within the possibilities of actual law, however, is debatable.[1] There were likewise exercises of impersonation, *prosopopoeiae*, which aimed at appropriateness of characterization, at speaking as Priam, Sulla, or Helen would have spoken. *Prosopopoeia* was thus intimately related to *suasoria* and *controversia* and often included by them.[2]

---

1 On this question see S. F. Bonner, *Roman Declamation in the Late Republic and Early Empire* (Liverpool, 1949), pp. 84–132. He concludes that most of the laws in the Senecan *controversiae* are "far closer to Roman Law than has been generally supposed" (p. 131). Bonner's book has a valuable bibliography.

2 The most important collections of *suasoriae* and *controversiae* are those of Seneca the Elder (ed. H. Bornecque [Paris, 1932]; see also *The Suasoriae of Seneca the Elder*, ed. and trans. William A. Edward [Cambridge, 1928]) and two collections formerly ascribed to Quintilian (*Declamationes maiores* and *Declamationes minores*; cf. M. L. Clarke, *Rhetoric at Rome* [London, 1953], pp. 126–29). For description and criticism, Quintilian, *Inst.*, passim; Tacitus, *Dial.*, xxxi–xxxv; Philostratus, *Vitae soph.*; *Rhet. Her.*, passim. Useful modern studies besides those of Bonner and Clarke mentioned above: H. Bornecque, *Les déclamations et les déclamateurs d'après Sénèque le père* (Lille, 1902); C. S. Baldwin, *Ancient*

When properly controlled, declamation must have had some measure of utility as an instrument of education, but we find repeated complaints by Roman critics that *controversiae* degenerated too often into extravagant, unrealistic performances. Far from testing the argumentative competence of the speaker, they tended to become mere exhibitions of his virtuosity. Their wildly improbable themes and situations draw severe condemnation from Quintilian and Tacitus. Juvenal assures us that the professors were bored to death by them.[1] Quintilian thinks such exercises are good if used sensibly but an utter waste of time unless applicable to real life and real law.[2] How most of the examples in the collection of Seneca could have applied to real life is not easy to understand, filled as they are with adulterers, pirates, tyrants, and a nightmarish assortment of children and parents. "Children are required by law to support their parents or be imprisoned. Two brothers quarreled. One had a son. When his uncle became destitute, the boy rescued him despite his father's opposition. For this act he was disinherited, but he was then adopted by the uncle. The uncle inherited a fortune. The boy's father became destitute, and despite the uncle's opposition the boy went to his father's assistance. He was disinherited."[3] Another Senecan *controversia* accomplishes the questionable feat of including in one theme parents, children, pirates, adulterers, and tyrants: "Children are required by law to support their parents or be imprisoned. A man killed one of his brothers as a tyrant. His other brother he caught in adultery and killed, despite the father's plea. Then he himself was captured by pirates. He wrote to his father for ransom, but the father promised the pirates twice the sum if they would cut off the son's hands. The pirates released him. He refused to help his father when the latter became destitute."[4] A woman who is raped may demand

Rhetoric and Poetic (New York, 1924); J. Wight Duff, *A Literary History of Rome in the Silver Age*, ed. A. M. Duff (New York, 1960); D. L. Clark, *Rhetoric in Greco-Roman Education* (New York, 1957); H. I. Marrou, *A History of Education in Antiquity*, trans. G. Lamb (London, 1956), pt. 2, ch. 10. On Lucian's declamations see Bompaire, *Lucien écrivain.* On his *Tyrannicida,* see Charles S. Rayment, "The *Tyrannicida* of Erasmus: Translated Excerpts with Introduction and Commentary," *Speech Monographs, 26* (1959), 233–47; cited hereafter as "Rayment, '*Tyrannicida.*'"

1 *Sat.*, vii, 150–70.

2 "Nam si foro non praeparat, aut scenicae ostentationi aut furiosae vociferationi simillimum est" (*Inst.*, II, x, 8).

3 I, i.

4 I, vii.

by law that her attacker be killed or that he marry her without a dowry. One man raped two women in one night; one demands his death, the other a marriage: what shall the court decide?[1] It is not hard to see why Quintilian would have had the gravest doubts about the propriety of this sort of thing as a training for young minds. Tacitus[2] mentions rewards for tyrannicide as an example of the absurd topics assigned for declamations by teachers who misconceive the true purpose of the genre or wilfully abuse it. Absurd or not, rhetorical performances with such topics helped Lucian to earn a living.

We are almost constrained to say that in many of the declamations of classical rhetoric, improbability is the guide of life. We may say of these productions that, in Santayana's words, the performance may be astonishing but the achievement is mean. Still, banality, sophistry, and pedantry in competitive discourse are not limited to classical declamations. These characteristics are easy to find in pedagogical exercises and formal academic discourses in every century; and many lines of connection, direct or indirect, run between the ancient varieties and the speeches and *disputationes* common in mediaeval and Renaissance universities. And to think that most of More's educated contemporaries doubted the utility of rhetorical accomplishments or did not take pleasure in them would be a very provincial judgment. We have not the slightest reason for doubting either that Erasmus and More enjoyed writing their speeches in reply to Lucian's or that their readers enjoyed reading them.

We know More had a dramatic flair, a fondness for acting parts.[3] Erasmus says in a familiar passage that More as a young man delighted in literary exercises of all sorts and took special pleasure in declamations, in which he sharpened his wits by tackling difficult questions.[4] We can guess, too, that to write a forensic speech opposing

---

[1] I, v.

[2] *Dial.*, xxxv.

[3] For a good example see Erasmus' colloquy, *Exorcism* (*Colloquies of Erasmus*, pp. 230–37). Roper's passage about how More would "steppe in among the players" at Christmas entertainments is well known (*Lyfe of Sir Thomas Moore, Knighte,* ed. E. V. Hitchcock; Early English Text Society, original series, 197 [London, 1935], p. 5).

[4] "Primam aetatem carmine potissimum exercuit, mox diu luctatus est vt prosam orationem redderet molliorem, per omne scripti genus stilum exercens. . . . Declamationibus praecipue delectatus est, et, in his, materiis adoxis, quod in his acrior sit ingeniorum

the argument of Lucian's claimant in *Tyrannicida* would have appealed to More's professional interest in legal distinctions and procedures. Neither his legal nor his literary abilities could have been widely known beyond London in 1505, but the wit, eloquence, and readiness in speaking that were to become part of the tradition about him were already known to those in what we would be tempted today to call the "Establishment" in London—and to Erasmus, who did so much to make More's qualities known to Europeans.

Erasmus, who on more than one occasion had to defend his own writings from critics by insisting on the distinction between personal opinions and those which are dramatically or rhetorically appropriate in certain modes but are not necessarily the author's, has much to say about the theory and practice of declamation as a literary form. He defines it as "argumentum fictum, quod exercendae dictionis gratia tractatur in utramque partem. . . . Qui declamationem profitetur, ipse sibi fidem abrogat, nec potest nisi de ingenio periclitari."[1] Again, when answering attacks on his declamation on marriage: "Quis enim nescit, declamationes exercitandi ingenii gratia in fictis themis versari? Quod Graeci magis ipso vocabulo testantur, μελέτας eas appellantes, quasi dicas exercitamenta."[2] Obviously such distinctions might be crucial to a man who wrote as many declamations, or so-called declamations, as Erasmus did[3] and became imbroiled in so many controversies over them. To what extent his protests were dictated by sincerity or by convenience is an important and complicated question for his biographers, but about the definition of *declamatio* he was surely correct. The essential fact about *declamatio* is that its author professedly commits himself to an *imagined*, *fictive* argument and thereby claims immunity from being

---

exercitatio. Vnde adolescens etiamnum dialogum moliebatur, in quo Platonis communitatem ad vxores vsque defendit. . . . Vix alium reperias qui felicius dicat ex tempore: adeo felici ingenio felix lingua subseruit. Ingenium praesens et vbique praeuolans, memoria parata; quae cum omnia habeat velut in numerato, prompte et incontanter suggerit quicquid tempus aut res postulat. In disputationibus nihil fingi potest acutius" (*EE*, *4*, 21.247–66). Cf. Roper, p. 22.

[1] *Appendix de scriptis Iodoci Clithovei* (*Erasmi opera omnia*, ed. J. Clericus, Leiden, 1703–1706, *9*, 812F–813A. Cited hereafter as "*LB*").

[2] *Apologia pro declamatione matrimonii* (*LB*, *9*, 108A).

[3] *E.g. Encomium matrimonii*, *Moriae encomium*, *Encomium artis medicae*, *Declamatio de morte*, *De contemptu mundi*, *De pueris instituendis*. We hear of others that were unfinished or unpublished: on nature, on grace (*EE*, *1*, 19.14), on why a papal war should be waged against Venice, on why it should not be waged (ibid., *1*, 37.7–10).

taken literally. Should *Utopia* be treated as a *declamatio*? The second book only? Certain portions of the second book? For example, we are warned that the passage on permissive suicide and euthanasia must be read as a *declamatio.*[1] No doubt this is so; but the ambiguities, the levels and nuances of interpretation possible, are part of the charm of *Utopia*, as of other books in which imagination, irony, and dramatic invention are so artistically blended.

The *declamatio* by More in reply to Lucian's is not a thing to hold children from play or old men from the chimney corner. No student of More's literary career may ignore it; few but specialists would care to read it twice. To treat it too seriously as law or logic would be misguided, of course, but as a *controversia* it is a good specimen of Latin rhetoric as practiced by a sixteenth-century humanist. The classical ideal of eloquence was still a fundamental aim of education, and in More's time education still meant chiefly training in letters; which in turn required command of the principles and procedures, strategy and tactics, of formal rhetoric. These statements are commonplaces, but worth repeating whenever we think about what the sixteenth century meant by literature, English as well as Latin. Criticism relied on the vocabulary of rhetoric. To assess the enthymemes and *colores*, the schemes and tropes, and all the other abundant, delightful flowers of rhetoric the Latinist was heir to, gave to cultivated readers what we must believe was authentic pleasure.[2] We may be confident that the speeches in which Erasmus

---

[1] Edward Surtz, *The Praise of Wisdom* (Chicago, 1957), pp. 90–91; and see *Renaissance Quarterly*, *22* (1969), 329–33.

[2] Surtz provides helpful analyses of More's Latin style in *Utopia* (*CW 4*, 579–82; and *Studies in the Renaissance*, *14*, 1967, 93–109), and many of his observations are applicable also to this declamation. On the other hand, a forensic speech, which includes questions addressed directly to the speaker's opponent and to the jury, and is delivered in a formal setting, does not and cannot have the easy, colloquial character or the extensive narrative and descriptive passages found in *Utopia*. Rhetorical figures are plentiful, because the speaker must convey emotion as a patriot besides persuading as a litigant.

More's Latinity was admired. So far as I am aware, we have no grounds for believing he valued it less than his English style. His skill in Latin prose is usually, and rightly, judged by accomplishments more substantial than his reply to *Tyrannicida*, above all by *Utopia*; but like all good writers he adapted his language to the subject and the situation. Erasmus, a sensitive and authoritative judge of Latinity, held that if allowances were made for the fact (a rather unfortunate fact, he seems to think) that More was a lawyer, and that from the standpoint of letters nothing is more barbarous than English law, his literary talents were remarkable (*Ciceronianus*, *LB*, *1*, 1012F–1013A). Writing in 1528, he regrets that More's immersion in public life does not allow him more literary activity.

and More answered Lucian's *Tyrannicida* were liked by sixteenth-century readers, who responded to these *tours de force* in the common sixteenth-century ways.

More's speech, twice as long as Lucian's,[1] is the work of a man who is well practiced in Latin, resourceful in argument, and fond of disputation. It may be sophistical on the whole, and at times bathetic—as when the speaker objects that payment of the reward for tyrannicide would strain the government's treasury[2]—but it has a few passages in which the language seems to express genuine feeling, even attaining to a certain eloquence.[3] The main arguments in More's and Erasmus' speeches are similar, but Erasmus' is three times as long[4] and more copious and detailed;[5] he likes to give two or three illustrations instead of one. Both writers insist that since the claimant did not kill the tyrant (as the terms of the reward require) but his son, this claimant was not directly responsible for the tyrant's death and therefore is not entitled to the reward; liberation was the gift of the gods. Erasmus praises More's speech warmly. He accepted More's challenge, he says, not for the sake of victory over so keen a rival but for the pleasure of the contest and because he believes such exercises ought to be encouraged.[6] He invited a common friend,

---

His judgment of More's oratorical style is interesting: "Dicendi genus quod assequutus est magis vergit ad Isocraticam structuram ac dialecticam subtilitatem quam ad fusum illud Ciceronianae dictionis flumen, quanquam urbanitate nihilo M. Tullio inferior est" (ibid., *1*, 1013A).

[1] More notes elsewhere that it is the custom in all courts to allow more time to the man who answers (*Responsio ad Lutherum*, ed. John M. Headley, trans. Sister Scholastica Mandeville, the Yale Edition of the Complete Works of St. Thomas More, vol. 5 [New Haven and London, 1969] 693/13–15; cited hereafter as "*CW 5*"). He counters all of the claimant's main arguments, arranges and emphasizes them to suit his own tactical purposes, denies some of his opponent's assertions, questions others, and insists that the laws be interpreted strictly and literally.

[2] Not quite so ridiculous when we recall that only two years before writing this speech More had been deeply involved in a disagreement between Parliament and Henry VII over a large grant demanded by the king (R. W. Chambers, *Thomas More* [London, 1948], p. 87). Erasmus too objects to the financial strain of paying the reward (*LB*, *1*, 273A).

[3] As in some of the dicta on tyrants and tyranny, e.g.: "Intestatus semper Tyrannus moritur, quippe legibus ab illo captiuis, quae solae ratum facere testamentum possunt. Proinde qui defuncti locum Tyranni subit, haeres non est, sed nouus Tyrannus. Non enim succedit, sed inuadit" (104/22–25).

[4] For an English translation of the principal parts of Erasmus' declamation see Rayment, "*Tyrannicida*," pp. 237–47.

[5] As he acknowledges in the speech, *LB*, *1*, 285B.

[6] *EE*, *1*, 422.1–423.26.

Richard Whitford, to whom he dedicated his declamation, to compare it with More's,[1] but what Whitford thought of them we are not told. Those of More's biographers who express an opinion of it find it meritorious, even impressive, but to call it a "masterpiece" as one[2] does is hagiography rather than criticism.

Although we are not likely to mistake patently rhetorical compositions for essays in civil law or political science when reading Lucian's *Tyrannicida* and More's and Erasmus' replies, we should bear in mind that these productions belong to a tradition which originated in reactions to actual situations or events and to subsequent analyses or recollections of them.[3] Amusing or boring as the extravagances of *controversiae* on tyrants may be, even *controversiae* were but judicial speeches gone wild or carried to extremes. In the classroom, however, they became remote from political actualities.

To know the extent of More's acquaintance with classical and Christian works on tyranny, and his reflections on them in 1506, would be gratifying. The limited evidence available consists of inferences about his reading. That he knew Augustine's *De civitate Dei*, Plato, Aristotle, Plutarch, Thucydides, Sallust, Livy, Suetonius, and Tacitus is very likely. Whether he knew them all, particularly Suetonius and Tacitus, as early as 1506 is less probable. In the texts of these historians and philosophers he would have met many examples of despotism, and his reading is reflected in *Richard III*, as Professor Sylvester has demonstrated.[4] *Richard III* and *Utopia*[5] are the only prose writings in which he can be said to have commented on political topics, including that of tyranny. Since these books were written later than 1506, they do not show us how much More had thought about such subjects by, or at, that time when his attention was occupied by Lucian. We do know that he chose out of the *Greek Anthology* some poems on tyrants, and on contrasts between good and

---

[1] "Hortor autem vt et Moricam conferas, itaque iudices numquid in stilo sit discriminis inter hos quos tu ingenio, moribus, affectibus, studiis vsque adeo similes esse dicere solebas, vt negares vllos gemellos magis inter se similes reperiri posse" (ibid., *1*, 423.28–32).

[2] T. E. Bridgett, *Life and Writings of Sir Thomas More* (London, 1891), p. 82.

[3] Cf. Bompaire, *Lucien écrivain*, pp. 337–39.

[4] *Richard III*, ed. Richard S. Sylvester, The Yale Edition of the Complete Works of St. Thomas More, vol. 2 (New Haven and London, 1963), lxxxv–cii; cited hereafter as "*CW 2*."

[5] On tyranny in *Utopia* see *CW 4*, 502.

bad rulers, to translate.[1] If it is objected that this material was literature, not historiography or political philosophy, the answers are, first, that More's choice testifies at any rate to some degree of interest in them and in the topic; secondly, that in his intellectual world historiography, literature, and philosophy were not so rigidly divided as they are now. Considering his reading and writing from 1506 to 1520, we are justified in saying that some of his early Latin poems, his work on Lucian, his *Richard III*, and *Utopia* establish sufficiently that—to put it in no stronger terms—he had a perceptible interest in the topic of tyranny. As scholar and lawyer he would have been familiar with the commonplaces of the subject; and, I think, more than that. To what degree and in what fashion his own experiences in later years affected this interest, transforming it into something more personal, is irrelevant here. But More's biographers do not fail to note Erasmus' remark (1519) that More always had a special loathing of tyranny.[2]

In all probability More and Erasmus translated from the text of the Aldine edition, 1503.[3] Because of his later friendship with Aldus and his respect for the famous Venetian printer's services to learning,[4] it is hard to conceive of Erasmus using the other and generally less accessible text of 1496; though we have to remember that he did not become acquainted with Aldus personally until after he had completed his work on Lucian for the 1506 volume. We know that

---

[1] See Bradner and Lynch, pp. 138–43, 146, 161, 171–73, 174–75, 180, 204, 205, 217, 218.

[2] ". . . illi semper peculiariter inuisa fuerit tyrannis, quemadmodum aequalitas gratissima" (*EE*, *4*, 15.87–89). Robert P. Adams, *The Better Part of Valor* (Seattle, 1962), pp. 35–36, questions an earlier opinion of mine that More's interest in tyranny, in 1506, was literary rather than personal or political. (Cf. also *CW 2*, xcix–cii.) It would have been more accurate to say that although some of his poems speak strongly of tyrants and tyranny (see commentary, below, p.155), and to that extent may reflect a political mood as well as literary interest, we must be cautious about reading biography into his poetry. Even more must we resist any temptation, when reading his *declamatio* of 1506, to think ahead to More's career in the service of the Crown. Lucian's tyrant is not a Henry VII or Henry VIII.

[3] "All the sixteenth-century Latin translations, those of Erasmus, of Thomas More, of Richard Pace, of Pirckheimer and of many others, are made from the Aldine edition" (Goldschmidt, "Lucian's *Calumnia*," p. 244). To say "all" is hazardous, but that most were made from *1503* is probable.

[4] See his tribute to Aldus in the 1508 and subsequent editions of the *Adagia*, under "Festina lente," *LB*, *2*, 402B–406A; for a translation, *The Adages of Erasmus*, trans. M. M. Phillips (Cambridge, 1964), pp. 179–87.

in later years his library contained a copy of an Aldine edition of Lucian.[1] We are told that the Utopians possess Aldine editions of some Greek authors. True, the Aldine edition of Lucian is not named specifically when More mentions their enjoyment of Lucian, but it is tempting to surmise that they read him in the 1503 text. As for More's own reading—assuming he consistently used a printed and not a manuscript version—we are not limited to surmises. When *1496* and *1503* differ and we can judge which of these texts More followed, it seems clear that he used *1503*.[2]

By Tudor standards, at any rate, More was a careful, conscientious translator, accurate and resourceful: a man who respected his text and wanted to render it correctly. He tries to include everything in his Latin which is in his original; sometimes he tries too hard, e.g. in *Philopseudes* (77/19) he translates Lucian's *κἄν τινα ὁ δηχθεὶς ἄνθρωπος δάκῃ* as "si quem mordicus homo morsus momorderit," a clause whose repetition of *-mor* must have pleased the More who wrote it—was he having his little joke? Sometimes he changes constructions, as we would expect him to do;[3] at other times he tries to render phrases idiomatically;[4] but on the whole his translation, like others by him but unlike so many other sixteenth-century ones, is fairly close, sometimes even literal.[5] One of the seventeenth-century translators of Lucian into English, Ferrand Spence (1684), found More too literal: "too superstitious and has purely and slavishly rendered

---

[1] Fritz Husner, "Die Bibliothek des Erasmus," *Gedenkschrift zum 400. Todestage des Erasmus von Rotterdam* (Basel, 1936), p. 239, no. 123; cited hereafter as "Husner."

[2] Thus at 73/14, More's *pureque lingua Graeca* agrees with *1503*; but *1496* contains a negative particle and says the man spoke imperfect Greek. At 91/15, More's *metu* translates a word omitted in *1496* but present in *1503*. In *Menippus*, the name of the second speaker first appears abbreviated as *φι* in *1496*; in *1503* and in More it is spelled out, *φιλωνίδης*, when first used. Speakers' names are sometimes omitted in *1496*, e.g. in parts of *Cynicus*.

The Harleian collection in the British Museum contains an important early manuscript of Lucian (No. 5694), but there is no evidence that this manuscript, which is incomplete, was in England in the sixteenth century. It does not include any of the works translated by More. For description see *A Catalogue of the Harleian Manuscripts* (London, 1808–12), *3*, 288.

[3] To emphasize an interpretation: thus for Lucian's *τὴν ἐλευθέριον ἐκείνην καὶ ἐπινίκιον σπονδήν* he has "libertatis & uictoriae parentem Libitinam" (93/23). In another passage (67/27) he expands Lucian's *κυνίδιον* to "caniculus, qui mihi in delitijs erat."

[4] Thus "ne diem narrando conteram" (53/24) for *ἵνα μὴ διατρίβω λέγων*.

[5] As in "correpto in manum quam maxime horrendo carmine" (71/1–2) for *προχειρισάμενος τὴν φρικωδεστάτην ἐπίρρησιν*.

Lucian word for word."[1] On the other hand, a seventeenth-century scholar who turned Lucian into Latin thought More's version a model.[2] As Erasmus had remarked (1503), when learning the craft of translation, "nihil esse difficilius quam ex bene Graecis bene Latina reddere."[3] For More, *Philopseudes* must have been the most difficult dialogue; and this is probably the reason his translation of it was singled out for praise by Paulus Bombasius, who was professor of Greek at Bologna when the 1506 volume appeared.[4]

iii

After this review of the facts about More's translating of Lucian, we may now ask what were the purpose and profit of this undertaking. Why read and translate Lucian, and what did More learn, or use, as a result? Our primary concern has been with four works, *Cynicus*, *Menippus*, *Philopseudes*, and *Tyrannicida*, but More must have known many others, beginning with all those translated by Erasmus.

In their estimates of Lucian's substance and style, More and Erasmus agree. First, Lucian is fun: a fellow of infinite jest, of wit, of invention, with good stories and entertaining dialogue. That is why he is a favorite of the Utopians, who set a high value on Greek literature and "Luciani quoque facetijs ac lepore capiuntur."[5] Second, translating Lucian is a good way to improve one's control of Greek and to practice Latin composition. But, as Lupton remarked long ago, More had another and "deeper object" than purely literary exercise in choosing Lucian.[6] Lupton identifies this activity

---

1 Quoted by Hardin Craig, "Dryden's Lucian," 144.

2 *Luciani Samosatensis opera, ex versione Ioannis Benedicti* (Amsterdam, 1687; first published Saumur, 1619), 1, preface.

3 *EE*, *1*, 393.100–1. On the title page of the Froben, 1521, edition of these translations, it is stated that an attentive reader ". . . facile cognoscet, arbitror, cuiusmodi res sit peregrinam linguam, ut in aliam quamuis, ita in Latinam bene ac fideliter uertere." This sounds like Beatus Rhenanus.

The editorial office of the Yale Edition has a microfilm of a manuscript copy of *Cynicus* and *Menippus* in More's translation (Württembergische Landesbibliothek, Cod. theol. et phil. 4° 11, fols. 211r–226v, 238r–264r), thought to have been made in the sixteenth century, probably from a printed edition.

4 Richard Pace, *De fructu qui ex doctrina percipitur*, ed. and trans. Frank Manley and Richard S. Sylvester (New York, 1967), p. 104; cited hereafter as "Pace, *De fructu*."

5 *CW 4*, 182/2–3.

6 Introduction to his edition of *Utopia* (Oxford, 1895), pp. xxii–xxiii.

of More's with "the spirit of the New Learning in its better and purer aspect." We would not put it in quite the same fashion, but the point is sound. Lucian, according to Erasmus, is "adamantinus omnium superstitionum insectator";[1] the reading of Lucian, More tells us, is not merely amusing but rewarding, because Lucian is so good at exposing superstition and fraud and satirizing hypocrisy.[2] When he does these things, he is fundamentally a moral writer. And although it is the follies and foibles of pagans and pagan religion he satirizes, Christians too can learn from him to be on guard against the corruptions that creep even into the one true religion.[3] Similarly More and Erasmus, in their social and satirical commentaries, are fundamentally moral writers, whose motive is reform. James K. McConica, among other recent writers on Tudor humanism, has stressed the "essentially Lucianic" character of *Moriae encomium*, *Colloquia*, and *Utopia*. Of the translations from Lucian he says: "It is not possible to read them and mistake the work for a purely literary exercise. The application to contemporary religious decay is quite explicit, and the targets are identified as falsehood and pretence, both learned and popular."[4] That *Utopia* is *essentially* Lucianic is perhaps debatable, depending on strict definition of "essential," but there can be no quarrel with the assertion that the translations of Lucian apply explicitly to contemporary ills.

This explicitness is brought out in More's prefatory letter, addressed to Thomas Ruthall. The letter is undated but was written in 1506, perhaps in April or May but in any event before he had translated *Tyrannicida* and replied to it. What we notice first of all is More's strong endorsement of Lucian's method. Lucian does not simply dogmatize or pronounce in an *ipse dixi* fashion, nor does he resort to obscenities. Instead he presents dramatically, through dialogue, what

---

1 *LB*, 2, 294A.

2 In addition to the varieties of fraud and superstition More names in his letter to Ruthall, it is probable that he had astrology in mind. For his poems satirizing astrologers see Bradner and Lynch, pp. 33–35, 51, 72, 75–76; and cf. C. A. J. Armstrong, "An Italian Astrologer at the Court of Henry VII," *Italian Renaissance Studies*, ed. E. F. Jacob (London, 1960), pp. 453–54. Erasmus translated Lucian's *De astrologia*.

3 Lucian not only ridiculed religion in general, as in *De sacrificiis* and *Iupiter tragoedus*, but in *Mors Peregrini* made fun of the Christian sect. Even worse, he was thought in the Renaissance to have been the author of *Philopatris*, a dialogue interpreted as vilifying Christian beliefs.

4 *English Humanists and Reformation Politics* (Oxford, 1965), pp. 15–16.

he wants us to see and to think about. More praises, because he values, this *literary* mode of moral teaching, a mode utilizing satire and irony but not malevolence.

In explaining why he thinks *Cynicus*, *Menippus*, and *Philopseudes* are worth reading, More is at pains to disarm critics who may object to Lucian's paganism. He insists on the propriety of disregarding the paganism of ancient authors in favor of the benefits they confer. Though brief, the conviction and clarity of this letter make it a notable example of Christian humanism, if by that term we signify the reaction of Christian scholars, *both* as Christians and as scholars, to classical civilization. Too often a vague or superfluous phrase, "Christian humanism" is in this instance appropriate, even if defined so broadly, because More is commenting on Lucian both as an appreciative reader and as a discriminating Christian. To approach every classical text in the same way he treats Lucian would be as tedious or pedantic as the passion for allegorizing in mediaeval exegetes, but the letter to Ruthall is justified by More's purpose and —we suspect—by the character of the person to whom the letter is addressed.[1]

Clever, witty, and entertaining though Lucian is, More does not suggest that pleasure should be the main reason for reading him. Pleasure is mentioned only in the opening lines, where he alludes to the Horatian maxim about the twofold aim of poetry. Lucian's dialogues are defended chiefly because of their moral worth. If read correctly, their effect will be salutary, despite the writer's paganism. Ignore the paganism but enjoy, and take to heart, his exposure of fraud and hypocrisy. This discrimination by More is important, but we must repeat that his letter dwells on the *utile* rather than the *dulci* of Horace's phrase. In both respects it is characteristic of the more impressive apologies for literature, including pagan literature, that we meet in the sixteenth century. To teach delightfully is the highest aim, and the best justification, of literature: this is the doctrine we meet in Erasmus, in Sidney, in Spenser.[2] "Artistic means to

[1] More's recommendation and defense of a Greek writer, particularly this Greek writer, at this date deserves notice also, for in 1506 Greek had as yet few friends and fewer students in England. Half a century later the situation would be very different, but in 1506 Greek was still a novelty. A dozen years after More's Lucian was published, a group of diehards at Oxford still opposed the study of Greek. See above, p. xxv, n. 3.

[2] Craig R. Thompson, "Better Teachers than Scotus or Aquinas," *Medieval and Renaissance Studies* No. 2, ed. John L. Lievsay (Durham, N.C., 1968), pp. 114–45.

ethical ends" sums up the method, value, and pleasure of literary art, in the judgment of the humanists. They were better informed about ancient literatures than their mediaeval predecessors and correspondingly more sophisticated and more critical about language and style, but in their presuppositions about the purposes and utility of literature they had more in common with their mediaeval predecessors than with us. Where More seems a truer humanist, perhaps, is in his admonitions on testing a text for genuine and spurious contents and judging it from different standpoints. He is too sensitive and too scholarly to be patient with the palpable fictions so common in saints' lives. Truth is not served by pious frauds or faked miracles.

The diversity of Lucian's writings furnished opportunities for both friendly and hostile critics. These dialogues are acceptable; those must on no account be read by schoolboys. "It were better that a childe shuld neuer rede any parte of Luciane than all Luciane" was the way Elyot (1531) put it.[1] Lucian's *Amores* or *Lucius sive asinus* were certainly unsuitable for schoolboys; *Mors Peregrini* gave offense to sensitive Christians; some of the dialogues of courtesans were scandalous. Erasmus, who was attacked more than once because of his approbation of Lucian,[2] retorted that his literary merits and (a point not emphasized by More) his pedagogical utility outweigh whatever is objectionable in his pagan morals. For in addition to being an admirable satirist and entertainer, he is an excellent model for style.[3] Erasmus can praise the style of Chrysostom by saying

---

[1] *The Governour*, ed. H. H. S. Croft (London, 1883), *1*, 58.

[2] By Luther, for example, who declared Erasmus laughed at religion, like Lucian, and was in fact far worse than Lucian. See *Luthers Werke*, Weimar edition (1883–). *Briefwechsel*, *5*, 88; *Tischreden*, *3*, 136–37; and cf. *Tischreden*, *1*, 397; *2*, 146, 410; *3*, 214, 215; *4*, 543; *6*, 252. For Erasmus' comment on such libels see *Hyperaspistes* (1526–27), *LB*, *10*, 1260E–1261A.

[3] "Omne tulit punctum (vt scripsit Flaccus) qui miscuit vtile dulci. Quod quidem aut nemo, mea sententia, aut noster hic Lucianus est assecutus, qui priscae comoediae dicacitatem, sed citra petulantiam referens, Deum immortalem, qua vafricie, quo lepore, perstringit omnia, quo naso cuncta suspendit, quam omnia miro sale perfricat. . . . Tantum obtinet in dicendo gratiae, tantum in inueniendo felicitatis, tantum in iocando leporis, in mordendo aceti, sic titillat allusionibus, sic seria nugis, nugas seriis miscet; sic ridens vera dicit, vera dicendo ridet; sic hominum mores, affectus, studia quasi penicillo depingit, neque legenda, sed plane spectanda oculis exponit, vt nulla comoedia, nulla satyra cum huius dialogis conferri debeat, seu voluptatem spectes, seu spectes vtilitatem" (*EE*, *1*, 425.26–426.50). This passage states the case for Lucian as well as it is stated anywhere in the sixteenth century.

that it has the *facilitas*, *perspicuitas*, *suavitas*, and *copia* of Lucian.[1] When in *De ratione studii* he recommends Greek prose writers for study, Lucian is first on the list, followed by Demosthenes and Herodotus.[2] Defending his recommendations against a critic, he allows that Lucian scoffs at the gods, but those were pagan gods; this very scoffing, which won Lucian the name of "atheist," assures that Christian readers will avoid any danger of learning respect for paganism from Lucian. (Are Plato and Aristotle to be shunned because they wrote seriously about the pagan gods?) If someone objects to Lucian, are we to forbid Homer, Catullus, Juvenal, Martial—and are we to prefer moderns like Poggio or Pontano?[3] If Lucian made fun of Christianity, what of Pliny, Suetonius, Tacitus? Were Jerome and Augustine heretics because they were students of literature?

Erasmus' endorsement, with careful reservations, of Lucian for schools would hardly have been acceptable to his friend Dean Colet of St. Paul's, although Colet came to recognize the value of Greek. When he refounded St. Paul's School (1509–12) and wrote its statutes (1518), he stipulated that the master be a man learned in Latin "and also in greke yf suyche may be gotten."[4] He did find a capable man, William Lily, who had collaborated with More in translating epigrams from the *Greek Anthology*. Colet's statutes provided that Greek as well as Latin should be taught, but they say nothing further about Greek. That the language was actually taught at St. Paul's is an inference from our knowledge of Lily's attainments. Colet himself knew very little Greek, but if we may judge by his cautions about the choice of Latin authors we have no reason to think he would have taken a chance on Lucian. For his statutes have

---

1 *EE*, *6*, 50.251–52.

2 *LB*, *1*, 521D. Linacre writes to John Claymond, President of Magdalen College (1504–16) and later of Corpus Christi, Oxford, that if he will only read a little Lucian every day he will learn Greek with pleasure (P. S. Allen, *Erasmus* [Oxford, 1934], p. 153).

3 *Apologia in dialogum Latomi* (1519), *LB*, *9*, 92B–E. If a young man is tainted with lasciviousness, his confessor will rashly blame his reading of Virgil or Lucian instead of his youth or moral weakness (*Adagia*, *LB*, *2*, 1053D).

4 The statutes are reprinted by J. H. Lupton, *A Life of John Colet, D.D.*, 2d ed. (Hamden, Conn., 1961), pp. 271–84. Erasmus had close ties with St. Paul's School. He helped to write a grammar for use there; dedicated his influential *De copia* to Colet; wrote a sermon, prayers, poems, and a catechism for the pupils; and corresponded with Colet about the school. For a pleasant though idealized picture of one of the boys, see Erasmus' colloquy, *Confabulatio pia* (*Colloquies of Erasmus*, pp. 30–41).

unusual and explicit recommendation of Christian Latin authors: Lactantius, Prudentius, Proba, Sedulius, Juvencus, Baptista Mantuanus.

> As towchyng in this scole what shalbe taught of the Maisters and lerynd of the scolers it passith my wit to devyse and determyn in particuler but in generall to speke and sum what to saye my mynde, I wolde they were taught all way in good litterature both laten and greke, and goode auctors suych as haue the veray Romayne eliquence joyned withe wisdome specially Cristyn auctours that wrote theyre wysdome with clene and chast laten other in verse or in prose, for my entent is by thys scole specially to incresse knowledge and worshipping of god and oure lorde Crist Jesu and good Cristen lyff and maners in the Children And for that entent I will the Chyldren lerne ffirst aboue all the Cathechyzon in Englysh and after the accidence that I made or sum other yf eny be better to the purpose to induce chyldren more spedely to laten spech And thanne Institutum Christiani homines [*sic*] which that lernyd Erasmus made at my request and the boke called Copia of the same Erasmus And thenne other auctours Christian as lactancius prudentius and proba and sedulius and Juuencus and Baptista Mantuanus and suche other as shalbe t[h]ought convenyent and moste to purpose vnto the true laten spech all barbary all corrupcion all laten adulterate which ignorant blynde folis brought into this worlde and with the same hath distayned and poysenyd the olde laten spech and the veray Romayne tong which in the tyme of Tully and Salust and Virgill and Terence was vsid, whiche also seint Jerome and seint ambrose and seint Austen and many hooly doctours lerynd in theyr tymes. I say that ffylthynesse and all such abusyon which the later blynde worlde brought in which more ratheyr may be callid blotterature thenne litterature I vtterly abbanysh and Exclude oute of this scole and charge the Maisters that they teche all way that is the best and instruct the chyldren in greke and Redyng laten in Redyng vnto them suych auctours that hathe with wisdome joyned the pure chaste eloquence.[1]

---

[1] Lupton, *Life of Colet*, pp. 279–80. Some words seem to be omitted between "the true laten spech" and "all barbary" in the next to last sentence.

We have no conclusive evidence as to whether the Christian authors were in fact read, or for how long. The distance between programs or statutes and actual practice in school was probably as great then as it is now. If Colet feared the paganism of standard Latin authors, it is hard to believe that he could have taken any interest in Lucian. Scholarly but not literary, lacking the kind of imagination Erasmus and More had, he would not have responded to Lucianic wit. Neither Erasmus nor More dedicated any of their translations to him.

What did More learn from Lucian? The activity of translating and the letter to Ruthall prove that for some months in 1506, Lucian occupied his leisure and his thoughts. It does not follow, however, that we could draw up a list of parallel passages, reminiscences, quotations, and the like showing that More borrowed extensively from Lucian in later writings. Even an author who means much to a reader—and he must mean much to one who takes the considerable trouble of translating him into another language—may gradually be forgotten, or superseded by newer interests after the translation is finished and published. Yet it is not likely that a man of More's mind and temperament, who so obviously enjoyed Lucian, simply forgot him or failed to learn from him, even if "learning" means nothing more than recognition or recollection of Lucian's adroitness in producing those effects which More himself sought in his poems, satires, jokes, allusions, epigrams, and letters. This is but another way of saying that More's debt to Lucian is too subtle, too elusive, to be appraised simply by a count of specific instances. We may notice in *Utopia* a Latinized Greek word (*morosophis*)[1] taken from Lucian, who appears to have invented it (*Alexander*, xl). We find in *Utopia* many fanciful names coined from Greek (e.g. Achorians, Alaopolitans, Amaurotum, Anemolians, Anydrus, Barzanes, Buthrescae, Cynemerni, Macarians, Nephelogetes, Polylerites, Syphogrants, Tranibors, Trapemerni, Utopia, Zapoletans)—a Lucianic trick, though Aristophanic as well. We meet in *Richard III* and again in *The Four Last Things*[2] a famous metaphor from Lucian's *Menippus*, a variant of "All the world's a stage"; and probably though not certainly *Menippus* is where More first read it. We meet a few pas-

---

[1] *CW 4*, 64/2.

[2] See commentary, below, on 37/21.

sages in *Responsio ad Lutherum*[1] that may echo Lucian's *Adversus indoctum* and other writings (including the *Philopseudes*, translated by More), but these might have been remembered just as easily from Erasmus' *Adagia*. We hear from Pace that More gibed at two Scotist divines by telling them, "One of you milks a he-goat while the other holds a sieve," a pleasantry from Lucian's *Demonax*,[2] xxviii. All evidence of this kind is interesting, but there is not a great deal of it, and it is not very important. On the other hand, generalizations about "influence" have their own hazards, for however plausible to the critic enunciating them, they often appear less than convincing to others, who have no axes to grind. We must state our reasoned convictions and take our chances.

Influence of one common sort exists when a writer imitates plots or passages or scenes found in another author and there is no doubt about the source of his material, however he adapts or elaborates it; for example the indebtedness of Ulrich von Hutten or Rabelais to Lucian.[3] Or the later writer may keep referring to the earlier one and invoke him as an example, as Erasmus names Lucian in *Moriae encomium*. Or, third, there is influence which is the sum total of effects from an author read and liked, perhaps years earlier; and recalled and exploited, perhaps unconsciously, but mingled with many other books and memories, in one's own writing. This is the kind of influence—or of elective affinities—most significant in *Utopia* so far as Lucian is concerned. In assessing such influence scholars disagree, as they do about so many other aspects of *Utopia*. McConica finds *Utopia* "essentially" Lucianic. I suspect that the latest and most erudite commentator on the text, Father Surtz, would demur. Although he appears to accept the view that "familiarity with Lucian which the translations compelled and which they attest . . . contributed something to the verisimilitude of the wonderful *Utopia*," he

---

[1] *CW* 5, 80/2–3, 128/26, 146/13, 178/2, 214/28–29, 268/19, 292/25, 366/1, and see notes on these passages.

[2] Pace, *De fructu*, pp. 104, 106. Pace says this incident occurred when More was still a boy, *adhuc puer*. If *puer* is to be taken strictly, More must have found the illustration somewhere else than in Lucian's Greek. Or, more likely, Pace may have been mistaken about the time. The notion of the boy More talking to his elders so freely strains credulity.

Pace made a Latin version of *Demonax*, printed sometime after 1510 with translations of two works by Plutarch (Goldschmidt, *The First Cambridge Press in Its European Setting*, p. 17).

[3] For details see Jean Plattard, *L'oeuvre de Rabelais* (Paris, 1910), pp. 204–14.

concludes that the Lucianic dialogues "closest to the subject of More's work, namely, *A True History* and *Icaromenippus*, are far from the realism of the *Utopia*."[1] Bland descriptions of strange customs, whimsical humor,[2] a beguiling narrative art suggesting, as Swift says of *Gulliver's Travels*, "an air of truth apparent through the whole": these are qualities present also in Lucian's sketches and tales, and could have taught More (as I believe they did teach him) some of the techniques and strategems he uses so aptly in *Utopia*. But the question involves more than so-called realism. *Utopia* has, I think, besides Lucianic touches in dialogue and narrative,[3] a Lucianic spirit. To say this is not to affirm that it is "essentially" Lucianic; nor could such a claim be pressed without seeming to exclude other and equally important sources or influences.[4] *Utopia* is Lucianic—but it is also Platonic, also Plutarchan. It is many things, but *essentially* it is Morean, for it is unique. I should not wish to underestimate the contributions of Lucian, but in my judgment these must be said to

---

[1] *CW 4*, p. clxii. Professor A. E. Barker, in his review of the Yale edition, implies doubt that the influence of Lucian on *Utopia* has been exaggerated (*Journal of English and Germanic Philology*, *65* [1966], 329–30).

[2] Read *Utopia* "si quando voles ridere," Erasmus tells a friend (*EE*, *2*, 483.17). *Utopia* has what C. S. Lewis terms "different levels of seriousness" (*English Literature in the Sixteenth Century* [Oxford, 1954], p. 169), which are explicated with acuteness by recent scholars, but Lewis was right to remind us that Erasmus and other sixteenth-century readers were attracted first of all by its paradoxes and witty invention; in short, by what may be called its Lucianic character.

[3] For example, the manner in which More arouses our interest in *Utopia* is much the same as that at the opening of *Philopseudes*, which he had translated. Hythloday makes a passing reference to Utopia; later the name turns up again, when he tells us the Macarians live near Utopia. A page or two later he says the principles of Plato's ideal state are actually practiced in Utopia. By this time we are eager to hear about the place, and after dinner Hythloday begins his description of it. When *Philopseudes* opens, Tychiades asks his friend Philocles why it is that people are so fond of lying. But he does not tell him immediately of his recent experience at the house of Eucrates. Only after conversing with Philocles for a few moments does he say he has just come from Eucrates' home and that he left because he was fed up with the lies heard there. Philocles replies that Eucrates is well known to be a venerable philosopher who would not tolerate that sort of thing. Thereupon Tychiades relates how he had gone to Eucrates' house to look for a friend, failed to find him, but met other acquaintances who happened to be talking about unusual cures for diseases. By this time Philocles' curiosity is aroused and he wants to know what it was Tychiades heard.

[4] J. A. K. Thomson finds that *Utopia* "has all the marks which . . . were taken over from the Mime into the Lucianic Dialogue" ("Erasmus in England," pp. 79–80), but remarks of this kind do not help unless we are shown that the "marks" could not easily have had any other source than Lucian.

consist principally of conception, tone, approach, invention; and these are matters which cannot be tabulated or proven in court. A reader of More's Latin text, who knows Lucian thoroughly, will undoubtedly be reminded of the Greek writer many times when going through the second book of *Utopia*. If in addition he is aware of More's friendship with Erasmus and their work on Lucian some ten years before the writing of *Utopia*, he will have no difficulty in perceiving that *Utopia* is Lucianic, while acknowledging that it is also much else.[1]

One familiar, pervasive characteristic of Lucian's outlook and style is irony. It seems to me as certain as any biographical and critical inference can be that More, whose gift of *festivitas* was so well known, was attracted by this hallmark of Lucianic writing. "Irony" is meant in the usual senses: first, ironical speech, (a) the rhetorical tactic of saying one thing while meaning another and usually contrary thing, e.g. praising when one is blaming and vice versa;[2] (b) understatement or litotes; (c) intentional over-simplifica-

---

[1] T. S. Dorsch argues that "we shall not understand Book II of *Utopia* unless we read it in the same way as we read Lucian—and as we read *Gulliver's Travels*" ("Sir Thomas More and Lucian: An Interpretation of *Utopia*," *Archiv für das Studium der neueren Sprachen und Literaturen, 203* [1966–67], 362). That is, we must read More "in reverse, as we read Lucian—and Swift" (p. 357). I agree with much of what Dorsch, following C. S. Lewis, says about Lucianic qualities in *Utopia*; but in reaction against interpretations that find profound seriousness as well as comic elements in the book, he goes too far. Why can't we have it both ways? It may indeed be true that More's contemporaries read it "as they read Lucian" (p. 350), but is that enough? Maybe it is a more complex work than it seemed. We respect the seventeenth century's response to *Hamlet* and the eighteenth century's to *Gulliver's Travels*, but surely we are not limited to their interpretations of those works. A book that continues to interest and puzzle readers after four centuries may prove less simple and clear-cut to later generations than to its first readers, whose reactions to it may have been correct but necessarily limited. Similarly with respect to "as we read *Gulliver's Travels*." As *who* reads *Gulliver's Travels*—an undergraduate, a biographer of Swift, a specialist in eighteenth-century social or political history, a literary critic, a psychiatrist?

For further criticism of Dorsch's views, see R. S. Sylvester, "Si Hythlodaeo credimus: Vision and Revision in Thomas More's *Utopia*," *Soundings*, published by the Society for Religion in Higher Education, New Haven, Conn. (formerly *The Christian Scholar*), *51* (1968), 272–89.

[2] If irony, sometimes defined as the "dry mock," is taken or mistaken for merely sardonic or sarcastic speech, it invites censure. Edward Hall the chronicler, More's contemporary, writes of him that his "wytte was fine, and full of imaginacions, by reason wherof, he was to muche geven to mockinge, whyche was to his gravitie a great blemishe. . . . I cannot tell whether I shoulde call him a foolishe wyseman, or a wise foolishman, for undoubtedly he beside his learnyng, had a great witte, but it was so myngled with

tion; second, an habitual manner or cast of mind, specifically an assumed self-depreciation such as that practiced by Socrates; third, the irony of situation or fortune, when decisions and actions planned or carried out for supposedly sound, logical, dependable reasons produce instead wholly unforeseen and often catastrophic results. As a rhetorical technique, a tone, a mode of expression, irony in Lucian's dramatic dialogues, and to a lesser extent in his non-dramatic discourses, is a device More and Erasmus admired and, in their own ways and for their own purposes, practiced. In their own ways too they grasped, or shared, the Lucianic irony as a quality of mind, a temperament, indicative of (and to some degree conditioning) one's outlook on the world and society. This irony, the reflection of Lucian's skepticism, appears as an amused tolerance of human foibles, a pretended ignorance, and sometimes a cool rationalism; often it is the accompaniment of satire, as in *Moriae encomium.*

How much might Erasmus and More have learned about the rhetorical uses of irony, in its several senses, from their reading of Lucian? And how much did this experience contribute, some years later, to *Moriae encomium*, *Iulius exclusus* (the perfect Lucianic dialogue), and *Utopia*, and through these to the main stream of European literature? Legitimate questions, surely, but here again we have to go by impressions gained after wide and careful reading, not by statistical tables. Erasmus praises Lucian for mixing the serious with the entertaining, speaking truth while he laughs and laughing while

---

tauntyng and mockyng, that it semed to them that best knew him, that he thought nothing to be wel spoken except he had ministred some mocke in the communicacion . . . wyth a mocke he ended hys lyfe" (*Henry VIII*, ed. Charles Whibley [London, 1904], *2*, 158, 265–66). E. E. Reynolds, who quotes these passages, speaks of Hall's "tribute" to More (*Thomas More and Erasmus* [London, 1965], p. 242), but Hall seems rather to be damning with faint praise. More, he suggests, was a man of intelligence and learning, but through a culpable addiction to "mocking" (the modern "wisecrack"), brought trouble on himself. This may be the opinion of a man incapable of appreciating irony, but Hall was not alone in censuring More for mockery. Tyndale, for example, complains that it "is no christian manner" to "trifle out the truth with taunts and mocks, as M. More doth" (*The Supper of the Lord*, ed. Henry Walter, Parker Society edition [Cambridge, 1850], p. 263).

In the *Dialogue Concerning Heresies* the Messenger says to More: "But ye use (my maister sayth) to loke so sadly whan ye mene merely [merrily], that many times men doubte whyther ye speke in sporte, whan ye mene good ernest" (*The Workes . . . . in the Englysh Tonge*, London, 1557, sig. i_4, p. 127B; cited hereafter as "*EW*, 1557").

On litotes, see the recent study by Elizabeth McCutcheon, "More's Use of Litotes in *Utopia*," *Moreana*, *31–32* (1971), 107–21.

he speaks truth,[1] and tells us he and More are accustomed to doing the same.[2] In the preface dedicating his *Moriae encomium* to More, Erasmus declares nothing is more frivolous than to treat serious matters triflingly, yet nothing more delightful than to treat trifling topics as though one seems to have been anything but trifling.[3] Appreciation of the just mode of balancing the serious and the non-serious, of combining them artistically, that is, and for moral ends, is the key to understanding *Moriae encomium*—and, I think, much of *Utopia* as well. Not for nothing did the title page of *Utopia* promise the reader that this book was "nec minus salutaris quam festiuus." To affirm that Erasmus, with the help of More, "brought back irony into literature," that "to forge out of irony a literary instrument capable of sustained and extensive use, and so used, was a thing which had not really been done since Lucian,"[4] is a challenging if over-simplified thesis; but irony did become increasingly important to More and Erasmus in the first decade of the sixteenth century, and thereby to literature. And they did find and enjoy irony in Lucian especially.

More's *Richard III*, written sometime between 1514 and 1518 so far as we can tell,[5] bears some marks of ironical method and of Lucianic influence. Dean, who has analyzed varieties of irony in *Richard III*, distinguishes Erasmian from Lucianic techniques and concludes that the predominant kind of irony in *Richard III* is closer

---

[1] *EE*, *1*, 425.45–426.46.

[2] Ibid., *1*, 422.16.

[3] "Vt enim nihil nugacius quam seria nugatorie tractare, ita nihil festiuius quam ita tractare nugas vt nihil minus quam nugatus fuisse videaris" (ibid., *1*, 461.50–52). More seems to be paraphrasing or recalling this sentence when he writes to his children instructions for composition (Rogers, 257/44–48). Erasmus himself repeats the first part of it at the end of his *Convivium fabulosum* (*Colloquies of Erasmus*, p. 266).

We do not have a complete or exact account of the connection between More and the writing of *Moriae encomium*, but we have enough to be certain that the passage in which Erasmus calls him the *autor* of that Lucianic composition means More inspired it: ". . . et Luciano cum primis est delectatus; quin et mihi vt Morias Encomium scriberem, hoc est vt camelus saltarem, fuit autor" (*EE*, *4*, 16.119–20). Of the Lucianic character of *Moriae encomium* there can be no doubt; it is Lucianic in conception, form, and tone, written by a man who had Lucian in mind when writing it, and written moreover in the home of his collaborator in Lucianic studies.

[4] Thomson, "Erasmus in England," p. 67.

[5] *CW 2*, lxiii–lxv.

to the Erasmian type.[1] Whether these types are so clearly separable or not, we need to remember that neither Lucian nor Erasmus confines himself to a single kind of irony, or ironical method. Dean calls attention also to the relevance, for More's *Richard III*, of Lucian's most extended piece of literary criticism, *Quomodo historia conscribenda sit*.[2] In this readable essay on historiography, which More must have known, Lucian has much to say about style as well as substance. He exalts the historian over the mere chronicler or compiler. The ideal historian must be gifted with political insight (the gift of nature) and facility of expression (which can be learned), be a man of independent spirit, be obsessed with lucidity, and write for posterity.

iv

We do not read More's translations as an introduction to Lucian but to learn what they tell us about More and about English humanism in the early sixteenth century. Some recent writers on More and Erasmus, as we have noted, feel that their interest in Lucian meant more to them than the publication of a volume of translations; that it must be connected in one way or another with their lasting literary achievements, *Moriae encomium* and *Utopia*; that the translations somehow pointed the way to those books. This conviction explains why one scholar finds that "the most profitable approach to *Utopia* may be by way of More's fondness for Lucian."[3] Another calls these translations "a literary landmark."[4] A third,

---

[1] Leonard F. Dean, "Literary Problems in More's *Richard III*," *PMLA*, *58* (1943), 22–41. "Verbal and Socratic irony chiefly distinguish the dialogues of Lucian" (p. 29), but the Erasmian kind in *Moriae encomium*, which More's more nearly resembles, is an "irony of complexity." By means of this Erasmus "is able to examine in all its difficult complications a central human problem: the relation between comfortable conformity and the painful independence of wisdom. We are convinced, consequently, that his choice is neither that of a dreamy idealist nor of a rigid moralist. It is a kind of irony consonant with Erasmus' character and with the common quality of most forms of Renaissance humanism, namely, that attitude towards life which is comprehensive and flexible without being irresponsible. It is this kind of irony, furthermore, which pervades *Richard III*" (pp. 31–32).

[2] The dedicatory letter to the most familiar English translation of *Utopia*, Ralph Robinson's (1551), opens with a story from *Quomodo historia conscribenda sit*, iii.

[3] Dorsch, "Sir Thomas More and Lucian," p. 347.

[4] Adams, *The Better Part of Valor*, p. 33.

H. A. Mason,[1] submits that the central document here, with respect to More, is not his translations themselves but the prefatory letter to Ruthall. Mason's argument is not always easy to follow, but his essay is stimulating and has the merit of taking More's attention to Lucian seriously. He himself does not seem to think highly of Lucian; More's interest in *Tyrannicida* he regards as a "darker note."[2] But this very fact that humanists could esteem inferior authors is a problem for literary historians to ponder.

The humanists' approach to the classics, we are told, was "essentially trivial" and could not help being trivial; not because they themselves were trivial-minded but because they "were fatally without roots in the civilisation into which they were born." This odd assertion seems to mean they did not have sense enough to know that the future lay with the vernacular tongues. They "failed to see the true relations of literature and civilisation."[3] Worst of all, they did not understand the function of literature: "They could find no justification for literature other than its moral instructiveness."[4] Nevertheless More and Erasmus, exceptional men, were "guided by a right instinct in turning to Lucian,"[5] because "through Lucian they came to understand the basic principle of Roman literary theory: that literature is justified because it combines pleasure and instruction."[6] Others had read Horace's and Quintilian's words; More and Erasmus understood their spirit. They made a breakthrough because "they grasped the real relation of these two functions, instruction and pleasure."[7] "In short, what I am arguing is that the start of a positive answer to the question: where does new literature *begin* in the sixteenth century? is not in the translations More and Erasmus made from Lucian, but in *the reasons they gave for making them*. Consequently, the prefaces More and Erasmus wrote for their translations of Lucian are primary documents in the history of *real thinking* about literature in this century."[8] Their translations

---

1 *Humanism and Poetry in the Early Tudor Period*, p. 67.
2 Ibid., pp. 60, 72–73.
3 Ibid., p. 66.
4 Ibid., p. 66.
5 Ibid., p. 67.
6 Ibid., p. 70.
7 Ibid., p. 70.
8 Ibid., p. 67.

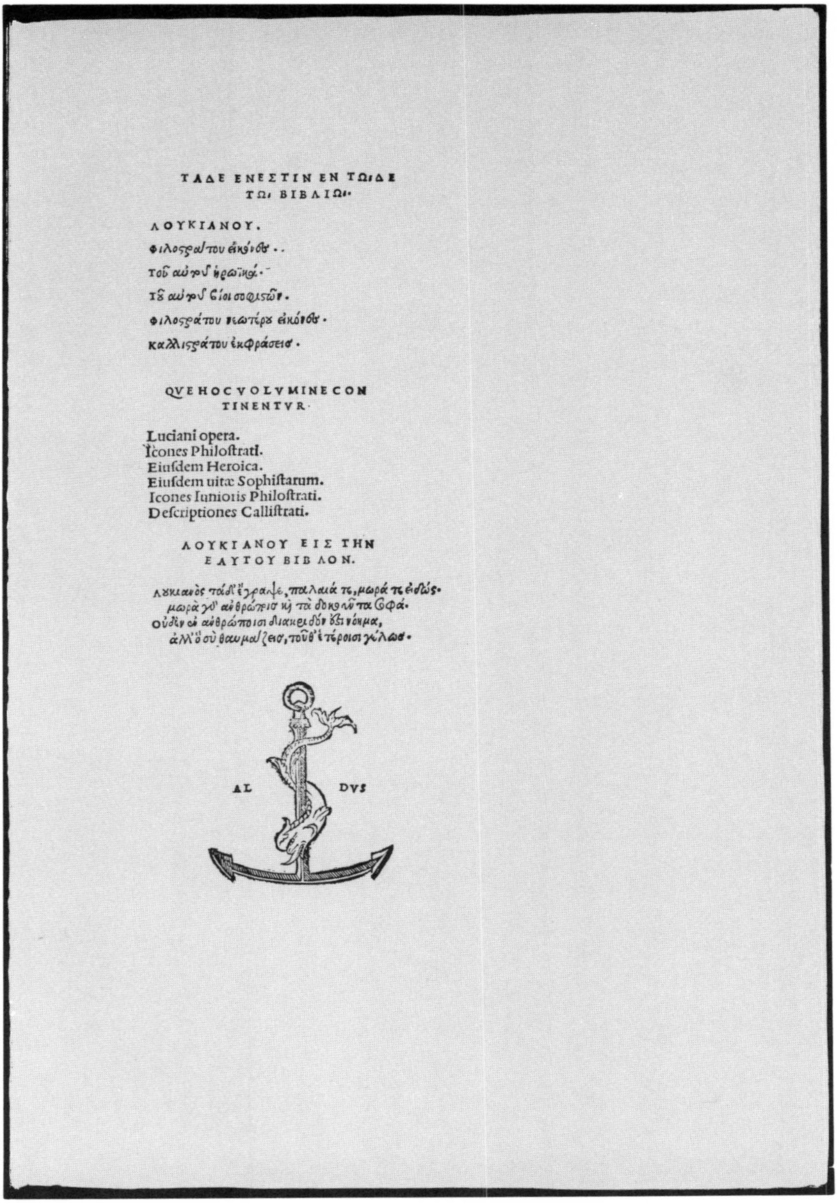

ΤΑΔΕ ΕΝΕΣΤΙΝ ΕΝ ΤΩΙΔΕ ΤΩΙ ΒΙΒΛΙΩΙ.

ΛΟΥΚΙΑΝΟΥ.

Φιλοστράτου εἰκόνες.

Τοῦ αὐτοῦ ἡρωϊκά.

Τοῦ αὐτοῦ βίοι σοφιστῶν.

Φιλοστράτου νεωτέρου εἰκόνες.

Καλλιστράτου ἐκφράσεις.

QVE HOC VOLVMINE CONTINENTVR.

Luciani opera.
Icones Philoſtrati.
Eiuſdem Heroica.
Eiuſdem uitæ Sophiſtarum.
Icones Iunioris Philoſtrati.
Deſcriptiones Calliſtrati.

ΛΟΥΚΙΑΝΟΥ ΕΙΣ ΤΗΝ ΕΑΥΤΟΥ ΒΙΒΛΟΝ.

Λουκιανὸς τάδ' ἔγραψε, παλαιά τε, μωρά τε εἰδώς·
μωρὰ γὰρ ἀνθρώποις καὶ τὰ δοκοῦντα σοφά·
οὐδὲν ἐν ἀνθρώποισι διακριδόν ἐστι νόημα,
ἀλλ' ὃ σὺ θαυμάζεις, τοῦθ' ἑτέροισι γέλως.

Lucian, title page of the Aldine edition, 1503 (reduced)

are dead, but the fruits of positive thinking—*Moriae encomium* and *Utopia*—are still alive.

That "new literature" in the sixteenth century begins with the prefaces to More's and Erasmus' translations of Lucian is a provocative suggestion, though not self-authenticating. We can agree about the importance of the fact that their attitude toward Lucian involved literary response as well as ethical approval. Other men had not said the same things about Lucian, or said them in the same way. But take a second look. More praises the wit and instructiveness he finds in Lucian, true. Yet he seems to me to emphasize the instructiveness more than Mason allows. In fact most of the letter to Ruthall is taken up with it. Entertaining as the wit and satire may be, they are means to a serious end.

However we connect the 1506 publication with later literature and literary theory in the sixteenth century, we are on safe ground if we think of More's work on Lucian as a true testimonial of his humanism early in his literary career and early in the history of Renaissance letters in England. The More who in 1516 skirted the "margins of modernity"[1] in *Utopia* was "modern" in 1506 because he liked Lucian enough to turn his Greek into Latin.

THE TEXT

This summary deals with editions published before 1535, the year of More's death; of later editions or reprints only two require brief notice. The textual and bibliographical history of the early editions has many uncertainties, though few of these are of much importance. Except for what the books themselves reveal about the text, virtually the only useful information available comes from Erasmus. More himself does not refer to his translations of Lucian, I believe, in his other writings or in his correspondence after 1506. A very few passages contain probable allusions to Lucian's dialogues, but on the making and printing of his own versions he is silent.

1506 PARIS, BADIUS ASCENSIUS (78)[2]

Nothing is known about the manuscripts of Erasmus' and More's translations. Did More keep a copy, we wonder, or did Erasmus

[1] The phrase is Hexter's, *CW 4*, p. cviii.

[2] The Gibson and Patrick numbers are added after each entry.

carry off the sole manuscript to Paris when he left England in late May or early June of 1506? After two months in Paris, Erasmus departed for Italy.[1] He must have left More's translations, and some of his own, with the printer in Paris. This printer, Josse Badius Ascensius, had other work by Erasmus in hand that summer: Latin verse translations of Euripides' *Hecuba* and *Iphigenia in Aulide*.[2] These appeared in September. They were followed a few months later by Erasmus' and More's versions of Lucian: *Luciani viri quam disertissimi compluria opuscula longe festiuissima ab Erasmo Roterodamo & Thoma moro interpretibus optimis in latinorum linguam traducta*. . . . Colophon: Ex officina Ascensiana ad Idus Nouemb. MDVI.[3]

To this volume Erasmus contributed, in all, translations of eighteen short dialogues and ten longer ones; More furnished four, *Cynicus*, *Menippus*, *Philopseudes*, *Tyrannicida*; and each supplied a *declamatio* answering Lucian's *Tyrannicida*, the only composition translated by both men. Some of Erasmus' versions[4] were printed by November 1 (so the *first* colophon, sig. Ii_6 verso) and all of More's by November 13 (the date of the *second* colophon, sig. CCc_5 verso); but the volume was not in fact complete until a second set of translations,[5] lately received from Erasmus, with a prefatory letter (dated November 17 from Bologna) addressed to Jerome Busleiden,[6] had been inserted.

---

1 *EE*, *1*, 426, introduction to *ep*. 194.

2 Ibid., *1*, 417.

3 On the press of Badius Ascensius see Ph. Renouard, *Bibliographie des impressions et des oeuvres de Josse Badius Ascensius* (Paris, 1908); on this volume of translations by Erasmus and More, *3*, 26–27.

4 *Toxaris*, *Alexander*, *Gallus*, *Timon*, *Tyrannicida* (with Erasmus' *declamatio* in reply), *De iis qui mercede conducti degunt; Dialogi mortuorum* iii, vii, viii, xvii, xviii, xxii; and a poem by Erasmus, *De senectute*.

5 *Dialogi mortuorum*, ix, xi, xiii, xxi, xxiv, xxv, xxvi; *Dialogi deorum*, xii, xix, xxi, xxiv; *Dialogi marini*, i; and *Hercules*, *Eunuchus*, *De sacrificiis*, *Convivium*.

On a translation of the *Longaevi* attributed to Lucian, made by Erasmus in 1505 or 1506, or earlier, but printed much later and without authorization, see Craig R. Thompson, "Erasmus' Translation of Lucian's *Longaevi*," *Classical Philology*, *35* (1940), 397–415; and cf. the new (Amsterdam) edition of *Erasmi opera omnia* (1969–), vol. I, pt. 1, pp. 372–73.

6 *EE*, *1*, 435.33–37. The colophon to these (sig. Ll_6 verso) has no date. Many years later Erasmus says in a letter (ibid., *11*, 184.508–512, written 1535) that his work on Lucian—which means the volume of 1506—was published (*aeditis*) before he reached the borders of Italy. Strictly speaking, this is not correct. He was in Italy by early September (ibid., *1*, 432), but the Lucian volume was not issued until November.

Erasmus' translations of Lucian, ed. Christopher Robinson, are included in vol. I, pt. 1, pp. 361–627 of *Erasmi opera omnia* (Amsterdam, 1969).

More's translations occupy unnumbered leaves AAa–CCc_5 verso. The order is: letter to Ruthall, *Cynicus*, *Menippus*, *Philopseudes*, *Tyrannicida*, declamation in reply to *Tyrannicida*. This order differs from that announced on the title page, where *Tyrannicida* and the declamation precede the others. Immediately before the colophon on sig. CCc_5 verso are these lines:

ASCENSIVS MORO SVO. S.D.

Laudabunt alii clarum vi laudis Erasmum:
  Dulcisonaque lyra grandisonaque tuba.
At te si merita celebrarent More camoena:
  Multum sudarent Flaccus & ipse Maro.
Tu siquidem illustreis olimiam Marte Britannos:
  Ditasti Latio protinus eloquio.

Others will heap praise on the famous Erasmus with dulcet lyre and resounding trumpet; but were they to laud you, More, with appropriate verse, Horace and Virgil himself would labor prodigiously. The Britons, though renowned of old for their prowess in arms, you have enriched from this time forth with Latin eloquence.

At this date Erasmus' reputation with the reading public rested mainly on the first edition of *Adagia*, 1500; a volume of *Lucubratiunculae*, 1503, which included *Enchiridion*; a panegyric on Philip of Burgundy, 1504; an edition of Lorenzo Valla's *Annotationes* on the New Testament, 1505; the recent translations of Euripides, 1506; and a few letters and poems. Badius Ascensius was printer and publisher of the Valla, Euripides (September 1506), and Lucian (November), and he was to issue a new edition[1] of the *Adagia* in December 1506. Although he had therefore a strong interest in puffing his author, and although a publisher is not on oath in his advertising, it is worth notice that in 1506 Badius can call Erasmus eminent or famous, *clarum*. His extravagant language about More is based on nothing but the versions of Lucian and the *declamatio*.

1514 Paris, Badius Ascensius (79)

Besides the translations printed in the volume of 1506, Erasmus

[1] *EE*, *4*, 429.89–93; Renouard, *Bibliographie des impressions et des oeuvres de Josse Badius Ascensius*, *2*, 415–17.

made Latin versions of seven other Lucianic pieces: *Saturnalia*, *Cronosolon*, *Epistolae Saturnales*, *De luctu*, *Abdicatus*, *Icaromenippus*, *De astrologia*. These had been dispatched to Badius Ascensius by May 19, 1512, and Erasmus furnished a dedicatory preface dated April 29, addressed to Archbishop Warham.[1] For reasons unknown to us, and perhaps not clear to Erasmus himself,[2] publication of a new edition was delayed until June 1, 1514. Accordingly Erasmus supplied a new dedicatory letter to Warham,[3] but Badius unaccountably omitted this and printed the earlier one instead.

Title: *Luciani Erasmo interprete Dialogi & alia emuncta. Quorum quaedam recentius quaedam annos abhinc octo sunt versa: sed nuper recognita. . . . Quaedam etiam a Thoma Moro latina facta: & Quaedam ab eodem concinnata. Vaenundantur in aedibus Ascensianis.* The book has two colophons. The first, on fol. CXXXV verso, is dated May 30; the second, June 1, follows *De astrologia* and a table of contents. The printer informs us on fol. CXXXIX (misnumbered, because CXXXVI is blank) that *De astrologia* was received too late to be inserted in its proper place.

The *1514* text was set from *1506*. It corrects at least thirty plain errors and misprints in the *1506* text of More's versions, but retains other errors.

One surviving copy of this *1514* edition has special interest because of its connection with the Froben editions, of which the first appeared in 1517. Before proceeding to that subject, we may notice an intervening edition.

1516 VENICE, ALDUS MANUTIUS (80)

Title: *Luciani opuscula Erasmo Roterodamo interprete . . . Eiusdem Luciani Thoma Moro Interprete. . . .* Colophon: Venetiis in Aedibus Aldi, et Andreae Soceri Mense Maio. M.D. XVI. More's translations are on pp. 187 verso–236 verso.

We learn nothing of the circumstances attending this publication, that is, whether Erasmus had been aware of Aldus' plans or was consulted about them, but a member of the firm reports that Erasmus

---

[1] *EE*, *1*, 512; 514 n. 2.
[2] Ibid., *1*, 517.22–23.
[3] Ibid., *1*, 562.

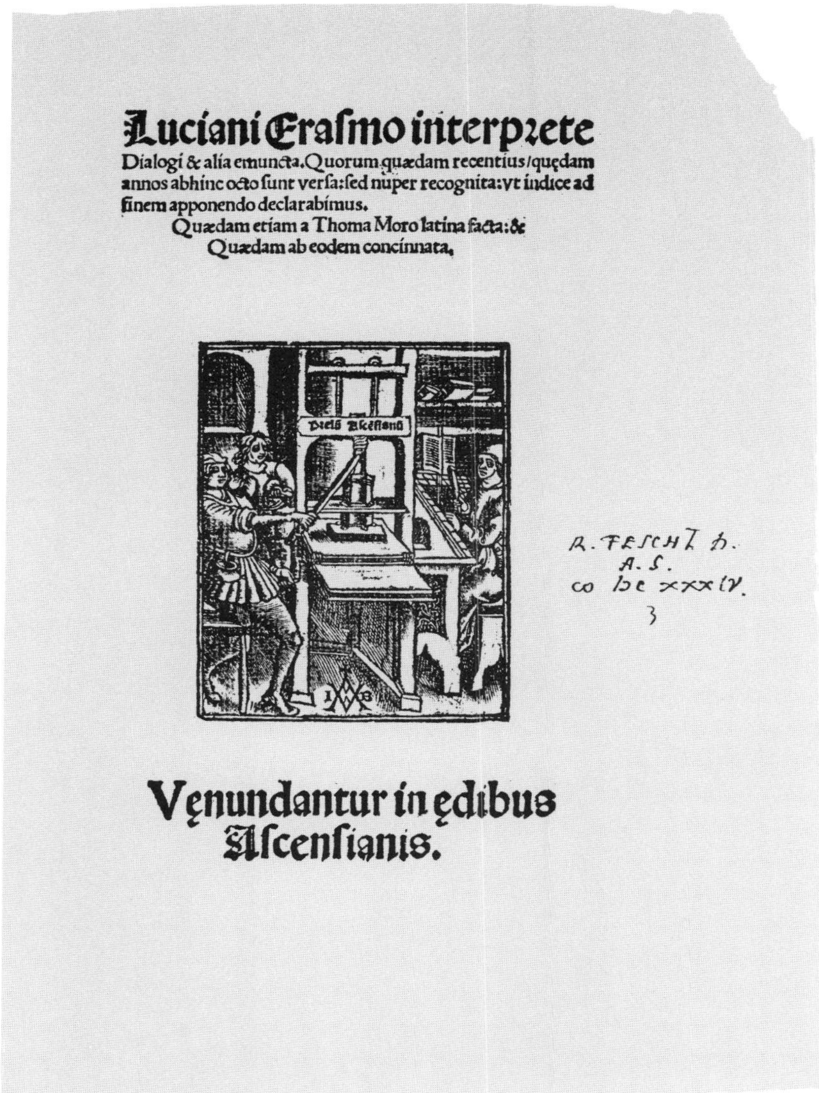

Luciani Erasmo interprete
Dialogi & alia emuncta. Quorum quædam recentius/quędam annos abhinc octo sunt versa: sed nuper recognita: vt indice ad finem apponendo declarabimus.
Quædam etiam a Thoma Moro latina facta: & Quædam ab eodem concinnata.

Vęnundantur in ędibus Ascensianis.

Title page of second edition (Erasmus' copy), 1514, Paris, Josse Badius Ascensius (reduced)

was pleased with the book.[1] It may be regarded as a reprint, with minor changes, of *1506*. Usually, therefore, this text agrees with *1506*, sometimes agreeing in error (e.g. 25/5 *vestiblum*, 53/1 *Dimoniachus*). Where *1506* and *1514* differ, *1516* often agrees with *1506*: at least forty times in the passages checked. Some misspellings in *1506* (e.g. 2/25 *acermi*, 17/26 *earnibus*, 17/31 *craterae*, 25/13 *tenebratum*, 45/28 *Erodotus*, 51/5 *ceruiua*, 55/2 *Babylonis*, 67/18 *quemadmonum*, 67/30 *quoitdieque*, 77/16 *Tychade*, 122/22 *numirium*) are correct in *1516*; though all but one of these words, 55/2 *Babylonis*, *1506*, had been rectified already in *1514*. These errors were so obvious that the Aldine printers or correctors would surely have detected them without aid from *1514*. At least two errors in *1506*, 25/5 *vestiblum* and 53/1 *Dimoniachus*, amended in *1514*, remain corrupt in *1516*. But *1516* was the first edition to print 55/16 *carbatinis* and 59/11 *Dinonis* correctly.

1517 BASEL, J. FROBEN (81)

After *1514* the next edition in which Erasmus was personally involved—and possibly More as well—was Froben's of December 1517. More's versions, which fill pp. 542–642, are preceded by a separate title page: *Luciani Cynicus, Menippus siue Necromantia, Philopseudes siue incredulus, Tyrannicida, Mori Declamatio Lucianicae respondens, Thoma Moro Britanno vicecomite et ciue Londinensi interprete*; and the colophon to this portion of the book is dated Basel, December 6, 1517.

It is clear that the text of this edition was set from a copy of *1514* belonging to Erasmus and supplied by him to Froben. This copy is now in the Universitätsbibliothek, Basel.[2] The last leaf in this copy contains his familiar "Sum Erasmi." Marginal corrections and additions to the text, in Erasmus' hand, are scattered throughout the volume. Twenty of these affect More's text and all twenty are adopted in the 1517 edition.[3] Furthermore most pages in the Basel copy of *1514* indicate, by marginal marks or the underscoring of

---

[1] Andreas Asolanus, father-in-law and partner of Aldus Manutius (see colophon, above); ibid., *2*, 589.3–5.

[2] As was reported by Husner, p. 258. In the seventeenth century the book was owned by the Basel collector, Rem. Fäsch.

[3] See textual notes to 2/2, 17/2, 19/24, 23/28, 23/31, 27/19–20, 33/11, 33/12, 43/8, 47/34, 53/21–22, 55/2, 55/5, 81/3, 83/8–9, 83/19, 83/34, 85/17, 87/19–20, 89/2–3. One change, at 55/5, merely corrects a printer's error.

words or syllables, the catchwords guiding Froben's printers in page division. Such indicators seldom appear in the first third of the Basel volume, but from fol. XLII verso to the end, including the pages containing More's translations, they are found fairly regularly.

Other proofs that this copy was intended for Froben's use are the marginal directions by Erasmus. On fol. CIIII verso, where his translation of *Convivium seu Lapithae* begins, we find: "Adde hic praefationem ad Eutychium," i.e. the dedicatory letter addressed to John Huttich (*EE*, *2*, 502–03). At the bottom of fol. CX verso is: "Adde hic de astrologia," a Lucianic essay translated by Erasmus. Badius Ascensius says that by some mistake the manuscript of this translation went to Basel before finally reaching him in Paris.[1]

In the Erasmus part of the book (fols. I verso–CX verso) are about a hundred marginal emendations. The More part (fols. CXI–CXXXV verso), as noted, has twenty. All but a very few of the marginalia are in the same hand. Those few exceptions or possible exceptions (e.g. on fols. II, XLVIII, XCVII verso) are in the Erasmus part of the book.

A note in the front of the Basel Universitätsbibliothek copy states that the emendations were made by Erasmus *manu propria*, and calls attention to the inscription "Sum Erasmi" at the end of the volume. Another note, in a different hand, says Froben used this copy for the edition of 1517. Both statements are unsigned and undated, without authority, but correct. Comparison with authentic specimens of Erasmus' hand gives confidence that ascription of the marginalia in this volume, including those in the More part, to him is quite sound. He did not always write the same hand—that depended on whether he was hurried and whether he was preparing a rough draft for a secretary or making a fair copy—but the evidence can only lead to the conclusion that the marginalia here are by him. That none is in More's hand seems to me certain. Nor do I think they are by Beatus Rhenanus or some other associate of the Froben firm.[2]

Since the corrections made in these marginalia are required, in virtually all instances, by the Greek text of Lucian probably used

---

[1] 1514 edition, fol. CXXXIX (misnumbered). Cf. *EE*, *1*, 519.

[2] Perhaps Beatus Rhenanus did write the postscript to Erasmus' translations in the printed volume of December 1517, p. 540, calling attention to several errors which would have been corrected "si in tempore nos quidam amicus noster monuisset."

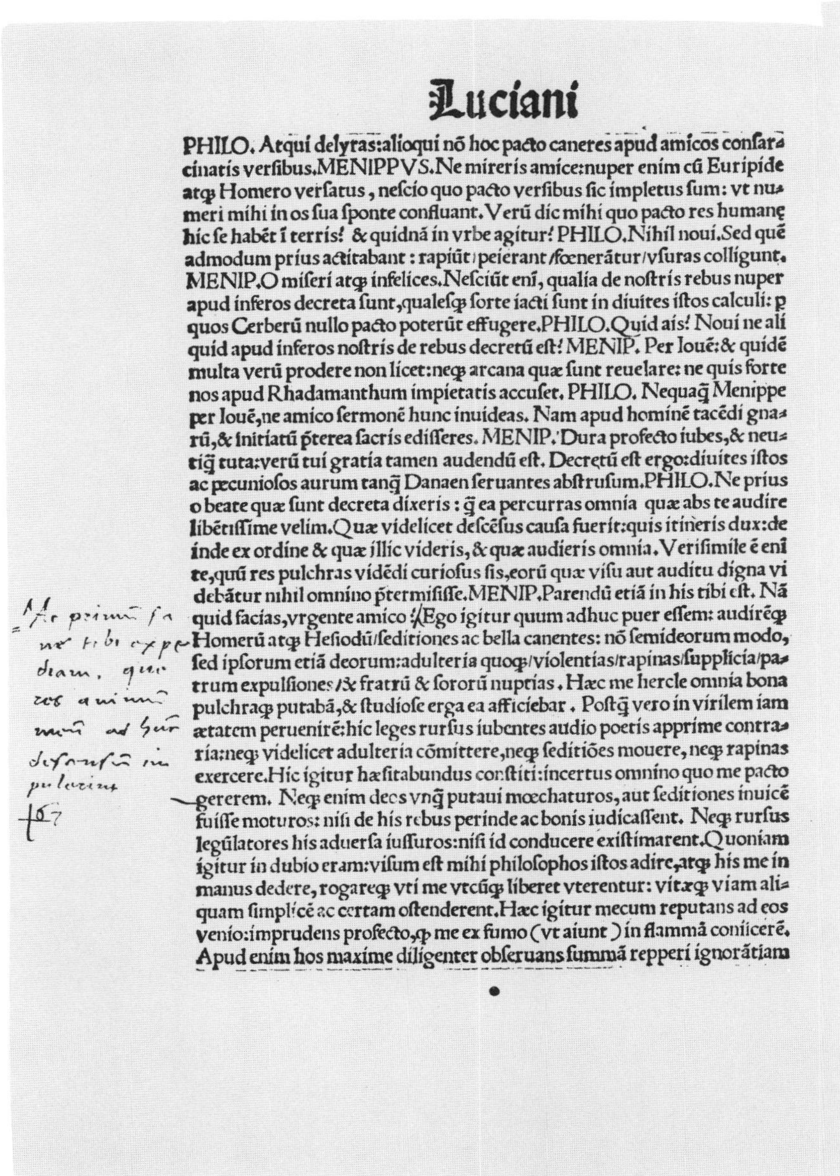

Luciani

PHILO. Atqui delyras:alioqui nõ hoc pacto caneres apud amicos consar=
cinatis versibus.MENIPPVS.Ne mireris amice:nuper enim cũ Euripide
atq; Homero versatus , nescio quo pacto versibus sic impletus sum: vt nu=
meri mihi in os sua sponte confluant. Verũ dic mihi quo pacto res humanę
hic se habẽt ĩ terris? & quidnã in vrbe agitur? PHILO.Nihil noui.Sed quẽ
admodum prius actitabant : rapiũt/peierant/fœnerãtur/vsuras colligunt.
MENIP.O miseri atq; infelices.Nesciũt enĩ, qualia de nostris rebus nuper
apud inferos decreta sunt,qualesq; sorte iacti sunt in diuites istos calculi: p
quos Cerberũ nullo pacto poterũt effugere.PHILO.Quid ais? Noui ne ali
quid apud inferos nostris de rebus decretũ est? MENIP. Per Iouẽ:& quidẽ
multa verũ prodere non licet:neq; arcana quæ sunt reuelare: ne quis forte
nos apud Rhadamanthum impietatis accuset. PHILO. Nequaq̃ Menippe
per Iouẽ,ne amico sermonẽ hunc inuideas. Nam apud hominẽ tacẽdi gna=
rũ,& initiatũ p̃terea sacris edisseres. MENIP. Dura profecto iubes,& neu=
tiq̃ tuta:verũ tui gratia tamen audendũ est. Decretũ est ergo:diuites istos
ac pecuniosos aurum tanq̃ Danaen seruantes abstrusum.PHILO.Ne prius
o beate quæ sunt decreta dixeris : q̃ ea percurras omnia quæ abs te audire
libẽtissime velim.Quæ videlicet descẽsus causa fuerit:quis itineris dux:de
inde ex ordine & quæ illic videris, & quæ audieris omnia. Verisimile ẽ enĩ
te,quũ res pulchras vidẽdi curiosus sis,eorũ quæ visu aut auditu digna vi
debãtur nihil omnino p̃termisisse.MENIP.Parendũ etiã in his tibi est. Nã
quid facias,vrgente amico ?/Ego igitur quum adhuc puer essem: audirẽq;
Homerũ atq; Hesiodũ/seditiones ac bella canentes: nõ semideorum modo,
sed ipsorum etiã deorum:adulteria quoq;/violentias/rapinas/supplicia/pa=
trum expulsiones/& fratrũ & sororũ nuptias . Hæc me hercle omnia bona
pulchraq; putabã,& studiose erga ea afficiebar . Postq̃ vero in virilem iam
ætatem peruenirẽ:hic leges rursus iubentes audio poetis apprime contra=
ria:neq; videlicet adulteria cõmittere,neq; seditiões mouere, neq; rapinas
exercere.Hic igitur hæsitabundus constiti:incertus omnino quo me pacto
gererem. Neq; enim deos vnq̃ putaui mœchaturos, aut seditiones inuicẽ
fuisse moturos: nisi de his rebus perinde ac bonis iudicassent. Neq; rursus
legũlatores his aduersa iussuros:nisi id conducere existimarent.Quoniam
igitur in dubio eram:visum est mihi philosophos istos adire,atq; his me in
manus dedere, rogareq; vti me vtcũq; liberet vterentur: vitæq; viam ali=
quam simplicẽ ac certam ostenderent.Hæc igitur mecum reputans ad eos
venio:imprudens profecto,q; me ex fumo (vt aiunt) in flammã conicerẽ.
Apud enim hos maxime diligenter obseruans summã repperi ignorãtiam

Fol. CXV verso of second edition, 1514, with marginal addition by Erasmus (reduced)

by More[1] and are incorporated in the edition of December 1517, that edition, in these passages at any rate, is superior to *1514*.

By the spring of 1517, Erasmus was thinking apparently of a new edition of the translations from Lucian, to be published by Froben. The translations were to be accompanied by his *Querela pacis*, epigrams, and *Declamatio de morte*, together with More's epigrams and *Utopia*. In late May, Erasmus writes to More that he has sent the latter's epigrams and *Utopia* to Froben,[2] and when he writes to More again about this matter, in July, he specifically includes Lucian.[3] At this time Erasmus was acting for More in negotiations with the Froben firm, so it is not at all surprising that he should have taken the initiative in preparations for a new edition of their versions of Lucian. But are the marginalia in *1514* to be regarded as changes authorized or requested by More? It seems reasonable enough to surmise that the two friends had discussed plans for a new edition of *Utopia*, the epigrams, and Lucian; yet we hear very little about Lucian in their correspondence of 1516 and 1517. Erasmus had been living in Basel since August 1514, except for two brief visits to England in late April and May of 1515,[4] and from approximately the middle of July until late August of 1516.[5] More was in London until May 12, 1515, when he left for Bruges as ambassador.[6] Erasmus stayed with More during his 1516 visit.[7] They must have had ample opportunity on those occasions to talk about publishing plans; and again when they met in Flanders.[8]

With respect to literary work, More's time in 1516 was taken up with *Nusquama* or *Utopia*.[9] He sent the manuscript, with a letter, to Erasmus early in September 1516.[10] The letter shows also (lines 20–28, "Si edas posthac . . . ingenio") that Erasmus had power to decide whether other writings besides *Utopia* should be published. That he was in charge of arrangements for the publication of *Utopia* is clear

---

[1] One, however, *referrent* to *referret* at 47/34, does not improve the sense of the passage; in *1521*, *referrent* is restored.

[2] *EE*, *2*, 576.15–17.

[3] Ibid., *3*, 6.43–44.

[4] Ibid., *2*, 67, introduction to *ep*. 332; *2*, 91.20–22.

[5] Ibid., *2*, 281, introduction to *ep*. 441.

[6] Ibid., *2*, 195.94 n.

[7] Ibid., *2*, 317.19–20.

[8] Ibid., *2*, 194.33.

[9] For details see Surtz and Hexter, *CW 4*, clxxxiii f.

[10] *EE*, *2*, 339.1–3.

beyond doubt.[1] The first edition (Louvain, Martens), came out in December 1516; the second (Paris, Gilles de Gourmont) sometime in the latter part of 1517; the third (Basel, Froben) in March 1518.

More kept in touch with Erasmus about the text of the second and third editions. On March 1, 1517, and again a week later, Erasmus wrote to him for a corrected copy of *Utopia*, to be used in the next (second) edition.[2] Whether this edition was to be published in Paris or Basel was still undecided. In the end, Thomas Lupset took over the arrangements and had the book printed in Paris.[3] Surtz conjectures that More sent a corrected copy to Paris for this purpose.[4]

For the third edition, which was expected to be part of the Froben volume of December 1517 that included Erasmus' and More's Lucian, Erasmus had sent a corrected copy of *Utopia* to Basel by May 30, 1517.[5] As stated above, the volume issued in December by Froben was to include, and did include, other writings besides Erasmus' and More's renderings of Lucian.[6] But because all this material filled 642 pages even without *Utopia*, Froben informs the reader (p. 643, dated December 6, 1517) that he will issue More's *Utopia* and *Epigrammata* in another volume shortly. This promised volume appeared in March 1518.

Although the translations of Lucian are not named among those works intended for the volume of December 1517 until July 1517,[7] inclusion of them was already implied some months earlier. If the prefatory letter to Erasmus' version of *Convivium*[8] was written in or near March 1517, as P. S. Allen believed, it is virtual proof that Erasmus was then thinking of a new edition. For this preface had not been printed earlier, whereas the translation of *Convivium* itself had appeared in the 1506 volume, without any dedication. An allusion to Erasmus' Lucian in a letter from Beatus Rhenanus in April 1517[9] confirms, or strongly suggests, that there had been talk

[1] Ibid., *2*, 346.13–347.23; 359.5–6; 375.1–4; 380.1–7; 385.13.

[2] Ibid., *2*, 494.11–13; 496.5.

[3] Ibid., *3*, 240.50–53; for Lupset's part, *3*, 90.26–30.

[4] *CW 4*, clxxxv–clxxxvi, 569.

[5] *EE*, *2*, 576.15–16; cf. *3*, 57.16–19.

[6] In a note of ca. December 9, 1517, probably written when he supposed the book was still in the press, Erasmus indicates that he wants his and More's translations to be printed together, "sicut hactenus fuerunt." *EE*, *3*, 163.19–20.

[7] Ibid., 3, 6.44.

[8] Ibid., 2, 502–503.

[9] Ibid., 2, 552.56–57.

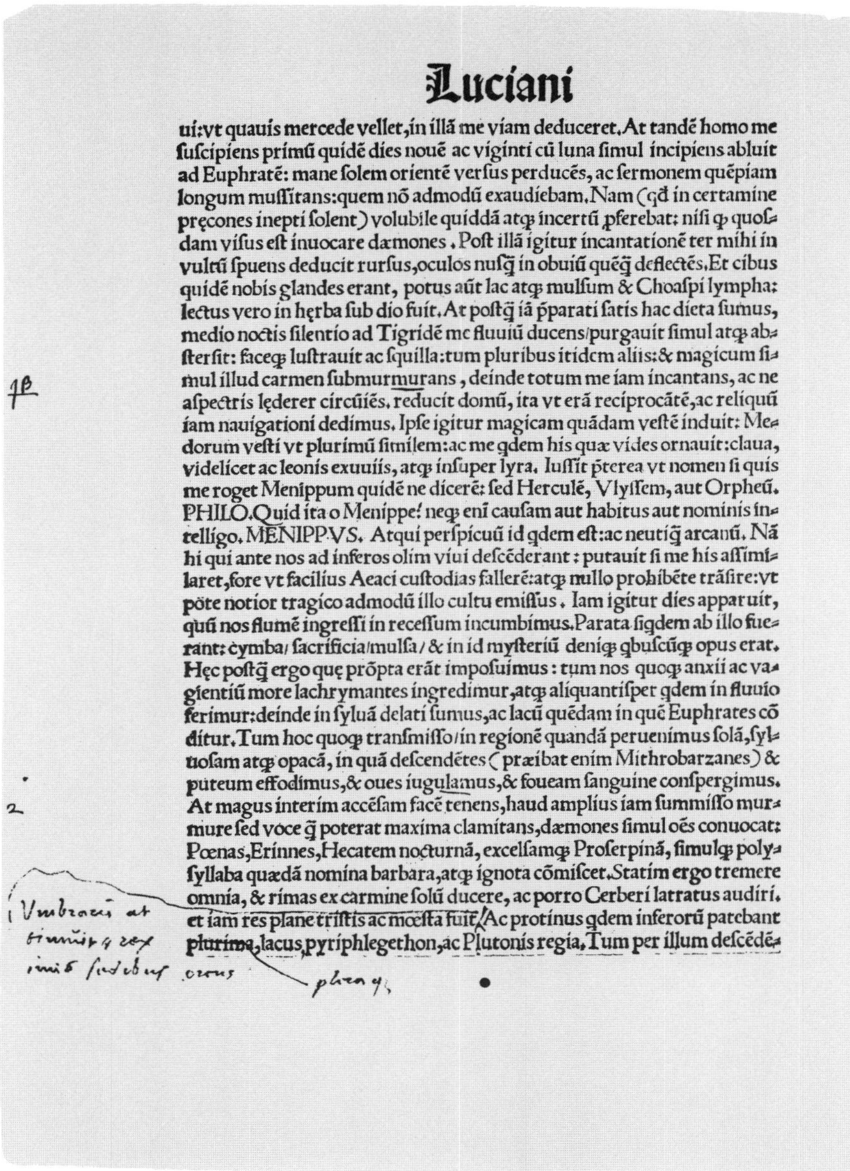

Luciani

ui:vt quauis mercede vellet,in illã me viam deduceret.At tandẽ homo me suscipiens primũ quidẽ dies nouẽ ac viginti cũ luna simul incipiens abluit ad Euphratẽ: mane solem orientẽ versus perducẽs, ac sermonem quẽpiam longum mussitans:quem nõ admodũ exaudiebam.Nam (qđ in certamine pręcones inepti solent) volubile quiddã atq; incertũ ꝓferebat: nisi ꝙ quos=dam visus est inuocare dæmones. Post illã igitur incantationẽ ter mihi in vultũ spuens deducit rursus,oculos nusq̃ in obuiũ quẽq̃ deflectẽs.Et cibus quidẽ nobis glandes erant, potus aũt lac atq; mulsum & Choaspi lympha: lectus vero in hęrba sub dio fuit.At postq̃ iã ꝑparati satis hac dieta sumus, medio noctis silentio ad Tigridẽ me fluuiũ ducens/purgauit simul atq; ab=stersit: faceq; lustrauit ac squilla:tum pluribus itidem aliis:& magicum si=mul illud carmen submurmurans, deinde totum me iam incantans, ac ne aspectris lęderer circũiẽs, reducit domũ, ita vt erã reciprocãtẽ,ac reliquũ iam nauigationi dedimus. Ipse igitur magicam quãdam vestẽ induit: Me=dorum vesti vt plurimũ similem:ac me q̃dem his quæ vides ornauit:claua, videlicet ac leonis exuuiis, atq; insuper lyra. Iussit p̄terea vt nomen si quis me roget Menippum quidẽ ne dicerẽ: sed Herculẽ, Vlyssem, aut Orpheũ. PHILO.Quid ita o Menippe? neq; enĩ causam aut habitus aut nominis in=telligo. MENIPPVS. Atqui perspicuũ id q̃dem est:ac neutiq̃ arcanũ. Nã hi qui ante nos ad inferos olim viui descẽderant: putauit si me his assimi=laret,fore vt facilius Aeaci custodias fallerẽ:atq; nullo prohibẽte trãsire:vt põte notior tragico admodũ illo cultu emissus. Iam igitur dies apparuit, quũ nos flumẽ ingressi in recessum incumbimus.Parata siqdem ab illo fue=rant: cymba/ sacrificia/mulsa/ & in id mysteriũ deniq; q̃buscũq; opus erat. Hęc postq̃ ergo quę prõpta erãt imposuimus: tum nos quoq; anxii ac va=gientiũ more lachrymantes ingredimur,atq; aliquantisper q̃dem in fluuio ferimur:deinde in syluã delati sumus,ac lacũ quẽdam in quẽ Euphrates cõditur.Tum hoc quoq; transmisso/in regionẽ quandã peruenimus solã,syl=uosam atq; opacã, in quã descendẽtes (præibat enim Mithrobarzanes) & puteum effodimus,& oues iugulamus,& foueam sanguine conspergimus. At magus interim accẽsam facẽ tenens,haud amplius iam summisso mur=mure sed voce q̃ poterat maxima clamitans,dæmones simul oẽs conuocat: Pœnas,Erinnes,Hecatem nocturnã, excelsamq; Proserpinã, simulq; poly=syllaba quædã nomina barbara,atq; ignota cõmiscet.Statim ergo tremere omnia, & rimas ex carmine solũ ducere, ac porro Cerberi latratus audiri. et iam res plane tristis ac mœsta fuit.Ac protinus q̃dem inferorũ patebant plurima,lacus,pyriphlegethon,ac Plutonis regia.Tum per illum descẽdẽ=

Fol. CXVI verso of second edition, 1514, with marginal addition and correction by Erasmus (reduced)

of a new edition. Some weeks later Erasmus tells More that he has sent *Utopia*, More's *Epigrammata*, "vna cum meis aliquot lucubrationibus," to Basel.[1] "Lucubrationibus" must include, I think, his versions of Lucian as well as *Querela pacis* and *Declamatio de morte*. In another letter to More, July 1517, More's writings which Erasmus had sent to Basel are said clearly to include Lucian.[2]

If More took trouble with corrections to *Utopia*, as we know he did, it is possible that in 1517 he could have done the same with his translations of Lucian, which were intended for publication with *Utopia* in Froben's new edition. That we hear nothing about those translations in his letters to Erasmus might be attributed to Erasmus' presence in London during most of April 1517. How much of that month he spent with More we cannot tell, but if corrections to Lucian were discussed, we are at liberty to conjecture that the corrections, now found in Erasmus' hand in the Basel Universitätsbibliothek copy of *1514*, were sent to him by More in the spring of 1517 or given to him by More during Erasmus' April visit. But it must be emphasized that this is conjecture only. I believe it is safer to think the main responsibility for these corrections belongs to Erasmus.

In More's part of the volume, *1517* agrees with *1514* (i.e. *1514* as corrected by marginalia), against *1506*, at least sixty times. It differs from *1514* (as corrected by marginalia) at least forty times. Most of the differences are minor ones; some merely represent divergences between the practices of printing houses. On the other hand, all but one of the changes contributed by *1514* marginalia and printed for the first time in *1517* are desirable improvements; e.g. at 27/19–20, *1517* prints a sentence omitted by *1506*; at 33/11 translates a verse (but prints it as prose) previously omitted; at 53/21–22 makes a partial correction of a passage; at 87/19–20 changes the phrasing; at 89/2–3 adds two clarifying words. None of the marginal or interlinear corrections or additions in *1514* affects More's declamation replying to Lucian's *Tyrannicida*. That was an original composition which in the successive editions contained a few printer's errors but apparently received no changes from the author.[3]

---

[1] Ibid., 2, 576.15–17.

[2] Ibid., *3*, 6.43–44.

[3] Absence of significant changes in the text of the declamation may be an additional indication, therefore, that the marginal changes in More's translations were due to

1519 Florence, Giunta (82)

This volume, *Luciani opuscula Erasmo Roterodamo interprete . . . Eiusdem Luciani Thoma Moro interprete . . .*, contains *Utopia* also. More's Lucian occupies pp. 172–216. Colophon: Impressum Florentiae per heredes Philippi Iuntae. Anno D.XIX. a christiana salute supra mille mense Iulio, Leone X. Pontifice. The publisher gives no information about the text used. He may have used more than one; if so, probably *1506* and *1516*. Where *1506* differs from *1517*, *1519* usually agrees with *1506*. Also it often agrees with *1514* or *1516*, but only once (96/1), I think, with *1517* alone. In a few places *1519* agrees with *1514* and *1517* against *1506* and *1516* (e.g. at 37/35 *efficitur*, 61/6 *Minoem*, 71/7 *Eubatidem*, 104/23 *solae*). But it agrees with *1516* and *1517* against *1506* and *1514* at 17/33 *posset* and with *1516* alone at 11/3 *Interlocutores* (again at 25/3), and at 33/38, 45/1–3, 59/23–24. Both *1516* and *1519* read *Dimoniachus* at 53/1, with *1506*, although elsewhere in *Philopseudes* they print the name correctly, *Dinomachus*. *1506*, *1516*, *1519* likewise agree in error at 61/16–17. *1519* agrees with *1506* and *1516* against *1514* at 81/22 *esset*, 91/31 *deos*, 104/2 *videor*, 116/17 *ineuitabile*, 118/4 *festinaret effugere*, 124/19 *charissimae*, 124/31 *indigne*. *1519* was the first to contribute to the text one reading which must be correct: 4/5 *uia* in More's prefatory letter to Ruthall.

1521 Basel, J. Froben (83)

Luciani Samosatensis . . . Des. Erasmo Roterod. Interprete. Aliquot item ex eodem commentarij, Thoma Moro interprete. . . . Colophon: Basiliae apud Ioannem Frobenium mense Augusto An. M.D XXI.

The translations by Erasmus are listed on the title page; More's, called "commentarij," are not; nor are these preceded by a separate title page as in *1517*. More's fill pages 244–98. The book itself says nothing about the source of the text, but evidently it was set from *1517*. In the collations attached to the present edition, *1517* and *1521* will be found to agree far more often than they disagree; yet more disagreement occurs than is implied by Allen's assertion that

---

Erasmus. For if More made those corrections, it would be surprising that he made none at all in his declamation. It is not surprising that, if Erasmus made them, he nevertheless refrained from improving More's composition.

1521 is reprinted from *1517* "with slight alterations."[1] They differ in at least forty places. When they disagree, *1521* is generally right. It has fewer misprints, and its punctuation is better than that of *1517*. In one place (17/23–24) it supplies a word, *illinc*, representing a Greek word left untranslated by all previous editions. At 53/21–22 half a dozen words previously untranslated are now represented. Other new and (except at 31/33) improved readings occur at 2/19, 27/3, 31/22, 31/33, 31/37, 35/9, 35/29, 39/3, 43/8, 51/20, 61/9, 63/25, 67/30–31, 96/9, 96/19, 100/19, 100/21, 100/22.

The improvements must have been made by More, by Erasmus, or by a corrector at the press. We have absolutely no information, so far as I am aware, that they came from More. We hear nothing of this edition in his correspondence. He became Under-Treasurer in May 1521, and it is not hard to believe that the demands of public business left little leisure for improvements to Lucian. We cannot even be certain that he knew the edition of 1521 was planned. Conceivably a corrector at Froben's press could have made the changes, or some of them, but, considering Erasmus' part in the publishing arrangements for the other early editions of his and More's translations, it is more likely that he himself was responsible for the changes in this 1521 edition as well. We shall return to this subject in a moment.

Of the sixteenth-century editions published after 1521, two deserve mention because they appeared before 1535 and two others because they were included in editions of More's collected Latin writings.

1528 Lyons, Gryphius (85)

This volume is *Luciani Samosatensis Opuscula quaedam, Erasmo Rote. & Thoma Moro interpretib. . . .* Colophon: Sebastianus Gryphius Germanus excudebat Lugduni, Anno M. D. XXVIII. More's translations, here called (p. 2) "commentarij" as in *1521*, run from p. 403 to p. 490; they do not have a separate title page. The remainder of the book (pp. 490–526) is occupied by translations of Lucian's *De calumnia* by Melanchthon and of his *Adversus indoctum* by "Anastasius Q.," and by one of Erasmus' colloquies, *Charon*.

This edition, issued by a publisher who reprinted many of Erasmus' works, lacks the authorization enjoyed by Froben's editions but is a

[1] *EE*, *1*, 416.

satisfactory text on the whole. With very few changes (e.g. 2/10, 23/35–37, 43/9, 45/4, 53/2, 94/19) it follows *1521*, even in some significant errors (e.g. 11/17, 47/21, 47/34, 67/27). Like *1521* it differs from *1517* at 2/10, 2/19, 17/23–24, 23/6, 27/3, 31/31, 35/9, 35/29, 39/3, 47/21, 47/34, 51/20, 55/16, 61/8, 63/25, 81/7, 96/1, 96/9, 96/19, 100/19, 100/21, 100/22, 110/23, 118/31; and there are many other examples. It differs from all previous texts at 53/2, 94/19.

1534 Basel, H. Froben and Episcopius (86)

In this edition, *Luciani Samosatensis dialogi aliquot Des. Erasmo Roter. & Thoma Moro interpretibus* . . . , More's versions are on pp. 461–559; they are followed by Melanchthon's translation of *De calumnia.* Colophon: Basiliae, in officina Frobeniana per Hieronymum Frobenium & Nicolaum Episcopium M D XXXIIII.

This text differs from *1521* and *1528* (in a few places correcting them) at 4/5, 6/30, 11/3, 11/4, 11/6, 11/17, 13/9, 15/1, 25/4, 27/19–20, 29/6, 33/16, 35/31–32, 43/13–15, 45/23, 47/21, 47/34, 49/36, 53/19, 55/2, 55/5, 55/16, 59/11, 61/35, 67/27, 77/25, 79/29, 81/6, 87/9, 93/7, 93/17, 93/26, 93/31–32, 100/15, 106/20, 110/23, 122/3, 126/4–5. In a few places *1534* agrees with *1528* against *1521* (23/35–37, 27/35, 31/33, 43/9, 45/4, 108/31); in at least two *1534* agrees with *1521* against *1528* (53/2, 94/19). It is the first text to have the correct reading at 61/35.

1534 might have been printed from *1517*, *1521*, or *1528*. It is inherently more probable that the Froben firm would have used an earlier Froben edition, *1517* or *1521*, than that of a rival printer. Of these two, *1521* is the more likely.

1563 Basel, Episcopius (74)
1566 Louvain, Bogard (76a)

In More's *Lucubrationes* of 1563 his versions of Lucian are printed on pp. 273–364. The source of the text is not given, but the editor or editors claim that in this edition More's writings are "ab innumeris mendis repurgatae." The editors of the Louvain (Bogard) edition of More's *Omnia Latina opera*, 1565, 1566,[1] rewrote several lines in

[1] Gibson and Patrick, 75a, 76a. More's Latin works were issued at Louvain in 1565 by Bogard and also by Zangrius (75b) and reissued by these printers in 1566 (76a, 76b).

More's letter to Ruthall (see textual notes to 4/22–28 and 4/33–6/1), evidently to tone them down and make them more acceptable to pious ears. In some other passages too the editors felt free to emend the text, though seldom to its improvement. *1563* and *1566* usually agree and (except at 2/10, 21/1, 47/34, 53/2, 59/16, 61/9, 63/37, 79/29, 106/9, 110/31, 118/4, 120/17) both agree with *1534*; but *1563* differs from *1566* at 4/22–28, 4/33–6/1, 11/1, 15/18–19, 17/1, 19/16, 19/23, 23/26, 25/5, 29/31, 31/1, 37/13, 37/30, 39/31, 41/30, 45/1–3, 51/38, 55/13, 57/15, 57/31, 59/16, 59/23–24, 59/25, 59/32, 59/36, 61/4, 61/15, 61/36, 67/25, 75/24, 75/26, 79/4, 89/4, 93/23, 100/22, 102/7, 104/7, 106/9, 118/30, 122/11, 124/24. *1566* is the first edition to print *terroribus*, which is certainly correct, at 57/27; and *ingredientibus* at 59/25.[1]

THE PRESENT TEXT

Editorial decisions affecting the text of More's translations rest on the following considerations. The indubitably authorized editions were *1506*, *1514*, and *1517*. Erasmus, who had close connections with Badius Ascensius and later with Froben, made the arrangements for printing and supplied the copy-text; whether More took any part or contributed any corrections after *1506* appeared we can only guess.[2] For all practical purposes, Froben's edition of August 1521 can also be regarded as authorized. Admittedly we have no direct information about Erasmus' connection (let alone More's) with this edition. Erasmus was not living in Basel in 1519–20 and did not return until November 1521. It is unlikely, however, that Froben would have brought out this edition without Erasmus' consent, certainly not against his wishes. Yet this question of authorization need not be pressed too far. In the first place, such questions seldom had the rigor or preciseness—or fascination—for sixteenth-century

[1] Although *1563* and *1566* have, on the whole, little value for the text of the Lucian translations, the two collections containing these translations are important for students of More's reputation. On differences between purposes and policies governing the editing of *Lucubrationes* and *Omnia Latina opera* see McConica, *English Humanists and Reformation Politics*, pp. 285–94.

[2] In a letter to More, November 13, 1518 (Rogers, pp. 132–33), Froben alludes to Lucian, but this letter was written more than a year after the negotiations for the December 1517 edition. Moreover Froben does not refer to More's translations, although he mentions one by Erasmus.

authors or printers that they have for bibliographers and literary historians today. In the second place, we should remember that Erasmus had other and more urgent affairs than Lucian to occupy him in 1520 and 1521. If he made corrections to the *1517* text of Lucian after publication, as he had done to that of *1514*, he need not have waited until 1520 or 1521 to do so.

Although the printed text gradually improves, no single edition is without faults. All have errors requiring correction, and each new edition, while correcting errors of previous ones, contributes at least a few new errors of its own. *1506* has the undeniable interest and importance attaching to an authorized first edition, but it contains dozens of errors. Most of the obvious ones are emended in *1514*, but some remain. We have in Erasmus' hand twenty corrections for *1517*, yet many other passages in *1514* deserving correction do not receive it. Some of these errors persist in *1517*; others are finally corrected in *1521*. For example, *praeoptat* for *praeoptate*, near the opening of More's letter to Ruthall, is clearly needed but does not appear until *1521*.

We do not know whether Erasmus went through More's translations completely in preparation for the *1517* edition. The character of the corrections to *1514*, and of Erasmus' usual working habits, suggests that he did not. If the marginal changes he made came from More, Erasmus may have let the matter go at that. In either event he passed up many opportunities to make additional corrections in More's text. Errors in *1506* and *1514* left uncorrected by *1517* include such obvious ones as proper names—55/21 *Alexidis*, 55/35 *Anaxiclem*, 61/35 *Antiochus*—which Erasmus could hardly have missed if he had gone over the text thoroughly. Yet if More was responsible for the twenty corrections it is equally surprising that he did not change the readings just mentioned, and others as well. We may reasonably suppose that he cared as much as most writers for the accuracy of his published works. We know that he concerned himself with corrections to *Utopia*. In the controversy with Brixius (Germain de Brie) he was stung by his critic's charge, in the appendix to *Antimorus* (1519), that his *Epigrammata* of 1518 contained sixteen metrical errors and fifteen solecisms.[1] The quarrel with Brixius made

[1] See Bradner and Lynch, pp. xxix–xxxi; and for More's reply, Rogers, 224/412–227/536.

these thirty-one errors look important; and in a sixteenth-century literary quarrel over Latin verses such matters *were* important. In addition, this quarrel was absurdly complicated by national pride and personal pique. More observes in his defense that because his book was printed at Basel he himself had not had opportunity to read the proofs.[1] He had not furnished the texts of the poems to the printer; Froben had got them from others.

So our question must remain unanswered: If More was concerned about the accuracy of *Utopia* and of his epigrams, how can we account for the persistence of errors in the 1514 and 1517 editions of his Lucian, errors that first occurred in *1506*? Patriotism exalted the urgency of quarrels with a Frenchman, no doubt. And that in sixteenth-century opinion correctness was even more urgent in verse than in prose is perhaps demonstrable. That More would have made other corrections to Lucian besides those transmitted to Froben by Erasmus seems probable. But why just twenty were made (in Erasmus' hand), and others, including some that were badly needed, are missing until *1521* or even later, we cannot explain.

Occasionally reference to the 1503 Aldine text of Lucian from which it is likely the translations were made helps to determine which of the possible readings More probably intended.[2] What happened to the manuscript from which *1506* was set we do not know. Editions subsequent to *1506* were set from printed texts. As a rule, when the unique manuscript does not survive and we have no good reason to think an author has made substantive changes in the text after the first edition, then that edition is the only reliable one to reprint; later editions possess no authority. Yet the meager evidence available indicates that More himself had little or nothing to do with the printing of his translations, whether in 1506, 1514, 1517, or later. And More was busy about other things after 1516: "Morus

---

[1] Nor was it established practice then for an author to read proofs. Erasmus habitually left this work to others: *EE*, *5*, 529 n.; *11*, 209.1–210.12. It is rather ironical that Brixius once complained in a letter to Erasmus (1526) about the number of typographical errors in one of his own books. These he blamed on the carelessness of the printer's correctors, adding that he himself had been in the country and could not be troubled with the demeaning task (*molestiam indignitatemque*) of reading proofs (*EE*, *6*, 376.23–377.41). The printer in question was Josse Badius Ascensius, who twenty years earlier had published Erasmus' and More's translations of Lucian.

[2] All passages that are, for whatever reason, questionable have been checked against the 1496 Lucian as well as the Aldine text of 1503.

ipse totus est aulicus," Erasmus writes in April 1518.[1] At any rate it is fair to say that for each of these editions he was far removed from the printing house, and we know that arrangements for *1506*, *1514*, and *1517* were made through Erasmus. Hence we cannot rely on the first edition as we would in editing many other sixteenth-century texts. Nor can we place undue reliance on the "accidentals"—spelling, capitalization, punctuation and so on—of the first edition, as editors of Renaissance texts are sometimes tempted to do. We cannot even assume that the accidentals are the author's or were approved by him. In such matters printing houses followed their own practices, but these were not invariable. Thus differences in accidentals occur in *1506* and *1514*, though both editions were printed in Badius Ascensius' shop; and the same is true of Froben's editions.

A thoroughly critical text of More's Lucian is hardly possible without more knowledge than we possess concerning the transmission of corrections for successive editions and concerning proofreading. To know more about the making of the first edition, *1506*, would be particularly useful. Lacking such knowledge, the most practical decision, in my judgment, is to use *1521* as the basic text for the present edition, adopting readings from other editions where there appears sound reason for doing so. Of the various editions, *1521* and *1534* are the best (despite a mistake in speakers' names on the very first page of translations, 11/17, of *1521*!). *1528* is good but cannot claim the status of a Froben edition. An argument might be made for *1517*, on the ground that this first Froben edition may have received some personal attention from More, as we know it did from Erasmus. They *could* have discussed the Lucian portion of the *1517* volume, and More *could* have supplied Erasmus with corrections to *1514*. But there is no evidence that he did so. An argument could be made too for *1534*: if we have no really convincing evidence of More's part in correcting *1517* or *1521*, why not use the latest improved text issued in his lifetime? Because the later the improvements or apparent improvements, the farther from More they may be. Granted that similar objection might be made even to *1521*; but that edition is after all much closer in date to the first Froben edition (*1517*), which Erasmus had in charge and in which More was undoubtedly interested. On the whole, *1521*, corrected where

[1] *EE*, *3*, 286.5.

LVCIANI SAMO-
SATENSIS

Saturnalia,
Cronoſolon, id eſt, Satur-
nalium legum lator,
Epiſtolæ Saturnales,
De luctu,
Abdicatus,
Icaromenippus ſeu Hyper-
nephelus,
Toxaris ſiue Amicitia,
Alexāder ſeu Pſeudomātis,
Gallus ſeu Somnium,
Timon ſeu Miſanthropus,
Pro tyrānicida declamatio,
ERASMI declamatio, Lu-
cianicæ reſpondens,
De ijs qui mercede condu-
cti degunt,
Dialogi XVIII.
Hercules Gallicus,
Eunuchus ſeu Pamphilus,
De Sacrificijs,
Conuiuium ſeu Lapithæ.
De Aſtrologia,

DES. ERASMO ROTE-
ROD. INTERPRETE.

Aliquot item ex eodē com-
mentarij, Thoma Moro in-
terprete, quos in calce huius
libri numeratos reperies.

Quibus ſi græce ſcripta, quæ propediem, dijs propicijs adijcientur, conferat ſtudioſus lector, facile cognoſcet, arbitror, cuiuſmodi res ſit peregrinam linguam, ut in aliam quamuis, ita in Latinam bene ac fideliter uertere.

BASILEAE APVD IO. FROB. AN. M.D. XXI.

Apelles huiuſmodi pictura calumniam ultus eſt.

Lucian, 1521 edition, Basel, Froben (reduced)

necessary, seems to me the most satisfactory edition to use as a basic text. This, then, is the text here presented unless the critical apparatus indicates otherwise.

For this edition the texts of *1506*, *1514*, *1517*, *1521*, *1528*, *1534*, *1563*, and *1566* (Bogard) have been collated and all variants found in these checked against *1516* and *1519*. The following sigla have been adopted:

1506	Paris, Badius Ascensius, 1506
1514	Paris, Badius Ascensius, 1514
1516	Venice, Aldus Manutius, 1516
1517	Basel, J. Froben, 1517
1519	Florence, Giunta, 1519
1521	Basel, J. Froben, 1521
1528	Lyons, Gryphius, 1528
1534	Basel, H. Froben and Episcopius, 1534
1563	Basel, Episcopius, 1563
1566	Louvain, Bogard, 1566

Sources of editions used were: the Harvard copy of *1506* (once owned by the Jesuits of Cordova); Basel Universitätsbibliothek copy of *1514* (Erasmus' copy); Huntington copy of *1517* (once the property of Philip Melanchthon); Folger copies of *1516*, *1519*, *1534*, *1563*, *1566*; Folger and Yale copies of *1521*; British Museum copy of *1528*. For Greek texts I have relied on the Yale copy of *1496* and Yale and Pierpont Morgan copies of *1503*.

With each of the four dialogues translated by More the Greek text of the 1503 Aldine edition is reproduced (from the Pierpont Morgan copy) in photographic facsimile on the left-hand pages. The type-page in the 1503 folio measures five by nine and one-half inches, including page number and catchword; it has been reduced in this edition to four and one-fourth by seven and one-half inches with the Greek pages cut off horizontally so that the text they present may correspond with the parallel Latin version.

References to marginalia in *1514* mean those in the Basel Universitätsbibliothek copy, as previously explained; i.e. in 2/2, *1514*, like *1506* (and *1516*, *1519*), prints "Magistro," but this word was crossed out and "Thomae" substituted in Erasmus' hand.

The text is printed without paragraphing, as in all early editions. Punctuation is changed only in passages (identified in the textual

notes) where sixteenth-century usage might obscure the meaning. Ordinary contractions, except ampersands, are silently expanded; *s* is printed for long *s*; *u* and *v* are printed as found. In the text *i* and *j* also are printed as found. Variant spellings in other editions than the first (*1506*) and the copy-text (*1521*) are usually not recorded unless they affect meaning and are not mere misprints; but because More is known to have preferred *consydero* to *considero*,[1] I have felt justified in changing the *1521* spelling to conform at 11/28, 15/38, 19/3, 23/28, 41/35–36, 63/9, 63/25, 89/26, 100/13. The spelling of this word varies in other editions; both forms occur in *1506*.

In the textual notes,[2] agreement of *1521* with the other editions collated may be assumed unless different readings are printed or unless *1521* is itself emended.

Proper names are sometimes abbreviated differently in different editions, or even within the same edition, but these variants are not recorded. The signature numbers of *1521* are placed within square brackets in the text, immediately preceding the folios to which they refer.

---

[1] See Pace, *De fructu*, p. 68. Cf. *EE*, 2, 340.23.

[2] These notes to the Latin texts have been set at the foot of the Latin (left-hand) pages when More is composing originally in Latin (the *Letter to Ruthall* and the *Reply to the Tyrannicida*) and at the foot of the facsimile Greek pages when he is translating from Greek to Latin (*Cynicus*, *Menippus*, *Philopseudes*, and *Tyrannicida*).

TRANSLATIONS
OF
LUCIAN

ORNATISSIMO DOCTISSIMOQVE VIRO THOMAE RVTHALO REGIO APVD ANGLOS SECRETARIO, THOMAS MORVS S.P.D.

SI QVISQVAM fuit unquam uir doctissime, qui Horatianum praeceptum impleuerit, uoluptatemque cum utilitate coniunxerit, hoc ego certe Lucianum in primis puto praestitisse. Qui & superciliosis abstinens Philosophorum praeceptis, & solutioribus Poetarum lusibus, honestissimis simul & facetissimis salibus, uitia ubique notat atque insectatur mortalium. Idque facit tam scite, tantaque cum fruge, ut quum nemo altius pungat, nemo tamen sit, qui non aequo animo illius aculeos admittat. Quod quum nunquam non egregie faciat, fecisse tamen mihi singulari quodam modo uidetur in tribus his Dialogis, quos ob idipsum e tanto festiuissimorum numero potissimum delegi, quos uerterem, alijs tamen alios fortasse longe praelaturis. Nam ut e uirginibus non eandem omnes, sed alius aliam, pro suo cuiusque animo praefert, deamatque, non quam praecipuam tuto possit asserere, sed quae sibi uideatur, ita e lepidissimis Luciani dialogis, alius alium praeoptat, mihi certe isti praecipue placuerunt, neque temere tamen (uti spero) neque soli. Nam ut a breuissimo incipiam, qui Cynicus inscribitur, quique posse uideatur ipsa breuitate contemni, nisi nos Horatius admoneret, saepe etiam in exiguo corpore uires esse praestantiores, ipsique minimas etiam gemmas esse uideremus in precio. In eius ergo delectu honorifico calculo mecum suffragatus est diuus Ioannes Chrysostomus, uir acerrimi iudicij, doctorum ferme omnium Christianissimus, & Christianorum (ut ego certe puto) doctissimus, quem usqueadeo Dialogus hic delectabat, ut bonam eius partem in Homiliam quandam quam in Ioannis euangelium commentatus est, inseruit. Neque id immerito. Quid enim

2 THOMAE] Magistro *1506 1514* (*crossed out and* Thomae *inserted*) *1516 1519* 10 tam] *1506 1514 1516 1517 1519 1563 1566*, tanque *1521*, tamque *1528 1534* 19 praeoptat] praeoptate *1506 1514 1516 1517 1519* 21–22 breuitate] breuiter *1517* 25 acerrimi] acermi [*sic*] *1506* 28 Homiliam] Homeliam *1506* 29 inseruit] inseruerit *1506 1516 1519 1534 1563 1566*

TO THE MOST ILLUSTRIOUS AND LEARNED THOMAS RUTHALL, ENGLISH ROYAL SECRETARY, THOMAS MORE SENDS GREETING:

IF, most learned Sir, there was ever anyone who fulfilled the Horatian maxim and combined delight with instruction, I think Lucian certainly ranked among the foremost in this respect. Refraining from the arrogant pronouncements of the philosophers as well as from the wanton wiles of the poets, he everywhere reprimands and censures, with very honest and at the same time very entertaining wit, our human frailties. And this he does so cleverly and effectively that although no one pricks more deeply, nobody resents his stinging words. He is always first-rate at this, but in my opinion he has done it exceptionally well in these three dialogues, which for this very reason I have chosen, from such an abundance of exceedingly pleasant ones, to translate; though perhaps other persons might much prefer other dialogues. For just as, among girls, all men do not love the same one, but each has his own preference as fancy dictates and adores not the one he can prove is best but the one who seems best to him—so of the most agreeable dialogues of Lucian, one man likes a certain one best, another prefers another; and these have particularly struck my fancy, yet not without reason, I trust, nor mine alone.

For to begin with the shortest, which is called *Cynicus*, and which might appear unacceptable on account of its very brevity did not Horace remind us that the greater strength is often to be found in a slight body, and did not we ourselves see that even the smallest jewels are prized: my choice of it is endorsed by the estimable approval of St. John Chrysostom, a man of the most acute judgment, of all learned men perhaps the most Christian and (at least in my opinion) of all Christians the most learned. So much did this dialogue delight him that he introduced a large part of it into a homily he composed on the Gospel of St. John. And not without reason: for

placere magis uiro graui, uereque Christiano debuit, quam is dialogus, in quo dum aspera, paruoque contenta Cynicorum uita defenditur, mollis, atque eneruata delicatorum hominum luxuria reprehenditur? Nec non eadem opera, Christianae uitae simplicitas, temperantia, frugalitas, denique arcta illa atque angusta uia, quae ducit ad uitam, laudatur. Iam Necromantia (nam hic secundo dialogo titulus est) non satis auspicato uocabulo, sed materia tamen felicissima, quam salse taxat, uel Magorum praestigias, uel inania Poetarum figmenta, uel incertas quauis de re philosopho[x_3]rum inter se digladiationes? Superest Philopseudes, qui non sine Socratica ironia, totus uersatur (id quod titulus ipse declarat) in ridenda, coarguendaque mentiendi libidine, dialogus nescio certe lepidior ne, an utilior. In quo non ualde me mouet, quod eius animi fuisse uidetur, ut non satis immortalitati suae confideret, atque in eo fuisse errore, quo Democritus, Lucretius, Plinius, plurimique itidem alij. Quid enim mea refert quid sentiat his de rebus ethnicus, quae in praecipuis habentur fidei Christianae mysterijs? Hunc certe fructum nobis afferet iste dialogus, ut neque magicis habeamus praestigijs fidem, & superstitione careamus, quae passim sub specie religionis obrepit, tum uitam ut agamus minus anxiam, minus uidelicet expauescentes tristia quaepiam ac superstitiosa mendacia, quae plerunque tanta cum fide atque autoritate narrantur, ut beatissimo etiam patri Augustino, uiro grauissimo, hostique mendaciorum acerrimo, nescio quisnam ueterator persuaserit, ut fabulam illam de duobus Spurinis, altero in uitam redeunte, altero decedente, tanquam rem suo ipsius tempore gestam pro uera narraret, quam Lucianus in hoc dialogo, mutatis tantum nominibus, tot annis antequam Augustinus nasceretur, irrisit. Quo minus mireris, si pinguioris uulgi mentes suis figmentis afficiant ij, qui se tum demum rem magnam confecisse putant, Christumque sibi deuinxisse perpetuo, si commenti fuerint, aut de sancto aliquo uiro fabulam, aut de inferis tragoediam, ad quam uetula quaepiam aut delira lachrymetur, aut pauida inhorrescat. Itaque nullam fere martyris, nullam uirginis uitam praetermiserunt,

1 magis] *1506 1514 1516 1519*, *om.* *1517 1521 1528 1534 1563 1566*   5 uia] *1519 1534 1563 1566*, vita *1506 1514 1516 1517 1521 1528*   8 salse] false *1519*   13 uidetur] videatur *1534 1563 1566*   22–28 ut beatissimo . . . irrisit] vt viris grauissimis atque sanctissimis frequenter imponant *1566*   4/33–6/1 Itaque . . . inseruerint] Ita vt in plurimas martyrum aut virginum historias aliquid huiusmodi mendaciorum inseruerint *1566*

what should have pleased that grave and truly Christian man more than this dialogue in which, while the severe life of Cynics, satisfied with little, is defended and the soft, enervating luxury of voluptuaries denounced, by the same token Christian simplicity, temperance, and frugality, and finally that strait and narrow path which leads to Life eternal, are praised?

Next *Necromantia*, for this is what the second dialogue is called—not very auspicious in its title but felicitous in content—how wittily it rebukes the jugglery of magicians or the silly fictions of poets or the fruitless contentions of philosophers among themselves on any question whatever!

There remains *Philopseudes*, which, with a measure of Socratic irony, is entirely concerned (as its title indicates) with ridiculing and reproving the inordinate passion for lying. Whether this dialogue is more amusing or more instructive is hard to say. I'm not much troubled by the fact that the author seems to have been disposed to doubt his own immortality, and to have been in the same error as Democritus, Lucretius, Pliny, and many others likewise were. For what difference does it make to me what a pagan thinks about those articles contained in the principal mysteries of the Christian faith? Surely the dialogue will teach us this lesson: that we should put no trust in magic and that we should eschew superstition, which obtrudes everywhere under the guise of religion. It teaches us also that we should live a life less distracted by anxiety; less fearful, that is, of any gloomy and superstitious untruths. Very many of these are related with such a show of confidence and authority that some cunning rogue or other even induced the most blessed father Augustine, a man of complete sobriety and a zealous enemy of lies, to tell as a truth, as something that occurred in his own lifetime, that yarn about two Spurinnae—one coming back to life and the other departing from it—which Lucian made fun of in this dialogue, with only the names changed, so many years before Augustine was born.

You should not be surprised, therefore, if the common herd are taken in by the fictions of those who think they've done a great work, and put Christ in their debt forever, if they've feigned a story about a saint or a horrendous tale of hell to drive some old woman to tears or make her tremble with fear. And so there is scarcely a martyr's or a virgin's life which they have passed over without in-

in quam non aliquid huiusmodi mendaciorum inseruerint, pie scilicet, alioqui enim periculum erat, ne ueritas non posset sibi ipsa sufficere, nisi fulciretur mendacijs. Nec ueriti sunt eam religionem contaminare figmentis, quam ipsa ueritas instituit, & in nuda uoluit ueritate consistere, nec uiderunt usqueadeo nihil istiusmodi fabulas conducere, ut nihil perniciosius officiat. Nempe (ut memoratus pater Augustinus testatur) ubi admixtum subolet mendacium, ueritatis ilico minuitur ac labefactatur autoritas. Vnde saepe mihi suspicio suboritur, magnam huiusmodi fabularum partem, a uafris ac pessimis quibusdam nebulonibus, haereticisque confictam, quibus studium fuit, partim ex incauta, simplicium potius, quam prudentium credulitate, uoluptatem capere, partim fabularum fictarum commercio, fidem ueris Christianorum historijs adimere, quippe qui frequenter quaedam, his quae in sacra scriptura continentur, tam uicina confingunt, ut facile se declarent, adludendo lusisse. Quamobrem quas scriptura nobis historias diuinitus inspirata commendat, eis indubitata fides habenda est. Caeteras uero ad Christi doctrinam, tanquam ad Critolai regulam, applicantes caute & cum iudicio, aut recipiamus, aut respuamus, si carere uo[x3v]lumus, & inani fiducia, & supersticiosa formidine. Sed quo progredior? epistola fere iam librum superat: nec interim tamen uerbum de tuis laudibus ullum, in quas alius fortasse totus incubuisset: quarumque citra ullam adulandi suspicionem uberrimam mihi materiam praebuissent (ut caeteras uirtutes tuas omittam) uel egregia doctrina tua, summaque in rebus agendis prudentia: quam tot in diuersis nationibus, in tam arduis negocijs, tam feliciter actae legationes declarant: uel singularis fides, grauitasque: quam nisi satis perspectam, exploratamque habuisset, nunquam te prudentissimus princeps sibi a secretis esse uoluisset. Sed caeterarum uirtutum tuarum praedicationi unica modestia tua reluctatur: quae facit, ut quum laudanda tam libenter facias: fecisse te tamen non libenter audias. Parco igitur pudori tuo: hoc unum duntaxat abs te precatus: ut has in graecis literis studij

30 facit] faciat *1534 1563 1566*

serting some falsehoods of this kind—with pious intent, to be sure, for otherwise there was danger lest truth could not stand by its own strength but had to be bolstered with lies! They have not shrunk from defiling with their tales that religion which Truth itself established and which it intended to consist of truth unadorned; and they have not considered that fables of this kind, so far from helping at all, do more deadly harm than anything else. Surely, as the aforementioned father Augustine testifies, when the added falsehood is detected, the authority of truth is immediately diminished and weakened. Wherefore I have often suspected that a large portion of such fables has been concocted by certain crafty, wicked wretches and heretics whose object was partly to amuse themselves by the thoughtless credulity of the simple-minded (rather than the wise), partly to undermine trust in the true stories of Christians by traffic in mere fictions; since they often invent things so nearly resembling those in Sacred Scripture that they easily reveal that by playing upon those stories they have been ridiculing them. Therefore we ought to place unquestioning trust in the stories commended to us by divinely inspired Scripture, but testing the others carefully and deliberately by the teaching of Christ (as though applying the rule of Critolaus), we should either accept or reject them if we wish to free ourselves both from foolish confidence and superstitious dread.

But where am I headed? This epistle already rivals a book in length, yet I haven't said a word so far in praise of you; another man would have dwelt perhaps on that theme exclusively. I had abundant resources for doing so, without being open to the slightest suspicion of flattery. There is—quite apart from the rest of your virtues—your distinction in learning and your unsurpassed wisdom in practical affairs, attested by numerous diplomatic missions carried out in various lands with such difficult negotiations and with such success. Or there is your extraordinary trustworthiness and dignity. Unless he had regarded this as tried and tested, a sagacious prince would never have appointed you to be Secretary. But your singular modesty, which makes you unwilling to hear yourself praised for the praiseworthy things you so willingly do, balks at publication of your other virtues. Accordingly I spare your sense of propriety, begging only that you kindly accept these first fruits of my Greek studies

mei primitias aequo animo suscipias, sinasque ut qualecunque apud te sint amoris, officijque in te mei monumentum, quas tibi sim ausus eo maiori fiducia committere, quod &si tam acre tibi iudicium sit, ut quicquid erratum fuerit, nemo penetrantius uideat: is tamen est ingenij tui candor, ut nemo libentius conniueat. Vale.

2 sim] sum *1506 1514 1516 1519* 3 maiori] maiora *1506 1516*, maiore *1519*

and treat them as a token, in some sort, of my affection and my duty toward you. I have ventured to submit them to you with the greater confidence because, although your judgment is so keen that nobody would more quickly detect any error there may be, yet your nature is so kind that none would more readily condone it. Farewell.

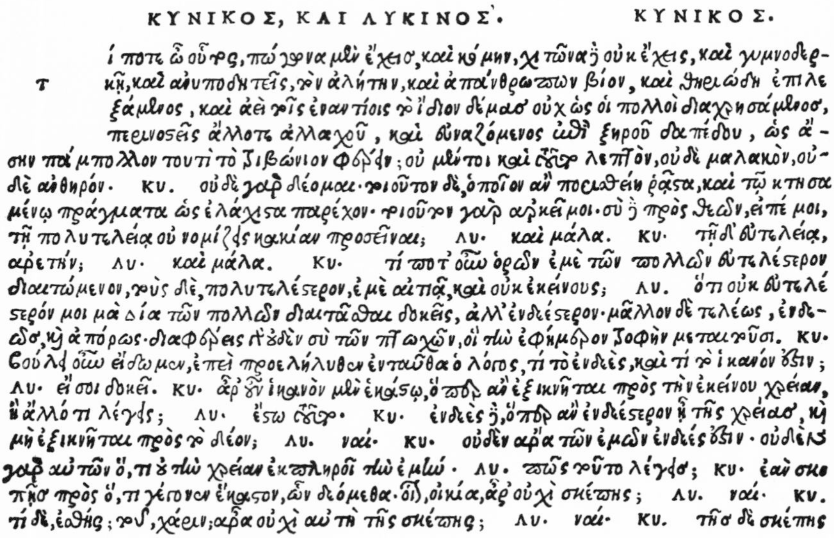

ΚΥΝΙΚΟΣ, ΚΑΙ ΛΥΚΙΝΟΣ. ΚΥΝΙΚΟΣ.

Τί ποτε ὦ οὗτος, πώγωνα μὲν ἔχεις, καὶ κόμην, χιτῶνα δὲ οὐκ ἔχεις, καὶ γυμνοδερκῇ, καὶ ἀνυποδητεῖς, τὸν ἀλήτην, καὶ ἀπάνθρωπον βίον, καὶ θηριώδη ἐπιλεξάμενος, καὶ ἀεὶ τοῖς ἐναντίοις τὸ ἴδιον δέμας οὐχ ὡς οἱ πολλοὶ διαχρησάμενος, περινοστεῖς ἄλλοτε ἀλλαχοῦ, καὶ εὐναζόμενος ἐπὶ ξηροῦ δαπέδου, ὡς ἄσην πάμπολλον τουτὶ τὸ τριβώνιον φορεῖν; οὐ μέντοι καὶ τοῦτο λεπτὸν, οὐδὲ μαλακὸν, οὐδὲ ἀνθηρόν. ΚΥ. οὐδὲ γὰρ δέομαι· τοιοῦτον δὲ, ὁποῖον ἂν πορισθείη ῥᾷστα, καὶ τῷ κτησαμένῳ πράγματα ὡς ἐλάχιστα παρέχον· τοιοῦτον γὰρ ἀρκεῖ μοι. σὺ δὲ πρὸς θεῶν, εἰπέ μοι, τῇ πολυτελείᾳ οὐ νομίζεις κακίαν προσεῖναι; ΛΥ. καὶ μάλα. ΚΥ. τῇ δ᾽ εὐτελείᾳ, ἀρετήν; ΛΥ. καὶ μάλα. ΚΥ. τί ποτ᾽ οὖν ὁρῶν ἐμὲ τῶν πολλῶν εὐτελέστερον διαιτώμενον, τοὺς δὲ, πολυτελέστερον, ἐμὲ αἰτιᾷ, καὶ οὐκ ἐκείνους; ΛΥ. ὅτι οὐκ εὐτελέστερόν μοι μὰ Δία τῶν πολλῶν διαιτᾶσθαι δοκεῖς, ἀλλ᾽ ἐνδεέστερον· μᾶλλον δὲ τελέως, ἐνδεῶς, καὶ ἀπόρως· διαφέρεις γὰρ οὐδὲν σὺ τῶν πτωχῶν, οἳ τὴν ἐφήμερον τροφὴν μεταιτοῦσι. ΚΥ. βούλει οὖν ἴδωμεν, ἐπεὶ προελήλυθεν ἐνταῦθα ὁ λόγος, τί τὸ ἐνδεὲς, καὶ τί τὸ ἱκανόν ἐστιν; ΛΥ. εἴ σοι δοκεῖ. ΚΥ. ἆρ᾽ οὖν ἱκανὸν μὲν ἑκάστῳ, ὅπερ ἂν ἐξικνῆται πρὸς τὴν ἐκείνου χρείαν, ἢ ἄλλο τι λέγεις; ΛΥ. ἔστω τοῦτο. ΚΥ. ἐνδεὲς δὲ, ὅπερ ἂν ἐνδεέστερον ᾖ τῆς χρείας, καὶ μὴ ἐξικνῆται πρὸς τὸ δέον; ΛΥ. ναί. ΚΥ. οὐδὲν ἄρα τῶν ἐμῶν ἐνδεές ἐστιν· οὐδὲν γὰρ αὐτῶν ὅ,τι οὐ τὴν χρείαν ἐκπληροῖ τὴν ἐμήν. ΛΥ. πῶς τοῦτο λέγεις; ΚΥ. ἐὰν σκοπῇς πρὸς ὅ,τι γέγονεν ἕκαστον, ὧν δεόμεθα· οἷον οἰκία, ἆρ᾽ οὐχὶ σκέπης; ΛΥ. ναί. ΚΥ. τί δὲ, ἐσθής; τοῦ χάριν; ἆρα οὐχὶ αὐτῆς τῆς σκέπης; ΛΥ. ναί. ΚΥ. τῆς δὲ σκέπης

1 LVCIANI CYNICVS] CYNICVS LVCIANI *1566* 3 Personae] *om.* *1534* *1563* *1566*, Interlocutores *1516* *1519* 4 LVCIANVS] *om.* *1534* *1563* *1566* 6 nudusque] nudus *1534* 17 LVCIANVS] Lu. *1506*, LVCIA. *1514* *1517* *1519*, Lucianus *1516*, LVCIAN. *1534*, LVC. *1563* *1566*, CYNICVS [*sic*] *1521* *1528* 20 diem.] diem: *1521* 28 ais] ait *1517* 28 consyderes] consideres *1521*

LVCIANI CYNICVS, THOMA MORO INTERPRETE.

Personae, LVCIANVS ET CYNICVS.

LVCIANVS.

QVID TV tandem? barbam quidem habes, & comam, tunicam non habes, nudusque conspiceris, ac sine calceis, delecta nimirum uaga, inhumanaque ac ferali uita, tum proprio corpore contra quam faciunt caeteri, semper usus incommode, nunc huc, nunc illuc circuis, in arido praeterea solo cubans, adeo ut plurimum etiam sordium, tritum isthoc pallium referat, alioqui nec ipsum, uel tenui filo, uel molle uel florulentum. CYNI. Neque enim indigeo, siquid est huiusmodi, ut comparetur facillime, dominoque minimum exhibeat negocij, id inquam mihi sufficit. At tu per Deos dic mihi, putas ne esse in luxu uitium? LVCIA. Immo admodum. CYN. Contra in frugalitate uirtutem? LVCIANVS. Admodum. CYNICVS. Cur igitur tandem quum me uideas uiuentem frugalius quam uulgo faciunt homines, eos uero sumptuosius, me, non illos arguis? LVCIANVS. Quia non frugalius per Iouem uideris mihi, sed egentius uiuere, immo uitam omnino egenam atque inopem. Nam tu nihil a mendicis differs, qui cibum mendicant [x_4] in diem. CYNICVS. Vis ergo uideamus (quandoquidem huc processit oratio) quidnam inopia sit, quidque rursus copia? LVCIA. Si tibi quidem ita uidetur. CYNICVS. Nunquid ergo satis id cuique est, quicquid ipsius explet necessitatem? an aliud quippiam dicis? LVCIANVS. Esto istud. CYNICVS. Indigentia uero quicquid cuiusquam usui deest, nec eo quo sit necesse peruenit? LVCIANVS. Scilicet. CYNI. Nihil igitur meis in rebus deest. Nihil enim in his est, quod necessitatem non expleat meam. LVCIA. Quo pacto istud ais? CYNICVS. Scies si consyderes in quem usum eorum quodque paratum est, quorum egemus, ut domus, an non tegumenti gratia? LVCIANVS. Maxime. CYNI. Quid uestis, cuius gratia? nonne tegumenti etiam ipsa? LVCIANVS. Sane.

αὐτῆς πρὸς θεῶν, τίνος ἐδεήθη μὴ ἕνεκα, οὐχ ὥστε ἄμεινον ἔχειν τὸν σκεπόμενον; ΛΥ. δοκεῖ μοι. ΚΥ. πότερον οὖν, τὼ πόδε χεῖρον ἔχειν δοκεῖ σοι; ΛΥ. οὐκ οἶδα. ΚΥ. ἀλλ' οὕτως ἂν μάθοις· τί ποδῶν ἐστ' ἔργον. ΛΥ. πορεύεσθαι. ΚΥ. χεῖρον οὖν πορεύεσθαί σοι δοκοῦσιν οἱ ἐμοὶ πόδες, ἢ οἱ τῶν πολλῶν; ΛΥ. τοῦτο μὲν, οὐκ ἴσως. ΚΥ. οὐ τοίνυν οὐδ' εἰ χεῖρον ἔχουσιν, ἢ μὴ χεῖρον, τὸ ἑαυτῶν ἔργον ἀποδιδόασιν. ΛΥ. ἴσως. ΚΥ. τοὺς μὲν δὴ πόδας, οὐδὲν φαίνομαι χεῖρον διακείμενος τῶν πολλῶν ἔχειν. ΛΥ. οὐκ ἔοικας. ΚΥ. τί δέ, τοὐμὸν σῶμα τῶν λοιπῶν ἆρα χεῖρον; εἰ γὰρ χεῖρον, καὶ ἀσθενέστερον. ἀρετὴ γὰρ σώματος, ἰσχύς. ἆρ' οὖν τὸ ἐμὸν ἀσθενέστερον; ΛΥ. οὐ φαίνεται. ΚΥ. οὐ τοίνυν οὔθ' οἱ πόδες φαίνονταί μοι σκέπης ἐνδεῶς ἔχειν, οὔτε τὸ λοιπὸν σῶμα. εἰ γὰρ ἐνδεῶς εἶχον, κακῶς ἂν εἶχον. ἡ γὰρ ἔνδεια, πανταχοῦ κακόν, καὶ χεῖρον ἔχειν ποιεῖ ταῦτα, οἷς ἂν προσῇ. ἀλλὰ μὴν, οὐδὲ τρέφεσθαί γε φαίνεται χεῖρον τὸ σῶμα τοὐμόν, ὅτι ἀπὸ τῶν τυχόντων τρέφεται. ΛΥ. δῆλον γάρ. ΚΥ. οὐδὲ εὔρωστον, εἰ κακῶς ἐτρέφετο. λυμαίνονται γὰρ αἱ πονηραὶ τροφαὶ τὰ σώματα. ΛΥ. ἔστι ταῦτα. ΚΥ. πῶς οὖν εἰπέ μοι τούτων οὕτως ἐχόντων, αἰτιᾷ μου, καὶ φαυλίζεις τὸν βίον, καὶ φῂς ἄθλιον; ΚΥ. ὅτι νὴ Δία τῆς φύσεως, ἣν σὺ τιμᾷς, καὶ τῶν θεῶν, γῆν ἐν μέσῳ κατατεθεικότων, ἐκ δ' αὐτῆς ἀναδεδωκότων πολλὰ κἀγαθά, ὥστ' ἔχειν ἡμᾶς πάντα ἄφθονα, μὴ πρὸς τὴν χρείαν μόνον, ἀλλὰ καὶ πρὸς ἡδονήν, σὺ πάντων τούτων, ἢ τῶν γε πλείστων ἄμοιρος εἶ, καὶ οὐδενὸς μετέχεις αὐτῶν, οὐδὲν μᾶλλον ἢ τὰ θηρία. πίνεις μὲν γὰρ ὕδωρ, ὅπερ καὶ τὰ θηρία· σιτῇ δέ, ὅπερ ἂν εὑρίσκῃς, ὥσπερ οἱ κύνες. εὐνὴν δὲ οὐδὲν κρείττω τῶν κυνῶν ἔχεις. χόρτος γὰρ ἀρκεῖ σοι, καθάπερ ἐκείνοις. ἔτι δὲ ἱμάτιον φορεῖς, οὐδὲν ἐπιεικέστερον ἀκλήρου. καίτοι εἰ σὺ τύχοις ἀρκούμενος ὀρθῶς φρονήσεις, ὁ θεὸς οὐκ ὀρθῶς ἐποίησε. τοῦτο μὲν, πρόβατα ποιήσας ἔμμαλλα. τοῦτο δ' ἀμπέλους ἡδυοίνους. τοῦτο δέ, τὴν ἄλλην παρασκευὴν θαυμαστῶς ποικίλην, καὶ ἔλαιον, καὶ μέλι, καὶ τὰ ἄλλα, ὥστ' ἔχειν μὲν ἡμᾶς σιτία παντοδαπά, ἔχειν δὲ ποτὸν ἡδύ, ἔχειν δὲ χρήματα, ἔχειν δ' εὐνὴν μαλακήν, ἔχειν δὲ οἰκίας καλάς, καὶ τὰ ἄλλα πάντα θαυμαστῶς κατεσκευασμένα. καὶ γὰρ αὖ τὰ τῶν τεχνῶν ἔργα, δῶρα τῶν θεῶν ἐστι. τὸ δὲ πάντων τούτων ζῆν ἀπεστερημένον, ἄθλιον

8 Fortasse] fortasse *1521* 9 affectis] affectus *1534 1563 1566*

CYNI. At ipso per Deos tegumento, cuius rei gratia indiguerimus, nonne ut melius se habeat id quod tegitur? LVCIA. Mihi quidem sic uidetur. CYNI. Vtrum igitur tibi peius se habere hi uidentur pedes? LVCIA. Nescio. CYNI. Atqui hoc pacto didiceris, quodnam pedum officium est? LVCIA. Ingredi. CYNI. An deterius ergo ingredi pedes tibi uidentur mei, quam aliorum? LVCIA. Istud uero fortasse non. CYNI. At non possent, seu sese melius seu deterius haberent, officium suum praestare? LVCIA. Fortasse. CYNICVS. Pedibus ergo nihilo peius affectis uideor, quam alij? LVCIANVS. Non uideris. CYNICVS. Quid corpus uero meum? Num deterius quam reliquorum? Nempe si deterius se haberet, esset idem imbecillius, corporis quippe uirtus robur est. An meum ergo debilius? LVCIANVS. Non uidetur. CYNI. Neque pedes ergo tegumento uidentur egere, neque reliquum corpus. Quippe si egerent, male haberent. Egestas etenim omnino mala, ac peius habere se facit, ea quibuscunque adfuerit. At ne ali quidem deterius corpus uidetur meum, quod quibuslibet cibis alitur. LVCIA. Manifestum est id quidem. CYNI. Nam nec uegetum esset, robustumque si aleretur male. Mala siquidem alimenta corpus tabefaciunt. LVCIA. Ista quidem ita se habent. CYNI. Quo pacto igitur, dic mihi, his ita se habentibus, me arguis, uitamque improbas meam, ac miseram praedicas? LVCIANVS. Ideo per Iouem, quod quum natura (quam tu colis) ac superi terram in communi statuerint, ex ea multa nimirum ac bona aediderint, ut nobis omnia superessent abunde, non in necessitatem modo: uerum in uoluptatem quoque, tu tamen horum omnium aut maximae saltem partis expers es, nec eorum quoquam frueris nihilo certe magis, quam ferae. Nempe aquam bibis, quam etiam bibunt ferae: Comedis uero quicquid offenderis, quemadmodum canes, tum cubile nihilo melius canibus habes: quandoquidem gramen tibi sufficit, quemadmodum & illis, pallium praeterea circumfers nihilo mendico decentius. Quanquam si tu [x4v] his contentus recte sapis, tum Deus profecto neutiquam recte fecit, primum quod oues effecit pingues, deinde uites dulcis uini feraces, ac reliquum deinde apparatum uarietate mirabilem, & oleum & mel & reliqua, omnia ut nos haberemus, edulia quidem omnigena haberemus, potum dulcem haberemus, pecunias haberemus, mollem lectum haberemus. Praeterea pulchras domos, ac reliqua demum omnia mirum in modum praeparata. Nam & ipsa quoque artium effecta deorum dona sunt. At uiuere omnibus huiusce bonis

μὲν, εἰ καὶ ὑπ' ἄλλου τινὸς ἀπεστέρητο, καθάπερ οἱ ἐν τοῖς δεσμωτηρίοις· πολὺ δὲ ἀθλιώτε-
ρον, εἴ τις αὐτὸς ἑαυτὸν ἀποστεροίη πάντων τῶν καλῶν· μανία τε ἤδη τοῦτό γε σαφής. ΚΥ.
ἀλλ' ἴσως ὀρθῶς λέγεις. ἐκεῖνο δέ μοι εἰπὲ, εἴ τις ἀνδρὸς πλουσίου προθύμως, καὶ φιλανθρώ-
πως, ἔτι τε φιλοφρόνως ἑστιῶντος, καὶ ξενίζοντος πολλοὺς ἅμα, καὶ παντοδαποὺς, τοὺς
μὲν, ἀσθενεῖς, τοὺς δὲ, ἐρρωμένους, κἄπειτα παραθέντος πολλὰ, καὶ παντοδαπὰ, πάντα
ἁρπάζοι, καὶ πάντα ἐσθίοι, μὴ τὰ πλησίον μόνον, ἀλλὰ καὶ τὰ πόρρω, τὰ τοῖς ἀσθενοῦσι
παρεσκευασμένα, ὑγιαίνων αὐτὸς, καὶ ταῦτα, μίαν μὲν κοιλίαν ἔχων, ὀλίγων δὲ ὥστε τρα-
φῆναι δεόμενος, ὑπὸ τῶν πολλῶν ἐπιτριβήσεσθαι μέλλων, οὗτος ὁ ἀνὴρ, ποῖός τις δοκεῖ σοι
εἶναι; ἆρά γε φρόνιμος; ΛΥ. οὐκ ἔμοιγε. ΚΥ. τί δὲ, σώφρων; ΛΥ. οὐδὲ τοῦτο.
ΚΥ. τί δὲ, εἴ τις μετέχων τῆς αὐτῆς ταύτης τραπέζης, τῶν μὲν πολλῶν, καὶ ποικίλων ἀ-
μελεῖ, ἓν δὲ τῶν ἔγγιστα κειμένων ἐπιλεξάμενος, ἱκανῶς ἔχων πρὸς τὴν ἑαυτοῦ χρείαν, τοῦτο ἐσθίοι κοσμίως, καὶ τούτῳ μόνῳ χρῷτο, τοῖς δὲ ἄλλοις οὐδὲ προσβλέποι, τοῦτον οὐχ ἡγῇ
σωφρονέστερον, καὶ ἀμείνω ἄνδρα ἐκείνου; ΛΥ. ἔγωγε. ΚΥ. πότερον οὖν, συνίης, ἢ ἐμὲ δεῖ
λέγειν; ΛΥ. τὸ ποῖον; ΚΥ. ὅτι ὁ μὲν θεὸς, τῷ ξενίζοντι καλῶς ἐκείνῳ ἔοικε, παρατιθεὶς πολλὰ, καὶ ποικίλα, καὶ παντοδαπὰ, ὅπως ἔχωσιν ἁρμόζοντα· τὰ μὲν, ὑγιαίνουσι· τὰ δὲ, νοσοῦσι. καὶ
τὰ μὲν, ἰσχυροῖς· τὰ δὲ, ἀσθενοῦσιν· οὐχ ἵνα χρώμεθα ἅπασι πάντες, ἀλλ' ἵνα τοῖς καθ' ἑαυτὸν ἕ-
καστος, καὶ τῶν καθ' ἑαυτὸν, ὅτουπερ ἂν τύχοι μάλιστα δεόμενος· ὑμεῖς δὲ, τῷ δι' ἀπληστίαν τε, καὶ
ἀκρασίαν ἁρπάζοντι πάντα, τούτῳ μάλιστα ἐοίκατε, πᾶσι χρῆσθαι ἀξιοῦντες, καὶ τοῖς ἀ-
πανταχοῦ, μὴ τοῖς παρ' ὑμῖν μόνον, οὐ γῆν, οὐ θάλασσαν τὴν καθ' αὑτοὺς αὐτάρκη νομίζον-
τες, ἀλλ' ἀπὸ περάτων γῆς ἐμπορευόμενοι τὰς ἡδονὰς, καὶ τὰ ξενικὰ τῶν ἐπιχωρίων ἀεὶ προτιμῶν-
τες, καὶ τὰ πολυτελῆ τῶν εὐτελῶν, καὶ τὰ δυσπόριστα τῶν εὐπορίστων· καθόλου δὲ, πράγματα,
καὶ κακὰ ἔχειν μᾶλλον ἐθέλοντες, ἢ δίχα πραγμάτων ζῆν. τὰ γὰρ δὴ πολλὰ, καὶ τίμια, καὶ
εὐδαιμονικὰ παρασκευάσματα, ἐφ' οἷς ἀγάλλεσθε, διὰ πολλῆς ὑμῖν ταῦτα κακοδαιμονίας,
καὶ ταλαιπωρίας παραγίνεται. σκόπει γὰρ εἰ βούλει, τὸν πολύευκτον χρυσὸν, καὶ τὸν ἄργυρον·
σκόπει τὰς οἰκίας τὰς πολυτελεῖς· σκόπει τὰς ἐσθῆτας τὰς ἐσπουδασμένας· σκόπει τὰ
τούτοις ἀκόλουθα πάντα, πόσων πραγμάτων ἐστὶν ὤνια, πόσων πόνων, πόσων κινδύνων, μᾶλλον δὲ,

1 aliquo] alio *1534 1563 1566* 5 istuc] istud *1506 1514 1516 1519* 18–19 hunc temperatiorem] hunc & temperatiorem *1506 1516 1519*, hunc temperantiorem *1563* 38 consydera . . . consydera . . . consydera] considera . . . considera . . . considera *1521*

priuatum, id fuerit profecto miserum, etiam si ab aliquo quopiam priueris. Quemadmodum hi qui seruantur in uinculis. Longe uero miserius, siquis ipse sese omnibus bonis priuet. Nam ea demum manifesta insania est. CYNI. Et recte quidem fortasse dicis. Verum istuc dic mihi: Siquis diuite quopiam alacriter atque humane, quin prolixe quoque exhibente conuiuium, tum hospites excipiente, & multos simul, & omnigenos, alios quidem imbecillos, alios autem robustos, deinde apponente multa, atque omnigena, siquis, inquam, omnia corripiat, omniaque deglutiat, non ea tantum quae uicina sunt, sed ea quoque quae procul absunt, praeparata uidelicet inualidis, ipse tamen ualens, quum unum duntaxat uentrem habeat, nec multis ut nutriatur indigeat, diutius tamen quam alij multi immoretur, hic uir cuiusmodi tibi uidetur esse? probus ne? LVCIA. Non mihi quidem. CYN. Quid uero, num temperans? LVCIA. Ne id quidem. CYN. Quid uero siquis eiusdem mensae particeps, multa illa ac uaria negligat, uno quopiam ex his quae proxime apponuntur, electo, quum satis in suam habeat necessitatem, id decenter edat, eoque solo utatur: caetera illa ne respiciat quidem, an non hunc temperatiorem & meliorem uirum illo putabis? LVCIA. Ego certe. CYN. Vtrum ergo iam intelligis, an me oportet dicere? LVCIA. Quid nam? CYN. Quod Deus illi quidem pulchre conuiuium instruenti similis est, ut qui apposuerit multa ac uaria, atque omnigena, uti essent quae cuique conueniant, alia quippe ualentibus, alia rursus aegrotantibus, atque alia quidem robustis, alia uero inualidis, non ut omnibus utamur omnes, sed ut his utantur singuli, quae suae cuiusque naturae conueniunt, & ex his ipsis, quacunque re maxime quemque indigere contigerit. At uos illum qui per insatiabilitatem atque incontinentiam omnia corripit refertis, ut qui rebus uti uelitis omnibus, & undecunque partis, non solis contenti praesentibus, existimantes propriam quidem neque terram, ne mare sufficere, sed importantes ab ipsis usque terrae finibus uoluptates, patrijsque rebus peregrina praeferentes, sumptuosaque frugalibus, atque ea quae difficile comparantur his quae sunt comparatu facilia. In summa denique molestias, malaque potius eligentes, quam absque molestijs uiuere. At isti quidem plu[x_5]rimi ac preciosi, beatique apparatus, quibus exultatis, per magnam ad uos miseriam, erumnamque perueniunt. Aurum ipsum tam optabile, si libet, argentumque consydera: domus consydera sumptuosas, uestes operosas consydera: atque eius generis omnia, quanto negocio emuntur, quot laboribus,

αἵματος, καὶ θανάτου, καὶ διαφθορᾶς ἀνθρώπων πόσης; οὐ μόνον ὅτι πλέοντες ἀπόλλυνται διὰ ταῦτα
πολλοί, καὶ ζητοῦντες, καὶ δημιουργοῦντες, δεινὰ πάσχουσιν, ἀλλ' ὅτι καὶ πολυμάχητά ἐστι,
καὶ ἐπιβουλεύουσιν ἀλλήλοις διὰ ταῦτα, φίλοις φίλοι, καὶ πατράσι παῖδες, καὶ γυναῖκες
ἀνδράσιν· οὕτως οἶμαι καὶ τὴν Εριφύλην, διὰ τὸν χρυσὸν προδοῦναι τὸν ἄνδρα· καὶ ταῦτα
μέντοι πάντα γίνεται, τῶν μὲν ποικίλων ἱματίων, οὐδέν τι μᾶλλον θάλπειν δυναμένων·
τῶν δὲ χρυσορόφων οἰκιῶν, οὐδέν τι μᾶλλον σκεπουσῶν· τῶν δὲ ἐκπωμάτων τῶν ἀργυρῶν, οὐκ
ὠφελούντων τὸν πότον, οὐδὲ τῶν χρυσῶν, οὐδὲ τῶν ἐλεφαντίνων αὖ κλινῶν, τὸν ὕπνον ἡδίω
παρεχομένων· ἀλλ' ὄψει πολλάκις ἐπὶ τῆς ἐλεφαντίνης κλίνης, καὶ τῶν πολυτελῶν στρω
μάτων, τοὺς εὐδαίμονας, ὕπνου λαχεῖν οὐ δυναμένους· ἔτι δὲ καὶ αἱ παντοδαπαὶ περὶ τὰ
βρώματα πραγματεῖαι, τρέφουσι μὲν οὐδὲν μᾶλλον, λυμαίνονται δὲ τὰ σώματα, καὶ τοῖς
σώμασι νόσους ἐμποιοῦσι· τί δὲ δεῖ λέγειν ὅσα τῶν ἀφροδισίων ἕνεκα πράγματα ποιοῦσί τε,
καὶ πάσχουσιν οἱ ἄνθρωποι; καίτοι ῥᾴδιον θεραπεύειν ταύτην τὴν ἐπιθυμίαν, εἰ μή τις ἐθέ
λοι τρυφᾶν· καὶ οὐδ' εἰς ταύτην ἡ μανία, καὶ διαφθορὰ φαίνεται τοῖς ἀνθρώποις ἀρκεῖν· ἀλλ'
ἤδη καὶ τῶν ὄντων τὴν χρῆσιν ἀναστρέφουσιν, ἑκάστῳ χρώμενοι, πρὸς ὃ μὴ πέφυκεν, ὥσπερ εἴ
τις ἀνθ' ἁμάξης ἐθέλοι τῇ κλίνῃ χρήσασθαι, καθάπερ ἁμάξῃ. λυ. καὶ τίς οὗτος; κυ. ὑμεῖς,
οἱ τοῖς ἀνθρώποις ἅτε ὑποζυγίοις χρῆσθε, κελεύετε δὲ αὐτοὺς ὥσπερ ἁμάξας τὰς κλίνας
τοῖς τραχήλοις ἄγειν· αὐτοὶ δ' ἄνω κατάκεισθε τρυφῶντες, καὶ ἐκεῖθεν, ὥσπερ ὄνους ἡνιοχεῖτε
τοὺς ἀνθρώπους, ταύτην, ἀλλὰ μὴ ταύτην τρέπεσθαι κελεύοντες· καὶ οἱ ταῦτα μάλιστα ποιοῦντες, μάλιστα μακαρίζεσθε. οἱ δὲ τοῖς κρέασι, καὶ μὴ τροφῇ χρώμενοι μόνον, ἀλλὰ καὶ βαφὰς μηχα
νώμενοι δι' αὐτῶν, οἷοί γέ εἰσιν οἱ τὴν πορφύραν βάπτοντες, οὐχὶ καὶ αὐτοὶ παρὰ φύσιν χρῶν
ται τοῖς τοῦ θεοῦ κατασκευάσμασι; λυ. νὴ Δία· δύναται γὰρ βάπτειν, οὐκ ἐσθίεσθαι μόνον τὸ
τῆς πορφύρας κρέας. κυ. ἀλλ' οὐ πρὸς τοῦτο γέγονεν· ἐπεὶ καὶ τῷ κρατῆρι δύναιτ' ἄν τις
βιαζόμενος, ὥσπερ χύτρᾳ χρήσασθαι· πλὴν οὐ πρὸς τοῦτο γέγονεν· ἀλλὰ γὰρ πῶς ἅπασαν
τὴν τούτων τις κακοδαιμονίαν διελθεῖν δύναιτ' ἄν; τοσαύτη τίς ἐστι· σὺ δέ μοι διότι μὴ βούλο
μαι ταύτης μετέχειν ἐγκαλεῖς; ζῶ δὲ καθάπερ ὁ κόσμιος ἐκεῖνος, εὐωχούμενος τοῖς κατ'
ἐμαυτὸν, καὶ τοῖς εὐτελεστάτοις χρώμενος. τῶν δὲ ποικίλων, καὶ παντοδαπῶν, οὐκ ἐφιέμενος.
κἄπειτα θηρίου βίον, βραχέων δεόμενος, καὶ ὀλίγοις χρώμενος, δοκῶ σοι ζῆν, κινδυνεύουσιν
οἱ θεοὶ καὶ τῶν θηρίων εἶναι χείρονες, κατά γε τὸν σὸν λόγον· οὐδενὸς γὰρ δέονται. ἵνα δὲ κατα-

1 quantoque] quandoque *1563* 2 pereunt conplures] pereunt *1506 1514* (*with* complures *added in margin*) *1516 1519* 6 Eriphylen] Eriphilen *1506* 23–24 atque illinc homines] atque homines *1506 1514 1516 1517 1519* 26 carnibus] earnibus [*sic*] *1506* 31 cratere] craterae *1506* 33 possit] *1506 1514*, posset *1516 1517 1519 1521 1528 1534 1563 1566* 34 nolo] volo *1506 1516 1519*

periculis: imo sanguine, ac caede quantoque hominum interitu: non ideo solum quod dum nauigant, propter ista pereunt conplures: ac dum quaerunt, parantque, grauia perferunt: sed ob id quoque quod digladiationes multas pariunt, quodque ob ea insidiantur inuicem & amicis amici, & parentibus liberi, & maritis coniuges. Sic opinor Eriphylen quoque auri gratia prodidisse maritum. Atque haec quidem omnia fiunt, quum tamen uestes illae uariae nihilo magis quicquam queant calefacere, aurataque illa aedificia nihilo prorsus magis tegant, nec pocula illa argentea potui quicquam magis conducant. Sed nec aurei illi, nec eburnei item lectuli, somnum suauiorem praebeant, imo uidebis frequenter in eburneo lecto, sumptuosisque stromatibus, beatis illis somnum contingere non posse. Praeterea omnigenae illae circa edulia curae, nihilo magis alunt, quin tabefaciunt potius corpora, ijsdemque morbos ingenerant. Quid autem dicere attinet, libidinis gratia quantas molestias mortales & faciunt, & patiuntur? quanquam facile est isti cupiditati mederi, nisi quis uelit indulgere delitijs. At ne haec quidem insania, corruptelaque sufficere uidetur mortalibus, sed iam rerum etiam usum peruertunt, singulis rebus ad id utentes, ad quod minime paratae sunt, quemadmodum lecto siquis uti carpenti loco uelit, ac tanquam curru. LVCIA. Quisnam is est? CYN. Vos, inquam, qui hominibus tanquam iumentis utimini. Nam eos iubetis, ut lecticas tanquam currus in ceruicibus ferant. Ipsi uero in sublimi residetis delicati, atque illinc homines perinde tanquam asinos aurigamini, imperantes ut hac, non illac eant, & qui haec facitis maxime, ijdem maxime beati uidemini. Tum hi qui piscium carnibus non tantum ut alimentis utuntur, uerum tincturas etiam quasdam ex his machinantur, eos dico, qui purpuram tingunt, nonne & hi praeter naturam his utuntur, quae a deo praeparata sunt? LVCIA. Non per Iouem, siquidem tingere etiam potest non comedi tantum purpurae caro. CYN. At non in id tamen nata est. Nam & cratere quispiam, si praeter naturam detorqueat, ollae loco posset uti, nec in id tamen paratus erat. Sed quo pacto possit quispiam uniuersam illorum infelicitatem percurrere, quae tanta est? At tu me quoque quod nolo eius esse particips, incusas. Viuo ego tamen quemadmodum modestus ille, his uidelicet duntaxat, quae mihi apponuntur uescens, ac frugalissimis utens. Varijs uero illis atque omnigenis minime inhians. Ac deinde quum paucis egeam, ac minime multis utar, ferinam tibi uideor uitam uiue[x_5v]re. Atqui hac ratione tua Dij profecto in periculum

μάθῃς ἀκριβέστερον τό, τε ὀλίγων, καὶ τὸ πολλῶν δεῖσθαι, ποῖόν τι ἑκάτερόν ἐστιν, ἐννόησον ὅτι δέονται πλειόνων οἱ μὲν παῖδες, τῶν τελείων· αἱ δὲ γυναῖκες, τῶν ἀνδρῶν. οἱ δὲ νοσοῦντες, τῶν ὑγιαινόντων· καθόλου δὲ πανταχοῦ τὸ χεῖρον τοῦ κρείττονος πλειόνων δεῖται. διὰ τοῦτο, θεοὶ μὲν, οὐδενός· οἱ δ' ἔγγιστα θεῶν, ἐλαχίστων δέονται. ἢ νομίζεις τὸν Ἡρακλέα τῶν πάντων ἀνθρώπων ἄριστον, θεῖον δὲ ἄνδρα, καὶ θεὸν ὀρθῶς νομισθέντα, διὰ κακοδαιμονίαν περινοστεῖν γυμνὸν, δέρμα μόνον ἔχοντα, καὶ μηδενὸς τῶν αὐτῶν ὑμῖν δεόμενον; ἀλλ' οὐ κακοδαίμων ἦν ἐκεῖνος, ὃς καὶ τῶν ἄλλων ἀπήμυνε τὰ κακά· οὐδ' αὖ πένης, ὃς γῆς, καὶ θαλάττης ἦρχεν· ἐφ' ὅ, τι γὰρ ὁρμήσειεν, ἁπανταχοῦ πάντων ἐκράτει, καὶ οὐδενὶ τῶν τότε ἐνέτυχεν ὁμοίῳ, οὐδὲ κρείττονι ἑαυτοῦ, μέχρι περ ἐξ ἀνθρώπων ἀπῆλθεν. ἢ σὺ δοκεῖς στρωμάτων, καὶ ὑποδημάτων ἀπόρως ἔχειν, καὶ διὰ τοῦτο περιιέναι τοιοῦτος; οὐκ ἔστιν εἰπεῖν, ἀλλ' ἐγκρατὴς, καὶ καρτερικὸς ἦν, καὶ κρατεῖν ἤθελε, καὶ τρυφᾶν οὐκ ἐβούλετο. ὁ δὲ Θησεὺς ὁ τούτου μαθητὴς, οὐ βασιλεὺς μὲν ἦν πάντων Ἀθηναίων, υἱὸς δὲ Ποσειδῶνος ὥς φασιν, ἄριστος δὲ τῶν καθ' αὑτόν; ἀλλ' ὅμως κἀκεῖνος ἤθελεν ἀνυπόδητος εἶναι, καὶ γυμνὸς βαδίζειν· καὶ πώγωνα, καὶ κόμην ἔχειν, ἤρεσκεν αὐτῷ· καὶ οὐκ ἐκείνῳ μόνον, ἀλλὰ καὶ πᾶσι τοῖς παλαιοῖς ἤρεσκεν. ἀμείνους γὰρ ἦσαν ὑμῶν· καὶ οὐκ ἂν ὑπέμειναν οὐδὲ εἷς αὐτῶν οὐδὲν μᾶλλον, ἢ τῶν λεόντων τις ξυρώμενος· ὑγρότητα γὰρ, καὶ λειότητα σαρκὸς, γυναιξὶ πρέπειν ἡγοῦντο· αὐτοὶ δ' ὥσπερ ἦσαν, καὶ φαίνεσθαι ἄνδρες ἤθελον· καὶ τὸν πώγωνα, κόσμον ἀνδρὸς ἐνόμιζον, ὥσπερ καὶ ἵππων χαίτην, καὶ λεόντων γένεια· οἷς ὁ θεὸς ἀγλαΐας, καὶ κόσμου χάριν προσέθηκέ τινα· οὕτω δὲ καὶ τοῖς ἀνδράσι τὸν πώγωνα προσέθηκεν. ἐκείνους οὖν ἐγὼ ζηλῶ τοὺς παλαιοὺς, καὶ ἐκείνους μιμεῖσθαι βούλομαι. τοὺς δὲ νῦν, οὐ ζηλῶ τῆς θαυμαστῆς ταύτης εὐδαιμονίας, ἣν ἔχουσι. καὶ περὶ τραπέζας, καὶ ἐσθῆτας, καὶ λεαίνοντες, καὶ ψιλούμενοι πᾶν τοῦ σώματος μέρος, καὶ μηδὲ τῶν ἀπορρήτων οὐδὲν, ᾗ πέφυκεν ἔχειν ἐῶντες. εὔχομαι δέ μοι τοὺς μὲν πόδας, ὁπλῶν ἱππείων οὐδὲν διαφέρειν, ὥσπερ φασὶ Χείρωνος. αὐτὸς δὲ μὴ δεῖσθαι στρωμάτων, ὥσπερ οἱ λέοντες, οὔτε τροφῆς δεῖσθαι πολυτελοῦς μᾶλλον, ἢ οἱ κύνες· εἴη δέ μοι, γῆν μὲν ἅπασαν εὐνὴν αὐτάρκη ἔχειν, οἶκον δὲ τὸν κόσμον νομίζειν, τροφὴν δὲ αἱρεῖσθαι τὴν ῥάστην πορισθῆναι· χρυσοῦ δὲ, καὶ ἀργύρου, μὴ δεῖ

3 consydera] considera *1521* 16 mundum] nudum *1566* 23 omnibus etiam] etiam omnibus *1566* 24 uos] nos *1506 1514* (*corrected in margin to* vos) *1516 1519 1563* 39 ea] ca [*sic*] *1506*

ueniunt, ne & ipsi sint feris etiam deteriores, quippe qui rei nullius indigent. Verum ut exactius intelligas, cuiusmodi horum utrunque sit, uel paucis uidelicet egere, uel multis, consydera quod pluribus egent, primum pueri quam adulti, deinde mulieres quam uiri, tum aegroti quam ualentes, atque omnino in summa, inferiora quaelibet praestantioribus plurium indigent, proinde Dij omnino nullius egent rei, qui uero ad Deos accedunt proxime quam minimis egent. An Herculem putas omnium hominum praestantissimum, quippe diuinum uirum, deumque recte creditum miserum tunc fuisse, quum circuiret nudus, pelle duntaxat indutus, harum rerum nostrarum nihil desiderans? At ille miser profecto non erat, quippe qui miseriam ab alijs propulsabat, neque rursus pauper, qui terra, marique dominabatur. Nempe quocunque intendisset impetum, omnes quaquauersum superabat, nec in quenquam sui temporis incidit, qui se uel aequarit unquam, uel uicerit, quoad ex humanis excessit. At tu illi stromata putas, calceosque defuisse? atque ob id mundum obambulasse tantum uirum? Dicendum profecto non est. Sed continens erat ac fortis, & moderate uiuere uolebat, non indulgere delitijs. Quid Theseus eius discipulus? An non rex erat Atheniensium omnium, ac filius etiam, ut ferunt, Neptuni, sua certe tempestate fortissimus? Attamen ille quoque uoluit sine calceis esse, ac nudus ingredi, barbamque & comam nutrire placuit ei, nec ei tamen solum, sed omnibus etiam ueteribus placuit, nempe meliores erant quam uos, atque adeo ne sustinuisset quidem eorum quisquam aliquid huiusmodi, nihilo profecto magis quam leo quispiam sese tonderi. Siquidem carnis molliciem ac laeuorem decere mulieres existimabant, ipsi uero sicuti erant, ita uideri quoque uiri uolebant, ac barbam quidem cultum uiri ducebant, quem admodum in equis iubam, in leonibus barbam, quibus deus splendoris quandam atque ornamenti uenustatem dedit, sic & uiris barbam adiunxit. Illos igitur ego aemulor, ueteres, inquam, illos imitari uolo, huius uero tempestatis homines non aemulor mirabilis huius felicitatis nomine, quam in epulis & uestibus habent, dum poliunt ac laeuigant singulas corporis partes, ac ne secretiorum quidem ullam, ita ut instituit natura, dimittentes. At mihi certe pedes opto, ut nihil equinis differant, quales Chironis fuisse ferunt. Tum ut ipse stromatis non egeam more leonum, nec cibo egeam magis exquisito, quam canes. Contingat praeterea mihi, ut terra quaeuis mihi per se pro cubili sufficiat. Domum uero ut mundum hunc existimem. Alimenta demum ut ea

θείην, μήτ' οὖν ἐγώ, μήτε τῶν ἐμῶν φίλων μηδείς. πάντα γὰρ τὰ κακὰ τοῖς ἀνθρώποις ἐκ τῆς τούτων ἐπιθυμίας φύονται, καὶ στάσεις, καὶ πόλεμοι, καὶ ἐπιβουλαί, καὶ σφαγαί. ταῦτα πάντα, πηγὴν ἔχει τὴν ἐπιθυμίαν τοῦ πλείονος. ἀλλ' ἡμῶν αὕτη ἀπείη, καὶ πλεονεξίας μήποτε ὀρεχθείην. μειονεκτῶν δ' ἀνέχεσθαι δυναίμην. τοιαῦτά σοι τά γε ἡμέτερα. πολὺ δήπου δὲ ἀφωνα τοῖς τῶν πολλῶν βουλήμασι. καὶ θαυμαστὸν οὐδέν, εἰ τῷ σχήματι διαφέρομεν αὐτῶν, ὁπότε καὶ τῇ προαιρέσει τοσοῦτον διαφέρομεν. θαυμάζω δέ σου πῶς ποτε κιθαρῳδοῦ μέν τινα νομίζεις στολὴν, καὶ σχῆμα, καὶ αὐλητοῦ νὴ Δία σχῆμα, καὶ στολὴν τραγῳδοῦ, ἀνδρὸς δὲ ἀγαθοῦ σχῆμα, καὶ στολὴν, οὐκ ἔτι νομίζεις, ἀλλὰ τὴν αὐτὴν αὐτὸν οἴει δεῖν ἔχειν τοῖς πολλοῖς. καὶ ταῦτα, τῶν πολλῶν κακῶν ὄντων. εἰ μὲν δεῖ ἑνὸς ἰδίου σχήματος τοῖς ἀγαθοῖς, τί πρέποι ἂν μᾶλλον, ἢ τοῦθ', ὅπερ ἀναιδέστατον μᾶλλον τοῖς ἀκολάστοις ἐστί, καὶ ὅπερ ἀπεύξαιντ' ἂν οὗτοι μάλιστα ἔχειν. οὐκοῦν τό γε ἐμὸν σχῆμα, τοιοῦτόν ἐστιν, αὐχμηρὸν εἶναι, λάσιον εἶναι, τρίβωνα ἔχειν, κομᾶν, ἀνυποδητεῖν. τὸ δ' ὑμέτερον, ὅμοιον τῷ τῶν κιναίδων. καὶ διακρίνειν οὐδὲ εἷς ἂν ἔχοι, οὐ τῇ χροιᾷ τῶν ἱματίων, οὐ τῇ μαλακότητι, οὐ τῷ πλήθει τῶν χιτωνίσκων, οὐ τοῖς ἀμφιάσμασιν, οὐχ ὑποδήμασιν, οὐ κατασκευῇ τριχῶν, οὐκ ὀδμῇ. καὶ γὰρ ἀπόζετε ἤδη παραπλήσιον ἐκείνοις, οἱ εὐδαιμονέστατοι οὗτοι μάλιστα. καίτοι, τί ἂν δῴη τις ἀνδρὸς τὴν αὐτὴν τοῖς κιναίδοις ὀδμὴν ἔχοντος; τοιγαροῦν, τοὺς μὲν πόνους, οὐδὲν ἐκείνων μᾶλλον ἀνέχεσθε. τὰς δὲ ἡδονάς, οὐδὲν ἐκείνων ἧττον. καὶ τρέφεσθε τοῖς αὐτοῖς, καὶ κοιμᾶσθε ὁμοίως, καὶ βαδίζετε. μᾶλλον δὲ βαδίζειν οὐκ ἐθέλετε. φέρεσθε δέ, ὥσπερ τὰ φορτία. οἱ μὲν, ὑπ' ἀνθρώπων. οἱ δὲ, ὑπὸ κτηνῶν. ἐμὲ δ' οἱ πόδες φέρουσιν ὅποι περ ἂν δέωμαι. κἀγὼ μὲν ἱκανὸς καὶ ῥίγους ἀνέχεσθαι, καὶ θάλπος φέρειν, καὶ τοῖς τῶν θεῶν ἔργοις μὴ δυσχεραίνειν, διότι ἄθλιός εἰμι. ὑμεῖς δέ, διὰ τὴν εὐδαιμονίαν, οὐδενὶ τῶν γιγνομένων ἀρέσκεσθε, καὶ πάντα μέμφεσθε. καὶ τὰ μὲν παρόντα, φέρειν οὐκ ἐθέλετε. τῶν δὲ ἀπόντων, ἐφίεσθε. χειμῶνος μὲν εὔχεσθαι θέρος, θέρους δὲ χειμῶνα. καὶ καύματος μὲν ῥῖγος, ῥίγους δὲ καῦμα, καθάπερ οἱ νοσοῦντες δυσάρεστοι, καὶ μεμψίμοιροι ὄντες. αἰτία δὲ ἐκείνοις μὲν, ἡ νόσος. ὑμῖν δέ, ὁ τρόπος. κἄπειτα δὲ ἡμᾶς μετατίθεσθαι, καὶ ἐπανορθοῦν τὰ ἡμέτερα ἀλλήλοις ἐπιτιμῶμεν, κακῶς βουλευομένοις πολλάκις περὶ ὧν πράττουσιν, αὐτοὶ ἄσκεπτοι ὄντες περὶ τῶν ἰδίων, καὶ μηδὲν αὐτῶν κρίσει, καὶ λογισμῷ ποιοῦντες, ἀλλ' ἔθει, καὶ ἐπι-

1 deligam] delegam *1563 1566* 9 ab] ad *1514* 9–10 differimus] deferimus *1506*

deligam, quae facillime comparari possint. Aurum uero, argentumque ne desiderem unquam, neque ego, [x_6] neque meorum amicorum quisquam. Omnia nanque mala inter homines ex horum cupiditate nascuntur, & seditiones, & bella, & insidiae, & caedes. Haec omnia fontem habent plus habendi cupidinem. At haec a nobis abscedat procul, ne unquam plus satis appetam, minus uero quum habeam, ferre aequo animo ualeam. Nostra quidem ita se habent. Plurimum profecto a uulgi sententijs ista dissentiunt. Neque quicquam ergo mirandum est, si ab his differimus habitu, a quibus tantum differimus instituto. Sed te demiror, quonam pacto quum suam quandam citharoedo uestem tribuas, cultumque, atque adeo tibicini suum, & tragoedo suum, bono uiro cultum, uestemque propriam nullam existimas, sed eandem ei cum uulgo habendam censes, idque quum uulgus malum sit. Quod si bonorum cultus proprius debet esse ullus, quinam deceat magis quam hic meus, qui maxime luxuriosis pudendus sit? quemque illi maxime auersentur? Cultus ergo meus huiusmodi est, squalidum esse, hirsutum esse, tritum pallium indui, comam producere, ac sine calceis ingredi. Vester uero Cinaedorum ornatui simillimus est, nec dignoscere uos quisquam ab illis possit, neque colore uestium, neque mollicie, neque camisiarum numero, neque lacernis, neque calceis, neque capillorum cura, neque odore. Nam & redoletis ut illi, iam praesertim uos qui estis felicissimi. Et quidem quid facias, quum uir eundem cum Cinaedis odorem oleat? Etenim in ferendis laboribus nihil illis praestatis. Voluptatibus uero nihilominus quam illi superamini, eadem comeditis, eodem modo dormitis, atque inceditis, imo uero incedere non uultis, sed gestari potius, tanquam sarcinae, alij ab hominibus, alij uero a iumentis. At me pedes ipsi gestant quocunque sit opus. Egoque & frigus tolerare sufficio, & calorem pati, eaque quae dij obtulerint, minime moleste ferre, ideo uidelicet, quia miser sum. Vos uero propter hanc felicitatem nulla estis fortuna contenti, sed omnium poenitet, ac praesentia ferre non potestis, absentia desideratis, hyeme quidem optantes aestatem, aestate rursus hyemem, atque in calore frigus, in frigore uicissim calorem, quemadmodum aegrotantes, morosi semper & queruli, quod in illis quidem facit morbus, in uobis uero mores. Atque haec ita quum sint, iam nos in uitam uestram traducere aequum censetis, nostramque corrumpere, quum saepe male consulta sint, quae facitis, ipsique sitis in uestris ipsorum negocijs minime circumspecti, nihilque eorum iudicio ac ratione,

θυμίᾳ. τοιγαροῦν οὐδὲν ὑμεῖς διαφέρετε τῶν ὑπὸ χειμάρρου φερομένων. ἐκεῖνοί τε γὰρ
ὅπου ἂν ἴοι τὸ ῥεῦμα, ἐκεῖ φέρονται. καὶ ὑμεῖς, ὅπου ἂν αἱ ἐπιθυμίαι. πάσχετε δὲ παραπλή-
σιόν τι, ὅ φασι παθεῖν τινὰ ἐφ' ἵππον ἀναβάντα, μαινόμενον. ἁρπάσας γὰρ αὐτὸν, ἔφερεν
ἄρα ὁ ἵππος. ὁ δ' οὐκ ἔτι καταβῆναι, τοῦ ἵππου θέοντος, ἐδύνατο. καί τις ἀπαντήσας, ἠ-
ρώτησεν αὐτὸν, ποῖ ἄπεισιν. ὁ δὲ, εἶπεν, ὅπου ἂν τούτῳ δοκῇ, δεικνὺς τὸν ἵππον. καὶ ὑμᾶς
ἄν τις ἐρωτᾷ ποῖ φέρεσθε, τἀληθὲς ἐθέλοντες λέγειν, ἐρεῖτε, ἁπλῶς μὲν, ὅπου περ ἂν
ταῖς ἐπιθυμίαις δοκῇ. κατὰ μέρος δὲ, ὅπου περ ἂν τῇ ἡδονῇ. ποτὲ δὲ, ὅπου τῇ δόξῃ. ποτὲ δὲ αὖ, τῇ φιλοκερδείᾳ. ποτὲ δὲ, ὁ θυμὸς, ποτὲ δὲ, ὁ φόβος, ποτὲ δὲ, ἄλλο τι τοιοῦτον ὑ-
μᾶς ἐκφέρειν φαίνεται. οὐ γὰρ ἐφ' ἑνὸς, ἀλλ' ἐπὶ πολλῶν γε ὑμεῖς τε ἵππων βεβηκότες, ἄλλοτε ἄλλων, καὶ μαινομένων πάντων, φέρεσθε. τοιγαροῦν ἐκφέρουσιν ὑμᾶς εἰς βάραθρα, καὶ
κρημνούς. ἴστε δ' οὐδαμῶς πρὶν πεσεῖν, ὅτι πεσεῖσθαι μέλλετε. ὁ δὲ τρίβων οὗτος, οὗ κατα-
γελᾶτε, καὶ ἡ κόμη, καὶ τὸ σχῆμα τοὐμὸν, τηλικαύτην ἔχει δύναμιν, ὥστε παρέχειν μοι
ζῆν ἐφ' ἡσυχίας, καὶ πράττοντι ὅ, τι βούλομαι, καὶ συνόντι οἷς βούλομαι. τῶν γὰρ ἀμα-
θῶν ἀνθρώπων, καὶ ἀπαιδεύτων, οὐδεὶς ἂν ἐθέλοι μοι προσιέναι διὰ τὸ σχῆμα. οἱ δὲ μαλακοὶ,
καὶ πάνυ πόρρωθεν ἐκτρέπονται. προσίασι δὲ οἱ κομψότατοι, καὶ ἐπιεικέστατοι, καὶ ἀρετῆς
ἐπιθυμοῦντες. οὗτοι μάλιστά μοι προσίασι. τοῖς γὰρ τοιούτοις ἐγὼ χαίρω συνών. θύρας δὲ τῶν καλουμένων ἀνθρώπων, οὐ θεραπεύω. τοὺς δὲ χρυσοῦς στεφάνους,
καὶ τὴν πορφύραν, τῦφον νομίζω, καὶ τῶν ἀνθρώπων καταγελῶ. ἵνα δὲ
μάθῃς περὶ τοῦ σχήματος, ὡς οὐκ ἀνδράσι μόνον ἀγαθοῖς, ἀλλὰ καὶ
θεοῖς πρέποντος, ἔπειτα καταγελᾷς αὐτοῦ, σκέψαι τὰ ἀ-
γάλματα τῶν θεῶν, πότερά σοι δοκοῦσιν ὁμοίως ἔχειν
ὑμῖν, ἢ ἐμοί. καὶ μὴ μόνον γε τῶν Ἑλλήνων, ἀλλὰ
καὶ τῶν βαρβάρων τοὺς ναοὺς ἐπισκόπει
περιϊὼν, πότερον αὐτοὶ οἱ θεοὶ κομῶ-
σι, καὶ γενειῶσιν ὡς ἐγὼ, ἢ καθάπερ
ὑμεῖς, ἐξυρημένοι πλάττον-
ται, καὶ γράφονται. καὶ μέν-
τοι καὶ ἀχίτωνας ὄψει τοὺς πολλοὺς, ὥσπερ ἐμέ. τί ἂν οὖν
ἔτι τολμῴης περὶ τούτου τοῦ σχήματος λέ-
γειν ὡς φαύλου, ὁπότε καὶ θεοῖς
φαίνεται πρέπον;

6 desilire] desilere *1506 1514 1517* 8 quocunque] quocun *1517* 26 non] num *1563* 28 consydera] considera *1521* 28 uobis] tibi *1506 1514* (*changed to* vobis *in margin*) *1516 1519* 31 plurimos] plurima *1506 1514* (*changed to* plurimos *in margin*) *1516 1519* 35–37 LVCIANI . . . FINIS] *om. 1516 1519 1528 1534 1563 1566*, Cynici finis Thoma Moro interprete *1506 1514*

sed consuetudine cupiditatis faciatis. Quamobrem nihil profecto differtis uos, ab his qui torrente feruntur. Illi quippe quocunque fluxus intenderit, eo rapiuntur, & uos itidem quocunque libidines. At similiter quidem uobiscum agitur, ut cum quodam qui equum insanum ascenderat. [x_6v] Equus igitur uirum corripiens abstulit. Hic uero amplius iam desilire equo currente non poterat. Quidam uero quum occurrisset ei, rogauit quonam tenderet? Hic respondit, quocunque huic uidetur, equum demonstrans. Quod si uos quisquam roget, quo feramini, si uerum uultis dicere, dicetis in uniuersum quidem quocunque uideatur affectibus, sigillatim uero, interdum quocunque uoluptati, interdum quocunque ambitioni, interdum rursus quo lucri studio. Quin interdum ira, interdum metus interdum aliud quippiam huiusmodi uos auferre uidetur. Neque enim unum duntaxat equum uos, sed multos insilientes, nunc hunc, nunc illum, furiosos quidem omnes auehimini. Auferunt ergo uos in barathrum, ac praerupta. Vos tamen priusquam cadatis casuros uos esse nescitis, at hoc detritum pallium quod uos ridetis comaque habitusque meus tantam habet uim, ut uitam mihi quietam praebeat, utque agam quicquid uolo, uerserque cum quibus uolo. Nempe ex indoctis, atque ineruditis hominibus nemo me adire uoluerit, ob hunc habitum. At molles etiam qui sunt adhuc admodum procul declinant. Congrediuntur uero scitissimi atque modestissimi, & qui uirtutem cupiunt, hi potissimum congrediuntur mecum, horum ego consuetudine delector. Eorum uero fores qui homines uocantur, non obseruo, tum coronas aureas ac purpuram pro fastu habeo, atque homines ipsos derideo. At ut cultum hunc intelligas, non bonos modo uiros, sed ipsos etiam deos decere, atque eum deinde, si libet, irrideas, deorum statuas consydera, utri uideantur uobis ne, an mihi similiores, neque Graecorum solum, sed barbarorum etiam templa circumspicias, utrum ipsi dij, ut ego, comati, barbatique sunt, an quemadmodum uos, rasi finguntur atque pinguntur. Quin plurimos etiam sine tunicis conspicies, ut me nunc esse uides. Quo pacto igitur audeas posthac hunc habitum uitio dare, quum deos etiam decere uideatur?

LVCIANI CYNICI, THOMA MORO
INTERPRETE,
FINIS. [y_1]

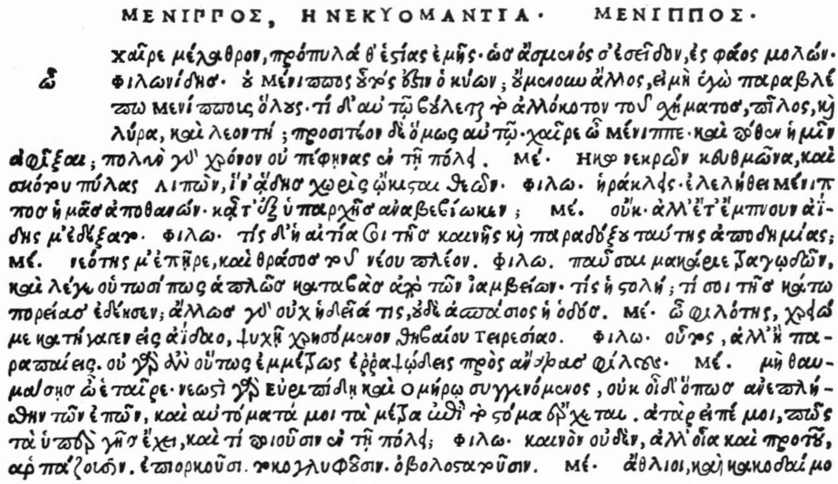

ΜΕΝΙΠΠΟΣ, Η ΝΕΚΥΟΜΑΝΤΙΑ· ΜΕΝΙΠΠΟΣ·

ὦ χαῖρε μέλαθρον, πρόπυλά θ' ἑστίας ἐμῆς· ὡς ἀσμενός σ' ἐσεῖδον, ἐς φάος μολών·
φιλωνίδης· οὐ Μένιππος οὗτός ἐστιν ὁ κύων; οὐ μὲν οὖν ἄλλος, εἰ μὴ ἐγὼ παραβλέ
πω Μένιππος ὅλος. τί δ' αὐτῷ βούλεται τὸ ἀλλόκοτον τοῦ σχήματος, πῖλος, καὶ
λύρα, καὶ λεοντῆ; προσιτέον δὲ ὅμως αὐτῷ. χαῖρε ὦ Μένιππε· καὶ πόθεν ἡμῖν
ἀφῖξαι; πολὺν γὰρ χρόνον οὐ πέφηνας ἐν τῇ πόλει. Με· ἥκω νεκρῶν κευθμῶνα, καὶ
σκότου πύλας λιπών, ἵν' ἅδης χωρὶς ᾤκισται θεῶν· φιλω· ἡράκλεις· ἐλελήθει Μένιπ
πος ἡμᾶς ἀποθανών· κᾆτ' ἐξ ὑπαρχῆς ἀναβεβίωκεν; Με. οὐκ· ἀλλ' ἔτ' ἔμπνουν ἀΐ-
δης μ' ἐδέξατο· φιλω· τίς δ' ἡ αἰτία σοι τῆς καινῆς καὶ παραδόξου ταύτης ἀποδημίας;
Με. νεότης μ' ἐπῆρε, καὶ θράσος τοῦ νέου πλέον. φιλω. παῦσαι μακάριε τραγῳδῶν,
καὶ λέγε οὑτωσί πως ἁπλῶς καταβὰς ἀπὸ τῶν ἰαμβείων· τίς ἡ στολή; τί σοι τῆς κάτω
πορείας ἐδέησεν; ἄλλως γὰρ οὐχ ἡδεῖά τις, οὐδὲ ἀσπάσιος ἡ ὁδός. Με· ὦ φιλότης, χρειὼ
με κατήγαγεν εἰς ἀΐδαο, ψυχῇ χρησόμενον θηβαίου τειρεσίαο. φιλω· οὗτος, ἀλλ' ἦ πα-
ραπαίεις. οὐ γὰρ ἂν οὕτως ἐμμέτρως ἐρραψῴδεις πρὸς ἄνδρας φίλους· Με. μὴ θαυ-
μάσῃς ὦ ἑταῖρε· νεωστὶ γὰρ εὐριπίδῃ καὶ ὁμήρῳ συγγενόμενος, οὐκ οἶδ' ὅπως ἀνεπλή-
σθην τῶν ἐπῶν, καὶ αὐτόματά μοι τὰ μέτρα ἐπὶ τὸ στόμα ἔρχεται. ἀτὰρ εἰπέ μοι, πῶς
τὰ ὑπὲρ γῆς ἔχει, καὶ τί ποιοῦσιν ἐν τῇ πόλει; φιλω· καινὸν οὐδέν, ἀλλ' οἷα καὶ πρὸ τοῦ,
ἁρπάζουσιν. ἐπιορκοῦσι. τοκογλυφοῦσιν. ὀβολοστατοῦσιν. Με· ἄθλιοι, καὶ κακοδαίμο

3 MENIPPVS, PHILONIDES] Personae Menippus Philonides *1506*, INTERLOCUTORES, MENIPPVS, PHILONIDES *1516 1519* 4 MENIPPVS] *om. 1534 1563 1566* 5 atrium] artium *1566* 5 uestibulum] vestiblum [*sic*] *1506 1516* 13 tenebrarum] tenebratum *1506* 18 causa tibi] tibi causa *1506 1516 1519* 24 uia?] via. *1506 1514 1516 1519*

MENIPPVS SIVE NECROMANTIA LVCIANI THOMA MORO INTERPRETE. MENIPPVS, PHILONIDES.

MENIPPVS.

SALVE atrium, domusque uestibulum meae:
Vt te lubens aspicio luci redditus.

PHILO. Num nam hic Menippus est canis ille? Non hercle alius, nisi ego forte ad Menippos omneis hallucinor. At quid sibi uult habitus huius insolentia? claua, lyra, leonis exuuiae? Adeundus tamen est. Salue Menippe. Vnde nobis aduenisti? diu est quod in urbe non uidimus.

MENIP. Adsum reuersus mortuorum e latibulis,
Foribusque tristium tenebrarum nigris:
Manes ubi inferi manent superis procul.

PHILO. O Hercules clam nobis Menippus uita functus est, reuixitque denuo?

MENIP. Non, sed me adhuc uiuum recepit tartarus.

PHILO. Quaenam causa tibi fuit nouae huius atque incredibilis uiae?

MENI. Iuuenta me incitauit, atque audacia:
Quam pro iuuenta haud paululum impotenior.

PHILO. Siste o beate Tragica, & ab iambis descendens sic potius simpliciter eloquere, quaenam haec uestis, quae causa tibi itineris inferni fuit, quum alioqui neque iucunda neque delectabilis sit uia?

MENIP. Res dilecte grauis me infernas egit ad umbras,
Consulerem manes ut uatis Tiresiai.

PHILO. Atqui deliras, alioqui non hoc pacto caneres apud amicos consarcinatis uersibus. MENIP. Ne mireris amice, nuper enim cum Euripide atque Homero uersatus, nescio quo pacto uersibus sic impletus sum, ut numeri mihi in os sua sponte confluant. Verum dic mihi quo pacto res humanae hic se habent in terris? & quid nam in urbe agitur? PHILO. Nihil noui. Sed quemadmodum prius actitabant, rapiunt, peierant, foenerantur, usuras colligunt. MENIP. O

νεσ. οὐ γὰρ ἴσασιν οἷα ἔναγχος κεκύρωται παρὰ τοῖς κάτω, καὶ οἷα κεχειροτόνηται τὰ ψηφίσματα κατὰ τῶν πλουσίων, ἃ μὰ τὸν κέρβερον, οὐδεμία μηχανὴ τοῦ διαφυγεῖν αὐτούς. φιλω. τί φής; δέδοκταί τι νεώτερον τοῖς κάτω περὶ τῶν ἐνθάδε; με. νὴ δία καὶ πολλά· ἀλλ' οὐ θέμις ἐκφέρειν αὐτὰ πρὸς ἅπαντας, οὐδὲ τὰ ἀπόρρητα ἐξαγορεύειν, μὴ καί τις ἡμᾶς γράψεται γραφὴν ἀσεβείας ἐπὶ τοῦ ῥαδαμάνθυος. φιλω. μηδαμῶς ὦ μένιππε πρὸς τοῦ διός, μὴ φθονήσῃς τῶν λόγων φίλῳ ἀνδρί. πρὸς γὰρ εἰδότα σιωπᾶν ἐρεῖς. τά τ' ἄλλα, καὶ πρὸς μεμυημένον. με. χαλεπὸν μὲν ἐπιτάττεις τοὐπίταγμα, καὶ οὐ πάντῃ ἀσφαλές. πλὴν, ἀλλὰ σοῦ γε ἕνεκα, τολμητέον. ἔδοξε δὴ τοὺς πλουσίους τούτοις, καὶ πολυχρημάτοις, καὶ τὸ χρυσίον κατάκλειστον, ὥσπερ τὴν δανάην φυλάττοντας. φιλω. μὴ πρότερον εἴπῃς ὦ 'γαθὲ τὰ δεδογμένα, πρὶν ἐκεῖνα διελθεῖν, ἃ μάλιστ' ἂν ἡδέως ἀκούσαιμί σου, ἥτις αἰτία σοι τῆς καθόδου ἐγένετο, τίς δὲ ὁ τῆς πορείας ἡγεμών. εἶθ' ἑξῆς ἅ τε εἶδες, ἅ τε ἤκουσας παρ' αὐτοῖς. εἰκὸς γὰρ δὴ φιλόκαλον ὄντα σε, μηδὲν τῶν ἀξίων θέας ἢ ἀκοῆς παραλιπεῖν. με. ὑπουργητέον καὶ ταῦτά σοι. τί γὰρ ἂν καὶ πάθοι τις, ὁπότε φίλος ἀνὴρ βιάζοιτο; καὶ δὴ πρῶτά σοι δίειμι τὴν γνώμην τὴν ἐμήν, καὶ ὅθεν ὡρμήθην πρὸς τὴν κατάβασιν. ἐγὼ γὰρ ἄχρι μὲν ἐν παισὶν ἦν, ἀκούων ὁμήρου, καὶ ἡσιόδου, πολέμους, καὶ στάσεις διηγουμένων, οὐ μόνον τῶν ἡμιθέων, ἀλλὰ καὶ αὐτῶν ἤδη τῶν θεῶν, ἔτι δὲ καὶ μοιχείας αὐτῶν, καὶ βίας, καὶ ἁρπαγάς, καὶ δίκας, καὶ πατέρων ἐξελάσεις, καὶ ἀδελφῶν γάμους, πάντα ταῦτα ἡγούμην εἶναι καλά, καὶ οὐ παρέργως ἐκινούμην πρὸς αὐτά. ἐπεὶ δὲ εἰς ἄνδρας τελεῖν ἠρξάμην, πάλιν αὖ ἐνταῦθα ἤκουον τῶν νόμων, τἀναντία τοῖς ποιηταῖς κελευόντων, μήτε μοιχεύειν, μήτε στασιάζειν, μήτε ἁρπάζειν. ἐν μεγάλῃ οὖν καθειστήκειν ἀμφιβολίᾳ, οὐκ εἰδὼς ὅ, τι χρησαίμην ἐμαυτῷ. οὔτε γὰρ τοὺς θεοὺς ἄν ποτε ἡγούμην μοιχεῦσαι, καὶ στασιάσαι πρὸς ἀλλήλους, εἰ μὴ ὡς περὶ καλῶν τούτων ἐγίνωσκον, οὔτ' ἂν τοὺς νομοθέτας τἀναντία τούτοις παραινεῖν, εἰ μὴ λυσιτελεῖν ὑπελάμβανον. ἐπεὶ δὲ διηπόρουν, ἔδοξέ μοι ἐλθόντα παρὰ τοὺς καλουμένους τούτους φιλοσόφους, ἐγχειρίσαι τε ἐμαυτόν, καὶ δεηθῆναι αὐτῶν χρῆσθαί μοι ὅ, τι βούλοιντο, καί τινα ὁδὸν ἁπλῆν καὶ βεβαίαν ὑποδεῖξαι τοῦ βίου. ταῦτα μὲν δὴ φρονῶν, προσῄειν αὐτοῖς. ἐλελήθειν δ' ἐμαυτὸν εἰς αὐτό φασι τὸ πῦρ ἐκ τοῦ καπνοῦ βιαζόμενος. παρὰ γὰρ δὴ τούτοις μάλιστα εὕρισκον ἐπισκοπῶν τὴν ἄγνοιαν, καὶ τὴν ἀπορίαν πλείονα. ὥστε μοι

3 quos per] per quos *1506 1514 1516 1517 1519* 12 abstrusum—] abstrusum. *1521* 19–20 Ac primum . . . impulerint] *so 1534 1563 1566 excepting* impulerit *for* impulerint, *om. 1506 1514* (*but added in margin*) *1516 1519* 24 nuptias: Haec] nuptias. Haec *1521* 35 uitaeque] *1506 1514 1516 1517 1519 1528 1534 1563 1566*, uitaequae *1521*

miseri atque infelices. Nesciunt enim, qualia de nostris rebus nuper apud inferos decreta sunt, qualesque sorte iacti sunt in diuites istos calculi, quos per Cer[y_1v]berum nullo pacto poterunt effugere. PHILO. Quid ais? Noui ne aliquid apud inferos nostris de rebus decretum est? MENIP. Per Iouem, & quidem multa, uerum prodere non licet; neque arcana quae sunt reuelare, ne quis forte nos apud Rhadamanthum impietatis accuset. PHILO. Nequaquam Menippe per Iouem, ne amico sermonem hunc inuideas. Nam apud hominem tacendi gnarum, & initiatum praeterea sacris edisseres. MENIPPVS. Dura profecto iubes, & neutiquam tuta, uerum tui gratia tamen audendum est. Decretum est ergo, diuites istos ac pecuniosos aurum tanquam Danaen seruantes abstrusum—PHILO. Ne prius o beate quae sunt decreta dixeris, quam ea percurras omnia quae abs te audire libentissime uelim: Quae uidelicet descensus causa fuerit, quis itineris dux, deinde ex ordine, & quae illic uideris, & quae audieris omnia. Verisimile est enim te, quum res pulchras uidendi curiosus sis, eorum quae uisu aut auditu digna uidebantur nihil omnino praetermisisse. MENIP. Parendum etiam in his tibi est. Nam quid facias, urgente amico? Ac primum sane tibi expediam, quae res animum meum ad hunc descensum impulerint. Ego igitur quum adhuc puer essem, audiremque Homerum atque Hesiodum, seditiones ac bella canentes, non semideorum modo, sed ipsorum etiam deorum, adulteria quoque, uiolentias, rapinas, supplicia, patrum expulsiones, & fratrum & sororum nuptias: Haec me hercle omnia bona pulchraque putabam, & studiose erga ea afficiebar. Postquam uero in uirilem iam aetatem peruenirem, hic leges rursus iubentes audio poetis apprime contraria, neque uidelicet adulteria committere, neque seditiones mouere, neque rapinas exercere. Hic igitur haesitabundus constiti, incertus omnino quo me pacto gererem. Neque enim deos unquam putaui moechaturos, aut seditiones inuicem fuisse moturos, nisi de his rebus perinde ac bonis iudicassent. Neque rursus legumlatores his aduersa iussuros, nisi id conducere existimarent. Quoniam igitur in dubio eram, uisum est mihi philosophos istos adire, atque his me in manus dedere, rogareque uti me utcunque liberet uterentur, uitaeque uiam aliquam simplicem ac certam ostenderent. Haec igitur mecum reputans ad eos uenio, imprudens profecto, quod me ex fumo (ut aiunt) in flammam conijcerem. Apud enim hos maxime diligenter obseruans summam repperi ignorantiam, omniaque magis incerta, adeo, ut prae his

τάχιστα χρυσοῦν ἀπέδειξαν ἤτοι τὸν τῶν ἰδιωτῶν βίον. ἀμέλει, ὁ μὲν αὐτῶν, παρῄνει τὸ
πᾶν ἥδεσθαι, καὶ μόνον τοῦτο ἐκ παντὸς μετιέναι· τοῦτο γὰρ εἶναι τὸ εὔδαιμον. ὁ δέ τις
ἔμπαλιν, πονεῖν τὰ πάντα, καὶ μοχθεῖν, καὶ τὸ σῶμα καταναγκάζειν, ῥυπῶντα, καὶ αὐ-
χμῶντα, καὶ πᾶσι δυσαρεστοῦντα, καὶ λοιδορούμενον, συνεχὲς ἐπιρραψῳδῶν τὰ πάν-
δημα ἐκεῖνα τοῦ Ἡσιόδου περὶ τῆς ἀρετῆς ἔπη, καὶ τὸν ἱδρῶτα, καὶ τὴν ἐπὶ τὸ ἄκρον ἀνάβα-
σιν. ἄλλος καταφρονεῖν χρημάτων παρεκελεύετο, καὶ ἀδιάφορον οἴεσθαι τὴν κτῆσιν αὐτῶν. ὁ δέ
τις αὖ πάλιν, ἀγαθὸν εἶναι καὶ τὸν πλοῦτον αὐτὸν ἀπεφαίνετο. περὶ μὲν γὰρ τοῦ κόσμου, τί χρὴ
καὶ λέγειν; ὅς γε ἰδέας, καὶ ἀσώματα, καὶ ἀτόμους, καὶ κενά, καὶ τοιοῦτόν τινα ὄχλον ὀνομάτων ὁ-
σημέραι παρ' αὐτῶν ἀκούων ἐναντίων, καὶ τὸ πάντων δεινῶν ἀτοπώτατον, ὅτι περὶ τῶν
ἐναντιωτάτων ἕκαστος αὐτῶν λέγων, σφόδρα νικῶντας καὶ πιθανοὺς λόγους ἐπορίζετο,
ὥστε μήτε τῷ θερμὸν τὸ αὐτὸ πρᾶγμα λέγοντι, μήτε τῷ ψυχρὸν, ἀντιλέγειν ἔχειν, καὶ ταῦτα,
εἰδότα σαφῶς, ὡς οὐκ ἄν ποτε θερμόν τι εἴη καὶ ψυχρὸν ἐν ταυτῷ χρόνῳ, ἀτεχνῶς οὖν ἔπασχον
τοῖς νυστάζουσι τούτοις ὅμοιον, ἄρτι μὲν, ἐπινεύων, ἄρτι δὲ, ἀνανεύων ἔμπαλιν. ἔτι δὲ πολλῷ τούτων ἐκείνων ἀτοπώτερον, τοὺς γοῦν αὐτοὺς τούτους εὕρισκον ἐπιτηρῶν, ἐναντιώτατα
τοῖς αὐτῶν λόγοις ἐπιτηδεύοντας. τοὺς γοῦν καταφρονεῖν παραινοῦντας χρημάτων, ἑώρων
ἀπρὶξ ἐχομένους αὐτῶν, καὶ περὶ τόκων διαφερομένους, καὶ ἐπὶ μισθῷ παιδεύοντας, καὶ πάντα ἕνεκα τούτων ὑπομένοντας. τούς τε τὴν δόξαν ἀποβαλλομένους, αὐτῆς ἕνεκα πάντα ἐ-
πιτηδεύοντας. ἡδονῆς τε αὖ σχεδὸν ἅπαντας κατηγοροῦντας, ἰδίᾳ δὲ, μόνῃ ταύτῃ προσηρ-
τημένους. σφαλεὶς οὖν καὶ ταύτης τῆς ἐλπίδος, ἔτι μᾶλλον ἐδυσχέραινον ἠρέμα παραμυθούμενος ἐμαυτὸν, ὅτι μετὰ πολλῶν, καὶ σοφῶν, καὶ σφόδρα ἐπὶ συνέσει διαβεβοημένων, ἀνό-
ητός τέ εἰμι, καὶ τἀληθὲς ἔτι ἀγνοῶν περιέρχομαι. καί μοι ποτὲ διαγρυπνοῦντι τούτων
ἕνεκα, ἔδοξεν ἐς Βαβυλῶνα ἐλθόντα, δεηθῆναί τινος τῶν μάγων τῶν Ζωροάστρου μαθητῶν, καὶ
διαδόχων. ἤκουον δ' αὐτοὺς ἐπῳδαῖς τε καὶ τελεταῖς τισιν ἀνοίγειν τε τοῦ ᾅδου τὰς πύλας, καὶ κατάγειν ὃν ἂν βούλωνται ἀσφαλῶς, καὶ ὀπίσω αὖθις ἀναπέμπειν. ἄριστον οὖν ἡγούμην εἶναι παρά τινος τούτων διαπραξάμενον τὴν κατάβασιν, ἐλθόντα παρὰ Τειρεσίαν τὸν
Βοιώτιον, μαθεῖν παρ' αὐτοῦ, ἅτε μάντεως καὶ σοφοῦ, τίς ἐστιν ὁ ἄριστος βίος, καὶ ὃν ἄν τις ἕλοιτο

6 sudorem] *1506 1514 1516 1519 1534 1563 1566*, sudorum *1517 1521 1528*
22 spernendam] spernendum *1506 1516 1519* 31 uere] viae *1566*

ilico mihi uel idiotarum uita iam aurea uideretur. Alius etenim soli me iussit uoluptati studere, atque ad eum scopum uniuersum uitae cursum dirigere. In eo ipsam sitam esse felicitatem. Alius rursus omni[y_2]no laborare, corpusque siti, uigilijs, ac squalore subigere, misere semper adfectum, contumelijsque obnoxium assidue, Hesiodi sedulo inculcans celebria illa de uirtute carmina, & sudorem uidelicet, & accliuem in uerticem montis ascensum. Alius contemnere iubet pecunias, earumque possessionem indifferentem putare. Alius contra bonas ipsas etiam diuitias esse pronunciat. De mundo uero quid dicam? de quo ideas incorporeas, substantias, atomos, & inane, ac talem quandam pugnantium inuicem nominum turbam in diem audiebam. & quod absurdorum omnium maxime fuit absurdum, de contrarijs unusquisque quum diceret, inuincibiles admodum rationes ac persuasibiles adferebat, ut nec ei qui calidum, nec ei qui frigidum idem prorsus esse contenderent, contra quicquam hiscere potuerim, atque id, quum tamen manifeste cognoscerem fieri nunquam posse, ut eadem res calida simul frigidaque sit. Prorsum igitur tale quiddam mihi accidebat, quale solet dormitantibus, ut interdum capite annuerem, interdum contra abnuerem. Praeterea quod multo erat istis absurdius, uitam eorum diligenter obseruans, comperi eam cum ipsorum uerbis praeceptisque summopere pugnare. Eos enim qui spernendam censebant pecuniam, auidissime conspexi colligendis diuitijs inhiare, de foenore litigantes, pro mercede docentes. Omnia denique nummorum gratia tolerantes. Ii uero qui gloriam uerbis aspernabantur, omnem uitae suae rationem in gloriam referebant. Voluptatem rursus omnes ferme palam incessebant. Clanculum uero ad eam solam libenter confluebant. Ergo hac quoque spe frustratus magis adhuc aegre molesteque tuli. Aliquantulum tamen inde memet consolabar, quod una cum multis & sapientibus & celeberrimis uiris ipse insipiensque essem, atque uere adhuc ignarus oberrarem. Peruigilanti mihi tandem, atque hisce de rebus mecum cogitanti, uenit in mentem, ut Babylonem profectus magorum aliquem ex Zoroastri discipulis ac successoribus conuenirem. Audieram siquidem eos inferni portas carminibus quibusdam ac mysterijs aperire, & quem libuerit illuc tuto deducere, ac rursus inde reducere. Optime ergo me facturum putaui, si cum horum quopiam de descensu paciscens Tiresiam Boeotium consulerem, ab eoque perdiscerem (quippe qui uates fuerit & sapiens) quae uita sit optima, quanque sapientissimus quisque potissimum

δυσφορῶν. καὶ δὴ ἀναπηδήσας ὡς εἶχον τάχους, ἔτεινον εὐθὺ Βαβυλῶνος. ἐλθὼν δὲ, συγγίνομαί τινι τῶν Χαλδαίων σοφῷ ἀνδρὶ, καὶ θεσπεσίῳ τὴν τέχνην, πολιῷ μὲν τὴν κόμην, γένειον δὲ μάλα σεμνὸν καθειμένῳ. τοὔνομα δὲ ἦν αὐτῷ, Μιθροβαρζάνης. δεηθεὶς δὲ καὶ καθικετεύσας, μόλις ἔτυχον παρ' αὐτοῦ, ἐφ' ὅτῳ βούλοιτο μισθῷ καθηγήσασθαί μοι τῆς ὁδοῦ. παραλαβὼν δέ με ὁ ἀνὴρ, πρῶτα μὲν ἡμέρας ἐννέα καὶ εἴκοσιν ἅμα τῇ σελήνῃ ἀρξάμενος, ἔλουε, κατάγων ἐπὶ τὸν Εὐφράτην, ἕωθεν πρὸς ἀνατέλλοντα τὸν ἥλιον, ῥῆσίν τινα μακρὰν ἐπιλέγων, ἧς οὐ σφόδρα κατήκουον· ὥσπερ γὰρ οἱ φαῦλοι τῶν ἐν τοῖς ἀγῶσι κηρύκων, ἐπίτροχόν τι, καὶ ἀσαφὲς ἐφθέγγετο· πλὴν, ἀλλ' ἐῴκει γέ τινας ἐπικαλεῖσθαι δαίμονας. μετὰ γοῦν τὴν ἐπῳδὴν, τρὶς ἄν μου πρὸς τὸ πρόσωπον ἀποπτύσας, ἐπανῄει πάλιν, οὐδένα τῶν ἀπαντώντων προσβλέπων. καὶ σιτία μὲν ἡμῖν, τὰ ἀκρόδρυα, ποτὸν δὲ, γάλα, καὶ μελίκρατον, καὶ τὸ τοῦ Χοάσπου ὕδωρ. εὐνὴ δὲ ὑπαίθριος ἐπὶ τῆς πόας. ἐπεὶ δὲ ἅλις εἶχε τῆς προδιαιτήσεως, περὶ μέσας νύκτας ἐπὶ τὸν Τίγρητα ποταμὸν ἀγαγὼν, ἐκάθηρέ τέ με, καὶ ἀπέμαξε, καὶ περιήγνισε δᾳδὶ, καὶ σκίλλῃ, καὶ ἄλλοις πλείοσιν, ἅμα καὶ τὴν ἐπῳδὴν ἐκείνην ὑποτονθορύσας. εἶτα ὅλον με καταμαγεύσας, καὶ περιελθὼν, ἵνα μὴ βλαπτοίμην ὑπὸ τῶν φασμάτων, ἐπανάγει ἐς τὴν οἰκίαν, ὡς εἶχον ἀναποδίζοντα. καὶ τὸ λοιπὸν, ἀμφὶ πλοῦν εἴχομεν. αὐτὸς μὲν οὖν μαγικήν τιν' ἐνέδυ στολὴν, τὰ πολλὰ ἐοικυῖαν τῇ Μηδικῇ. ἐμὲ δὲ τουτοισὶ φέρων ἐνεσκεύασε, τῷ πίλῳ, καὶ τῇ λεοντῇ, καὶ προσέτι τῇ λύρᾳ. καὶ παρεκελεύσατο, ἤν τις ἔρηταί με τοὔνομα, Μένιππον μὴ λέγειν, Ἡρακλέα δὲ, ἢ Ὀδυσσέα, ἢ Ὀρφέα. ΦΙΛΩ. ὡς δὴ τί τοῦτο ὦ Μένιππε; οὐ γὰρ συνίημι τὴν αἰτίαν οὔτε τοῦ σχήματος, οὔτε τῶν ὀνομάτων. ΜΕ. καὶ μὴν πρόδηλόν γε τοῦτο, καὶ οὐ παντελῶς ἀπόρρητον. ἐπεὶ γὰρ οὗτοι πρὸ ἡμῶν ζῶντες, ἐς ᾅδου κατεληλύθεσαν, ἡγεῖτο εἴ με ἀπεικάσειεν αὐτοῖς, ῥᾳδίως ἂν τὴν τοῦ Αἰακοῦ φρουρὰν διαλαθεῖν, καὶ ἀκωλύτως παρελθεῖν, ἅτε συνηθέστερον, τραγικῶς μάλα παραπεμπόμενον ὑπὸ τοῦ σχήματος. ἤδη δ' οὖν ὑπέφαινεν ἡμέρα· καὶ κατελθόντες ἐπὶ τὸν ποταμὸν, περὶ ἀναγωγὴν ἐγιγνόμεθα. παρεσκεύαστο δ' αὐτῷ καὶ σκάφος, καὶ ἱερεῖα, καὶ μελίκρατα, καὶ ἄλλα, ὅσα πρὸς τὴν τελετὴν χρήσιμα. ἐμβαλόμενοι οὖν ἅπαντα τὰ παρεσκευασμένα, οὕτω δὴ καὶ αὐτοὶ βαίνομεν ἀχνύμενοι, θαλερὸν κατὰ δάκρυ χέοντες. καὶ μέχρι μέν τινος ὑπεφερόμεθα ἐν τῷ ποταμῷ. εἶτα δ' εἰσεπλεύσαμεν ἐς τὸ ἕλος, καὶ τὴν λίμνην, ἐς ἣν ὁ Εὐφράτης ἀφανίζεται. περαιωθέντες δὲ καὶ ταύτην, ἀφικνούμεθα ἔς τι χωρίον ἔρη

1 celerrime] celerrima *1566* 17 Tigridem] Tigredem *1506* 21 eram, reciprocantem] eram reciprocantem *1521* 22 reliqua . . . praeparauimus] reliquum iam nauigationi dedimus *1506 1514 1516 1517 1519* (*see commentary*) 31 transirem] transire *1514 1517* 33 nos ad flumen] nos flumen *1506 1514 1516 1517 1519* 33 ingressi] *1506 1514 1516 1517 1519 1528 1534 1563 1566*, priongressi [*sic*] *1521* 37 Ingredimur . . . obortis] anxii, ac vagientium more lachrymantes ingredimur *1506 1514 1516 1517 1519*

elegerit. Ac statim quidem exiliens quam poteram celerrime Babylonem uersus recta contendi. Quo quum uenio, diuersor apud Chaldaeorum quendam hominem certe sapientem, atque arte mirabilem, coma quidem canum, admodumque promissa barba uenerabilem. [y_2v] Nomen autem illi fuit Mithrobarzanes. Orans igitur obsecransque uix exoraui, ut quauis mercede uellet, in illam me uiam deduceret. At tandem homo me suscipiens primum quidem dies nouem ac uiginti cum luna simul incipiens abluit ad Euphratem, mane solem orientem uersus perducens, ac sermonem quempiam longum mussitans, quem non admodum exaudiebam. Nam (quod in certamine praecones inepti solent) uolubile quiddam atque incertum proferebat, nisi quod quosdam uisus est inuocare daemones. Post illam igitur incantationem ter mihi in uultum spuens deducit rursus, oculos nusquam in obuium quenquam deflectens. Et cibus quidem nobis glandes erant, potus autem lac atque mulsum & Choaspi lympha, lectus uero in herba sub dio fuit. At postquam iam praeparati satis hac diaeta sumus, medio noctis silentio ad Tigridem me fluuium ducens, purgauit simul atque abstersit, faceque lustrauit ac squilla, tum pluribus itidem alijs, & magicum simul illud carmen submurmurans, deinde totum me iam incantans, ac ne a spectris laederer circumiens, reducit domum, ita ut eram, reciprocantem, ac reliqua noctis parte nauigationi nos praeparauimus. Ipse igitur magicam quandam uestem induit, Medorum uesti ut plurimum similem, ac me quidem his, quae uides ornauit, claua uidelicet, ac leonis exuuijs, atque insuper lyra. Iussit praeterea ut nomen si quis me roget, Menippum quidem ne dicerem, sed Herculem, Vlyssem, aut Orpheum. PHILO. Quid ita o Menippe? neque enim causam aut habitus, aut nominis intelligo. MENIPPVS. Atqui perspicuum id quidem est, ac neutiquam arcanum. Nam hi qui ante nos ad inferos olim uiui descenderant, putauit si me his assimilaret, fore ut facilius Aeaci custodias fallerem, atque nullo prohibente transirem, utpote notior tragico admodum illo cultu emissus. Iam igitur dies apparuit, quum nos ad flumen ingressi in recessum incumbimus. Parata siquidem ab illo fuerant, cymba, sacrificia, mulsa, & in id mysterium denique quibuscunque opus erat. Haec postquam ergo quae prompta erant imposuimus, tum nos quoque

Ingredimur tristes lachrymisque implemur obortis.

Atque aliquantisper quidem in fluuio ferimur, deinde in syluam delati sumus, ac lacum quendam in quem Euphrates conditur. Tum

μον, καὶ ὑλῶδες, καὶ ἀνήλιον· ἐς ὃ ἀποβάντες, ἡγεῖτο δὲ ὁ Μιθροβαρζάνης, βόθρον τε ὠρυ-
ξάμεθα, καὶ τὰ μῆλα ἐσφάξαμεν, καὶ τὸ αἷμα περὶ τὸν βόθρον ἐσπείσαμεν. ὁ δὲ μάγος, ἐν
τοσούτῳ δᾷδα καιομένην ἔχων, οὐκ ἔτ' ἠρεμαίᾳ τῇ φωνῇ, παμμέγεθες δὲ ὡς οἷός τε ἦν ἀ-
νακραγὼν, δαίμονάς τε ὁμοῦ πάντας ἐπεβοᾶτο, καὶ ποινὰς, καὶ Ἐρριννύας, καὶ νυχίαν
Ἑκάτην, καὶ αἰπεινὴν Περσεφόνειαν, παραμιγνὺς ἅμα βαρβαρικά τινα καὶ ἄσημα ὀνόματα,
καὶ πολυσύλλαβα. εὐθὺς οὖν πάντα ἐκεῖνα ἐσαλεύετο, καὶ ὑπὸ τῆς ἐπῳδῆς τοὔδαφος ἀ-
νερρήγνυτο· καὶ ἡ ὑλακὴ τοῦ Κερβέρου, πόρρωθεν ἠκούετο, καὶ τὸ πρᾶγμα ὑπερκατηφὲς ἦν,
καὶ σκυθρωπόν· ἔδδεισεν δ' ὑπένερθεν ἄναξ ἐνέρων Ἀϊδωνεύς· κατεφαίνετο γὰρ ἤδη τὰ
πλεῖστα, καὶ ἡ λίμνη, καὶ ὁ Πυριφλεγέθων, καὶ τοῦ Πλούτωνος τὰ βασίλεια. κατελθόντες
δ' ὅμως διὰ τοῦ χάσματος, τὸν μὲν Ῥαδάμανθυν εὕρομεν τεθνεῶτα μικροῦ δεῖν ὑπὸ τοῦ δέους·
ὁ δὲ Κέρβερος, ὑλάκτησε μέν τοι, καὶ παρεκίνησε. ταχὺ δέ μου κρούσαντος τὴν λύραν, πα-
ραχρῆμα ἐκοιμήθη ὑπὸ τοῦ μέλους. ἐπεὶ δὲ πρὸς τὴν λίμνην ἤλθομεν, μικροῦ μὲν οὐδ' ἐπε-
ραιώθημεν· ἦν γὰρ ἤδη πλῆρες τὸ πορθμεῖον, καὶ οἰμωγῆς ἀνάπλεων· τραυματίαι δὲ πάντες ἐπέπλεον· ὁ μὲν, τὸ σκέλος, ὁ δὲ, τὴν κεφαλὴν, ὁ δὲ, ἄλλο τι συντετριμμένος· ἐμοὶ δοκεῖν,
ἔκ τινος πολέμου παρόντες. ὅμως δ' οὖν ὁ βέλτιστος Χάρων ὡς εἶδε τὴν λεοντῆν, οἰηθείς
με τὸν Ἡρακλέα εἶναι, εἰσεδέξατό με, καὶ διεπόρθμευσέ τε ἄσμενος· καὶ ἀποβᾶσι, διεσήμαινε
τὴν ἀτραπόν. ἐπεὶ δὲ ἦμεν ἐν τῷ σκότῳ, προῄει μὲν ὁ Μιθροβαρζάνης, εἱπόμην δ' ἐγὼ κατό-
πιν ἐχόμενος αὐτοῦ, ἕως πρὸς λειμῶνα μέγιστον ἀφικνούμεθα, τῷ ἀσφοδέλῳ κατάφυ-
τον· ἔνθα δὴ περιεπέτοντο ἡμᾶς τετριγυῖαι τῶν νεκρῶν αἱ σκιαί· κατ' ὀλίγον δὲ προϊόντες,
παραγινόμεθα πρὸς τὸ τοῦ Μίνω δικαστήριον· ἐτύγχανε δὲ, ὁ μὲν, ἐπὶ θρόνου τινὸς ὑψηλοῦ
καθήμενος· παρειστήκεισαν δὲ αὐτῷ ποιναὶ, καὶ ἀλάστορες, καὶ Ἐριννύες. ἑτέρωθεν δὲ, προ-
σήγοντο πολλοί τινες ἐφεξῆς ἁλύσει μακρᾷ δεδεμένοι· ἐλέγοντο δὲ εἶναι μοιχοὶ, καὶ πορνο-
βοσκοὶ, καὶ τελῶναι, καὶ κόλακες, καὶ συκοφάνται, καὶ τοιοῦτος ὅμιλος τῶν πάντα
κυκώντων ἐν τῷ βίῳ. χωρὶς δὲ, οἵ τε πλούσιοι, καὶ τοκογλύφοι προσῄεσαν, ὠχροὶ, καὶ προ-
γάστορες, καὶ ποδαγροὶ, κλοιὸν ἕκαστος αὐτῶν, καὶ κόρακα διτάλαντον ἐπικείμενος. ἐφε-
στῶτες οὖν ἡμεῖς, ἑωρῶμέν τε τὰ γιγνόμενα, καὶ ἠκούομεν τῶν ἀπολογουμένων· κατηγό-
ρουν δὲ αὐτῶν καινοί τινες καὶ παράδοξοι ῥήτορες. ΦΙΛ. Τίνες οὗτοι πρὸς Διός; μὴ
γὰρ ὀκνήσῃς καὶ τοῦτο εἰπεῖν. ΜΕ. Οἶσθά που ταυτασὶ τὰς πρὸς τὸν ἥλιον ἀποτελου-

11 Vmbrarum . . . Orcus] *printed as prose 1517, om. 1506 1514* (*but added in margin*) *1516 1519* 12 pleraque] plurima *1506 1514* (*crossed out and* pleraque *added in margin*) *1516, 1519* 12–13 lacus, pyriphlegethon] lacus pyriphlegethon *1521* 16 celerrime] *1534 1563 1566* celeberrime *1506 1514 1516 1517 1519 1521 1528* 38 hi] hii *1506*, ii *1516 1519*

hoc quoque transmisso, in regionem quandam peruenimus solam, syluosam atque opacam, in quam descendentes (praeibat enim Mithrobarzanes) & puteum effodimus, & oues iugulamus, & foueam sanguine conspergimus. At magus interim accensam facem tenens, haud amplius iam summisso murmure, sed uoce quam poterat maxima clamitans, daemo[y3]nes simul omnes conuocat, Poenas, Erinnes, Hecaten nocturnam, excelsamque Proserpinam, simulque polysyllaba quaedam nomina barbara, atque ignota commiscet. Statim ergo tremere omnia, & rimas ex carmine solum ducere, ac porro Cerberi latratus audiri, & iam res plane tristis ac moesta fuit,

Vmbrarum at timuit rex imis sedibus Orcus.

Ac protinus quidem inferorum patebant pleraque, lacus, pyriphlegethon, ac Plutonis regia. Tum per illum descendentes hiatum, Rhadamanthum propemodum metu reperimus extinctum. Ac Cerberus primum quidem latrabat commouitque sese. At quum ego lyram celerrime correptam pulsassem, cantu statim sopitus obdormit, deinde posteaquam ad lacum uenimus, tranare fere non licuit. Iam enim onustum erat nauigium, & eiulatu certe plenum. Vulnerati quippe in ea nauigabant omnes, hic femur, ille caput, alius alio quopiam membro luxatus, usqueadeo, ut mihi certe ex bello quopiam adesse uiderentur. At optimus Charon quum leonis uideret exuuias, esse me ratus Herculem recepit, transque uexit libens, tum exeuntibus quoque nobis monstrauit semitam. Sed quoniam iam eramus in tenebris, praecedit quidem Mithrobarzanes, ego autem a tergo continuus illi comes adhaereo, quoad in pratum quoddam uenimus maximum, asphodelo consitum, ubi circumfusae undique mortuorum stridulae nos sequuntur umbrae. Tum paulo procedentes longius ad ipsum Minois tribunal accessimus. Erat ipse quidem in solio forte quodam sublimi sedens. Astabant autem illi Poenae, Tortores, mali Genij, Furiae. Ex altera parte plurimi quidam adducti sunt ex ordine longa fune uincti. Dicebantur autem adulteri, lenones, moechi, homicidae, adulatores, sycophantae, ac talis hominum turba quiduis in uita patrantium. Seorsum autem diuites ac foeneratores prodibant pallidi, uentricosi, ac podagrici, quorum quisque trabe uinctus erat, ferri pondere duorum talentorum imposito. Nos igitur astantes, & quae fiunt omnia conspicimus, & quae dicuntur auscultamus. Accusant autem noui quidam atque admirabiles rhetores. PHILO. Quinam ergo hi per Iouem sunt, ac ne isthuc quidem te pigeat dicere. MENIPPVS. Vmbras ne unquam

μιᾶς σκιᾶς ἀπὸ τῶν σωμάτων; ΦΙΛΩ. πάνυ μὲν οὖν. ΜΕ. αὗται τοίνυν, ἐπειδὰν ἀποθάνωμεν, κατηγοροῦσί τε, καὶ καταμαρτυροῦσι, καὶ διελέγχουσι τὰ πεπραγμένα ἡμῖν παρὰ τὸν βίον. καὶ σφόδρα τινὲς αὐτῶν ἀξιόπιστοι δοκοῦσιν, ἅτε ἀεὶ συνοῦσαι, καὶ μηδέποτε ἀφιστάμεναι τῶν σωμάτων. ὁ δ' οὖν Μίνως ἐπιμελῶς ἐξετάζων, ἀπέπεμπεν ἕκαστον ἐς τὸν τῶν ἀσεβῶν χῶρον, δίκην ὑφέξοντα κατ' ἀξίαν τῶν τετολμημένων. καὶ μάλιστα ἐκείνων ἥπτετο, τῶν ἐπὶ πλούτοις τε καὶ ἀρχαῖς τετυφωμένων, καὶ μονονουχὶ καὶ προσκυνεῖσθαι περιμενόντων, τήν τε ὀλιγοχρόνιον ἀλαζονείαν αὐτῶν, καὶ τὴν ὑπεροψίαν μυσαττόμενος· καὶ ὅτι μὴ ἐμέμνηντο θνητοί τε ὄντες αὐτοί, καὶ θνητῶν ἀγαθῶν τετυχηκότες. οἱ δέ, ἀποδυσάμενοι τὰ λαμπρὰ ἐκεῖνα πάντα, πλούτους λέγω, καὶ γένη, καὶ δυναστείας, γυμνοὶ κάτω νενευκότες, παρειστήκεσαν, ὥσπερ τινὰ ὄνειρον ἀναπεμπαζόμενοι τὴν παρ' ἡμῖν εὐδαιμονίαν· ὥστε ἔγωγε ταῦθ' ὁρῶν, ὑπερέχαιρον· καὶ εἴ τινα γνωρίσαιμι αὐτῶν, προσιὼν ἂν ἡσυχῇ πως, ὑπεμίμνησκον οἷος ἦν παρὰ τὸν βίον, καὶ ἡλίκον ἐφύσα τότε, ἡνίκα πολλοὶ μὲν ἕωθεν ἐπὶ τῶν πυλώνων παρειστήκεσαν, τὴν πρόοδον αὐτοῦ περιμένοντες, ὠθούμενοί τε, καὶ ἀποκλειόμενοι πρὸς τῶν οἰκετῶν, ὁ δέ, μόγις ἄν ποτε ἀνατείλας αὐτοῖς πορφυροῦς τις, ἢ περίχρυσος, ἢ διαποίκιλος, εὐδαίμονας ᾤετο καὶ μακαρίους ἀποφαίνειν τοὺς προσειπόντας, ἢν τὸ στῆθος, ἢ τὴν δεξιὰν προτείνων δοίη καταφιλεῖν. ἐκεῖνοι μὲν οὖν ἠνιῶντο ἀκούοντες. τῷ δὲ Μίνωι, μία τις καὶ πρὸς χάριν ἐδικάσθη δίκη· τὸν γάρ τοι Σικελιώτην Διονύσιον, πολλὰ καὶ ἀνόσια ὑπό τε Δίωνος κατηγορηθέντα, καὶ ὑπὸ τῆς σκιᾶς καταμαρτυρηθέντα, παρελθὼν Ἀρίστιππος ὁ Κυρηναῖος, ἄγουσι δ' αὐτὸν ἐν τιμῇ, καὶ δύναται μέγιστον ἐν τοῖς κάτω, μικροῦ δεῖν τῇ Χιμαίρᾳ προσδεθέντα, παρέλυσε τῆς καταδίκης, λέγων πολλοῖς αὐτὸν τῶν πεπαιδευμένων πρὸς ἀργύριον γενέσθαι δεξιόν. ἀποστάντες δὲ ὅμως τοῦ δικαστηρίου, πρὸς τὸ κολαστήριον ἀφικνούμεθα. ἔνθα δή, ὦ φίλε, πολλὰ καὶ ἐλεεινὰ ἦν ἀκοῦσαί τε, καὶ ἰδεῖν. μαστίγων τε γὰρ ὁμοῦ ψόφος ἠκούετο, καὶ οἰμωγὴ τῶν ἐπὶ τοῦ πυρὸς ὀπτωμένων. καὶ στρέβλαι, καὶ κύφωνες, καὶ τροχοί. καὶ ἡ Χίμαιρα ἐσπάραττε, καὶ ὁ Κέρβερος ἐδάρδαπτε. ἐκολάζοντό τε ἅμα πάντες, βασιλεῖς, δοῦλοι, σατράπαι, πένητες, πλούσιοι, πτωχοί. καὶ μετέμελε πᾶσι τῶν τετολμημένων. ἐνίους δὲ αὐτῶν καὶ ἐγνωρίσαμεν ἰδόντες, ὁπόσοι ἦσαν τῶν ἔναγχος τετελευτηκότων. οἱ δέ, ἐνεκαλύπτοντο, καὶ ἀπεστρέφοντο. εἰ δὲ καὶ προσβλέποιεν, μάλα δουλοπρεπές τι, καὶ κολακευτικόν. καὶ ταῦτα, πῶς οἴει, βαρεῖς ὄντες, καὶ ὑπερόπται παρὰ τὸν βίον. τοῖς μέντοι πένησιν, ἡμιτέλεια τῶν κακῶν ἐδίδοτο. καὶ ἀναπαυόμενοι, πάλιν ἐκολάζοντο. καὶ μὴν κἀκεῖνα εἶδον τὰ μυθώδη,

4 dignae] digne *1517* 9 nimirum breui perituram] nimirum perituram *1506 1514 1516 1517 1519* 25 interueniens—Nam] interueniens: Nam *1521* 26 autoritas—ferme] autoritas, ferme *1521* 29 licuit] licuisset *1506 1514 1516 1517 1519* 29–30 Nam simul] Nam semel *1506 1516 1519* 31–32 lacerat, Chimaera] lacerat, & Chimaera *1534 1563 1566* 35 discesserant] decesserant *1506 1516 1519*

istas nosti, quas opposita soli reddunt corpora? PHILO. Quid ni? MENIPPVS. Hae nos igitur quum primum functi uita sumus accusant, testantur, atque redarguunt, quicquid in uita peccauimus, & sane quaedam ex his dignae admodum fide uidentur, utpote nobiscum uersatae semper, nostrisque nusquam digressae corporibus. Minos igitur curiose quemlibet examinans, impiorum relegabat in coetum, poenas ibi sceleribus suis dignas luiturum. In hos praecipue tamen incenditur, quos opes dum [y3v] uiuerent, ac dignitates inflauerant, quique adorari se fere expectabant, nimirum breui perituram eorum superbiam fastumque detestatus, quippe qui non meminissent mortales ipsi quum sint, sese bona quoque mortalia consequutos. At nunc splendida illa exuti omnia diuitias, inquam, genus, munia, nudi ac uultu demisso steterunt tanquam somnium quoddam humanam hanc felicitatem recogitantes, adeo ut haec dum conspicarer nimis quam delectatus fuerim. Et si quem eorum forte agnoueram accessi, atque in aurem silenter admonui, qualis in uita fuerat, quantopereque fuerat inflatus, tum quum plurimi mane fores eius obsidentes pulsi interim exclusique a famulis illius expectabant egressum. At ipse uix tandem illis exoriens puniceus, aureus aut uersicolor, felices ac beatos se facturum salutantes putabat, si pectus dextramue porrigens, permitteret osculandam. Illi uero audientes ista moleste ferebant. At Minos quiddam etiam iudicauit in gratiam. Quippe Dionysium Siciliae tyrannum multis & atrocibus criminibus & a Dione accusatum, & graui Stoicorum testimonio conuictum, Cyrenaeus Aristippus interueniens—Nam illum ualde suspiciunt inferi, eiusque plurimum ibi ualet autoritas—ferme iam Chimaerae alligatum absoluit a poena, asserens illum eruditorum nonnullos olim iuuisse pecunia. Tum nos a tribunali discedentes, ad supplicij locum peruenimus. Vbi o amice & multa, & miseranda audire simul, ac spectare licuit. Nam simul & flagrorum sonus auditur, & eiulatus hominum in igne flagrantium, tum rotae & tormenta, catenae, Cerberus lacerat, Chimaera dilaniat, crucianturque pariter omnes, captiui, reges, praefecti, pauperes, mendici, diuites, & iam scelerum omnes poenitebat. Et quosdam quidem eorum, dum intuemur, agnouimus, uidelicet qui nuper e uita discesserant. At hi se pudentes tum occulebant, nostroque subtrahebant aspectui, aut si nos aliquando respiciebant, id seruiliter admodum abiecteque faciebant, atque hi quidem quam olim putas onerosi fastosique in uita? At pauperibus malorum dimidium remittebatur, & quum interquieuissent, denuo repetebantur

τὸν Ἰξίονα, καὶ τὸν Σίσυφον, καὶ τὸν Φρύγα Τάνταλον χαλεπῶς ἔχοντα, καὶ τὸν γηγενῆ Τιτυόν· Ἡράκλεις ὅσος· ἔκειτο γοῦν τόπον ἐπέχων ἀγροῦ. διελθόντες δὲ καὶ τούτους, ἐς τὸ πεδίον ἐσβάλλομεν τὸ Ἀχερούσιον· εὑρίσκομέν τε αὐτόθι τοὺς ἡμιθέους τε, καὶ τὰς ἡρωΐνας, καὶ τὸν ἄλλον ὅμιλον τῶν νεκρῶν κατὰ ἔθνη καὶ φῦλα διαιτωμένους· τοὺς μὲν, παλαιούς τινας, καὶ εὐρωτιῶντας, καὶ ὥς φησιν Ὅμηρος, ἀμενηνούς· τοὺς δὲ, νεαλεῖς, καὶ συνεστηκότας· καὶ μάλιστα τοὺς Αἰγυπτίους αὐτοὺς, διὰ τὸ πολυαρκὲς τῆς ταριχείας. τὸ μέντοι διαγινώσκειν ἕκαστον, οὐ πάνυ τι ἦν ῥᾴδιον. ἅπαντες γὰρ ἀτεχνῶς ἀλλήλοις γίνονται ὅμοιοι, τῶν ὀστέων γεγυμνωμένων. πλὴν μόγις καὶ διὰ πολλοῦ ἀναθεωροῦντες αὐτοὺς ἐγινώσκομεν. ἔκειντο δὲ ἐπ' ἀλλήλοις ἀμαυροὶ, καὶ ἄσημοι, καὶ οὐδὲν ἔτι τῶν παρ' ἡμῖν καλῶν φυλάττοντες. ἀμέλει, πολλῶν ἐν ταὐτῷ σκελετῶν κειμένων, καὶ πάντων ὁμοίων, φοβερόν τι, καὶ διάκενον δεδορκότων, καὶ γυμνοὺς τοὺς ὀδόντας προφαινόντων, ἠπόρουν πρὸς ἐμαυτὸν ᾧτινι διακρίναιμι τὸν Θερσίτην ἀπὸ τοῦ καλοῦ Νιρέως, ἢ τὸν μεταίτην Ἶρον, ἀπὸ τοῦ Φαιάκων βασιλέως, ἢ Πυρρίαν τὸν μάγειρον, ἀπὸ τοῦ Ἀγαμέμνονος· οὐδὲν γὰρ ἔτι τῶν παλαιῶν γνωρισμάτων αὐτοῖς παρέμενεν, ἀλλ' ὅμοια τὰ ὀστᾶ ἦν, ἄδηλα, καὶ ἀνεπίγραφα, καὶ ὑπ' οὐδενὸς ἔτι διακρίνεσθαι δυνάμενα. τοιγάρτοι ἐκεῖνα ὁρῶντι, ἐδόκει μοι ὁ τῶν ἀνθρώπων βίος πομπῇ τινι μακρᾷ προσεοικέναι, χορηγεῖν δὲ καὶ διατάττειν ἕκαστα ἡ τύχη, διάφορα καὶ ποικίλα τοῖς πομπεύουσι σχήματα προσάπτουσα. τὸν μὲν γὰρ λαβοῦσα ἡ τύχη, βασιλικῶς διεσκεύασε, τιάραν τε ἐπιθεῖσα, καὶ δορυφόρους παραδοῦσα, καὶ τὴν κεφαλὴν στέψασα τῷ διαδήματι· τῷ δὲ, οἰκέτου σχῆμα περιέθηκε. τὸν δέ τινα, καλὸν εἶναι ἐκόσμησε. τὸν δὲ, ἄμορφον, καὶ γελοῖον παρεσκεύασε. παντοδαπὴν γὰρ οἶμαι δεῖν γενέσθαι τὴν θέαν. πολλάκις δὲ, διὰ μέσης τῆς πομπῆς μετέβαλε τὰ ἐνίων σχήματα, οὐκ ἐῶσα ἐς τέλος διαπομπεῦσαι ὡς ἐτάχθησαν· ἀλλὰ μεταμφιέσασα, τὸν μὲν Κροῖσον ἠνάγκασε τὴν τοῦ οἰκέτου καὶ αἰχμαλώτου σκευὴν ἀναλαβεῖν· τὸν δὲ Μαιάνδριον, τέως ἐν τοῖς οἰκέταις πομπεύοντα, τὴν Πολυκράτους τυραννίδα μετενέδυσε· καὶ μέχρι μέν τινος εἴασε χρῆσθαι τῷ σχήματι. ἐπειδὰν δ' ὁ τῆς πομπῆς καιρὸς παρέλθῃ, τηνικαῦτα ἕκαστος ἀποδοὺς τὴν σκευὴν, καὶ ἀποδυσάμενος τὸ σχῆμα μετὰ τοῦ σώματος, ὥσπερ ἦν πρὸ τοῦ, γίγνεται, μηδὲν τοῦ πλησίον διαφέρων. ἔνιοι δ' ὑπ' ἀγνωμοσύνης, ἐπειδὰν ἀπαιτῇ τὸν κόσμον, ἐπιστᾶσα ἡ τύχη, ἄχθονταί γε, καὶ ἀγανακτοῦσιν, ὥσπερ οἰκείων τινῶν στερισκόμενοι, καὶ οὐχ ἃ πρὸς ὀλίγον ἐχρήσαντο ἀποδιδόντες. οἶμαι δὲ καὶ τῶν ἐπὶ τῆς σκηνῆς πολλάκις ἑωρακέναι, τοὺς τρα-

13 simul] simnl [*sic*] *1506*, *om. 1566* 20 unquam] vsquam *1506 1516 1519* 30 ornatu] ornate *1566* 31 incedentem] incidentem *1506 1514 1516 1519* 35 efficitur] afficitur *1506 1516* 39 ut] prout *1506 1516 1519*

ad poenam. Sed illa quoque quae fabulis feruntur aspexi, Ixionem, Sisyphum, Phrygiumque grauiter affectum Tantalum, genitumque terra Tityum, Dij boni, quantum? Integrum stratus agrum occupabat. Hos tandem praetereuntes, in campum uenimus Acherusium, ubi semideos, heroidasque reperimus, atque aliam simul mortuorum turbam in gentes, tribusque dispositam, alios quidem uetulos, quosdam ac marcidos, atque (ut Homerus ait) euanidos, alios uero iuueniles & integros, & hos potissimum ob illam condiendi efficaciam Aegyptios. Verum dignoscere quemlibet haud procliue fuit, adeo nudatis ossibus omnes erant inuicem simillimi, nisi quod uix tandem eos diu intendentes agnouimus. Quippe conferti considebant obscuri atque ignobiles, nullumque seruantes amplius pristinae formae uestigium. Cum igitur multi simul ossei consisterent, inuicem [y_4] omnino similes, qui terrificum quiddam per cauos oculorum orbes transpicerent, dentesque nudos ostenderent, haesitabam certe mecum, quonam signo Thersitem a Nireo illo formoso discernerem, aut mendicum Irum a Phaeacum rege, aut Pyrrhiam coquum ab Agamemnone. Quippe quibus iam nihil ueteris permansit indicij, sed ossa fuerunt inter se similia, incognibilia, nullis inscripta titulis, nullique unquam dinoscenda. Haec igitur spectanti mihi, persimilis hominum uita pompae cuipiam longae uidebatur, cui praesit ac disponat quaeque fortuna, ex his qui pompam agunt, diuersos uariosque cuique habitus accommodans. Alium siquidem fortuna deligens, regijs ornat insignibus, & tiaram imponens, & satellites addens, & caput diademate coronans. Alium serui rursus ornatum induit, hunc formosum effigiat, hunc deformem atque deridiculum fingit: nam omnigenum, ut opinor, debet esse spectaculum. Quin habitus quorundam plerunque in media quoque pompa demutat, neque perpetuo eodem sinit ordine, cultuque progredi quo prodierant. Sed ornatu commutato Croesum quidem coegit serui, captiuique uestes induere. Maeandrium autem olim inter seruos incedentem, Polycratis uicissim ornat tyrannide. Et aliquantisper quidem eo cultu permittit uti, uerum ubi iam pompae tempus praeterijt, apparatum quisque restituens, & cum corpore simul exutus amictu, qualis ante fuit efficitur, nihilo a uicino differens. Quidam tamen ob inscitiam quum suos fortuna cultus exigit, aegreferunt atque indignantur, tanquam proprijs quibusdam bonis priuati, ac non potius alienis, quibus paulisper utebantur, exuti. Quin in scena quoque uidisse te plerunque puto histriones istos tragicos, qui (ut fabulae

γικοὺς ὑποκριτὰς τούτους πρὸς τὰς χρείας τῶν δραμάτων ἄρτι μὲν, κρέοντας, ἐνίοτε δὲ, Πριάμους γιγνομένους, ἢ Ἀγαμέμνονας. καὶ ὁ αὐτὸς, εἰ τύχοι μικρὸν ἔμπροσθεν μάλα σεμνῶς, τὸ τοῦ Κέκροπος ἢ Ἐρεχθέως σχῆμα μιμησάμενος, μετ' ὀλίγον οἰκέτης προῆλθεν ὑπὸ τοῦ ποιητοῦ κεκελευσμένος. ἤδη δὲ πέρας ἔχοντος τοῦ δράματος, ἀποδυσάμενος ἕκαστος αὐτῶν τὴν χρυσόπαστον ἐκείνην ἐσθῆτα, καὶ τὸ προσωπεῖον ἀποθέμενος, καὶ καταβὰς ἀπὸ τῶν ἐμβατῶν, πένης, καὶ ταπεινὸς περιέρχεται. οὐκ ἔτ' Ἀγαμέμνων ὁ Ἀτρέως, οὐδὲ Κρέων ὁ Μενοικέως, ἀλλὰ Πῶλος Χαρικλέους Σουνιεὺς ὀνομαζόμενος, ἢ Σάτυρος ὁ Θεογείτονος Μαραθώνιος. τοιαῦτα καὶ τὰ τῶν ἀνθρώπων πράγματά ἐστιν, ὥς τότε μοι ὁρῶντι ἔδοξεν. ΦΙΛΩ. εἰπέ μοι ὦ Μένιππε, οἱ δὲ τοὺς πολυτελεῖς τούτους καὶ ὑψηλοὺς τάφους ἔχοντες ὑπὲρ γῆς, καὶ στήλας, καὶ εἰκόνας, καὶ ἐπιγράμματα, οὐδὲν τιμιώτεροι παρ' αὐτοῖς εἰσι τῶν ἰδιωτῶν νεκρῶν; ΜΕ. ληρεῖς ὦ οὗτος. εἰ γοῦν ἐθεάσω τὸν Μαύσωλον αὐτὸν, λέγω δὲ τὸν Κᾶρα, τὸν ἐκ τοῦ τάφου περιβόητον, εὖ οἶδα ὅτι οὐκ ἂν ἐπαύσω γελῶν. οὕτω ταπεινῶς ἔρριπτο ἐν παραβύστῳ που, λανθάνων ἐν τῷ λοιπῷ δήμῳ τῶν νεκρῶν. ἐμοὶ δοκεῖν, τοσοῦτον ἀπολαύων τοῦ μνήματος, παρ' ὅσον ἐβαρύνετο τηλικοῦτον ἄχθος ἐπικείμενος. ἐπειδὰν γὰρ ὦ ἑταῖρε ὁ Αἰακὸς ἀπομετρήσῃ ἑκάστῳ τὸν τόπον, δίδωσι δὲ τὸ μέγιστον οὐ πλέον ποδὸς, ἀνάγκη ἀγαπῶντα κατακεῖσθαι, πρὸς τὸ μέτρον συνεσταλμένον. πολλῷ δ' ἂν οἶμαι μᾶλλον ἐγέλας, εἰ ἐθεάσω τοὺς παρ' ἡμῖν βασιλέας, καὶ σατράπας, πτωχεύοντας παρ' αὐτοῖς, καὶ ἤτοι ταριχοπωλοῦντας ὑπ' ἀπορίας, ἢ τὰ πρῶτα διδάσκοντας γράμματα, καὶ ὑπὸ τοῦ τυχόντος ὑβριζομένους, καὶ κατὰ κόρρης παιομένους, ὥσπερ τῶν ἀνδραπόδων τὰ ἀτιμότατα. Φίλιππον γοῦν τὸν Μακεδόνα ἐγὼ θεασάμενος, οὐδὲ κρατεῖν ἐμαυτοῦ δυνατὸς ἦν. ἐδείχθη δέ μοι ἐν γωνιδίῳ τινὶ μισθοῦ ἀκούμενος τὰ σαθρὰ τῶν ὑποδημάτων. πολλοὺς δὲ καὶ ἄλλους ἦν ἰδεῖν ἐν ταῖς τριόδοις μεταιτοῦντας, Ξέρξας λέγω, καὶ Δαρείους, καὶ Πολυκράτεις. ΦΙΛΩ. ἄτοπα διηγῇ τὰ περὶ τῶν βασιλέων. καὶ μικροῦ δεῖν, ἄπιστα. τί δὲ ὁ Σωκράτης ἔπραττε, καὶ Διογένης, καὶ εἴ τις ἄλλος τῶν σοφῶν; ΜΕ. ὁ μὲν Σωκράτης, κἀκεῖ περιέρχεται διελέγχων ἅπαντας. σύνεισι δ' αὐτῷ Παλαμήδης, καὶ Ὀδυσσεὺς, καὶ Νέστωρ, καὶ εἴ τις ἄλλος λάλος νεκρός. ἔτι μέντοι ἐπεφύσητο αὐτῷ, καὶ διῳδήκει ἐκ τῆς φαρμακοποσίας τὰ σκέλη. ὁ δὲ βέλτιστος Διογένης, παροικεῖ μὲν Σαρδαναπάλῳ τῷ Ἀσσυρίῳ, καὶ Μίδᾳ τῷ Φρυγὶ, καὶ ἄλλοις τισὶ τῶν πολυτελῶν. ἀκούων δὲ οἰμωζόντων αὐτῶν, καὶ τὴν παλαιὰν τύχην ἀναμετρουμένων, γελᾷ τε, καὶ τέρπεται. καὶ τὰ πολλὰ ὕπτιος κατακείμενος, ᾄδει μάλα τραχείᾳ καὶ ἀπηνεῖ τῇ φωνῇ, τὰς οἰμωγὰς αὐτῶν ἐπικαλύπτων, ὥστε ἀνιᾶσθαι τοὺς ἄνδρας, καὶ δια-

3 post] postea *1506 1514 1516 1517 1519* 31 obuersatur] observatur *1566* 38 ut plurimum] utplurimum *1521*

ratio poscit) modo Creontes, modo Priami fiunt, aut Agamemnones. Idemque (si sors tulerit) paulo ante tam grauiter Cecropis aut Erechthei formam imitatus, paulo post seruus, poeta iubente, progreditur. At quum fabulae iam finis affuerit, quisque auratas illas uestes exutus, personam deponens, & ab altis illis crepidis descendens, pauper atque humilis obambulat, haud amplius Agamemnon ille Atreo prognatus, aut Creon Menoecei filius, sed Polus filius Chariclei Suniensis, aut Satyrus filius Theogitonis Marathonius. Sic se mortalium res habent, quemadmodum mihi tum spectanti uidebatur. PHILO. Dic mihi Menippe, isti qui magnificos altosque tumulos habent super terram, & columnas, imagines, titulos, nihilo ne sunt apud inferos plebeis quibuslibet umbris honoratiores? MENIPPVS. Nugaris tu quidem, nam si uidisses Mausolum, Carem illum dico Pyramide celebrem, sat scio, nunquam ridere desijsses, ita in antrum quoddam abstrusum despectim abiectus est, in reliqua mortuorum turba delitescens. Hoc tantum commodi mihi uidetur ex monumento re[y4v]ferre, quod imposito tanto pondere, laborat magis & premitur. Nam quum Aeacus o amice, locum cuique metitur, dat autem cui plurimum haud amplius pedem necesse est eo iacere contentum, seseque ad loci modum contrahere. At uehementius multo risisses, opinor, si reges hosce nostros satrapasque uidisses apud eos mendicantes, & aut salsamenta uendentes, aut primas ipsas literas urgente inopia profitentes, & quemadmodum contumelijs a quouis afficiantur, atque in faciem caedantur perinde atque uilissima mancipia. Itaque Philippum Macedonem conspicatus, continere me certe non potui: ostensus est mihi in angulo quodam detritos calceos mercede resarciens. Quin alios praeterea multos erat uidere mendicantes in triuijs, Xerxes uidelicet, Darios, ac Polycrates. PHIL. Admiranda narras ista de regibus, peneque incredibilia. Socrates autem quid facit, ac Diogenes? & si quis est sapientum alius? MENIP. Socrates profecto etiam ibi obuersatur, omnesque redarguit: uersantur autem cum illo Palamedes, Vlysses, & Nestor, & quisquis est alius inter defunctos garrulus. Inflantur autem illi etiamnum, atque intumescunt, exhausto ueneno crura. At optimus Diogenes Sardanapalo uicinus Assyrio Midaeque Phrygio, atque alijs item pluribus ex istorum sumptuosorum numero manet, quos quum eiulantes audit, ueteris fortunae magnitudinem recogitantes, & ridet & delectatur, ac supinus cubans, ut plurimum cantat, aspera nimis atque iniucunda uoce illorum eiulatus obscurans, adeo ut id aegreferentes, nec

σκώπτεσθαι μετρικεῖν οὐ φέροντας τὸν Διογένην. ΦΙΛ. ταυτὶ μὲν ἱκανῶς. τί δὲ τὸ ψήφισμα ἦν, ὅπερ ἐν ἀρχῇ ἔλεγες κεκυρῶσθαι κατὰ τῶν πλουσίων; ΜΕ. εὖ γε ὑπέμνησας· οὐ γὰρ οἶδ' ὅπως περὶ τούτου λέγειν προθέμενος, πάμπολυ ἀπεπλανήθην τοῦ λόγου· διατρίβοντος γάρ μου παρ' αὐτοῖς, προὔθεσαν οἱ πρυτάνεις ἐκκλησίαν περὶ τῶν κοινῇ συμφερόντων· ἰδὼν οὖν πολλοὺς συνθέοντας, ἀναμίξας ἐμαυτὸν τοῖς νεκροῖς, εὐθὺς εἷς καὶ αὐτὸς ἦν τῶν ἐκκλησιαστῶν. διῳκήθη μὲν οὖν καὶ ἄλλα· τελευταῖον δὲ, τὸ περὶ τῶν πλουσίων. ἐπεὶ γὰρ αὐτῶν κατηγόρητο πολλὰ, καὶ δεινὰ, βία, καὶ ἀλαζονεία, καὶ ὑπεροψία, καὶ ἀδικία, τέλος, ἀναστάς τις τῶν δημαγωγῶν, ἀνέγνω ψήφισμα τοιοῦτον·

ΨΗΦΙΣΜΑ.

Πειδὴ πολλὰ καὶ παράνομα οἱ πλούσιοι δρῶσι παρὰ τὸν βίον, ἁρπάζοντες,
ἐ καὶ βιαζόμενοι, καὶ πάντα τρόπον τῶν πενήτων καταφρονοῦντες, δέδοκται
τῇ βουλῇ, καὶ τῷ δήμῳ, ἐπειδὰν ἀποθάνωσι, τὰ μὲν σώματα αὐτῶν, κολάζεσθαι, καθάπερ καὶ τὰ τῶν ἄλλων πονηρῶν. τὰς δὲ ψυχὰς, ἀναπεμφθείσας ἄνω ἐς τὸν βίον, καταδύεσθαι ἐς τοὺς ὄνους, ἄχρις ἂν ἐν τῷ τοιούτῳ διαγάγωσι μυριάδας ἐτῶν πέντε καὶ εἴκοσιν ὄνοι ἐξ ὄνων γιγνόμενοι, καὶ ἀχθοφοροῦντες, καὶ ὑπὸ τῶν πενήτων ἐλαυνόμενοι· τοὐντεῦθεν δὲ λοιπὸν, ἐξεῖναι αὐτοῖς ἀποθανεῖν· εἶπε τὴν γνώμην Κρανίων Σκελετίωνος Νεκυσιεὺς, φυλῆς ἀλιβαντίδος· τούτου ἀναγνωσθέντος τοῦ ψηφίσματος, ἐπεψήφισαν μὲν αἱ ἀρχαί· ἐπεχειροτόνησε δὲ τὸ πλῆθος, καὶ ἐνεβριμήσατο ἡ βριμὼ, καὶ ὑλάκτησεν ὁ κέρβερος. οὕτω γὰρ ἐντελῆ γίγνεται, καὶ κύρια τὰ ἀνεγνωσμένα. ταῦτα μὲν δή σοι τὰ ἐν τῇ ἐκκλησίᾳ. ἐγὼ δὲ, οὗπερ ἀφίγμην ἕνεκα, τῷ τειρεσίᾳ προσελθὼν, ἱκέτευον αὐτὸν τὰ πάντα διηγησάμενος, εἰπεῖν πρός με ποῖόν τινα ἡγεῖται τὸν ἄριστον βίον. ὁ δὲ, γελάσας, ἔστι δὲ τυφλόν τι γερόντιον, καὶ ὠχρὸν, καὶ λεπτόφωνον, ὦ τέκνον φησὶ, τὴν μὲν αἰτίαν οἶδά σου τῆς ἀπορίας, ὅτι παρὰ τῶν σοφῶν ἐγένετο, οὐ ταὐτὰ γιγνωσκόντων ἑαυτοῖς. ἀτὰρ οὐ θέμις λέγειν πρὸς σέ. ἀπείρηται γὰρ ὑπὸ τοῦ ῥαδαμάνθυος. μηδαμῶς ἔφην ὦ πατέριον, ἀλλ' εἰπὲ, καὶ μὴ περιίδῃς με σοῦ τυφλότερον περιιόντα ἐν τῷ βίῳ. ὁ δὲ, δή με ἀπαγαγὼν, καὶ πολὺ τῶν ἄλλων ἀποσπάσας, ἠρέμα προσκύψας πρὸς τὸ οὖς, φησὶν, ὁ τῶν ἰδιωτῶν, ἄριστος βίος, καὶ σωφρονέστερος, ὡς τῆς ἀφροσύνης παυσάμενος τοῦ μετεωρολογεῖν, καὶ τέλη, καὶ ἀρχὰς ἐπισκοπεῖν. καὶ καταπτύσας τῶν σοφῶν τούτων συλλογισμῶν, καὶ τὰ τοιαῦτα λῆρον ἡγησάμενος, τοῦτο μόνον ἐξ ἅπαντος θηράσῃ, ὅπως τὸ παρὸν εὖ θέμενος, παραδράμῃς γελῶν τὰ πολλὰ, καὶ περὶ μηδὲν ἐσπου-

30 id] *om. 1566* 31 inquam] *1506 1514 1516 1519*, inquit *1517 1521 1528 1534 1563 1566* 35–36 consyderatione] consideratione *1521*

Diogenem ferre ualentes, de mutanda sede deliberent. PHIL. De his iam satis quidem: caeterum quodnam illud decretum est, quod initio dixeras aduersus diuites esse sancitum? MENIPPVS. Bene admones: nescio enim quo pacto quum hac de re dicere proposuissem, ab instituto sermone procul aberraui. Dum igitur ibi uersabar, magistratus concionem aduocauerunt, his uidelicet de rebus, quae in commune conducerent. Conspiciens ergo multos concurrere, me quoque cum illis simul immiscens, unus de numero eorum qui in concione aderant, efficior. Agitata sunt igitur & alia multa: postremo uero de diuitibus negocium, in quos posteaquam plurima fuissent obiecta, uiolentia, superbia, fastus, iniuriae, assurgens tandem ex populo primas quidam, huiusmodi decretum legit: Quoniam, inquit, multa diuites perpetrant in uita rapientes, ac uim inferentes, inopesque omni modo despectui habentes, Curiae Populoque uisum est, ut quum functi uita fuerint, corpora quidem eorum poenas cum alijs sceleratorum corporibus luant: animae uero sursum remissae in uitam, in asinos demigrent, donec in tali rerum statu quinquies ac uicies decem annorum milia transegerint, asini semper ex asinis renati, onera ferentes, atque a pauperibus [y5] agitati. Dein ut liceat illis e uita excedere. Hanc sententiam dixit Caluarius, patre Aridello, patria Manicensis, tribu Stygiana. Hac igitur lege recitata, approbauerunt principes, sciuit plebs, adfremuit Proserpina, allatrauit Cerberus: sic enim rata quae inferi statuunt, autenticaque fiunt. Quae igitur in concione agebantur, erant huiusmodi. Tum ego statim, cuius gratia ueneram, Tiresiam adeo, atque illi re, uti erat, ordine narrata supplicaui, ut mihi diceret, quodnam optimum uitae genus putaret. Hic uero subridens (est autem seniculus quispiam caecus, pallidus, uoce gracili) o fili, inquit, causam tuae perplexitatis scio a sapientibus istis profectam, haudquaquam idem inuicem ijsdem de rebus sentientibus, uerum haud fas est id tibi proloqui: siquidem quod Rhadamanthus interdixit. Nequaquam, inquam, o patercule, sed dic amabo, neque me contemnas, qui in uita te etiam ipso caecior oberro. Abducens ergo me, procul ab alijs auferens, ad aures mihi inclinans: Optima est, inquit, idiotarum priuatorumque uita, ac prudentissima. Quamobrem ab hac uanissima sublimium consyderatione desistens, mitte principia semper ac fines inquirere, & uafros hosce syllogismos despuens, atque id genus omnia nugas aestimans, hoc solum in tota uita persequere, ut praesentibus bene compositis minime curiosus, nulla re sollicitus, quam plurimum potes hilaris

δακώς· ὡς εἰπὼν, πάλιν ὥρμα κατ' ἀσφοδελὸν λειμῶνα. ἐγὼ δὲ, καὶ γὰρ ἤδη ὀψὲ ἦν, ἄγε δὴ ὦ Μιθροβαρζάνη φημὶ, τί διαμέλλομεν, καὶ οὐκ ἄπιμεν αὖθις ἐς τὸν βίον; ὁ δὲ, πρὸς ταῦτα, θάρρει φησὶν ὦ Μένιππε, ταχεῖαν γάρ σοι καὶ ἀπράγμονα ὑποδείξω ἀτραπόν. καὶ δὴ ἀπαγαγών με πρός τι χωρίον τοῦ ἄλλου ζοφερώτερον, δείξας τῇ χειρὶ πόρρωθεν ἀμαυρόν τι καὶ λεπτὸν ὥσπερ διὰ κλειθρίας εἰσρέον φῶς, ἐκεῖνο ἔφη ἐστὶ τὸ ἱερὸν τοῦ Τροφωνίου, κἀκεῖθεν κατέρχονται οἱ ἀπὸ Βοιωτίας. ταύτην οὖν ἄνιθι, καὶ εὐθὺς ἔσῃ ἐπὶ τῆς Ἑλλάδος. ἡσθεὶς δὲ τοῖς εἰρημένοις ἐγὼ, καὶ τὸν μάγον ἀσπασάμενος, χαλεπῶς μάλα διὰ τοῦ στομίου ἀνερπύσας, οὐκ οἶδ' ὅπως ἐν Λεβαδείᾳ γίγνομαι.

8 Trophonij] Torphoni [*sic*] *1506 1514* (*changed in text to* Trophoni) *1516 1519*, Trophoni *1517* 9 ascendas] ascendes *1528 1534 1563 1566* 13–15 NECROMANTIAE . . . FINIS] Necromantiae seu Menippi Luciani finis *1506 1514*, *om.* *1516 1519 1534 1563 1566*

uitam ridensque traducas. Haec quum dixisset, rursus Asphodelorum in pratum sese corripuit. Ego igitur (nam & nunc uesper erat) age, inquam, o Mithrobarzane quid cunctamur? ac non hinc rursus abimus in uitam? Ad haec ille: confide, inquit, o Menippe, breuem quippe facilemque tibi monstrabo semitam, & me protinus abducens in regionem quandam magis priore tenebricosam, manu procul ostendens subobscurum tenueque, ac uelut per rimam influens lumen: Illud, inquit, Trophonij templum est, atque illac ad inferos e Boeotia descenditur, hac ascendas, atque illico fueris in Graecia. Ego igitur hoc sermone gauisus, salutato Mago difficile admodum per angustas antri fauces subrepens, nescio quo pacto, in Lebadiam perueni.

NECROMANTIAE SEV MENIPPI LVCIANI,
THOMA MORO INTERPRETE,
FINIS. [y5v]

ΦΙΛΟΨΕΥΔΗΣ, Η ΑΠΙΣΤΩΝ. ΤΥΧΙΑΔΗΣ.

Ἔχεις μοι ὦ Φιλόκλεις εἰπεῖν τί ποτε ἄρα τοῦτό ἐστιν, ὃ τοὺς πολλοὺς εἰς ἐπιθυμίαν τοῦ ψεύδους προάγεται, ὡς αὐτούς τε χαίρειν μηδὲν ὑγιὲς λέγοντας, καὶ τοῖς τὰ τοιαῦτα διεξιοῦσι μάλιστα προσέχειν τὸν νοῦν; ΦΙΛΟ. Πολλὰ ὦ Τυχιάδη ἐστὶν, ἃ τοὺς ἀνθρώπους ἐνίους ἀναγκάζει τὰ ψευδῆ λέγειν, ἐς τὸ χρήσιμον ἀποβλέποντας. ΤΥ. Οὐδὲν πρὸς ἔπος ταῦτα φασὶν, οὐδὲ περὶ τούτων ἠρόμην, ὁπόσοι τῆς χρείας ἕνεκα ψεύδονται. συγγνώμης τοιγαροῦν οὗτοί γε, μᾶλλον καὶ ἐπαίνου τινὲς αὐτῶν ἄξιοι, ὁπόσοι ἢ πολεμίους ἐξηπάτησαν, ἢ ἐπὶ σωτηρίᾳ τῷ τοιούτῳ φαρμάκῳ ἐχρήσαντο ἐν τοῖς δεινοῖς, οἷα πολλὰ καὶ Ὀδυσσεὺς ἐποίει, τήν τε αὑτοῦ ψυχὴν ἀρνύμενος, καὶ τὸν νόστον τῶν ἑταίρων. ἀλλὰ περὶ ἐκείνων ὦ ἄριστε φημὶ, οἳ αὐτὸ ἄνευ τῆς χρείας τὸ ψεῦδος περὶ πολλοῦ τῆς ἀληθείας τίθενται, ἡδόμενοι τῷ πράγματι, καὶ ἐνδιατρίβοντες ἐπ' οὐδεμιᾷ προφάσει ἀναγκαίᾳ· τούτους οὖν ἐθέλω εἰδέναι, τίνος ἀγαθοῦ τοῦτο ποιοῦσιν. ΦΙΛΟ. Ἤδη που κατανενόηκας ἤδη τινὰς τοιούτους, οἷς ἔμφυτος ὁ ἔρως οὗτός ἐστι πρὸς τὸ ψεῦδος; ΤΥ. Καὶ μάλα πολλοί εἰσιν οἱ τοιοῦτοι. ΦΙΛΟ. Τί δ' οὖν ἄλλο, ἢ ἄνοιαν χρὴ αἰτίαν εἶναι αὐτοῖς φάναι τοῦ μὴ ἀληθῆ λέγειν, εἴγε τὸ χεῖρον ἀντὶ τοῦ βελτίστου προαιροῦνται; ΤΥ. Οὐδὲν τοῦτο, ἐπεὶ πολλοὺς ἂν ἐγώ σοι δείξαιμι, συνετοὺς τἆλλα, καὶ τὴν γνώμην θαυμαστοὺς, οὐκ οἶδ' ὅπως ἑαλωκότας τούτῳ τῷ κακῷ, καὶ φιλοψευδεῖς ὄντας, ὡς ἀνιᾶσθαί με, εἰ τοιοῦτοι ἄνδρες ἄριστοι τὰ πάντα, ὅμως χαίρουσιν αὑτούς τε, καὶ τοὺς ἐντυγχάνοντας ἐξαπατῶντες. ἐκείνους μὲν γὰρ τοὺς παλαιοὺς πρὸ ἐμοῦ σε χρὴ εἰδέναι, τὸν Ἡρόδοτον, καὶ Κτησίαν τὸν Κνίδιον, καὶ πρὸ τούτων, τοὺς ποιητὰς, καὶ τὸν Ὅμηρον αὐτὸν, ἀοιδίμους ἄνδρας ἐγγράφῳ τῷ ψεύσματι κεχρημένους, ὡς μὴ μόνον ἐξαπατᾶν τοὺς τότε ἀκούοντας αὐτῶν, ἀλλὰ καὶ μέχρις ἡμῶν διικνεῖσθαι τὸ ψεῦδος, ἐκ διαδοχῆς ἐν καλλίστοις ἔπεσι, καὶ μέτροις φυλαττόμενον. ἐμοὶ γοῦν πολλάκις αἰδεῖσθαι ὑπὲρ

1–3 LVCIANI . . . INTERPRETE] Sequitur. LVCIANI PHILOPSEVDES siue INCREDVLVS ab eodem THOMA MORO in latinam linguam traductus *1506 1514*, LVCIANI PHILOPSEVDES, siue Incredulus ab eodem Thoma Moro in latinam linguam traductus *1516 1519*, PHILOPSEVDES LVCIANI, SIVE INCREDVlus, Thoma Moro interprete *1566* 4 Personae] *om. 1528 1534 1563 1566*, Interlocutores *1516 1519* 4 ac] & *1506 1514 1516 1519* 23 optimae] *1534 1563 1566*, optimi *1506 1514 1516 1517 1519 1521 1528* 28 Herodotus] Erodotus *1506*

LVCIANI PHILOPSEVDES SIVE INCREDVLVS, THOMA MORO INTERPRETE.

Personae, TYCHIADES ac PHILOCLES.

TYCHIADES.

POTES mihi Philocles dicere, quidnam id tandem sit, quod multos in mentiendi cupiditatem adducit, ut pariter gaudeant, quum & ipsi nihil sani loquuntur, & his qui talia narrant, maxime animum intendant? PHILOC. Multa Tychiade sunt, quae nonnullos mortales mentiri compellunt, quia in rem uident conducere. TYCH. Nihil ad rem haec (ut aiunt) neque enim de his rogabam, qui quum usus postulat mentiuntur, uenia nimirum hi, imo laude plerique eorum digni sunt, quicunque uel hostes fefellerunt, uel ad salutem tali quopiam pharmaco usi sunt in necessitatibus. Cuiusmodi multa Vlysses etiam fecit, ut & uitam suam, & sociorum reditum redimeret: sed de illis uir optime dico, qui nulla necessitate mendacium ipsum ueritati longe anteponunt, ipsa re uidelicet delectati, atque in ea sine ulla idonea occasione uersati. Isti ergo scire cupio, cuius commodi gratia istud agunt. PHILOC. An alicubi tales aliquos iam deprehendisti, quibus haec insita sit mentiendi libido? TYCH. Et quidem admodum multi sunt huiusmodi. PHILOC. Quid aliud ergo in causa sit, quod mentiuntur nisi dementia? siquidem rem pessimam, optimae loco praeoptant. TYCH. Hoc nihil est, nam ego tibi multos ostenderim ad caetera prudentes, ac sapientia mirabili: nescio tamen quo pacto captos hoc malo, mendacijque studiosos, adeo ut ego certe moleste feram, quod uiri tales, omnibus caeteris in rebus optimi, gaudent tamen & se, & eos in quos inciderint, fallere. Nam ueteres illi, id quod tibi notius est quam mihi, Herodotus, Ctesiasque Cnidius, atque his superiores, denique Homerus ipse, uiri celebres, mendacijs etiam scriptis utebantur, ut non solum eos fallerent, a quibus tunc audiebantur, uerum usque ad nos etiam mendacium per manus traditum perueniret, in pulcherrimis uersibus metrisque seruatum. Me ergo saepe illorum uersuum nomine subijt pudor, si quando

αὐτῶν ἔπεισιν, ὁπόταν οὐρανοῦ τομὴν, καὶ Προμηθέως δεσμὰ διηγῶνται, καὶ γιγάντων ἐπανάστασιν, καὶ τὴν ἐν ᾅδου πᾶσαν τραγῳδίαν, καὶ ὡς δι' ἔρωτα ὁ Ζεὺς ταῦρος, ἢ κύκνος ἐγένετο, καὶ ὡς ἐκ γυναικός τις, ἐς ὄρνεον, ἢ ἐς ἄρκτον μετέπεσεν. ἔτι δὲ πηγάσους, καὶ χιμαίρας, καὶ γοργόνας, καὶ κύκλωπας, καὶ ὅσα τοιαῦτα, πάνυ ἀλλόκοτα, καὶ τεράστια μυθίδια, παίδων ψυχὰς κηλεῖν δυνάμενα· ἔτι τὴν μορμὼ, καὶ τὴν λάμιαν δεδιότων. καίτοι τὰ μὲν τῶν ποιητῶν, ἴσως μέτρια· τὸ δὲ καὶ πόλεις ἤδη, καὶ ἔθνη πολλὰ, κοινῇ, καὶ δημοσίᾳ ψεύδεσθαι, πῶς οὐ γελοῖον, εἰ Κρῆτες μὲν τὸν Διὸς τάφον δεικνύοντες οὐκ αἰσχύνονται, Ἀθηναῖοι δὲ τὸν Ἐριχθόνιον ἐκ τῆς γῆς ἀναδοθῆναί φασι, καὶ τοὺς πρώτους ἀνθρώπους ἐκ τῆς Ἀττικῆς ἀναφῦναι, καθάπερ τὰ λάχανα· πολὺ σεμνότερον οὗτοι τῶν Θηβαίων, οἳ ἐξ ὄφεως ὀδόντων, σπαρτούς τινας ἀναβεβλαστηκέναι διηγοῦνται· ὃς δ' ἂν οὖν ταῦτα καταγέλαστα ὄντα, μὴ οἴηται ἀληθῆ εἶναι, ἀλλ' ἐμφρόνως ἂν ἐξετάζων ταῦτα, Κοροίβου τινὸς, ἢ Μαργίτου νομίζοι τὸ πείθεσθαι, ἢ Τριπτόλεμον ἐλάσαι διὰ τοῦ ἀέρος ἐπὶ δρακόντων ὑποπτέρων, ἢ Πᾶνα ἥκειν ἐξ Ἀρκαδίας σύμμαχον ἐς Μαραθῶνα, ἢ Ὠρείθυιαν ὑπὸ τοῦ βορέου ἀναρπασθῆναι, ἀσεβὴς οὗτός γε, καὶ ἀνόητος αὐτοῖς ἔδοξεν, οὕτω προδήλοις, καὶ ἀληθέσι πράγμασιν ἀπιστῶν· ἐς τοσοῦτον ἐπικρατεῖ τὸ ψεῦδος. ΦΙΛΟ. ἀλλ' οἱ μὲν ποιηταὶ ὦ Τυχιάδη, καὶ αἱ πόλεις δὲ, συγγνώμης τυγχάνοιεν ἄν· οἱ μὲν, τὸ ἐκ τοῦ μύθου τερπνὸν ἐπαγωγότατον ὂν, ἐγκαταμιγνύντες τῇ γραφῇ, οὗπερ μάλιστα δέονται πρὸς τοὺς ἀκροατάς. Ἀθηναῖοι δὲ, καὶ Θηβαῖοι, καὶ εἴ τινες ἄλλοι, σεμνοτέρας ἀποφαίνονται τὰς πατρίδας ἐκ τῶν τοιούτων. εἰ γοῦν τις ἀφέλοι τὰ μυθώδη ταῦτα ἐκ τῆς Ἑλλάδος, οὐδὲν ἂν κωλύσῃ λιμῷ τοὺς περιηγητὰς αὐτῶν διαφθαρῆναι, μηδὲ ἀμισθὶ τῶν ξένων τἀληθὲς ἀκούειν ἐθελησάντων. οἱ δὲ μηδεμιᾶς ἕνεκα τοιαύτης αἰτίας, ὅμως χαίροντες τῷ ψεύσματι, παγγέλοιοι εἰκότως δοκοῖεν ἄν. ΤΥ. εὖ λέγεις. ἐγὼ γὰρ παρὰ Εὐκράτους ἥκω σοι, τοῦ πάνυ πολλὰ τὰ ἄπιστα, καὶ μυθώδη ἀκούσας. μᾶλλον δὲ μεταξὺ λεγομένων, ἀπιὼν ᾠχόμην, οὐ φέρων τοῦ πράγματος τὴν ὑπερβολὴν, ἀλλά με ὥσπερ αἱ ἐρινύες ἐξήλασαν, πολλὰ τεράστια, καὶ ἀλλόκοτα διεξιόντες. ΦΙΛΟ. καίτοι ὦ Τυχιάδη, ἀξιόπιστος ὁ Εὐκράτης ἐστί. καὶ οὐδεὶς ἂν οὐδὲ πιστεύσειεν, ὡς ἐκεῖνος οὕτω βαθὺν πώγωνα καθειμένος, ἑξηκοντούτης ἀνὴρ, ἔτι καὶ φιλοσοφίᾳ ξυνὼν τὰ πολλὰ, ὑπομείνειεν ἂν καὶ ἄλλου τινὸς ψευδομένου ἀκοῦσαι παρὼν, οὐχ ὅπως αὐτός τι τολμῆσαι τοιοῦτον. ΤΥ. οὐ γὰρ οἶσθα ὦ ἑταῖρε, οἷα μὲν εἶπεν, ὅπως δὲ αὐτὰ ἐπιστώσατο, ὡς δὲ καὶ ἐπώμνυτο τ

12 ex] & *1506* 16 esse si] esse: si *1521* 21 PHILOC.] Phi. *1506 1516 1519*, PHILOCLES *1514*, PHIL. *1517 1534 1563 1566*, PHILOPS. [*sic*] *1521 1528* 29 ridiculi] riduculi [*sic*] *1506* 34 referrent] referret *1514* (*changed in margin from* referrent *by corrector*) *1517 1563 1566* (*see commentary*) 34 PHILOC.] Phi. *1506 1516 1519*, PHILO. *1514*, PHIL. *1517 1534 1563 1566*, PHILOPS. [*sic*] *1521 1528*

coeli sectionem, ac Promethei uincula recensent, gigantumque rebellionem, atque [y6] omnem illam de inferis tragoediam. Et quo pacto ob amorem Iupiter in taurum & cygnum uersus sit, & quemadmodum ex muliere quispiam in auiculam ursamue mutatus sit. Pegasos praeterea, Chimaerasque & Gorgonas, ac Cyclopas, atque id genus omnia, admodum absurdas monstrosasque fabulas, & quae mentes afficere puerorum queant, qui laruam adhuc lamiamque metuunt: quanquam poetica sint fortasse tolerabilia. At urbes iam gentesque totas una uoce ac publicitus mentiri, an non hoc ridiculum? Veluti quum Cretenses sepulchrum Iouis ostendere non pudet: Athenienses Ericthonium aeditum e terra ferunt, primosque illos homines in Attica olerum more ex terra emersisse. Hi tamen multo uerecundiores quam Thebani, qui ex serpentis dentibus satiuos quosdam progerminasse narrant: quod si quis haec, quum sint ridicula, uera esse non credat, sed ea prudenter examinans, Chorebi cuiuspiam, aut Margitae existimet esse si quis aut Triptolemum credat in alatis draconibus per aerem uectum esse, aut Pana quendam ex Arcadia in Marathonem uenisse auxilio, uel Orithyiam a Borea raptam esse, impius nimirum hic atque insanus uideatur eis: quippe qui tam manifesta ueraque non credat, usqueadeo obtinet mendacium. PHILOC. At poetis Tychiade, urbibusque fuerit fortassis ignoscendum: nam illi delectationem illam quae ex fabula proficiscitur, ut quae maxima sit illecebra, poematibus suis immiscent, qua potissimum erga auditores opus habent. Athenienses uero Thebanique, & si qui sunt alij, patriae suae plus maiestatis ex huiusmodi figmentis conciliant: quod si quis fabulas auferat e Graecia, nihil obstiterit quo minus earum narratores fame intereant, quando iam nemo futurus sit hospitum, qui uerum uel gratis audire uelit. At si qui nulla tali causa, gaudent tamen mendacio, hi omnino ridiculi merito uideantur. TYCHIADES. Recte dicis, nam ego protinus ab Eucrate illo celebri uenio, ubi multa incredibilia ac fabulosa quum audissem, imo uero medio in sermone discessi, non ferens narrationem tam supra fidem, sed me uelut furiae quaedam abegerunt, dum monstrosa multa atque absurda referrent. PHILOC. Atqui Tychiade, uir grauis Eucrates est, & nemo certe crediderit illum tam promissa barba uirum sexagenarium: & qui praeterea sit plurimum in philosophia uersatus, sustinuisse ut alium quenquam audiret se praesente mentientem, nedum ut ipse tale quicquam audeat. TYCH. At nescis amice qualia referebat: tum ea quam constanter asserebat: praeterea quam sancte

πλείστοις, παραστησάμενος τὰ παιδία, ὥστε με καὶ ἀποβλέποντα ἐς αὐτὸν, ποικίλα ἐννοεῖν. ἄρτι μὲν, ὡς μεμήνοι, καὶ ἔξω εἴη τοῦ καθεστηκότος· ἄρτι δὲ, ὡς γόης ὢν, ἄρα τοσοῦτον χρόνον ἐλελήθει με ὑπὸ τῇ λεοντῇ, γελοῖόν τινα πίθηκον περιστέλλων· οὕτως ἄτοπα διηγεῖτο. ΦΙΛΟ. τίνα ταῦτα πρὸς τῆς ἑστίας ὦ Τυχιάδη; ἐθέλω γὰρ εἰδέναι ἥντινα τὴν ἀλαζονείαν ὑπὸ τηλικούτῳ τῷ πώγωνι ἔσκεπεν. ΤΥ. εἰώθειν μὲν καὶ ἄλλοτε ὦ Φιλόκλεις, φοιτᾶν πρὸς αὐτὸν, εἴ ποτε πολλὴν τὴν σχολὴν ἄγοιμι. τήμερον δὲ, Λεοντίχῳ συγγενέσθαι δεόμενος, ἑταῖρος δέ μοι ὡς οἶσθα, ἀκούσας παρὰ τοῦ παιδὸς ὡς παρ' Εὐκράτην ἕωθεν ἀπέλθοι, νοσοῦντα ἐπισκεψόμενος, ἀμφοῖν ἕνεκα, ὡς καὶ τῷ Λεοντίχῳ συγγενοίμην, κἀκεῖνον ἴδοιμι, ἠγνοήκειν γὰρ ὡς νοσοίη, παραγίγνομαι πρὸς αὐτόν, εὑρίσκω δὲ αὐτόθι τὸν μὲν Λεόντιχον, οὐκ ἔτι. ἐφθάκει γὰρ ὡς ἔφασκον, ὀλίγον προεξεληλυθώς. ἄλλους δὲ συχνούς, ἐν οἷς Κλεόδημός τε ἦν ὁ ἐκ τοῦ περιπάτου, καὶ Δεινόμαχος ὁ στωϊκὸς, καὶ Ἴων. οἶσθα τὸν ἤδη τοῖς Πλάτωνος λόγοις θαυμάζεσθαι ἀξιοῦντα, ὡς μόνον ἀκριβῶς κατανενοηκότα τὴν γνώμην τοῦ ἀνδρὸς, καὶ τοῖς ἄλλοις ὑποφητεῦσαι δυνάμενον. ὁρᾷς οἵους ἄνδρας σοι φημὶ, πανσόφους, καὶ παναρέτους; ὅ τι περ τὸ κεφάλαιον αὐτὸ ἐξ ἑκάστης προαιρέσεως, αἰδεσίμους ἅπαντας, καὶ μονονουχὶ φοβεροὺς τὴν πρόσοψιν. ἔτι καὶ ὁ ἰατρὸς Ἀντίγονος παρῆν, κατὰ χρείαν οἶμαι τῆς νόσου ἐπικληθείς, καὶ ῥᾷον ἐδόκει ἤδη ἔχειν ὁ Εὐκράτης, καὶ τὸ νόσημα τῶν συντρόφων ἦν. τὸ ῥεῦμα γὰρ, ἐς τοὺς πόδας αὖθις αὐτῷ κατεληλύθει. καθέζεσθαι οὖν με παρ' αὐτὸν ἤδη τῇ κλίνῃ ὁ Εὐκράτης ἐκέλευσεν, ἠρέμα ἐγκλίνας τῇ φωνῇ ἐς τὸ ἀσθενικὸν, ὁπότε εἶδέ με. καίτοι βοῶντος αὐτοῦ, καὶ διατεινομένου, τί μεταξὺ εἰσιὼν ἐπήκουον. κἀγὼ μάλα πεφυλαγμένως μὴ ψαύσαιμι τῶν ποδῶν αὐτοῦ, ἀπολογησάμενος τὰ συνήθη ταῦτα, ὡς ἀγνοήσαιμι νοσοῦντα, καὶ ὡς ἐπεὶ ἔμαθον, δρομαῖος ἔλθοιμι, ἐκαθεζόμην πλησίον. οἱ μὲν δὴ ἐτύγχανον ἤδη ὑπὲρ τοῦ νοσήματος, τὰ μὲν, ἤδη προειρηκότες, τὰ δὲ, καὶ τότε διεξιόντες, ἔτι δὲ καὶ θεραπείας τινὰς ἕκαστος ὑποβάλλοντες. ὁ γοῦν Κλεόδημος, εἰ τοίνυν φησὶ τῇ ἀριστερᾷ τις ἀνελόμενος χαμόθεν τὸν ὀδόντα τῆς μυγαλῆς, οὕτω φονευθείσης ὡς προεῖπον, ἐνδήσειεν εἰς δέρμα λέοντος, ἄρτι ἀποδαρέντος, εἶτα περιάψειε περὶ τὰ σκέλη, αὐτίκα παύεται τὸ ἄλγημα. οὐκ εἰς λέοντος ἔφη ὁ Δεινόμαχος ἐγὼ ἤκουσα, ἐλάφου δὲ θηλείας, ἔτι παρθένου, καὶ ἀβάτου. καὶ τὸ πρᾶγμα οὕτω πιθανώτερον. ὠκὺ γὰρ ἡ ἔλαφος, καὶ ἔρρωται μάλιστα ἐκ τῶν ποδῶν καὶ ὁ λέων, ἄλκι-

36 illigauerit] alligauerit *1534 1563 1566*

in plerisque iurabat, admotis etiam filijs, adeo ut ego quum eum respicerem, uaria mecum cogitarem, interdum quidem illum insanire, neque animo constare: interdum uero ita cogitabam, fugisse me, quod impostor esset, ac tantum temporis sub leonis pelle ridiculam quandam [$y_{6}v$] simiam circumtulisset, adeo absurda narrabat. PHIL. Quaenam illa (per lares) sunt Tychiade? nam cupio cognoscere quamnam praestigiaturam sub tam longa barba occuluerit. TYCH. Solebam quidem etiam alias Philocles aliquoties eum interuisere, si quando uidelicet multo ocio abundarem. Hodie uero quum opus esset mihi conuento Leonthico (est autem, ut scis, amicus mihi) edoctus a puero, eum se ad Eucratem mane contulisse, ut eum morbi inspiciendi causa uiseret, amborum nomine, nempe ut & Leonthicum conuenirem, & Eucratem uiderem, ignoraueram autem quod aegrotaret, ad eum peruenio. At Leonthicum ibi iam non inuenio: nam paulo ante ut dicebant exiuerat, alios uero confertos reperio, in quibus erat & Cleodemus Peripateticus, & Dinomachus Stoicus, & Ion, nosti uirum? illum dico, qui ex Platonica doctrina magnam sui admirationem expectat, ut qui solus mentem uiri deprehenderit, quique eius oracula alijs quoque possit enarrare: uides quos tibi uiros nomino, nimirum omni sapientia atque omni uirtute praeditos, utpote ipsum ex quaque secta caput, reuerendos hercle omnes, atque aspectu propemodum terribiles. Aderat praeterea medicus Antigonus, ut usui in morbo esset aduocatus opinor: & melius iam habere se uidebatur Eucrates: ac morbus quidam ex familiaribus erat: humor enim rursus in pedes ei descenderat. Sedere me ergo Eucrates in lecto iuxta se iussit uoce languidule remissa paululum, quum me conspiceret: quanquam interim dum ingrederer, uociferantem eum ac uocem intendentem audieram: tamen ego admodum curiose cauens ne pedes eius tangerem, ubi me uulgaribus istis uerbis purgaueram, quod eum aegrotare nesciuerim: quod ubi rescissem, curriculo uenerim, adsedi prope, & illis quidem sermo iam de morbo erat, & quaedam iam ante dixerant, quaedam uero etiam tunc narrabant: praeterea medicamenta quaedam quisque proferebat. Cleodemus igitur: Si quis ergo (inquit) sinistra manu tollens humo mustelae dentem, sic interfectae, ut ante dixi, in leonis pellem illigauerit, nuper excoriati, ac deinde circum crura posuerit, illico sedatur dolor. Non in leonis pellem (inquit Dinomachus) ut ego audiui, sed in ceruae potius foemellae uirginis adhuc, & nondum initae, & res quidem magis est hoc pacto credibilis: uelox enim cerua est,

μος μὲν, καὶ τὸ λίθον αὐτοῦ, καὶ ἡ χεὶρ ἡ δεξιὰ, καὶ αἱ τρίχες ἐκ τοῦ πώγωνος αἱ ὀρθαὶ, μεγάλα δύναιντο, εἴ τις ἐπίσταιτο αὐτοῖς χρῆσθαι μετὰ τῆς οἰκείας ἐπῳδῆς ἑκάστῳ. τὸ δ' οὖν δὴ ἴασιν, ἥκιστα ἐπαγγέλλεται. καὶ αὐτὸς ἦ δ' ὃς ὁ Κλεόδημος, οὔπω πάλαι ἐγίγνωσκον ἐλάφου χρῆναι τὸ δέρμα εἶναι, διότι ὠκὺ ἔλαφος. ὁ Ἄγγος δὲ λίβυς ἀνὴρ σοφὸς τὰ τοιαῦτα, μετεδίδαξέ με, εἰπὼν ὠκυτέρους εἶναι τῶν ἐλάφων τοὺς λέοντας. ἀμέλει ἔφη, καὶ αἱροῦσιν αὐτὰς διώκοντες. ἐπῄνεσαν οἱ παρόντες, ὡς εὖ εἰπόντος τοῦ λίβυος. ἐγὼ δὲ, οἴεσθε γὰρ ἔφην ἐπῳδαῖς τισι τὰ τοιαῦτα παύεσθαι, ἢ τοῖς ἔξωθεν παραρτήμασι, τοῦ κακοῦ ἔνδον διατρίβοντος; ἐγέλασαν ἐπὶ τῷ λόγῳ μου, καὶ δῆλοι ἦσαν καταγνωκότες μου πολλὴν τὴν ἄνοιαν, ἐπεὶ μὴ ἐπισταίμην τὰ προδηλότατα. καὶ περὶ ὧν ἂν οὐδεὶς φρονῶν ἀντείποι, μὴ οὐχὶ οὕτως ἔχειν. ὁ μέντοι ἰατρὸς Ἀντίγονος, ἐδόκει μοι ἡσθῆναι τῇ ἐρωτήσει μου. πάλαι γὰρ ἠμελεῖτο οἶμαι, βοηθεῖν ἀξιῶν τῷ εὐκράτει μετὰ τῆς τέχνης, οἴνου τε παραγγέλλων ἀπέχεσθαι, καὶ λάχανα σιτεῖσθαι, καὶ ὅλως ὑφαιρεῖν τοῦ τόνου. ὁ γοῦν Κλεόδημος, ὑπομειδιῶν ἅμα, τί λέγεις ἔφη ὦ Τυχιάδη; ἄπιστον εἶναί σοι δοκεῖ τὸ ἐκ τῶν τοιούτων γίγνεσθαι τινὰς ὠφελείας ἐς τὰ νοσήματα; ἔμοιγε ἦν δ' ἐγὼ, εἰ μὴ πάνυ τὴν ῥῖνα κορύζης μεστὸς εἴην, ὡς πιστεύσειν τὰ ἔξω, καὶ μηδὲν κοινωνοῦντα τοῖς ἔνδοθεν, ἐπιχειρεῖν τὰ νοσήματα, μεθ' ῥημάτων ὥς φατε, καὶ γοητείας τινὸς ἐνεργεῖν, καὶ τὴν ἴασιν ἐπιπέμπειν προσαρτώμενα. τὸ δ' οὐκ ἂν γένοιτο, οὐδ' ἢν ἐς τοῦ νεμείου λέοντος τὸ δέρμα ἐνδήσῃ τις ἑκκαίδεκα ὅλας μυγαλᾶς. ἐγὼ γοῦν αὐτὸν τὸν λέοντα εἶδον πολλάκις χωλεύοντα ὑπ' ἀλγηδόνων, ἐν ὁλοκλήρῳ τῷ αὐτοῦ δέρματι. πάνυ γὰρ ἰδιώτης ἔφη ὁ Δεινόμαχος εἶ, καὶ τὰ τοιαῦτα οὐκ ἐμέλησέ σοι ἐκμαθεῖν, ὅντινα τρόπον ὠφελεῖ, τοῖς νοσήμασι προσφερόμενα. καί μοι δοκεῖς, οὐδὲ τὰ προφανέστατα ἂν παραδέξασθαι ταῦτα, τῶν ἐκ περιόδου πυρετῶν τὰς ἀποπομπὰς, καὶ τῶν ἑρπετῶν τὰς καταθέλξεις, καὶ βουβώνων ἰάσεις, καὶ τἆλλα, ὁπόσα καὶ αἱ γρᾶες ἤδη ποιοῦσιν. εἰ δὲ ἐκεῖνα γίγνεται ἅπαντα, τί δή ποτε οὐχὶ ταῦτα οἰήσῃ γίγνεσθαι ὑπὸ τῶν ὁμοίων; ἀπέραντα ἦν δ' ἐγὼ ξυμπεραίνῃ ὦ Δεινόμαχε, καὶ ἥλῳ φασὶν ἐκκρούεις τὸν ἧλον. οὐδὲ γὰρ ἃ φῂς, ταῦτα δῆλα μετὰ τοιαύτης δυνάμεως γιγνόμενα. ἢν γοῦν μὴ πείσῃς πρότερον ἐπάγων τὸν λόγον διότι φύσιν ἔχει γίγνεσθαι, τοῦ τε πυρετοῦ, καὶ τοῦ οἰδήματος δεδιότος, ἢ ὄνομα θεσπέσιον, ἢ ῥῆσιν βαρβαρικὴν, καὶ διὰ τοῦτο ἐκ τοῦ βουβῶνος δραπετεύοντος, ἔτι σοι γραῶν μῦθοι

4 inquit Cleodemus] inquit, Cleodemus *1521* 5 ceruina] ceruiua [*sic*] *1506* 20 aduersus] apud *1506 1514 1516 1517 1519* 24 immittere; id] immittere, id *1521* 38 uereatur] vertatur *1566*

maximeque ualet pedibus: & leo quidem fortis est, pinguedoque eius ac manus dextra, pilique qui recti e barba prominent, magnam uim obtinent, si quis uti nouerit, cum proprio cuique carmine, at pedum curam minime pollicentur. Et ipse quoque, inquit Cleodemus, olim sic putabam ceruina pelle utendum, propterea quod cerua uelox esset. At nuper uir quidam Libycus, peritus profecto in rebus huiusmodi contra me docuit, ceruis ostendens ueLociores esse leones: quippe qui eas, inquit, etiam persequendo capiunt. Laudabant qui ade[z_1]rant, tanquam recte dixisset Libycus ille: Tum ego: Putatis, inquam, incantamentis quibusdam sedari talia: aut foris admotis appendiculis, quum intus malum grassetur? Riserunt hunc sermonem meum: & palam in me magnam damnabant amentiam, qui apertissimas res ignorarem, & quibus nemo qui sapiat, contradicat: quin sic se habeant. At medicus certe Antigonus delectari mihi uisus est hac rogatione mea. Iamdudum autem neglectui habitus fuerat, opinor, quum opem Eucrati ferre ex arte uellet, denuncians uidelicet uino ut abstineret: atque oleribus uesceretur, & uigorem animo omnino minueret. Cleodemus ergo subridens interim, Quid ais, inquit, Tychiade? incredibile tibi uidetur esse, ut ex rebus huiuscemodi parentur quaedam aduersus morbos remedia? Mihi certe uidetur inquam, ego: nisi naribus adeo mucosis sim, ut credam ea quae foris applicantur, nihilque cum his quae morbos excitant, intus communicant: per uerbula tamen, ut dicitis, ac praestigiaturam operari: & quum appenduntur, sanitates immittere; id profecto nunquam fieri possit: nec si quis uel in Nemei leonis pellem sedecim mustelas integras insuerit. Ego profecto leonem ipsum e doloribus saepe claudicantem uidi in uniuersa suijpsius pelle. Nimium idiota es, inquit Dinomachus, neque unquam tibi curae fuit, ut disceres quonam modo res istiusmodi aduersus morbos, quum adhibentur conferunt, ac mihi uideris ne notissima quidem ista recepturus: febrium uidelicet istarum profligationes, quae certo quodam ambitu recurrunt, tum serpentum demulsiones, ac bubonum sanationes, & caetera: quaecunque anus etiam iam faciunt: quod si illa fiunt omnia, quur tandem non putabis haec etiam similibus rebus fieri? Infinita congeris, inquam, Dinomache, clauumque, ut aiunt, clauo extrudis. Neque enim constat ea quae commemoras, eiusmodi ui fieri. Quamobrem nisi reddita ratione persuaseris primum natura fieri posse, ut febris tumorque uereatur, aut nomen aliquod diuinum, aut dictionem aliquam barbaricam: ob idque ex inguine fugiat: aniles adhuc fabulae

τὰ λεγόμενα ᾄδειν. σύ μοι δοκεῖς ἦ δ' ὃς ὁ Δινόμαχος τὰ τοιαῦτα λέγων, οὐδὲ θεοὺς εἶναι
πιστεύειν, εἴ γε μὴ οἴει τὰς ἰάσεις οἷόν τε εἶναι ὑπὸ ἱερῶν ὀνομάτων γίγνεσθαι. τοῦτο μὲν ἦν
δ' ἐγώ, μὴ λέγε ὦ ἄριστε· κωλύει γὰρ οὐδὲν καὶ θεῶν ὄντων, ὅμως τὰ τοιαῦτα ψευδῆ εἶναι.
ἐγὼ δὲ καὶ θεοὺς σέβω, καὶ ἰάσεις αὐτῶν ὁρῶ, καὶ ἃ εὖ ποιοῦσι τοὺς κάμνοντας, ὑπὸ φαρ
μάκων, καὶ ἰατρικῆς ἀνιστάντες. ὁ γοῦν Ἀσκληπιὸς αὐτὸς, καὶ οἱ παῖδες αὐτοῦ, ἤπια φάρ
μακα πάσσοντες, ἐθεράπευον τοὺς νοσοῦντας, οὐ λέοντας, καὶ μυγαλᾶς περιάπτοντες·
ἔα τοῦτον ἔφη ὁ Ἴων· ἐγὼ δὲ ὑμῖν θαυμάσιόν τι διηγήσομαι. ἦν μὲν ἐγὼ μειράκιον ἔτι, ἀμφὶ τὰ τέτταρα, καὶ δέκα ἔτη σχεδόν· ἧκε δέ τις ἀγγέλλων τῷ πατρὶ, Μίδαν τὸν ἀμπελουρ
γὸν ἐρρωμένον ἐς τὰ ἄλλα, οἰκέτην, καὶ ἐργατικὸν, ἀμφὶ πληθοῦσαν ἀγορὰν, ὑπὸ ἐχίδνης
δηχθέντα, κεῖσθαι ἤδη σεσηπότα τὸ σκέλος. ἀναδοῦντι γὰρ αὐτῷ τὰ κλήματα, καὶ ταῖς
χάραξι περιπλέκοντι, προσερπύσαν τὸ θηρίον, δακεῖν κατὰ τὸν μέγαν δάκτυλον. καὶ τὸ
μὲν, φθάσαι, καὶ καταδῦναι αὖθις ἐς τὸν φωλεόν· τὸν δὲ, οἰμώζειν, ἀπολλύμενον ὑπ' ἀλ
γηδόνων· ταῦτά τε οὖν ἀπηγγέλλετο· καὶ τὸν Μίδαν ἑωρῶμεν αὐτὸν ἐπὶ σκίμποδος ὑπὸ
τῶν ὁμοδούλων προσκομιζόμενον, ὅλον ᾠδηκότα, πελιδνὸν, μυδῶντα τὴν ἐπιφάνειαν,
ὀλίγον ἔτι ἐμπνέοντα. λελυπημένῳ δὴ τῷ πατρὶ, τῶν φίλων τις παρὼν, θάρρει ἔφη.
ἐγὼ γάρ σοι ἄνδρα Βαβυλώνιον τῶν Χαλδαίων ὥς φασιν, αὐτίκα μέτειμι, ὃς ἰάσεται
τὸν ἄνθρωπον. καὶ ἵνα μὴ διατρίβω λέγων, ἧκεν ὁ Βαβυλώνιος, καὶ ἀνέστησε τὸν Μίδαν, ἐ-
πῳδῇ τινι ἐξελάσας τὸν ἰὸν ἐκ τοῦ σώματος, ἔτι καὶ προσαναρτήσας τῷ ποδὶ τεθνηκυίας
παρθένου λίθον, ἀπὸ τῆς στήλης ἐκκολάψας· καὶ τοῦτο μὲν, ἴσως μέτριον· καίτοι ὁ Μίδας
αὐτὸς ἀράμενος τὸν σκίμποδα, ἐφ' οὗ ἐκεκόμιστο, ᾤχετο ἐς τὸν ἀγρὸν ἀπιών· τοσοῦτον ἡ
ἐπῳδὴ ἐδυνήθη, καὶ ὁ στηλίτης ἐκεῖνος λίθος· ὁ δὲ, καὶ ἄλλα ἐποίησε θεσπέσια ὡς ἀλη-
θῶς· ἐς γὰρ τὸν ἀγρὸν ἐλθὼν, ἕωθεν ἐπειπὼν ἱερατικά τινα ἐκ βίβλου παλαιᾶς ὀνόματα
ἑπτὰ, θείῳ, καὶ δᾳδὶ καθαγνίσας τὸν τόπον, περιελθὼν ἐς τρὶς, ἐξεκάλεσεν ὅσα ἦν ἑρπε
τὰ ἐντὸς τῶν ὅρων· ἧκον οὖν ὥσπερ ἑλκόμενοι πρὸς τὴν ἐπῳδὴν ὄφεις πολλοὶ, καὶ ἀσπίδες, καὶ
ἔχιδναι, καὶ κεράσται, καὶ ἀκοντίαι, φρῦνοί τε, καὶ φύσαλοι. ἐλείπετο δὲ εἷς δράκων πα
λαιὸς, ὑπὸ γήρως οἶμαι ἐξερπύσαι μὴ δυνάμενος, παρακούσας τοῦ προστάγματος· ὁ δὲ μά
γος, οὐκ ἔφη παρεῖναι ἅπαντας, ἀλλ' ἕνα τινὰ τῶν ὄφεων τὸν νεώτατον χειροτονήσας, πρε
σβευτὴν ἔπεμψεν ἐπὶ τὸν δράκοντα. καὶ μετὰ μικρὸν ἧκε κἀκεῖνος. ἐπεὶ δὲ συνηλίσθη

1 Dinomachus] Dimoniachus [*sic*] *1506 1516 1519* 2 putes] putas *1528 1563 1566* 9–10 inquit Ion] inquit, Ion *1521* 19 in] *om.* *1534 1563 1566* 19 a] e *1506 1516 1519* 21–22 ferret, amicorum quispiam, qui tum forte aderat, Bono animo es, inquit] ferret: inquit *1506 1514* (amicorum quispiam *added after* ferret *in margin*) *1516 1519*, ferret amicorum quispiam, inquit *1517* (*see commentary*)

sunt quaecunque retulisti. Tu mihi uideris, inquit Dinomachus, quum ista dicas, ne deos quidem esse credere. Siquidem putes fieri non posse, ut per sacra nomina remedia morbis adferantur. Hoc, inquam ego, uir optime ne dixeris, nihil enim prohibet quo minus, etiam si maxime dij sint, ista tamen sint uana. Ego uero & deos colo, & medelas eorum uideo, & leuamenta quae laborantibus conferunt, pharmacis uidelicet, atque arte medica restituentes. Itaque Aesculapius ipse eiusque posteri salutaria pharmaca admouentes medebantur aegrotis: non leones, aut mustelas circumligantes. Mitte hunc, inquit Ion. At ego uobis mirabile quiddam narrabo. Eram adhuc adolescentulus: annos natus ferme quatuordecim: quum quidam ad patrem meum uenit nuncians ei, Midam uitis cul[z_1v]torem seruum, etiam alijs in rebus robustum atque industrium, circa plenum iam forum a uipera morsum iacere iam putrefacto crure. Etenim dum ligaret palmites, ac uallis circumplicaret, adrepentem bestiolam maximum ei pedis momordisse digitum. Tum illam quidem ilico aufugisse, & sese rursus in latebram condidisse. Illum uero eiulare perditum e doloribus. Haec ergo quum nunciarentur, iam Midam ipsum uidebamus in lectica domum a conseruis adportari: inflatum totum, liuidum, ac superficie tabefactum, uix iam spirantem. Pater ergo quum id moleste ferret, amicorum quispiam, qui tum forte aderat, Bono animo es, inquit. Ego enim uirum quendam Babylonium ex Chaldaeis, quos uocant, protinus huc adducam, qui sanabit hominem: & ne diem narrando conteram, uenit Babylonius, ac Midam restituit: effugato ex corpore ueneno, quadam incantatione, & ad pedem eius appenso uirginis defunctae lapillo, quem e columna exciderat. Atque istud quidem hactenus forsan mediocre fuerit. Tum Midas iam ipse sublato, in quo allatus erat scabello, discessit in agrum: tantum potuit incantatio, & columnaris ille lapis. At idem iste Babylonius alia praeterea diuina plane fecit. Nempe in agrum profectus mane, quum pronunciasset sacra quaedam ex uetusto codice, septem nomina, sulphure ac face lustrato loco in orbem ter obambulans, serpentes omneis inuitos exciuit: quicunque intra eam regionem erant. Veniebant ergo tanquam ad incantationem tracti, serpentes multi, atque aspides, & uiperae, & cerastae, & iaculi, phrynique, ac physali: relinquebatur autem unus draco, annosus, prorepere (ut opinor) ob senectam non ualens, qui non fuerat audiens dicto. At magus, Non adsunt omnes inquit. Tum unum quendam ex serpentibus eum uidelicet qui natu minimus erat, selectum legatum mittebat

σαν, ἐνεφύσησε μὲν αὐτὰ ὁ βαβυλώνιος, τὰ δὲ, αὐτίκα μάλα κατεκαύθη ἅπαντα ὑπὸ τῷ φυσήματι. ἡμεῖς δὲ ἐθαυμάζομεν. εἰπέ μοι ὦ ἴων ἦν δ' ἐγὼ, ὁ ὄφις ὁ πρεσβύτης ὁ νέος, ἆρα καὶ ἐχειραγώγει τὸν δράκοντα ἤδη ὡς φὴς γεγηρακότα, ἢ σκίπωνα ἔχων ἐκεῖνος, ἐπεστηρίζετο· σὺ μὲν παίζεις ἔφη ὁ κλεόδημος· ἐγὼ δὲ καὶ αὐτὸς ἀπιστότερος ὢν σοῦ πάλαι τὰ τοιαῦτα, ᾤμην γὰρ οὐδενὶ λόγῳ δυνατὸν γίγνεσθαι ἂν αὐτὰ πιστεῦσαι, ὅμως ὅτε τὸ πρῶτον εἶδον πετόμενον τὸν ξένον τὸν βάρβαρον, ἐξ ὑπερβορέων δὲ ἦν ὡς ἔφασκεν, ἐπίστευσα, καὶ ἐνικήθην, ἐπὶ πολὺ ἀντισχών. τί γὰρ ἔδει ποιεῖν, αὐτὸν ὁρῶντα διὰ τοῦ ἀέρος φερόμενον, ἡμέρας οὔσης, καὶ ἐφ' ὕδατος βαδίζοντα, καὶ διὰ πυρὸς διεξιόντα, σχολῇ, καὶ βάδην· σὺ ταῦτα ἦν δ' ἐγὼ εἶδες, τὸν ὑπερβόρειον ἄνδρα πετόμενον, ἢ ἐπὶ τοῦ ὕδατος βεβηκότα; καὶ μάλα ἦ δ' ὅς ὑποδεδεμένον γε καρβατίνας, οἷα μάλιστα ἐκεῖνοι ὑποδοῦνται. τὰ μὲν γὰρ σμικρὰ ταῦτα, τί χρὴ καὶ λέγειν, ὅσα ἐπεδείκνυτο, ἔρωτας ἐπιπέμπων, καὶ δαίμονας ἀνάγων, καὶ νεκροὺς ἑώλους ἀνακαλῶν, καὶ τὴν ἑκάτην αὐτὴν ἐναργῆ παριστὰς, καὶ τὴν σελήνην κατασπῶν. ἐγὼ γοῦν διηγήσομαι ὑμῖν ἃ εἶδον γιγνόμενα ὑπ' αὐτοῦ ἐν γλαυκίου τοῦ ἀλεξικλέους. ἄρτι γὰρ ὁ γλαυκίας τοῦ πατρὸς ἀποθανόντος, παραλαβὼν τὴν οὐσίαν, ἠράσθη χρυσίδος τῆς δημαινέτου θυγατρός. ἐμοὶ δὲ διδασκάλῳ ἐχρῆτο πρὸς τοὺς λόγους· καὶ εἴ γε μὴ ὁ ἔρως ἐκεῖνος ἀπησχόλησεν αὐτὸν, ἅπαντα ἂν ἤδη τὰ τοῦ περιπάτου ἠπίστατο· ὃς καὶ ὀκτωκαιδεκαέτης ὢν, ἀνέλυε· καὶ τὴν φυσικὴν ἀκρόασιν μετεληλύθει εἰς τέλος. ἀμηχανῶν δὲ ὅμως τῷ ἔρωτι, μηνύει μοι τὸ πᾶν. ἐγὼ δὲ ὥσπερ εἰκὸς ἦν, διδάσκαλον ὄντα τὸν ὑπερβόρειον ἐκεῖνον μάγον, ἄγω πρὸς αὐτὸν, ἐπὶ μναῖς τέτταρσι μὲν τὸ παραυτίκα. ἔδει γὰρ προτελέσαι τι πρὸς τὰς θυσίας· ἑκκαίδεκα δὲ, εἰ τύχοι τῆς χρυσίδος. ὁ δὲ, αὐξομένην τηρήσας τὴν σελήνην, τότε γὰρ ὡς ἐπὶ τὸ πολὺ τὰ τοιαῦτα τελεσιουργεῖται, βόθρον τε ὀρυξάμενος ἐν αἰθρίῳ τινὶ τῆς οἰκίας, περὶ μέσας νύκτας ἀνεκάλεσεν ἡμῖν, πρῶτον μὲν, τὸν ἀναξικλέα τὸν πατέρα τοῦ γλαυκίου, πρὸ ἑπτὰ μηνῶν τεθνεῶτα· ἠγανάκτει δὲ ὁ γέρων ἐπὶ τῷ ἔρωτι, καὶ ὠργίζετο· τὰ τελευταῖα δὲ, ὅμως ἐφῆκεν αὐτῷ ἐρᾶν· μετὰ δὲ, τὴν ἑκάτην τε ἀνήγαγεν, ἐπαγομένην τὸν κέρβερον, καὶ τὴν σελήνην κατέσπασε. πολύμορφόν τι θέαμα, καὶ ἄλλοτε ἀλλοῖόν τι φανταζόμενον. τὸ μὲν γὰρ πρῶ-

2 Babylonius] Babylonis *1506*, Babyloniis *1514* (*corrected interlinearily to* Babylonius) 2 eos] *1534 1563 1566*, eas *1506 1514 1516 1517 1519 1521 1528* 5 illum dico] illum co *1514* (*corrected in margin to* illum dico) 5 perduxit] deduxit *1534 1563 1566* 13 incedentem] incendentem *1566* 16 carbatinis] carbatiuis [*sic*] *1506 1514 1517*, carbatinas *1534 1563 1566* 21 Alexiclis] Alexidis *1506 1514 1516 1517 1519 1521 1528 1534 1563 1566* (*see commentary*) 23 disciplinas] *1506 1514 1516 1519*, disciplina *1517 1521 1528 1534 1563 1566* 35 Alexiclem] Anaxiclem *1506 1514 1516 1517 1519 1521 1528 1534 1563 1566* (*see commentary*) 37 permisit ut] permisit: ut *1521*

ad draconem: ac paulo post uenit etiam ille. At postquam iam collecti constitissent, Babylonius in eos insibulauit. Atque illi repente admodum omnes ab eius flatu incensi sunt, nobis interim admirantibus. Tum ego, dic mihi inquam Ion. Serpens ille legatus, iuuenem illum dico, utrum manu perduxit draconem, qui iam (ut ais) senuerat, an ille baculum gestans innitebatur? Ludis tu quidem, inquit Cleodemus. At ego, qui & ipse quoque olim minus talia credebam, quam nunc tu, putabam enim nulla ratione fieri posse, ut ea crederem: tamen quum uolantem primum conspicerem, peregrinum illum barbarum (erat autem ut ferebant ex Hyperboreis) credidi, ac uictus sum: quum tamen multum diuque repugnassem, nam quid facerem quum eum cernerem in aere uolantem, atque id interdiu, ac super aquam ingredientem, atque per medium ignem incedentem, idque lente ac sensim? Tu ne, inquam ego, ista uidebas, uirum Hyperboreum uolantem, aut super aquas ambulantem: & maxime, inquit [z2] ille, carbatinis indutum, quo calceamenti genere illi potissimum utuntur. Nam minutula ista, quid attinet referre, quaecunque fecit, quo pacto amores immiserit, ac daemones exegerit, mortuosque marcidos in uitam reuocauerit, atque Hecaten ipsam palam conspectibus exhibuerit, lunamque e coelo detraxerit? Quin ego uobis referam, quae ab eo fieri conspexi in Glaucia Alexiclis filio. Glaucias hic quum patris nuper defuncti substantiam suscepisset, Chrysidem amabat Demaeneti filiam, ac me quidem praeceptore in disciplinas utebatur: ac nisi amor ille a studio deduxisset eum, uniuersam Peripateticorum doctrinam perdidicisset: ut qui octo & decem quum esset annorum, iam absoluerat analytica: tum physicam auscultationem in finem usque percurrerat. Amore tamen uictus, mihi rem omnem significat. Ego uero quemadmodum par erat, quippe qui praeceptor eram, Hyperboreum illum magum ad eum duco: conductum quatuor ilico minis in manum datis: oportebat enim praeparari quiddam ad sacrificia, tum sedecim praeterea, si Chryside potiretur. Ille uero crescentem obseruans lunam (Nam tunc ut plurimum huiusmodi sacra peraguntur) fossam quum effodisset in aperto quodam loco domus, sub dio circa mediam noctem, euocauit nobis primum quidem Alexiclem Glauciae patrem, ante septem menses uita defunctum. Succensebat autem ob amorem senex, atque indignabatur. Tandem tamen ei permisit ut amaret. Postea uero Hecaten quoque eduxit: adferentem una Cerberum, tum lunam detraxit multiforme quoddam spectaculum, & quod alias aliud apparebat. Primum

τι, γυναικείαν μορφὴν ἐπιδείκνυτο. εἶτα βοῦς ἐγένετο πάγκαλος. εἶτα σκύλαξ ἐφαίνετο. τέλος δ' οὖν, ὁ ὑπερβόρεος ἐκ πηλοῦ ἐρώτιόν τι ἀναπλάσας, ἄπιθι ἔφη, καὶ ἄγε Χρυσίδα. καὶ ὁ μὲν πηλὸς, ἐξέπτατο. καὶ μετὰ μικρὸν δὲ, ἐπέστη κόπτουσα τὴν θύραν ἐκείνη. καὶ εἰσελθοῦσα, περιβάλλει τὸν Γλαυκίαν, ὡς ἂν ἐμμανέστατα ἐρῶσα. καὶ συνῆν, ἄχρι δὴ ἀλεκτρυόνων ἠκούσαμεν ᾀδόντων. τότε δὴ ἥ τε σελήνη ἀνέπτατο εἰς τὸν οὐρανὸν, καὶ ἡ Ἑκάτη ἔδυ κατὰ τῆς γῆς, καὶ τὰ ἄλλα φάσματα ἠφανίσθη, καὶ τὴν Χρυσίδα ἐξέπεμψαμεν περὶ αὐτό που σχεδὸν τὸ λυκαυγές. εἰ ταῦτα εἶδες ὦ Τυχιάδη, οὐκ ἂν ἔτι ἠπίστησας εἶναι πολλὰ ἐν ταῖς ἐπῳδαῖς χρήσιμα. λέγεις ἦν δ' ἐγώ. ἐπίστευον γὰρ ἂν, εἴπερ εἶδον αὐτά. νῦν δὲ συγγνώμη οἶμαι, εἰ μὴ τὰ ὅμοια ὑμῖν ὀξυδερκεῖν ἔχω. πλὴν ἀλλ' οἶδα γὰρ τὴν Χρυσίδα ἣν λέγεις, ἐραστὴν γυναῖκα, καὶ πρόχειρον, οὐχ ὁρῶ δὲ τίνος ἕνεκα ἐδεήθητε ἐπ' αὐτὴν τοῦ πηλίνου πρεσβευτοῦ, καὶ μάγου τοῦ ἐξ Ὑπερβορέων, καὶ σελήνης αὐτῆς, ἣν εἴκοσι δραχμῶν ἀγαγεῖν εἰς Ὑπερβορέους δυνατὸν ἦν. πάνυ γὰρ ἐνδίδωσι πρὸς ταύτην τὴν ἐπῳδὴν ἡ γυνὴ, καὶ τὸ ἐναντίον τοῖς φάσμασι πέπονθεν. ἐκεῖνα μὲν γὰρ ἢν ψόφον ἀκούσῃ χαλκοῦ, ἢ σιδήρου, πέφευγε. καὶ ταῦτα γὰρ ὑμεῖς φατε. αὕτη δὲ, ἂν ἀργύριόν που ψοφῇ, ἔρχεται πρὸς τὸν ἦχον. ἄλλως τε, καὶ θαυμάζω αὐτοῦ τοῦ μάγου, εἰ δυνάμενος αὐτὸς ἐρασθῆναι πρὸς τῶν πλουσιωτάτων γυναικῶν, καὶ τάλαντα ὅλα παρ' αὐτῶν λαμβάνειν. ὁ δὲ, τεττάρων μνῶν πάνυ σμικρολόγος ὢν, Γλαυκίαν ἐπέρασον ἐργάζεται. γελοῖα ποιεῖς ἔφη ὁ Ἴων, ἀπιστῶν ἅπασιν. ἐγὼ γοῦν ἡδέως ἂν ἐροίμην σε τί περὶ τούτων φῄς, ὅσοι τοὺς δαιμονῶντας ἀπαλλάττουσι τῶν δειμάτων, οὕτω σαφῶς ἐξάδοντες καὶ τὰ φάσματα. καὶ ταῦτα οὐκ ἐμὲ χρὴ λέγειν, ἀλλὰ πάντες ἴσασι τὸν Σύρον τὸν ἐκ τῆς Παλαιστίνης, τὸν ἐπὶ τούτων σοφιστὴν, ὅσους παραλαβὼν καταπίπτοντας πρὸς τὴν σελήνην, καὶ τὼ ὀφθαλμὼ διαστρέφοντας, καὶ ἀφροῦ πιμπλαμένους τὸ στόμα, ὅμως ἀνίστησι, καὶ ἀποπέμπει ἀρτίους, ἐπὶ μισθῷ μεγάλῳ ἀπαλλάξας τῶν δεινῶν. ἐπειδὰν γὰρ ἐπιστῇ κειμένοις, καὶ ἔρηται ὅθεν εἰσεληλύθασιν εἰς τὸ σῶμα, ὁ μὲν νοσῶν αὐτὸς, σιωπᾷ. ὁ δαίμων δὲ, ἀποκρίνεται, ἑλληνίζων, ἢ βαρβαρίζων, ἢ ὅθεν ἂν αὐτὸς ᾖ, ὅπως τε, καὶ ὅθεν εἰσῆλθεν ἐς τὸν ἄνθρωπον. ὁ δὲ, ὅρκους ἐπάγων, εἰ δὲ μὴ πεισθείη, καὶ ἀπειλῶν, ἐξελαύνει τὸν δαίμονα. ἐγὼ γοῦν καὶ εἶδον ἐξιόντα μέλανα, καὶ καπνώδη τὴν χροιάν. οὐ μέγα ἦν δ' ἐγὼ τὰ τοιαῦτά σε ὁρᾶν ὦ Ἴων, ᾧ γε καὶ αἱ ἰδέαι αὐταὶ φαίνονται, ἃς ὁ πατὴρ ὑμῶν Πλάτων δείκνυσιν ἀ-

3 Cupidinem, Abi] Cupidinem. Abi *1521* 15 legato] ligato *1566* 27 terroribus] *1566*, erroribus *1506 1514 1516 1517 1519 1521 1528 1534 1563* (*see commentary*) 31 os] *om. 1566* 36 expellit] expellitque *1506 1516 1519* 39 o] *1506 1516 1519*, *om. 1514 1517 1521 1528 1534 1563 1566* 39 ipsae] ipse *1506*

quidem muliebrem formam referebat: deinde in uaccam formosam uertebatur: Postremo uero catula uidebatur. Hyperboreus ille tandem, quum finxisset quendam e luto Cupidinem, Abi, inquit, atque huc perducas Chrysidem: ac lutum quidem protinus euolabat: paulo post autem affuit illa pulsans ostium. Tum ingressa Glauciam complectitur, eum quam insanissime deperiens, & cum eo uersata est, quoad gallos canentes audiuimus. Tum uero luna subuolabat in coelum, atque Hecate subijt terram, caeteraque spectra disparuerunt: & Chrysidem tandem emisimus circa ipsum ferme diluculum. Haec Tychiades si conspexisses, haud quaquam amplius dubitasses, esse multa in carminibus istis commoda. Bene dicis, inquam, ego credidissem equidem, si uidissem ea: nunc uero ignoscendum mihi puto, si qualia uos uidetis, acute perspicere non possum: uerumtamen Chrysidem illam quam dicis, noui, mulierem plane meretricem ac facilem: nec uideo sane cuius gratia ad illam egueritis luteo illo legato magoque ex Hyperboreis usque, atque ipsa insuper luna. Quippe quam uiginti drachmis ducere in Hyperboreos usque potuisses. Mirifice enim sese offert ad hanc incantationem mulier. Et contrarium quiddam spectris istis habet. Nam ea quidem aeris ferriue sonum [z_2v] si audierint fugiunt (nam id uos praedicatis) illa uero si argentum uspiam sonuerit, accurrit ad tinnitum. Praeterea ipsum etiam magum admiror: quod cum ditissimas mulieres in amorem sui possit elicere, atque ab eis solida talenta suscipere, is tamen ob quatuor minas admodum tantilli lucelli auidus Glauciam amoris compotem fecerit. Ridicule facis, inquit Ion, qui nihil credis. Ego te libenter ergo rogauerim quid de his respondeas, qui daemoniacos liberant terroribus, adeo manifeste spectra illa carminibus eijcientes? Atque haec me dicere non opus est, uerum omnes nouerunt: Syrus ille ex Palestina, qui harum rerum artifex est, quammultos mortales suscipiat, qui ad lunam concidant, oculosque distorqueant, spumaque os oppleant: quos tamen erigit ac sanos remittit, magna accepta mercede, diris eos malis liberans. Etenim quum iacentibus instet, rogaueritque, unde sint in corpus ingressi: aegrotus quidem ipse tacet, at daemon uero respondet (aut lingua Graeca loquens, aut barbarica, aut undecunque fuerit ipse) & quomodo & unde intrauit in hominem. Ille uero adiurans eum, ac ni paruerit minitans etiam, expellit abigitque daemonem. Quin ego quoque daemonem quendam exeuntem uidi nigrum certe & colore fumidum. Non magnum erat, inquam ego, talia te o Ion cernere: cui ipsae etiam apparent Ideae,

μαυρόν τι θέαμα, ὡς πρὸς ἡμᾶς τοὺς ἀμβλυώττοντας. μόνος γὰρ Ἴων ἔφη ὁ Εὐκράτης τὰ τοιαῦτα εἶδεν, οὐχὶ δὲ καὶ ἄλλοι πολλοὶ δαίμοσιν ἐντετυχήκασιν· οἱ μὲν, νύκτωρ· οἱ δὲ, μεθ' ἡμέραν; ἐγὼ δὲ οὐχ ἅπαξ, ἀλλὰ μυριάκις ἤδη τὰ τοιαῦτα τεθέαμαι· καὶ τὸ μὲν πρῶτον, ἐταραττόμην πρὸς αὐτά· νῦν δὲ ὑπὸ τοῦ ἔθους, οὐδέν τι παράλογον ὁρᾶν μοι δοκῶ· καὶ νῦν μάλιστα, ἐξ οὗ μοι τὸν δακτύλιον ὁ Ἄραψ ἔδωκε, σιδήρου τοῦ ἐκ τῶν σταυρῶν πεποιημένον, καὶ τὴν ἐπῳδὴν ἐδίδαξε τὴν πολυώνυμον, ἐκτὸς εἰ μὴ κἀμοὶ ἀπιστήσεις ὦ Τυχιάδη. καὶ πῶς ἄν ἦν δ' ἐγὼ ἀπιστήσαιμι Εὐκράτει τῷ Δείνωνος, σοφῷ ἀνδρὶ μάλιστα, καὶ ἐλευθερίως τὰ δοκοῦντά οἱ λέγοντι οἴκοι παρ' αὐτῷ μετ' ἐξουσίας; τὸ γοῦν περὶ τοῦ ἀνδριάντος ἦ δ' ὃς ὁ Εὐκράτης, ἅπασι τοῖς ἐν τῇ οἰκίᾳ, ὅσαι νύκτες φαινόμενον, καὶ παισὶ, καὶ νεανίαις, καὶ γέρουσι, τοῦτο οὐ παρ' ἐμοῦ μόνον ἀκούσειας ἄν, ἀλλὰ καὶ παρὰ τῶν ἡμετέρων ἁπάντων. ποίου ἦν δ' ἐγὼ ἀνδριάντος; οὐχ ἑώρακας ἔφη εἰσιὼν ἐν τῇ αὐλῇ, ἑστῶτα πάγκαλον ἀνδριάντα, Δημητρίου ἔργον τοῦ ἀνθρωποποιοῦ; μῶν τὸν δισκεύοντα ἦν δ' ἐγὼ φῄς, τὸν ἐπικεκυφότα κατὰ τὸ σχῆμα τῆς ἀφέσεως, ἀπεστραμμένον εἰς τὴν δισκοφόρον, ἠρέμα ὀκλάζοντα τῷ ἑτέρῳ, ἐοικότα ξυναναστησομένῳ μετὰ τῆς βολῆς; οὐκ ἐκεῖνον ἦ δ' ὅς, ἐπεὶ τῶν Μύρωνος ἔργων ἓν καὶ τοῦτό ἐστιν, ὁ δισκοβόλος, ὃν λέγεις. οὐδὲ τὸν παρ' αὐτὸν φημὶ τὸν διαδούμενον τὴν κεφαλὴν τῇ ταινίᾳ, τὸν καλόν. Πολυκλείτου γὰρ τοῦτο ἔργον. ἀλλὰ τοὺς μὲν, ἐν δεξιᾷ εἰσιόντων, ἄφες, ἐν οἷς καὶ τὰ Κριτίου τοῦ Νησιώτου πλάσματα ἕστηκεν, οἱ τυραννοκτόνοι. σὺ δὲ εἴ τινα παρὰ τὸ ὕδωρ τὸ ἐπιρρέον εἶδες προγάστορα, φαλαντίαν, ἡμίγυμνον τὴν ἀναβολήν, ἠνεμωμένον τοῦ πώγωνος τὰς τρίχας ἐνίας, ἐπίσημον τὰς φλέβας, αὐτοανθρώπῳ ὅμοιον, ἐκεῖνον λέγω. Πέλιχος ὁ Κορίνθιος στρατηγὸς εἶναι δοκεῖ. νὴ Δί' ἦν δ' ἐγὼ, εἶδόν τινα ἐν δεξιᾷ τοῦ Κρόνου, ταινίας, καὶ στεφάνους ξηροὺς ἔχοντα, κεχρυσωμένον πετάλοις τὸ στῆθος. ἐγὼ δὲ ὁ Εὐκράτης ἔφη, ἐκεῖνα ἐχρύσωσα, ὁπότε μ' ἰάσατο διὰ τρίτης ὑπὸ τοῦ ἠπιάλου ἀπολλύμενον. ἦ γὰρ καὶ ἰατρὸς ἦν δ' ἐγὼ ὁ βέλτιστος οὗτος Πέλιχος; ἔστι, καὶ μὴ σκῶπτε ἦ δ' ὃς ὁ Εὐκράτης, ἤ σε οὐκ εἰς μακρὰν μέτεισιν ὁ ἀνήρ. οἶδα ἐγὼ ὅσον δύναται οὗτος ὁ ὑπὸ σοῦ γελώμενος ἀνδριάς. ἢ οὐ νομίζεις τοῦ αὐτοῦ εἶναι καὶ ἐπιπέμπειν ἠπιάλους, οἷς ἂν ἐθέλοι, εἴγε καὶ ἀποπέμπειν δυνατὸν αὐτῷ; ἵλεως ἦν δ' ἐγὼ ἔστω ὁ ἀνδριάς, καὶ ἤπιος, οὕτως ἀνδρεῖος ὤν. τί δ' οὖν καὶ ἄλλο ποιοῦντα ὁρᾶτε αὐτὸν ἅπαντες οἱ ἐν τῇ οἰκίᾳ; ἐπειδὰν τάχιστα ἔφη νὺξ γένηται, ὁ δὲ, καταβὰς ἀπὸ τῆς βάσεως, ἐφ' ἧς ἕστηκε, περίεισι

11 Dinonis] *1516 1519 1534 1563 1566*, diuonis [*sic*] *1506 1514 1517 1521 1528* 16 ingredereris] ingrederis *1563*, ingredieris *1566* 21 illam] *1506 1516 1519*, *om. 1514 1517 1521 1528 1534 1563*, illa *1566* 23–24 eum . . . illam] eam loquor, cui taeniis caput vinctum est, formosam illam *1516 1519*, cui tenijs caput vinctum est formosam loquor illam *1566* 24 Polycleti] Polecleti *1506* 25 ingredientibus] *1566*, egredientibus *1506 1514 1516 1517 1519 1521 1528 1534 1563* (*see commentary*) 32 triduo, febre] tertioque die epialo *1566* 36 febres] epialos *1566*

quas uestrae familiae parens ostendit Plato: rem uidelicet spectatu tenuem, atque euanidam: quantum ad nos homines lusciosos. Ita ne solus Ion, inquit Eucrates: istiusmodi uidit: ac non alij etiam multi inciderunt in daemones: alij noctu, alij etiam interdiu? Ego profecto non semel, sed millies iam talia conspexi, ac primum quidem turbabar ad ea: iam uero ob consuetudinem nihil nouum, aut prodigiosum mihi uidere uideor, maximeque nunc ex quo annulum mihi Arabs dedit ex ferro de cruce quapiam sumpto, factum carmenque docuit nominibus multis plenum, nisi forte ne mihi quidem fidem sis habiturus Tychiade. At qui fieri possit inquam, ut Eucrati non credam Dinonis filio: uiro in primis sapienti ac libere, quae sibi uidentur domi in priuato suo cum autoritate narranti? Illud ergo de statua, inquit Eucrates, quae omnibus qui in domo sunt singulis noctibus apparet: tum pueris, tum adolescentibus, tum senibus: hoc inquam, non a me duntaxat audieris, uerum etiam a nostris omnibus? De qua statua, inquam ego? Non uidisti (inquit) quum ingredereris statuam quandam in atrio collocatam, sane quam pulchram, opus Demetrij: qui statuas humana specie fingere consueuit? Nonne illam dicis, inquam, quae discum iacit: quae inclinata est ad emissuri gestum reflexa in eam quae discum fert, altero pede modice inflexo, quaeque se erectura uidetur una cum iactu? Non illam, inquit: nam unum est ex Myronis operibus ille disci iactator, quem dicis. Sed nec eam quae est ei proxima: eum loquor cui tenijs caput uin[z3]ctum est, formosam illam. Nam id Polycleti opus est: uerum eas quae a dextra sunt ingredientibus omitte, inter quas & tyrannicidae illi stant: Critiae Nesiotae plasmata: tu uero an non ad aquam illam quae influit, quampiam uidisti uentre prominulo, caluam, seminudatam, uulsis quibusdam barbae pilis, insignibus uenis, uero homini simillimam? Pelichus dux Corinthius esse uidetur. Per Iouem, inquam uidi quandam a dextra Saturni, quae tenias coronasque aridas habebat, pectoreque folia quaedam inaurata. Ego, inquit Eucrates, ea inauraui, quum me sanasset triduo, febre pereuntem. Erat ne igitur etiam medicus, inquam ego, optimus iste Pelichus? Est, neque ride, inquit Eucrates: alioqui homo te haud multo post inuadet. Noui ego certe quantum ualeat haec, quam tu rides statua. An non eiusdem putas esse immittere febres, in quos uoluerit quandoquidem potis est eijcere? Propitia, inquam, placataque sit haec statua mihi, quae tantum ualeat. Quidnam ergo aliud facientem eam uiderunt omnes qui in domo sunt? Quum primum nox est, inquit, haec e base

ἐν κύκλῳ τὴν οἰκίαν, καὶ πάντες ἐντυγχάνουσιν αὐτῷ, ἐνίοτε καὶ ᾄδοντι. καὶ οὐκ ἔστιν ὅντινα ἠδίκησεν· ἐκτρέπεσθαι γὰρ χρὴ μόνον· ὁ δὲ, παρέρχεται, μηδὲν ἐνοχλήσας τοὺς ἰδόντας· καὶ μὴν καὶ λούεται τὰ πολλὰ, καὶ παίζει δι' ὅλης νυκτὸς, ὥστε ἀκούειν τοῦ ὕδατος ψοφοῦντος. ὅρα τοίνυν ἦν δ' ἐγὼ, μὴ οὐχὶ Πέλιχος ὁ ἀνδριὰς, ἀλλὰ Τάλως ὁ Κρὴς ὁ τοῦ Μίνωος ᾖ· καὶ γὰρ ἐκεῖνος χαλκοῦς τις ἦν, τῆς Κρήτης περίπολος· εἰ δὲ μὴ χαλκοῦ ὦ Εὔκρατες, ἀλλὰ ξύλου ἐπεποίητο, οὐδὲν αὐτὸν ἐκώλυεν οὐ Δημητρίου ἔργον εἶναι, ἀλλὰ τῶν Δαιδάλου τεχνημάτων. δραπετεύει γοῦν ὡς φὴς ἀπὸ τῆς βάσεως καὶ οὗτος. ὅρα ἔφη ὦ Τυχιάδη, μή σοι μεταμελήσῃ τοῦ σκώμματος ὕστερον. οἶδα ἐγὼ οἷα ἔπαθεν ὁ τοὺς ὀβολοὺς ὑφελόμενος, οὓς κατὰ τὴν νουμηνίαν ἑκάστην τίθεμεν αὐτῷ. πάνδεινα ἐχρῆν ὁ Ἴων ἔφη, ἱερόσυλόν γε ὄντα. πῶς οὖν αὐτὸν ἠμύνατο ὦ Εὔκρατες; ἐθέλω γὰρ ἀκοῦσαι, εἰ καὶ ὅτι μάλιστα οὑτοσὶ Τυχιάδης ἀπιστήσει. πολλοὶ ἦ δ' ὃς ἔκειντο ὀβολοὶ πρὸς τοῖν ποδοῖν αὐτοῦ, καὶ ἄλλα νομίσματα ἔνια ἀργυρᾶ πρὸς τὸν μηρὸν, κηρῷ κεκολλημένα, καὶ πέταλα ἐξ ἀργύρου, εὐχαί τινος, ἢ μισθὸς ἐπὶ τῇ ἰάσει, ὁπόσοι δι' αὐτὸν ἐπαύσαντο πυρετῷ ἐχόμενοι. ἦν δὲ ἡμῖν Λίβυς τις οἰκέτης, κατάρατος, ἱπποκόμος. οὗτος ἐπεχείρησε νυκτὸς ὑφελέσθαι πάντα ἐκεῖνα, καὶ ὑφείλετο, καταβεβηκότα ἤδη τηρήσας τὸν ἀνδριάντα. ἐπεὶ δὲ ἐπανελθὼν τάχιστα ἔγνω περισεσυλημένος ὁ Πέλιχος, ὅρα ὅπως ἠμύνατο, καὶ κατεφώρασε τὸν Λίβυν. δι' ὅλης γὰρ τῆς νυκτὸς περιῄει ἐν κύκλῳ τὴν αὐλὴν, ὁ ἄθλιος ἐξελθεῖν οὐ δυνάμενος, ὥσπερ ἐς λαβύρινθον ἐμπεσών. ἄχρι δὴ κατελήφθη ἔχων τὰ φώρια, γενομένης τῆς ἡμέρας, καὶ τότε μὲν, πληγὰς οὐκ ὀλίγας ἔλαβεν ἁλούς. οὐ πολὺν δὲ ἐπιβιοὺς χρόνον, κακὸς κακῶς ἀπέθανε, μαστιγούμενος ὡς ἔλεγε, κατὰ τὴν νύκτα ἑκάστην, ὥστε καὶ μώλωπας ἐς τὴν ἐπιοῦσαν φαίνεσθαι αὐτοῦ ἐπὶ τοῦ σώματος. πρὸς ταῦτα ὦ Τυχιάδη, καὶ τὸν Πέλιχον σκῶπτε, κἀμὲ, ὥσπερ τὸν Μίνωος ἡλικιώτην παραπαίειν ἤδη δόκει. ἀλλ' ὦ Εὔκρατες ἦν δ' ἐγὼ, ἔστ' ἂν ὁ χαλκὸς μὲν, χαλκὸς, τὸ δὲ ἔργον, Δημήτριος ὁ Ἀλωπεκῆθεν εἰργασμένος ᾖ, οὐ θεοποιός τις, ἀλλ' ἀνθρωποποιὸς ὢν, οὔποτε φοβήσομαι τὸν ἀνδριάντα Πελίχου, ὃν οὐδὲ ζῶντα πάνυ ἐδεδίειν, ἀπειλοῦντά μοι. ἐπὶ τούτοις, Ἀντίγονος ὁ ἰατρὸς εἶπε. κἀμοὶ ὦ Εὔκρατες, Ἱπποκράτης ἐστὶ χαλκοῦς, ὅσον πηχυαῖος τὸ μέγεθος. ὃς μόνον ἐπειδὰν ἡ θρυαλλὶς ἀποσβῇ, περίεισι τὴν οἰκίαν ὅλην ἐν κύκλῳ, ψοφῶν, καὶ τὰς πυξίδας ἀνατρέπων, καὶ τὰ φάρμακα συγχέων, καὶ τὴν θύραν περιτρέπων, καὶ μάλιστα ἐπειδὰν τὴν θυσίαν ὑπερβαλώμεθα, ἣν κατὰ τὸ ἔτος ἕκαστον αὐτῷ θύομεν. ἀξιοῖ γὰρ ἤδη

4 infestans] infestant *1566* 6 Minoem] Ninoem [*sic*] *1506 1516* 8 nisi] *1506 1514 1516 1517 1519*, si non *1521 1528 1534 1563 1566* 9 quin] quum *1506 1514 1516 1517 1519*, qui *1563 1566* 15 quam] *om.* *1566* 16–17 numismata] numissimata [*sic*] *1506 1516 1519* 35 Antigonus] *1534 1563 1566*, Antiochus *1506 1514 1516 1517 1519 1521 1528* (*see commentary*) 36 tunc] nunc *1563*

descendens in qua steterat, in orbem totam domum circuit: omnes occurrunt ei interdum etiam canenti: nec quisquam est quem unquam laeserit, diuertere tantum oportet. Illa uero praeterit, nihil intuentes infestans, quum & lauat saepe, & tota nocte ludit, ut ex ipso aquae strepitu licet audire. Vide ergo inquam ego, ne forte non Pelichus haec statua sit, sed Talus potius Cretensis, qui apud Minoem fuisse dicitur. Nam & ille aereus quidam Cretae custos erat: quod nisi ex aere, non autem ex ligno facta esset, nihil eam prohiberet, quin non opus Demetrij, sed una potius ex Daedali machinis esse uideatur. E base nanque (ut ais) etiam ista fugit. Vide, inquit, o Tychiade, ne te posthac scommatis huius poeniteat. Noui quidem ego, quid illi euenerit, qui obolos surripuit, quos ei quoque nouilunio suspendimus. Prorsus atrocia, inquit Ion, oportebat accidere: quippe qui sacrilegus erat: quomodo ergo illum ultus est o Eucrates? Nam audire cupio, etiam si quam maxime Tychiades iste diffisurus est. Multi, inquit ille, ad pedes eius oboli iacebant, aliaque item numismata, quaedam argentea ad crus eius affixa caera, ac laminae quoque argenteae: uota cuiusque, aut merces ob sanationem eius, qui ab eo liberatus esset, quum febre detineretur. At erat nobis seruus quidam Libycus sceleratus, equorum curator. Hic noctu aggressus est ea auferre omnia, abstulitque digressam iam quum obseruasset statuam. At quum primum reuersus intellexit sacrilegio se compilatum Pelichus, uide quo pacto sese ultus est, atque furti prodidit Libycum. Tota nocte atrium obambulabat in orbem miser, exire non ualens, tanquam in Labyrinthum incidisset, quoad orta die iam deprehensus est, ea tenens quae furto abstulerat: ac tum quidem comprehensus, plagas non paucas recepit, nec temporis multum superstes [z3v] malus male perijt: uapulans, ut dicebat, singulis noctibus: adeo ut uibices postridie apparerent in corpore. I nunc & post ista quoque Tychiades Pelichum ride, ac me tanquam coaetaneum Minoi iam delirare puta. At o Eucrates, inquam ego, quam diu aes erit aes, operisque plastes Demetrius Alopecensis fuerit: qui non deos, sed homines fingere consueuit: Pelichi nunquam statuam uerebor: quippe qui nec ipsum etiam uiuentem, si mihi minaretur, admodum timuissem. Ad haec medicus Antigonus. Et mihi o Eucrates, inquit, Hippocrates aereus est magnitudine ferme cubitali: qui tunc dumtaxat quum lucerna extincta sit, totam in orbem domum ambit: perstrepens ac pyxides euertens, pharmacaque commiscens, atque ostia circumuertens: maximeque si quando sacrificia praetermitti-

δ' ἐγὼ καὶ Ἱπποκράτης ἤδη ὁ ἰατρὸς θύεσθαι αὐτῷ, καὶ ἀγανακτεῖ, ἣν μὴ κατὰ καιρὸν ἀφ' ἱερῶν τελείων ἐστιαθῇ; ὃν ἐχρῆν ἀγαπᾶν, εἴ τις ἐναπόσειεν αὐτῷ, ἢ μελίκρατον ἐπισπείσειεν, ἢ στεφανώσειε τὴν κεφαλήν. ἄκουε τοίνυν ἔφη ὁ Εὐκράτης, τοῦτο μὲν καὶ ἐπὶ μαρτύρων, ὃ πρὸ ἐτῶν πέντε εἶδον. ἐτύγχανε μὲν ἀμφὶ τρυγητὸν τὸ ἔτος ὄν, ἐγὼ δὲ ἀμφὶ τὸν ἀγρὸν μεσούσης τῆς ἡμέρας τρυγῶντας ἀφεὶς τοὺς ἐργάτας, κατ' ἐμαυτὸν εἰς τὴν ὕλην ἀπήειν, μεταξὺ φροντίζων τι, καὶ ἀνασκοπούμενος. ἐπεὶ δ' ἐν τῷ συνηρεφεῖ ἦν, τὸ μὲν πρῶτον, ὑλαγμὸς ἐγένετο κυνῶν, κἀγὼ εἴκαζον Μνάσωνα τὸν υἱόν, ὥσπερ εἰώθει, παίζειν, καὶ κυνηγετεῖν ἐς τὸ λάσιον μετὰ τῶν ἡλικιωτῶν παρελθόντα. τὸ δ' οὐκ εἶχεν οὕτως. ἀλλὰ μετ' ὀλίγον σεισμοῦ τινος γενομένου, καὶ βοῆς, οἷον ἐκ βροντῆς, γυναῖκα ὁρῶ προσιοῦσαν φοβεράν, ἡμισταδιαίαν σχεδὸν τὸ ὕψος. εἶχε δὲ καὶ δᾷδα ἐν τῇ ἀριστερᾷ, καὶ ξίφος ἐν τῇ δεξιᾷ, ὅσον εἰκοσάπηχυ. καὶ τὰ μὲν ἔνερθεν, ὀφιόπους ἦν. τὰ δὲ ἄνω, γοργόνι ἐμφερής, τὸ βλέμμα φημί, καὶ τὸ φρικῶδες τῆς προσόψεως. καὶ ἀντὶ τῆς κόμης, τοὺς δράκοντας βοστρυχηδὸν περιέκειτο, εἱλουμένους περὶ τὸν αὐχένα, καὶ ἐπὶ τῶν ὤμων ἐνίους ἐσπειραμένους. ὁρᾶτε ἔφη ὅπως ἔφριξα ὦ φίλοι, μεταξὺ διηγούμενος; καὶ ἅμα λέγων, ἐδείκνυεν ὁ Εὐκράτης τὰς ἐπὶ τοῦ πήχεος τρίχας, πᾶσιν ὀρθὰς ὑπὸ τοῦ φόβου. οἱ μὲν οὖν ἀμφὶ τὸν Ἴωνα, καὶ τὸν Δεινόμαχον, καὶ τὸν Κλεόδημον, κεχηνότες ἀτενές, προσεῖχον αὐτῷ γέροντες ἄνδρες, ἑλκόμενοι τῆς ῥινός, ἠρέμα προσκυνοῦντες οὕτως ἀπίθανον κολοσσόν, ἡμισταδιαίαν γυναῖκα, γιγάντειόν τι μορμολύκειον. ἐγὼ δέ, ἐνενόουν μεταξὺ οἷοι ὄντες αὐτοί, νέοις τε ὁμιλοῦσιν ἐπὶ σοφίᾳ, καὶ ὑπὸ πολλῶν θαυμάζονται, μόνῃ τῇ πολιᾷ, καὶ τῷ πώγωνι διαφέροντες τῶν βρεφῶν. τὰ δ' ἄλλα, καὶ αὐτῶν ἐκείνων εὐαγωγότεροι πρὸς τὸ ψεῦδος. ὁ γοῦν Δεινόμαχος, εἰπέ μοι ἔφη ὦ Εὔκρατες, οἱ κύνες δὲ τῆς θεοῦ, πηλίκοι τὸ μέγεθος ἦσαν; ἐλεφάντων ἦ δ' ὅς, ὑψηλότεροι τῶν ἰνδικῶν, καὶ μέλανες καὶ αὐτοί, καὶ λάσιοι, πιναρᾷ, καὶ αὐχμώσῃ τῇ λάχνῃ. ἐγὼ μὲν οὖν ἰδών, ἔστην, ἀναστρέψας ἅμα τὴν σφραγῖδα, ἥν μοι ὁ Ἄραψ ἔδωκεν εἰς τὸ εἴσω τοῦ δακτύλου. ἡ Ἑκάτη δὲ πατάξασα τῷ δρακοντείῳ ποδὶ τοὔδαφος, ἐποίησε χάσμα παμμέγεθες, ἡλίκον, ταρτάρειον τὸ μέγεθος. εἶτα ᾤχετο μετ' ὀλίγον ἁλλομένη ἐς τὸ αὐτό. ἐγὼ δὲ θαρσήσας, ἐπέκυψα, λαβόμενος δένδρου τινὸς πλησίον πεφυκότος, ὡς μὴ σκοτοδινιάσας, ἐμπέσοιμι ἐπὶ κεφαλήν. εἶτα ἑώρων τὰ ἐν ᾅδου ἅπαντα, τὸ

9 consyderans] considerans *1521* 25 Mormolycium] Mormolocium *1506 1514 1516 1517 1519* 25 consyderabam] considerabam *1521* 30 inquit, Eucrates] inquit Eucrates *1521* 31 inquit ille] inquit, ille *1521* 33 protinus] protenus *1506 1514* 37 apprensa] apprehensa *1516 1519 1563 1566*

mus: quibus in singulos annos ei sacrificamus. Postulat ergo, inquam ego, etiam Hippocrates medicus iam ut sibi sacrificetur: indignaturque nisi in tempore iustorum sacrificiorum epulis accipiatur: quem nimirum decebat boni consulere, si quis ei libauerit, aut mulsum insperserit, aut caput coronauerit. Audi ergo, inquit Eucrates: istud certe etiam testibus probauero, quod ante annos quinque uidi. Erat ferme uindemiae tempus. Ego uero in agrum circa meridiem uindemiatum dimissis operarijs, in syluam solus abibam: cogitans interim quiddam atque consyderans. At postquam in saltum perueni: canum primo latratus insonuit. Ego uero Mnasona filium meum, cum aequalibus uenientem, ludere uenarique (quemadmodum solebat) conijciebam. At res haudquaquam sic se habebat: uerum paulopost facto terraemotu, sonoque uelut e tonitru, mulierem aduenientem uideo terribilem: proceritate ferme semistadiali: habebat autem in sinistra facem: in dextra uero gladium uiginti circiter cubitorum. Et inferne quidem pedibus erat serpentinis, superne uero Gorgonem referens uultu uidelicet, atque aspectus horrore: pro coma quidem draconibus, tanquam caesarie circumcincta: alijs collum amplectentibus, alijs etiam per humeros sparsis. Videte, inquit, amici quo pacto etiam inter narrandum exhorrui: & simul haec dicens Eucrates, ostendit omnibus brachij sui setas erectas metu. Ion ergo ac Dinomachus, & Cleodemus uehementer inhiantes auscultabant eum uiri senes, tanquam naribus traherentur, adorantes apud sese tam incredibilem Colossum: mulierem semistadialem, giganteum quoddam Mormolycium. Ego uero consyderabam interim, cuiusmodi erant hi qui cum iuuenibus sapientiae nomine uersentur, uulgoque in admiratione habeantur: quum sola nimirum canicie barbaque ab ipsis differant infantibus: Caeterum etiam illis ipsis facilius ductiles ad credenda mendacia. Dinomachus ergo, dic mihi, inquit, Eucrates: illi canes deae, quanta magnitudine erant? Elephantis, inquit ille, proceri[z_4]ores Indicis, nigri & ipsi hirsutique sordido squalidoque uillo. Ego igitur quum uiderem, restiti, inuerso protinus in interiorem digiti partem (quod Arabs mihi dederat) sigillo. Hecate ergo percusso draconicis illis pedibus solo, hiatum effecit maximum: & qui immani magnitudine penitus aequaret tartarum. Deinde paulo post abijt in eum desiliens. Ego uero praesente animo porrecta ceruice inclinatus, inspexi apprensa arbore quapiam, quae uicina stabat, ne obortis mihi tenebris ac uertigine, in caput praeceps inciderem, deinde conspexi ea quae in inferno sunt

πυριφλεγέθοντα, τὴν λίμνην, τὸν κέρβερον, τοὺς νεκρούς, ὥστε γνωρίζειν ἐνίους αὐτῶν. τὸν γοῦν πατέρα εἶδον ἀκριβῶς αὐτὰ ἐκεῖνα ἔτι ἀμπεχόμενον, ἐν οἷς αὐτὸν κατεθάψαμεν. τί δὲ ἔπραττον ὁ Ἴων ἔφη ὦ Εὔκρατες αἱ ψυχαί; τί ἄλλο ἦ δ' ὅς, ἢ κατὰ φῦλα, καὶ φρήτρας μετὰ τῶν φίλων, καὶ συγγενῶν διατρίβουσιν ἐπὶ τοῦ ἀσφοδέλου κατακείμενοι; ἀντιλεγέτωσαν οὖν ἔτι ἦ δ' ὃς ὁ Ἴων οἱ ἀμφὶ τὸν Ἐπίκουρον τῷ ἱερῷ Πλάτωνι, καὶ τῷ περὶ τῶν ψυχῶν λόγῳ. σὺ δὲ μὴ καὶ τὸν Σωκράτην αὐτὸν, καὶ τὸν Πλάτωνα εἶδες ἐν τοῖς νεκροῖς; τὸν Σωκράτην ἔγωγε ἦ δ' ὅς, οὐδὲ τοῦτον σαφῶς, ἀλλὰ εἰκάζων ὅτι φαλακρὸς, καὶ προγάστωρ ἦν. τὸν Πλάτωνα δὲ, οὐκ ἐγνώρισα. χρὴ γὰρ οἶμαι πρὸς φίλους ἄνδρας τἀληθῆ λέγειν. ἅμα γοῦν ἔγωγε ἅπαντα ἀκριβῶς ἑωράκειν. καὶ τὸ χάσμα συνέμυε. καί τινες τῶν οἰκετῶν ἀναζητοῦντές με, καὶ Πυρρίας οὗτος ἐν αὐτοῖς, ἐπέστησαν οὔπω τέλεον μεμυκότος τοῦ χάσματος. εἰπὲ Πυρρία εἰ ἀληθῆ λέγω. νὴ Δί' ἔφη ὁ Πυρρίας, καὶ ὑλακῆς δὲ ἤκουσα διὰ τοῦ χάσματος, καὶ πῦρ τι ὑπολάμπειν ἀπὸ τῆς δᾳδός μοι ἐδόκει. κἀγὼ ἐγέλασα, ἐπιμετρήσαντος τοῦ μάρτυρος τὴν ὑλακὴν, καὶ τὸ πῦρ. ὁ Κλεόδημος δέ, οὐ καινὰ εἶπεν, οὐδὲ ἄλλοις ἀόρατα ταῦτα εἶδες, ἐπεὶ καὶ αὐτὸς οὐ πρὸ πολλοῦ νοσήσας, τοιόνδε τι ἐθεασάμην. ἐπεσκόπει δέ με, καὶ ἐθεράπευεν Ἀντίγονος οὗτος. ἑβδόμη μὲν ἦν ἡμέρα. ὁ δὲ πυρετὸς, οἷος, καῦσος σφοδρότατος. ἅπαντες δέ με ἀπολιπόντες ἐπ' ἐρημίας, ἐπικλεισάμενοι τὰς θύρας, ἔξω περιέμενον. οὕτω γὰρ ἐκέλευσας ὦ Ἀντίγονε, εἴ πως δυνηθείην εἰς ὕπνον τρέπεσθαι. τότε οὖν ἐφίσταταί μοι νεανίας ἐγρηγορότι, πάγκαλος, λευκὸν ἱμάτιον περιβεβλημένος. εἶτα ἀναστήσας, ἄγει διά τινος χάσματος ἐς τὸν ἅδην, ὡς αὐτίκα ἐγνώρισα Τάνταλον ἰδὼν, καὶ Τιτυὸν, καὶ Σίσυφον. καὶ τὰ μὲν ἄλλα, τί ἂν ὑμῖν λέγοιμι; ἐπεὶ δὲ κατὰ τὸ δικαστήριον ἐγενόμην, παρῆν δὲ καὶ ὁ Αἰακὸς, καὶ ὁ Χάρων, καὶ αἱ Μοῖραι, καὶ αἱ Ἐρινύες, ὁ μέν τις ὥσπερ βασιλεύς, ὁ Πλούτων μοι δοκεῖ καθῆστο, ἐπιλεγόμενος τῶν τεθνηξομένων τὰ ὀνόματα, οὓς ἤδη ὑπερημέρους τῆς ζωῆς συνέβαινεν εἶναι. ὁ δὲ νεανίσκος, ἐμὲ φέρων, παρέστησεν αὐτῷ. ὁ δὲ Πλούτων, ἠγανάκτησέ τε, καὶ πρὸς τὸν ἀγαγόντα με οὔπω πεπλήρωταί φησι τὸ νῆμα αὐτῷ. ὥστε ἀπίτω. σὺ δὲ δὴ τὸν χαλκέα Δημύλον ἄγε. ὑπὲρ γὰρ τὸν ἄτρακτον ἤδη βιοῖ. κἀγὼ ἄσμενος ἀναδραμὼν, αὐτὸς μὲν ἤδη ἀπύρετος ἦν, ἀπήγγελλον δ' ἅπασιν, ὡς τεθνήξεται Δημύλος. ἐν γειτόνων δὲ ἡμῖν ᾤκει, νοσῶν τι καὶ αὐτὸς ὡς ἀπηγγέλλετο. καὶ μετὰ μικρὸν ἠκούομεν οἰμωγῆς ὀδυρομένων ἐπ' αὐτῷ. τί θαυμαστὸν εἶπεν ὁ Ἀντίγονος; ἐγὼ γάρ τινα οἶδα μετὰ εἰκοστὴν ἡμέραν, ἧς ἐτάφη, ἀναστάντα, θεραπεύσας καὶ πρὸ τοῦ θανάτου, καὶ ἐπεὶ ἀνέστη, τὸν ἄνθρωπον. καὶ πῶς ἐν

13 plene] plane *1506 1514 1516 1519* 22 astitit] astetit *1506*

omnia: pyriphlegetontem, lacum, Cerberum, manes: adeo ut quosdam etiam eorum agnoscerem. Patrem ergo meum manifeste cernebam adhuc his ipsis amictum, quibus eum sepeliuimus. Quid agebant (inquit Ion) o Eucrates animae? Quid aliud, inquit ille, quam per tribus familiasque cum amicis cognatisque uersantur: in Asphodelo collocati? Contradicant ergo etiam nunc (inquit Ion) Epicurei sacro Platoni, eiusque de anima rationibus. At tu nonne Socratem etiam ipsum Platonemque uidebas inter manes? Socratem (inquit) uidi: neque illum tamen euidenter, nisi quod inde conieci, quoniam caluus, ac uentricosus erat. Platonem uero non cognoui: nam apud amicos nimirum uera fateri oportet. Simul ergo atque ego omnia conspexi, & hiatus coijt, & ex famulis meis quidam quaerentes me, atque in his Pyrrhias hic, superuenere hiatu nondum plene obducto: dic Pyrrhia, an non uera narro? Per Iouem (inquit Pyrrhias) & latratum audiui per hiatum: & ignis quidem a face mihi suffulgere uidebatur. Tum risi ego profecto, teste latratum ignemque in cumulum addente. Tum Cleodemus: haud quaquam noua ista, inquit, neque alijs inuisa uidisti. Nam & ipse haud ita pridem quum aegrotarem tale quiddam conspexi. Prospiciebat mihi curabatque Antigonus hic, ac septima dies erat: febrisque o qualis? incendio certe uehementior. Omnes ergo me relinquentes solum, clausis foribus foris manebant. Sic enim iusseras Antigone: si quo pacto possem obdormiscere. Tunc igitur astitit mihi iuuenis quidam uigilanti: pulcher admodum, ueste circumamictus candida. Ac me quum excitasset, per hiatum quendam ducit ad inferos: sicuti ilico cognoui: Tantalum quum uiderem ac Tityum Sisyphumque. At caetera uobis quid commemorem? Postquam uero ad tribunal perueni (aderat autem & Aeacus, & Charon, Parcaeque atque Erinnes) quidam uelut rex (Pluto certe mihi uidebatur) assedit singulorum nomina percensens, qui morituri erant: quos diem iam uitae praescriptum praeterijsse contigerat. Iuuenis ergo me, adducens illi exhibuit. At Pluto tunc incanduit, & ad eum qui me ducebat, nondum illi completum est stamen, inquit. Abeat ergo. Tu uero fabrum De[z4v]mylum adduc: iam siquidem ultra colum uiuit. Tum ego laetus recurrens, ipse quidem iam febre liber eram: denunciabam uero omnibus, quod Demylus esset moriturus. Manebat autem nobis in uicinia aegrotans, etiam ipse nonnihil ut renunciatum est. Ac paulo post audimus eiulatum eorum qui lugebant eum. Quid miri est, inquit Antigonus? Ego etenim quendam noui post uigesimum diem quam sepultus est, resurrexisse. Nam hominem & antequam moreretur, &

δ' ἑπτὰ καὶ εἴκοσιν ἡμέραις ὅτε ἐμύδησε τὸ σῶμα, ὅτε ἄλλως ὑπὸ λιμοῦ διεφθάρη, εἰ μή τινά γε Ἐπιμενίδην σύ γε ἐθεράπευες. ἅμα ταῦτα λεγόντων ἡμῶν, ἐπεισῆλθον οἱ τοῦ Εὐκράτους υἱοὶ ἐκ τῆς παλαίστρας, ὁ μὲν, ἤδη ἐξ ἐφήβων· ὁ δὲ ἕτερος, ἀμφὶ τὰ πεντεκαίδεκα ἔτη. καὶ ἀσπασάμενοι ἡμᾶς, ἐκαθέζοντο ἐπὶ τῆς κλίνης παρὰ τῷ πατρί· ἐμοὶ δέ, εἰσεκομίσθη θρόνος. καὶ ὁ Εὐκράτης ὥσπερ ἀναμνησθεὶς πρὸς τὴν ὄψιν τῶν υἱέων, οὕτως ὀναίμην ἔφη τούτων, ἐπιβαλὼν αὐτοῖν τὴν χεῖρα, ὡς ἀληθῆ ὦ Τυχιάδη πρὸς σὲ ἐρῶ. τὴν μακαρῖτίν μου γυναῖκα τὴν τούτων μητέρα, πάντες ἴσασιν ὅπως ἠγάπησα. ἐδήλωσα δέ, οἷς περὶ αὐτὴν ἔπραξα, οὐ ζῶσαν μόνον, ἀλλ' ἐπεὶ καὶ ἀπέθανε, τόν τε κόσμον ἅπαντα συγκατακαύσας, καὶ τὴν ἐσθῆτα, ᾗ ζῶσα ἔχαιρεν· ἑβδόμῃ δὲ μετὰ τὴν τελευτὴν ἡμέρᾳ, ἐγὼ μὲν ἐνταῦθα ἐπὶ τῆς κλίνης, ὥσπερ νῦν, ἐκείμην παραμυθούμενος τό γε πένθος· ἀνεγίγνωσκον γὰρ τὸ περὶ ψυχῆς τοῦ Πλάτωνος βιβλίον ἐφ' ἡσυχίας· ἐπεισέρχεται δὲ μεταξὺ ἡ Δημαινέτη αὐτὴ ἐκείνη, καὶ καθέζεται πλησίον, ὥσπερ νῦν Εὐκρατίδης οὑτοσί, δείξας τὸν νεώτερον τῶν υἱέων· ὁ δέ, αὐτίκα ἔφριξε μάλα παιδικῶς· καὶ πάλαι ἤδη ὠχρὸς ἦν πρὸς τὴν διήγησιν· ἐγὼ δ' ἦ δ' ὃς ὁ Εὐκράτης, ὡς εἶδον, περιπλακεὶς αὐτῇ, ἐδάκρυον ἀνακωκύσας· ἡ δέ, οὐκ εἴα βοᾶν· ἀλλ' ᾐτιᾶτό με ὅτι τὰ ἄλλα πάντα χαρισάμενος αὐτῇ, θάτερον τοῖν σανδάλοιν χρυσοῖν ὄντοιν, οὐ κατακαύσαιμι· εἶναι δὲ αὐτὸ ἔφασκε, παραπεσὸν ὑπὸ τῇ κιβωτῷ· καὶ διὰ τοῦτο ἡμεῖς οὐχ εὑρόντες, θάτερον μόνον ἐκαύσαμεν· ἔτι δὲ ἡμῶν διαλεγομένων, κατάρατόν τι κυνίδιον ὑπὸ τῇ κλίνῃ ὄν, μελιταῖον, ὑλάκτησεν. ἡ δέ, ἠφανίσθη πρὸς τὴν ὑλακήν· τὸ μέντοι σανδάλιον, εὑρέθη ὑπὸ τῇ κιβωτῷ, καὶ κατεκαύθη ὕστερον· ἔτι ἀπιστεῖν τούτοις ὦ Τυχιάδη ἄξιον ἐναργέσιν οὖσι, καὶ κατὰ τὴν ἡμέραν ἑκάστην φαινομένοις; μὰ Δί' ἦν δ' ἐγώ, ἐπεὶ σανδάλῳ γε χρυσῷ ἐς τὰς πυγάς, ὥσπερ τὰ παιδία, παίεσθαι ἄξιοι ἂν εἶεν οἱ ἀπιστοῦντες, καὶ οὕτως ἀναισχυντοῦντες πρὸς τὴν ἀλήθειαν· ἐπὶ τούτοις, ὁ Πυθαγορικὸς Ἀρίγνωτος εἰσῆλθεν, ὁ κομήτης, ὁ σεμνὸς ἀπὸ τοῦ προσώπου· οἶσθα τὸν ἀοίδιμον ἐπὶ τῇ σοφίᾳ, τὸν ἱερὸν ἐπονομαζόμενον. κἀγὼ μὲν ὡς εἶδον αὐτόν, ἀνέπνευσα· τοῦτ' ἐκεῖνο ἥκειν μοι νομίσας, πέλεκύν τινα κατὰ τῶν ψευσμάτων. ἐπιστομιεῖ γὰρ αὐτοὺς ἔλεγον ὁ σοφὸς ἀνήρ, οὕτω τεράστια διεξιόντας. καὶ τὸ τοῦ λόγου, θεὸν ἀπὸ μηχανῆς ἐπεισκληθῆναί μοι τοῦτον ᾤμην ἀπὸ τῆς

18 quemadmodum] quemadmonum [*sic*] *1506* 25 ob] *om. 1566* 27 quidam] *1506 1514 1516 1517 1519 1534 1563 1566*, quidem *1521 1528* 30 quotidieque] quoitdieque [*sic*] *1506* 30–31 obseruentur] seruantur *1506 1514 1516 1517 1519* 34 nosti] Nosti *1521*

postquam resurrexit, ipse curaui. Et quo pacto (inquam ego) in diebus uiginti, neque tabuit corpus, neque praeterea fame corruptum est, nisi fortassis Epimenidem quempiam tu curasti? Haec quum diceremus, protinus ingrediebantur Eucratis filij e palaestra redeuntes. Alter quidem iam ex ephebis excesserat, alter uero annos natus erat circiter quindecim. Tum salutatis nobis iuxta patrem adsidebant in lecto, ac mihi quidem sella illata est. Tum Eucrates tanquam e conspectu filiorum admonitus: sic his frui mihi contingat, inquit, simulque manum eis iniecit, ut apud te Tychiades uera narrabo. Felicis memoriae uxorem meam horum matrem nouerunt omnes, quo pacto dilexerim: Nam declaraui his rebus quas in eam feci, non modo dum uiueret: uerum etiam postquam uita functa est. Quippe qui mundum eius uniuersum uestemque qua dum uiueret, oblectabatur, in rogum illius iniecerim. Septima uero post mortem die, ego quidem hic in eundem lectum incumbebam: quemadmodum nunc, luctum eum mihi commitigans, quem de illa conceperam. Legebam enim tacitus Platonis illum de anima libellum. Ingreditur interim Demenete ea ipsa, atque adsidet iuxta: quemadmodum nunc Eucratides hic, minorem designans filium. Hic uero ilico tremuit admodum pueriliter, ac dudum ad narrationem pallebat. Ego uero (inquit Eucrates) ut conspexi, amplexus eam singultim lachrymabam. Illa uero me uociferari non patiebatur, uerum incusabat me, quod quum ei fuissem in reliquis gratificatus omnibus, e sandalijs aureis alterum non cremaueram, superesse autem id dicebat, quod sub arca ceciderat: atque ob id nos quum non inueniremus, alterum tantum cremaueramus. Nobis autem adhuc disserentibus scelestissimus quidam caniculus, qui mihi in delitijs erat, in lecto cubans allatrabat, ea uero ad latratum euanuit. At sandalium sub arca repertum est: posteaque a nobis incensum. An haec etiam Tychiades recusabis credere, quum tam sint euidentia, quotidieque obseruentur? Per Iouem, inquam ego, digni fuerint, quibus aureo sandalio nates puerorum more feriantur: si qui ista non credant, atque usque adeo impudenter uero resistant. Interea Pythagoricus intrabat Arignotus comatus ille, ab aspectu uenerabilis, nosti illum doctrinae nomine celebrem: qui cognominatur sacer. Atque ego quidem, ut eum conspexi, respiraui: hoc [z_5] ipsum, quod prouerbio dici solet, aduenisse mihi ratus: nempe securim quampiam aduersus mendacia: Occludet, inquam, eis ora uir sapiens: adeo monstrosa narrantibus: atque prorsus, iuxta uulgatum illud adagium, repente deum immissum

τύχης. ὁ δὲ, ἐπεὶ ἐκαθέζετο, ὑπεκστάντος αὐτῷ τοῦ κλεοδήμου, προσῆτα μὲν, περὶ τῆς νόσου ἤρετο· καὶ ὡς ῥᾷον ἤδη ἔχειν ἤκουσε παρὰ τοῦ Εὐκράτους, τί δὲ ἔφη πρὸς ἀλλήλους φιλοσοφεῖτε. μεταξὺ γὰρ εἰσιὼν, ἐπήκουσα· καί μοι δοκεῖτε εἰς καλὸν διατεθήσεσθαι τὴν διατριβήν· τί δ' ἄλλο εἶπεν ὁ Εὐκράτης, ἢ τουτονὶ τὸν ἀδαμάντινον πείθομεν, δείξας ἐμὲ, ἡγεῖσθαι δαίμονάς τινας εἶναι, καὶ φαντάσματα, καὶ νεκρῶν ψυχὰς περιπολεῖν ὑπὲρ γῆς, καὶ φαίνεσθαι οἷς ἂν ἐθέλωσιν· ἐγὼ μὲν οὖν ἠρυθρίασα, καὶ κάτω ἔνευσα, αἰδεσθεὶς τὸν Ἀρίγνωτον· ὁ δὲ, ὅρα ἔφη ὦ Εὔκρατες, μὴ τοῦτό φησι Τυχιάδης, τὰς τῶν βιαίως ἀποθανόντων μόνας ψυχὰς περινοστεῖν, οἷον εἴ τις ἀπήγξατο, ἢ ἀπετμήθη τὴν κεφαλὴν, ἢ ἀνεσκολοπίσθη, ἢ ἄλλῳ γέ τῳ τρόπῳ τοιούτῳ ἀπῆλθεν ἐκ τοῦ βίου, τὰς δὲ τῶν κατὰ μοῖραν ἀποθανόντων οὐκέτι· ἢν γὰρ τοῦτο λέγῃ, οὐ πάνυ ἀπόβλητα φήσει· μὰ Δί' ἦ δ' ὃς ὁ Δεινόμαχος, ἀλλ' οὐδὲ ὅλως εἶναι τὰ τοιαῦτα, οὐδὲ συνεστῶτα ὁρᾶσθαι οἴεται. πῶς λέγεις ἦ δ' ὃς ὁ Ἀρίγνωτος, δριμὺ ἀπιδὼν εἰς ἐμέ· οὐδέν σοι τούτων γίγνεσθαι δοκεῖ, καὶ ταῦτα, πάντων ὡς εἰπεῖν ὁρώντων; ἀπολελόγησθε ἦν δ' ἐγὼ ὑπὲρ ἐμοῦ, εἰ μὴ πιστεύω, διότι μὴ ὁρῶ μόνος τῶν ἄλλων· εἰ δὲ ἑώρων, καὶ ἐπίστευον ἂν δηλαδὴ, ὥσπερ ὑμεῖς· ἀλλὰ ἦ δ' ὃς ἤν ποτε ἐς Κόρινθον ἔλθῃς, ἐροῦ ἔνθα ἐστὶν ἡ Εὐβατίδου οἰκία· καὶ ἐπειδάν σοι δειχθῇ παρὰ τὸ Κράνειον, παρελθὼν ἐς αὐτὴν, λέγε πρὸς τὸν θυρωρὸν Τίβιον, ὡς ἐθέλοις ἰδεῖν ὅθεν τὸν δαίμονα ὁ Πυθαγορικὸς Ἀρίγνωτος ἀνορύξας, ἀπήλασε, καὶ πρὸς τὸ λοιπὸν οἰκεῖσθαι τὴν οἰκίαν ἐποίησε· τί δὲ τοῦτο ἦν ὦ Ἀρίγνωτε ἤρετο ὁ Εὐκράτης· ἀοίκητος ἦν ἦ δ' ὃς ἐκ πολλοῦ ὑπὸ δειμάτων. εἰ δέ τις οἰκήσειεν, εὐθὺς ἐκπλαγεὶς, ἔφευγεν ἐκδιωχθεὶς ὑπό τινος φοβεροῦ καὶ ταραχώδους φάσματος· συνέπιπτεν οὖν ἤδη, καὶ ἡ στέγη κατέρρει· καὶ ὅλως, οὐδεὶς ἦν ὁ θαρρήσων παρελθεῖν ἐς αὐτήν. ἐγὼ δὲ ἐπεὶ ταῦτα ἤκουσα, τὰς βίβλους λαβὼν, εἰσὶ δέ μοι αἰγύπτιαι μάλα πολλαὶ περὶ τῶν τοιούτων, ἧκον ἐς τὴν οἰκίαν περὶ πρῶτον ὕπνον, ἀποτρέποντος τοῦ ξένου, καὶ μονονοὺ ἐπιλαμβανομένου, ἐπεὶ ἔμαθεν οἷ βαδίζοιμι, ἐς προὖπτον κακὸν ὡς ᾤετο· ἐγὼ δὲ λύχνον λαβὼν, μόνος εἰσέρχομαι· καὶ ἐν τῷ μεγίστῳ οἰκήματι καταθεὶς τὸ φῶς, ἀνεγίγνωσκον ἡσυχῇ χαμαὶ καθεζόμενος. ἐφίσταται δὲ ὁ δαίμων, ἐπί τινα τῶν πολλῶν ἥκειν νομίζων, καὶ δεδίξεσθαι κἀμὲ ἐλπίζων, ὥσπερ τοὺς ἄλλους, αὐχμηρὸς, καὶ κομήτης, καὶ μελάντερος τοῦ ζόφου. καὶ ὁ μὲν, ἐπιστὰς, ἐπειρᾶτό μου πανταχόθεν προσβάλλων, εἴ ποθεν κρατήσειε· καὶ ἄρτι μὲν, κύων, ἄρτι δὲ, ταῦ

22 atque] Atque *1521* 25 reddiderit. Quidnam] reddiderit, Quidnam *1521* 30 sunt] Sunt *1521* 33 putabat, exitium] putabat exitium *1521* 36 quoque] quo que *1521*

esse mihi hunc a fortuna putabam. Hic uero postquam adsedit: assurgente ei ac cedente Cleodemo, primum de morbo percontatus est, seque audisse dicebat, Eucratem iam se melius habere. At quidnam inquit, inter uos philosophamini? Nam interim dum ingrediebar subauscultaui, ac mihi certe uidemini in re quapiam pulchra conuersari. Quid aliud, inquit Eucrates, quam ut huic adamantino persuadeamus (me demonstrans) ut daemones credat aliquos esse, phantasmataque, ac mortuorum animas super terram obambulare, & sese quibus libitum fuerit ostendere? Ego igitur erubui, uultumque deieci reueritus Arignotum. At ille, uide (inquit) Eucrates num hoc dicat Tychiades. Eorum tantum qui uiolenter interierint, animas errare, ueluti si quis suffocatus, aut capite truncatus, cruciue suffixus fuerit, aut alio quopiam istiusmodi modo e uita discesserit, eas uero quae fatali morte naturalique discesserint, haud quaquam amplius oberrare. Nam si hoc dicat, non usque adeo absurda dixerit. Per Iouem inquit Dinomachus, ne esse quidem istiusmodi, nec praesentia cerni putat. Quid ais, inquit Arignotus? in me torue aspiciens, nihil horum tibi uidetur fieri? praesertim quum omnes (ut ita dicam) uideant? Ignosces, inquam ego, mihi, si non credo, nam solus omnium non uideo. Quod si uidissem, profecto & credidissem quemadmodum & uos. Atqui, inquit ille, si quando Corinthum ueneris, roga ubi sit Eubatidae domus, atque ubi tibi fuerit indicata, nempe circa Craneum, in eam ingressus, dic ianitori Tibio, uelle te uidere, unde daemonem Pythagoricus Arignotus quum adduxisset, abegerit, ac deinceps habitabilem domum reddiderit. Quidnam hoc erat Arignote? rogabat Eucrates. Inhabitabilis erat, inquit ille, diu propter terricula, quod si quis inhabitasset, expauefactus ilico fugiebat exactus a quodam horrendo ac terribili spectro. Deciderat ergo iam, tectumque rumpebatur, neque quisquam erat omnino qui in eam ingredi fuerit ausus. Ego uero ubi haec audiui, libellos sumens (sunt autem Aegyptij mihi de talibus rebus admodum multi) ueni in domum circa primam uigiliam, dehortante hospite, ac ferme detinente, postquam didicerat quo iturus essem, in certum, ut putabat, exitium. At ego sumpta lucerna solus ingredior, atque in uastissimo atrio collocato lumine, humi sedens tacite legebam. Adest uero daemon ille, cum quopiam e uulgo se congressurum ratus, ac me quoque quemadmodum alios perterriturum squallidus, hirsutus, ac tenebris nigrior. Atque hic quum adstaret, undique me adsultim petens tentauit, si qua posset expugnare, ac modo in canem, modo in taurum, modo

ρος γιγνόμενος, ἢ λέων. ἐγὼ δὲ προχειρισάμενος τὴν φρικωδεστάτην ἐπίρρησιν, αἰγυπτιάζων τῇ φωνῇ, συνήλασα κατᾴδων αὐτὸν εἴς τινα γωνίαν σκοτεινοῦ οἰκήματος. ἰδὼν δὲ αὐτὸν οἷ κατέδυ, τὸ λοιπὸν ἀνεπαυόμην. ἕωθεν δὲ πάντων ἀπεγνωκότων, καὶ νεκρὸν εὑρήσειν με οἰομένων, καθάπερ τοὺς ἄλλους, προελθὼν ἀπροσδόκητος ἅπασι, πρόσειμι τῷ Εὐβατίδῃ, εὐαγγελιζόμενος αὐτῷ, ὅτι καθαρὰν αὐτῷ, καὶ ἀδείμαντον ἤδη ἕξει τὴν οἰκίαν οἰκεῖν. καὶ παραλαβὼν αὐτόν τε, καὶ τῶν ἄλλων πολλούς, εἵποντο γὰρ τοῦ παραδόξου ἕνεκα, ἐκέλευον ἀγαγὼν ἐπὶ τὸν τόπον, οὗ καταδεδυκότα τὸν δαίμονα ἑωράκειν, σκάπτειν, λαβόντας δικέλλας, καὶ σκαφεῖα. καὶ ἐπειδὴ ἐποίησαν, εὑρέθη ὡς ἐπ' ὀργυιὰν κατορωρυγμένος τις νεκρὸς ἕωλος, μόνα τὰ ὀστᾶ κατὰ σχῆμα συγκείμενος. ἐκεῖνον μὲν οὖν ἐθάψαμεν ἀνορύξαντες. ἡ οἰκία δὲ τὸ ἀπ' ἐκείνου ἐπαύσατο, ἐνοχλουμένη ὑπὸ τῶν φασμάτων. ὡς δὲ ταῦτα εἶπεν ὁ Ἀρίγνωτος, ἀνὴρ δαιμόνιος τὴν σοφίαν, καὶ ἅπασιν αἰδέσιμος, οὐδεὶς ἦν ἔτι τῶν παρόντων, ὃς οὐχὶ κατεγίγνωσκέ μου πολλὴν τὴν ἄνοιαν, τοῖς τοιούτοις ἀπιστοῦντος. καὶ ταῦτα, Ἀριγνώτου λέγοντος. ἐγὼ δὲ ὅμως οὐδὲν τρέσας, οὔτε τὴν κόμην, οὔτε τὴν δόξαν τὴν περὶ αὐτοῦ, τί τοῦτ' ἔφην ὦ Ἀρίγνωτε, καὶ σὺ τοιοῦτος ἦσθα, ἡ μόνη ἐλπὶς τῆς ἀληθείας, καπνοῦ μεστὸς, καὶ ἰνδαλμάτων; τὸ γοῦν τοῦ λόγου ἐκεῖνο, ἄνθρακες ἡμῖν ὁ θησαυρὸς πέφηνας. σὺ δὲ ἦ δ' ὃς ὁ Ἀρίγνωτος, εἰ μήτε ἐμοὶ πιστεύεις λέγοντι, μήτε Δεινομάχῳ, ἢ Κλεοδήμῳ τουτῳί, μήτε αὐτῷ Εὐκράτει, φέρε εἰπὲ τίνα περὶ τῶν τοιούτων ἀξιοπιστότερον ἡγῇ τἀναντία ἡμῖν λέγοντα. νὴ Δί' ἦν δ' ἐγὼ μάλα θαυμαστὸν ἄνδρα, τὸν Ἀβδηρόθεν ἐκεῖνον Δημόκριτον, ὃς οὕτως ἄρα ἐπέπειστο μηδὲν οἷόν τε εἶναι συστῆναι τοιοῦτον, ὥστ' ἐπειδὴ καθείρξας ἑαυτὸν ἐς μνῆμα ἔξω πυλῶν, ἐνταῦθα διετέλει γράφων, καὶ συντάττων καὶ νύκτωρ, καὶ μεθ' ἡμέραν. καί τινες τῶν νεανίσκων, ἐρεσχελεῖν βουλόμενοι αὐτὸν, καὶ δειματοῦν, σεσαγμένοι νεκρικῶς ἐσθῆτι μελαίνῃ, καὶ προσωπείοις ἐς τὰ κρανία μεμιμημένοις περιστάντες αὐτὸν, περιεχόρευον ὑπὸ πυκνῇ τῇ βάσει ἀναπηδῶντες. ὁ δὲ, οὔτε ἔδεισε τὴν προσποίησιν αὐτῶν, οὔτε ὅλως ἀνέβλεψε πρὸς αὐτούς. ἀλλὰ μεταξὺ γράφων, παύσασθε ἔφη παίζοντες. οὕτω βεβαίως ἐπίστευε μηδὲν εἶναι τὰς ψυχὰς ἔτι ἔξω γενομένας τῶν σωμάτων. τοῦτο φὴς ἦ δ' ὃς ὁ Εὐκράτης, ἀνόητόν τινα ἄνδρα καὶ τὸν Δημόκριτον γενέσθαι, εἴγε οὕτως ἐγίγνωσκεν. ἐγὼ δὲ ὑμῖν καὶ ἄλλο διηγήσομαι αὐτὸς παθὼν, οὐ παρ' ἄλλου ἀκούσας. τάχα γὰρ ἂν καὶ σὺ ὦ Τυχιάδη ἀκούων, προσβιβασθείης πρὸς

2 Aegyptiam, &] & egyptiam *1506*, egyptiam *1516 1519* 7 Eubatidem] Eubatedem *1506 1516* 11 suffoderent] suffoderenr [*sic*] *1521* 34–35 inquit, ineptire] inquit ineptire *1521*

in [z5v] leonem uertebatur. At ego correpto in manum quam maxime horrendo carmine, simulque uocem imitatus Aegyptiam, & incantans eum in domicilij tenebrosi angulum quendam compuli. At quum animaduertissem, ubi se in terram condidit, tum destiti. Mane autem desperantibus uniuersis, ac me quemadmodum alios mortuum sese reperturos putantibus, praeter omnium spem progrediens, Eubatidem adeo, feliciter illi adnuncians, quod puram sibi ac spectris liberam domum iam liceret incolere. Atque illum assumens aliosque multos (sequebantur autem huius inopinatae rei gratia) quum ad locum duxissem, ubi condentem se daemona conspexeram, iussi ut sumptis ligonibus matulisque suffoderent. Atque ubi id fecerant, inuentum est fere ad passum defossum cadauer quoddam marcidum, ossibus tantum humana specie cohaerentibus: Illud igitur effossum sepeliuimus, domus uero postea turbari prodigijs desijt. Haec ubi narrauit Arignotus, uir prodigiosa sapientia, ac reuerendus omnibus, nemo erat ex his qui aderant, qui non multam mihi imputaret insaniam, qui talia non credam, narrante praesertim Arignoto. Ego tamen nihil ueritus neque comam, neque illam quam de eo habebant opinionem. Quid hoc inquam Arignote? Etiam tu talis eras, in quo mihi sola spes fuit, fumo plenus ac simulacris? Illud ergo nobis in te quod dici solet, euenit: ut thesaurum quum sperauerimus, carbones offenderimus. At tu, inquit Arignotus, si neque mihi credis narranti, neque Dinomacho, aut huic Cleodemo, neque ipsi Eucrati, dic age quemnam digniorem, cui his de rebus fides habeatur, existimas: qui nobis dicat contraria? Per Iouem, inquam ego uirum apprime mirabilem Abdera oriundum illum Democritum, cui tam firmiter erat persuasum eiusmodi nihil esse in rerum natura posse, ut quum se in monimento extra portas clausisset, ibique degeret dies noctesque scribens atque componens, iuuenesque eum quidam illudere cupientes ac perterrefacere, nigra ueste in modum cadaueris ornati, ac personis in capita adfictis circumsistentes, illum circumsilirent, crebro subsilientes: hic neque eorum commenta pertimuerit, neque eos omnino respexerit, sed inter scribendum: desistite, inquit, ineptire. Adeo firmiter credidit animas nihil esse postquam e corporibus exierint. Hoccine ais, inquit Eucrates, dementem quempiam uirum esse Democritum? siquidem sic existimauit. Ego uero uobis etiam aliud referam, quod mihi ipsi contigit, non quod ab alio acceperim, fortassis etiam tu Tychiades quum audieris, compelleris

τὴν ἀλήθειαν τοῦ διηγήματος. ὁπότε γὰρ ἐν Αἰγύπτῳ διῆγον, ἔτι νέος ὤν, ὑπὸ τοῦ πατρὸς ἐπὶ παιδείας προφάσει ἀποσταλείς, ἐπεθύμησα ἐς Κοπτὸν ἀναπλεύσας, ἐκεῖθεν ἐπὶ τὸν Μέμνονα ἐλθὼν, ἀκοῦσαι τὸ θαυμαστὸν ἐκεῖνο ἠχοῦντα, πρὸς ἀνίσχοντα τὸν ἥλιον. ἐκείνου μὲν οὖν ἤκουσα, οὐ κατὰ τὸ κοινὸν τοῖς πολλοῖς, ἄσημόν τινα φωνήν, ἀλλά μοι καὶ ἔχρησεν ὁ Μέμνων αὐτός, ἀνοίξας τὸ στόμα ἐν ἔπεσιν ἑπτά. καὶ εἴ γε μὴ περιττὸν ἦν, αὐτὰ ἂν ὑμῖν εἶπον τὰ ἔπη. κατὰ δὲ τὸν ἀνάπλουν, ἔτυχεν ἡμῖν συμπλέων Μεμφίτης ἀνὴρ τῶν ἱερῶν γραμματέων, θαυμάσιος τὴν σοφίαν, καὶ τὴν παιδείαν πᾶσαν εἰδὼς τὴν αἰγύπτιον. ἐλέγετο δὲ τρία καὶ εἴκοσιν ἔτη ἐν τοῖς ἀδύτοις ὑπόγειος ᾠκηκέναι, μαγεύειν παιδευόμενος ὑπὸ τῆς Ἴσιδος. Παγκράτην ἔφη λέγεις ὁ Ἀρίγνωτος, ἐμὸν διδάσκαλον, ἱερὸν ἄνδρα, ἐξυρημένον ἐν ὀθονίοις, νοήμονα, καθαρῶς ἑλληνίζοντα, ἐπιμήκη, σιμόν, πρόχειλον, ὑπόλεπτον τὰ σκέλη. αὐτὸν ἦν δ' ὃς ἐκεῖνον τὸν Παγκράτην. καὶ τὰ μὲν πρῶτα, ἠγνόουν ὅστις ἦν. ἐπεὶ δὲ ἑώρων αὐτὸν, εἴποτε ὁρμίσαιμεν τὸ πλοῖον, ἄλλα τε πολλὰ τεράστια ἐργαζόμενον, καὶ δὴ καὶ ἐπὶ κροκοδείλων ὀχούμενον, καὶ συννέοντα τοῖς θηρίοις, τὰ δὲ, ὑποπτήσσοντα, καὶ σαίνοντα ταῖς οὐραῖς, ἔγνων ἱερόν τινα ἄνθρωπον ὄντα. καὶ κατὰ μικρὸν φιλοφρονούμενος, ἔλαθον ἑταῖρος αὐτῷ, καὶ συνήθης γενόμενος. ὥστε πάντων ἐκοινώνει μοι τῶν ἀπορρήτων. καὶ τέλος, πείθει με, τοὺς μὲν οἰκέτας ἅπαντας, ἐν τῇ Μέμφιδι καταλιπεῖν, αὐτὸν δὲ μόνον ἀκολουθεῖν μετ' αὐτοῦ, μὴ γὰρ ἀπορήσειν ἡμᾶς τῶν διακονησομένων. καὶ τὸ μετὰ τοῦτο, οὕτω διήγομεν. ἐπειδὴ δὲ ἔλθοιμεν εἴς τι καταγώγιον, λαβὼν ἂν ὁ ἀνὴρ τὸν μοχλὸν τῆς θύρας, ἢ τὸ κόρηθρον, ἢ καὶ τὸ ὕπερον, περιβαλὼν ἱματίοις, ἐπειπών τινα ἐπῳδὴν, ἐποίει βαδίζειν, τοῖς ἄλλοις ἅπασιν ἄνθρωπον εἶναι δοκοῦντα. τὸ δὲ, ἀπελθὸν, ὕδωρ τε ἀνήντλει, καὶ ὠψώνει, καὶ ἐσκεύαζε, καὶ ἐς πάντα δεξιῶς ὑπηρέτει, καὶ διηκονεῖτο ἡμῖν. εἶτα δὲ ἐπειδὴ ἅλις ἔχοι τῆς διακονίας, αὖθις κόρηθρον τὸ κόρηθρον, ἢ ὕπερον τὸ ὕπερον, ἄλλην ἐπῳδὴν ἐπειπὼν, ἐποίει ἄν. τοῦτο ἐγὼ πάνυ ἐσπουδακὼς, οὐκ εἶχον ὅπως ἐκμάθοιμι παρ' αὐτοῦ. ἐβάσκαινε γὰρ αὐτὸ, καίτοι πρὸς τὰ ἄλλα προχειρότατος ὤν. μιᾷ δέ ποτε ἡμέρᾳ λαθὼν, ἐπήκουσα τῆς ἐπῳδῆς, ἦν δὲ τρισύλλαβος, σχεδὸν ἐν σκοτεινῷ ὑποστάς. καὶ ὁ μὲν, ᾤχετο ἐς τὴν ἀγορὰν, ἐντειλάμενος τῷ ὑπέρῳ ἃ ἔδει ποιεῖν. ἐγὼ δὲ, ἐς τὴν ὑστεραίαν ἐκείνου τι κατὰ τὴν ἀγορὰν πραγματευομένου, λαβὼν τὸ ὕπερον, σχηματίσας, ὁμοίως ἐπειπὼν τὰς συλλαβὰς, ἐκέλευον ὑδροφορεῖν. ἐπεὶ δὲ ἐμπλη

3–4 Memnonem] Mennonem [*sic*] *1506*

accedere, ipsa narrationis ueritate coactus. Quum in Aegypto uersarer adhuc adolescens, a patre uidelicet doctrinae gratia transmissus, cupiebam nauigio profectus in Coptum illinc adiens Memnonem, miraculum illud audire, eum uidelicet sonum reddentem ad orientem solem. Illum igitur audiui non hoc [z_6] uulgari modo, quo audiunt alij sonum quempiam inanem, sed mihi oracula etiam aedidit Memnon ipse aperto ore septem uersibus, quod nisi esset superuacaneum, ipsos uobis uersus recenserem. Inter nauigandum uero incidit in nos una nauigans uir Memphiticus quidam, ex sacris illis scribis, mirabili sapientia, & qui uniuersam Aegyptiorum doctrinam callebat. Dicebatur autem tres ac uiginti annos in adytis subterraneis mansisse, Magiam interea doctus ab Iside. Pancratem dicis (inquit Arignotus) praeceptorem meum, uirum sacrum, rasum, lineis indutum, doctum, pureque lingua Graeca loquentem, procerum, simum, labijs promissis, cruribusque gracilibus. Illum ipsum inquit ille, Pancratem, ac primum quidem quis esset ignorabam. At postquam uidi eum, si quando in portum appulissemus, cum alia multa miracula facientem, tum crocodilis insidentem agitasse, & cum feris uersantem, illas uero reuerentes eum, caudisque adulantes, agnoui sacrum quempiam uirum esse, paulatimque comitate mea me in eius amicitiam ac familiaritatem insinuaui, adeo ut omnia arcana communicaret. Ac tandem mihi persuadet, ut famulis omnibus in Memphide relictis, se solus consequerer, neque enim defuturos nobis ministros. Atque ex eo tempore sic uitam duximus. Quum in diuersorium quodpiam ueniremus, homo accepto pistillo, scobinaue, aut pessulo, uestibus implicans, quum in id carmen quoddam dixisset, effecit ut ambularet, utque alijs omnibus homo uideretur. Illud ergo abiens, & aquam hauriebat, & coenam parabat, instruebatque, atque in omnibus commode subseruiebat ministrabatque nobis. Deinde postquam iam satis huius ministerij fuit, scobinam rursus scobinam, ac pessulum, pessulum aliud recitans carmen reddebat. Hoc ego uehementer conatus non reperiebam, quo pacto ab illo expiscarer. Nam id mihi inuidebat, quanquam in alijs esset facillimus. At quadam die in angulo quodam tenebricoso clam illo delitescens subauscultaui propius incantationem illam. Erat autem trisyllaba. Tum ille quum pistillo mandasset quae curanda erant, abijt in forum. At ego postridie illo apud forum occupato, acceptum pistillum quum ornassem, syllabas illas simili modo pronuncians, aquam iussi ut hauriret. Tum impletam amphoram quum tulisset,

σάμενος τὸν ἀμφορέα ἐκόμισε, πέπαυσο ἔφην, καὶ μηκέτι ὑδροφόρει, ἀλλ' ἴσθι αὖθις ὕπερον. τὸ δὲ, οὐκέτι μοι πείθεσθαι ἤθελεν, ἀλλ' ὑδροφόρει ἀεί, ἄχρι δὴ ἐνέπλησεν ἡμῖν ὕδατος τὴν οἰκίαν ἐπαντλοῦν. ἐγὼ δὲ ἀμηχανῶν τῷ πράγματι, ἐδεδίειν γὰρ μὴ ὁ Παγκράτης ἐπανελθὼν ἀγανακτήσῃ, ὅπερ καὶ ἐγένετο, ἀξίνην λαβὼν, διακόπτω τὸ ὕπερον εἰς δύο μέρη. τὰ δὲ, ἑκάτερον τὸ μέρος, ἀμφορέα λαβόντα, ὑδροφόρει, καὶ ἀνθ' ἑνὸς, δύο μοι ἐγένοντο οἱ διάκονοι. ἐν τούτῳ καὶ ὁ Παγκράτης ἐφίσταται. καὶ συνεὶς τὸ γενόμενον, ἐκεῖνα μὲν αὖθις ἐποίησε ξύλα, ὥσπερ ἦν πρὸ τῆς ἐπῳδῆς. αὐτὸς δὲ ἀπολιπών με λαθὼν, οὐκ οἶδ' ὅποι ἀφανὴς ᾤχετο ἀπιών. νῦν οὖν ἔφη ὁ Δεινόμαχος οἶσθα κἂν ἐκεῖνο ἄνθρωπον ποιεῖν ἐκ τοῦ ὑπέρου; νὴ Δί' ἦ δ' ὃς ἐξ ἡμισείας γε. οὐκέτι γὰρ εἰς τὸ ἀρχαῖον οἷόν τέ μοι ἀπάγειν αὐτό, ἢν ἅπαξ γένηται ὑδροφόρος, ἀλλὰ δεήσει ἡμῖν ἐπικλυσθῆναι τὴν οἰκίαν ἐπαντλουμένην. οὐ παύσεσθε ἦν δ' ἐγὼ τὰ τοιαῦτα τερατολογοῦντες γέροντες ἄνδρες; εἰ δὲ μή, ἀλλὰ κἂν τῶν μειρακίων τούτων ἕνεκα εἰς ἄλλον καιρὸν ὑπερβάλλεσθε τὰς παραδόξους ταύτας, καὶ φοβερὰς διηγήσεις, μή πως λάθωσιν ἡμῖν ἐμπλησθέντες δειμάτων, καὶ ἀλλοκότων μυθολογημάτων. φείδεσθαι οὖν χρὴ αὐτῶν, μηδὲ τοιαῦτα ἐθίζειν ἀκούειν, ἃ διὰ παντὸς τοῦ βίου ἐνοχλήσει συνόντα, καὶ ψοφοδεεῖς ποιήσει, ποικίλης τῆς δεισιδαιμονίας ἐμπιπλάντα. εὖ γε ὑπέμνησας ἦ δ' ὃς ὁ Εὐκράτης, εἰπὼν τὴν δεισιδαιμονίαν. τί γάρ σοι ὦ Τυχιάδη, περὶ τῶν τοιούτων δοκεῖ, λέγω δὴ χρησμῶν, καὶ θεσφάτων, καὶ ὅσα θεοφορούμενοί τινες ἀναβοῶσιν, ἢ ἐξ ἀδύτων ἀκούεται, ἢ παρθένος ἔμμετρα φθεγγομένη, προθεσπίζει τὰ μέλλοντα, ἢ δῆλα δὴ καὶ τοῖς τοιούτοις ἀπιστήσεις. ἐγὼ δὲ, ὅτι μὲν καὶ δακτύλιόν τινα ἱερὸν ἔχω, Ἀπόλλωνος τοῦ Πυθίου εἰκόνα ἐκτυποῦσαν τῆς σφραγῖδος, καὶ οὗτος ὁ Ἀπόλλων φθέγγεται πρὸς ἐμέ, οὐ λέγω, μή σοι ἄπιστα δόξω περὶ ἐμαυτοῦ μεγαλαυχεῖσθαι. ἃ δὲ ἐν Ἀμφιλόχου τε ἤκουσα ἐν Μαλλῷ τοῦ ἥρωος ὑπερδιαλεχθέντος μοι, καὶ συμβουλεύσαντος ὑπὲρ τῶν ἐμῶν, καὶ ἃ εἶδον αὐτός, ἐθέλω ὑμῖν εἰπεῖν. εἶτα ἑξῆς ἃ ἐν Περγάμῳ εἶδον, καὶ ἤκουσα ἐν Πατάροις. ὁπότε γὰρ ἐξ Αἰγύπτου ἐπανῄειν οἴκαδε, ἀκούων τὸ ἐν Μαλλῷ τοῦτο μαντεῖον, ἐπιφανέστατόν τε, καὶ ἀληθέστατον εἶναι, καὶ χρᾶν ἐναργῶς, πρὸς ἔπος ἀποκρινόμενον, οἷς ἂν ἐγγράψας τις εἰς τὸ γραμματεῖον παραδῷ τῷ προφήτῃ, καλῶς ἂν ἔχειν ἡγησάμην ἐν παράπλῳ πειραθῆναι τοῦ χρηστηρίου, καί τι περὶ μελλόντων συμβουλεύσασθαι τῷ θεῷ. ταῦτα ἔτι τοῦ Εὐκράτους λέγοντος, ἰδὼν οἷ τὸ πρᾶγμα προχωρήσειν ἔμελλε, καὶ ὡς οὐ περὶ μικρᾶς ἐνήρχετο τῆς περὶ τὰ χρηστήρια

8 superuenit] superauit *1516 1519* 24 numine] minime *1566* 26 praedicit] praecedit *1566* 30 Mallo, heroe] Mallo heroe, *1521*

desiste inquam, neque aquam amplius haurito, sed rursus esto pistillum. At illud mihi haud amplius iam obtemperare uolebat, sed aquam hauriebat continue, quoad hauriendo totam domum nobis impleret. At ego quum resistere huic rei non ualerem, timebam autem ne Pancrates reuersus (id quod etiam euenit) irasceretur, correpta secure pistillum in duas partes disseco. At utraque pars amphoram sumens hauriebat aquam, iamque unius loco duo mihi ministri esse coeperunt. Interea Pancrates superuenit, ac re intellecta illas quidem in ligna rursus, quemadmodum ante carmen erant, mutauit. At ipse me clanculum [z6v] relicto, nescio quo clanculum se subducens abijt. At possis istud etiam nunc inquit Dinomachus, hominem ex pistillo facere? Per Iouem inquit ille, dimidia ex parte scio, nam in priorem formam nunquam a me restitui potest, postquam semel aquarius esse coeperit. Sed deserenda nobis domus esset aquae iam impleta. Non desistitis inquam ego, huiusmodi monstrosa narrare uiri senes? Alioqui horum saltem adolescentium gratia incredibiles istas ac terribiles fabulas aliud in tempus omittite, ne clanculum terroribus ac prodigiosis fabulamentis impleantur. Parcere ergo eis oportet, ne talia consuescant audire, quae eos per totam uitam comitata perturbabunt, atque ad omnem strepitum meticulosos reddent, posteaquam eos omnigena superstitione impleuerint. Recte admonuisti me, inquit Eucrates, quum superstitionem dixisti. Nam quid tibi Tychiade de rebus huiusmodi uidetur: de oraculis loquor ac uaticinijs, & quaecunque quidam numine afflati proclamant, quaeue ex adytis audiuntur? aut quae uirgo numeris eloquens futura praedicit? an uidelicet nec talia credis? At ego quod anulum quendam sacrum habeo, Pythij Apollinis imaginem exprimente sigillo, quodque hic Apollo mecum loquitur, non dico, ne tibi uidear ad gloriam meam res incredibiles narrare. Caeterum quae apud Amphilochum audiui in Mallo, heroe mecum diu disserente, deumque meis de rebus consulente, tum quae ipse uidi, uolo uobis narrare. Deinde ex ordine & quae uidi in Pergamo, & quae audiui in Pataris. Itaque quum ex Aegypto redirem domum, audiremque illud in Mallo uaticinium apertissimum, simul ac uerissimum esse, tamen sic oracula dare, ut ad rem respondeat his, quaecunque prophetae quispiam in schedulam inscripta tradiderit, recte me facturum putaui, si dum praeternauigarem, experirer oraculum, deumque de futuris quippiam consulerem. Haec adhuc Eucrate dicente, quum uiderem quam longe res esset processura,

τραγῳδίας, οὐ δοκεῖ οἰηθεὶς δεῖν μόνος ἀντιλέγειν ἅπασιν, ἀπολιπὼν αὐτὸν ἔτι διαπλέοντα ἐξ Αἰγύπτου εἰς τὴν μαλλὸν, καὶ γὰρ συνίην ὅτι μοι ἄχθονται παρόντι, καθάπερ ἀντισοφιστῇ τῶν ψευσμάτων, ἀλλ' ἐγὼ ἄπειμι ἔφην Λεόντιχον ἐπιζητήσων· δέομαι γὰρ αὐτῷ τι συγγενέσθαι. ὑμεῖς δὲ, ἐπεὶ οὐχ ἱκανὰ ἡγεῖσθε τὰ ἀνθρώπινα εἶναι, καὶ αὐτοὺς ἤδη τοὺς θεοὺς καλεῖτε συνεπιληψομένους ὑμῖν τῶν μυθολογουμένων. καὶ ἅμα λέγων, ἐξῄειν· οἱ δὲ, ἄσμενοι ἐλευθερίας λαβόμενοι, εἱστίων ὡς τὸ εἰκὸς αὐτοὺς, καὶ ἐνεφοροῦντο τῶν ψευσμάτων· τοιαῦτά σοι ὦ Φιλόκλεις, παρὰ Εὐκράτει ἀκούσας, ἥκω νὴ τὸν Δία, ὥσπερ οἱ τοῦ γλεύκους πιόντες, ἐμπεφυσημένος τὴν γαστέρα, ἐμέτου δεόμενος· ἡδέως δ' ἂν ποθεν ὠνῆ πολλῷ ἐπριάμην ληθεδανόν τι φάρμακον, ὧν ἤκουσα, ὡς μή τι κακὸν ἐργάσηταί με ἡ μνήμη αὐτῶν ἐνοικουροῦσα· τέρατα γοῦν, καὶ δαίμονας, καὶ Ἑκάτας ὁρᾶν μοι δοκῶ· καὶ αὐτὸς ὦ Τυχιάδη, τοιοῦτόν τι ἀπήλαυσα τῆς διηγήσεως· φασὶ γέ τοι μὴ μόνον λυττᾶν, καὶ τὸ ὕδωρ φοβεῖσθαι, ὁπόσους ἂν οἱ λυττῶντες κύνες δάκωσιν, ἀλλὰ κἄν τινα ὁ δηχθεὶς ἄνθρωπος δάκῃ, ἴσα τῷ κυνὶ δύναται τὸ δῆγμα· καὶ τὰ αὐτὰ κἀκεῖνος φοβεῖται. καὶ σὺ τοίνυν ἔοικας αὐτὸς ἐν Εὐκράτους δηχθεὶς ὑπὸ πολλῶν ψευσμάτων, μεταδεδωκέναι κἀμοὶ τοῦ δήγματος· οὕτω δαιμόνων μοι τὴν ψυχὴν ἐνέπλησας. ἀλλὰ θαῤῥῶμεν ὦ φιλότης, μέγα τῶν τοιούτων ἀλεξιφάρμακον ἔχοντες τὴν ἀλήθειαν, καὶ τὸν ἐπὶ πᾶσι λόγον ὀρθόν. ᾧ χρωμένους ἡμᾶς, οὐδὲν οὐ μὴ ταράξῃ τῶν κενῶν καὶ ματαίων τούτων ψευσμάτων.

16 Tychiade] Tychade [*sic*] *1506* 25 habeamus] habemus *1534 1563 1566* 28–29 LVCIANI PHILOPSEVDVS SEV INCREDVLI, THOMA MORO INTERPRETE, FINIS] Luciani Philopseudus seu increduli finis *1506 1514*, *om.* *1516 1519 1534 1563 1566*
28 PHILOPSEVDVS Philopseudes *1528*

quodque non breuem incepisset de oraculo Tragoediam, ratus non expedire, uti solus contradicerem omnibus, relinquens eum ex Aegypto adhuc in Mallum nauigantem. Nam & intelligebam molestam illis esse praesentiam meam, utpote qui dissentirem refelleremque eorum mendacia. Atqui ego abeo, inquam, quaesiturus Leonticum, nam opus habeo cum eo congredi. At uos quandoquidem parum sufficere uobis res humanas putatis, ipsos etiam deos denique in fabularum uobis partem uocate. Atque haec simul ac dixi, discessi. Illi uero alacres iam libertatem nacti, ut est uerisimile, mutuo sese epulis accipiebant, ac mendacijs ingurgitabant. Talibus o Philocles apud Eucratem auditis, uenio per Iouem inflato uentre, non aliter quam hi qui musto poti sunt, opus habens uomitu. Tum libenter alicunde magno emerim pharmacum aliquod, quod mihi obliuionem induceret eorum, quae audiui, ne me non[A_1]nihil earum rerum laedat inhaerens memoria: nempe monstra, daemones, atque Hecates mihi uidere uideor. PHILO. Quin mihi quoque o Tychiade, tale quiddam hic sermo tuus attulit: aiunt etenim non solum in rabiem uerti, atque aquam formidare, quoscunque rabidi canes mordeant, uerumetiam si quem mordicus homo morsus momorderit, illum morsum quoque non minus canino ualiturum, atque eum etiam eodem modo formidaturum. Quin tu ergo uideris, quum sis ipse apud Eucratem a multis mendacijs morsus, mihi quoque morsum illum communicasse, adeo mihi mentem daemonibus impleuisti. TYCH. At bono animo simus amice, quum magnum aduersus huiusmodi res remedium habeamus, ueritatem rectamque omnibus in rebus rationem, quo si utamur, nullis huiusmodi uanis stultisque mendacijs turbabimur.

LVCIANI PHILOPSEVDVS SEV INCREDVLI, THOMA MORO INTERPRETE, FINIS.

ΤΥΡΑΝΝΟΚΤΟΝΟΣ·

Ἀνῆλθέ τις εἰς τὴν ἀκρόπολιν ὡς ἀποκτενῶν τὸν τύραννον· καὶ αὐτὸν μὲν οὐχ εὗρε· τὸν δὲ
υἱὸν αὐτοῦ ἀποκτείνας, κατέλιπε τὸ ξίφος ἐν τῷ σώματι· ἐλθὼν ὁ τύραννος, καὶ
τὸν υἱὸν ἰδὼν ἤδη νεκρὸν, τῷ αὐτῷ ξίφει ἑαυτὸν ἀπέκτεινεν. αἰτεῖ ὁ ἀνελ
θὼν, καὶ τὸν τοῦ τυράννου υἱὸν ἀνελὼν, γέρας, ὡς τυραννοκτόνος·

Υο τυράννους ἀποκτείνας ὦ ἄνδρες δικασταὶ μιᾶς ἡμέρας, τὸν μὲν, ἤδη πα-
δ ρηβηκότα, τὸν δὲ, ἀκμάζοντα, καὶ πρὸς διαδοχὴν τῶν ἀδικημάτων ἑτοιμότε-
ρον, ἥκω μίαν ὅμως ἐπ' ἀμφοτέροις αἰτήσων δωρεὰν, μόνος τῶν πώποτε τυραννοκτόνων πληγῇ μιᾷ δύο πονηροὺς ἀποσκευασάμενος, καὶ φονεύσας, τὸν
μὲν παῖδα, τῷ ξίφει· τὸν πατέρα δὲ, τῇ πρὸς τὸν υἱὸν φιλοστοργίᾳ· ὁ μὲν οὖν τύραννος, ἀνθ' ὧν
ἐποίησεν, ἱκανὴν ἡμῖν δέδωκε τιμωρίαν, ζῶν μὲν, τὸν υἱὸν ἐπιδὼν προανῃρημένον παρὰ τὴν
τελευτήν· τελευταῖον δὲ, ἠναγκασμένος τὸ παραδοξότατον αὐτὸς αὑτοῦ γενέσθαι τυ-
ραννοκτόνος· ὁ παῖς δὲ ὁ ἐκείνου τέθνηκε μὲν ὑπ' ἐμοῦ, ὑπηρέτησε δέ μοι καὶ ἀποθανὼν πρὸς
ἄλλον φόνον, ζῶντι μὲν συναδικῶν τῷ πατρὶ, μετὰ θάνατον δὲ πατροκτονήσας, ὡς ἐδύνατο. τὴν μὲν οὖν τυραννίδα ὁ παύσας εἰμὶ ἐγώ· καὶ τὸ ξίφος, ὁ πάντα εἴργασται, ἐμόν· τὴν δὲ
τάξιν ἐνήλλαξα τῶν φόνων, καὶ τὸν τρόπον ἐκαινοτόμησα τῆς τῶν πονηρῶν τελευτῆς· τὸν μὲν ἰσχυ-
ρότερον, καὶ ἀμύνασθαι δυνάμενον, αὐτὸς ἀνελών· τὸν γέροντα δὲ, μόνῳ παραχωρήσας τῷ ξί-
φει· ἐγὼ μὲν οὖν καὶ περιττότερόν τι ἐπὶ τούτοις ᾤμην γενήσεσθαί μοι παρ' ὑμῶν, καὶ δωρεὰς λή-
ψεσθαι ἰσαρίθμους τοῖς ἀνῃρημένοις, ὡς ἂν οὐ τῶν παρόντων ἀπαλλάξας ὑμᾶς μόνον, ἀλλὰ καὶ τῆς
τῶν μελλόντων κακῶν ἐλπίδος, καὶ τὴν ἐλευθερίαν βέβαιον παρασχὼν, οὐδενὸς παραλελειμμένου
κληρονόμου τῶν ἀδικημάτων. μεταξὺ δὲ κινδυνεύω, τοσαῦτα κατορθώσας, ἀγέραστος ἀπελ-

1 LVCIANI] Eiusdem Luciani *1506 1514 1516 1519* 2 THOMA] eodem *1506 1514 1516 1519* 4 DECLAMATIONIS] *om. 1566* 29 certam] certem *1534*, certe *1563 1566*

LVCIANI DECLAMATIO PRO TYRANNICIDA, THOMA MORO INTERPRETE.

ARGVMENTVM DECLAMATIONIS.

Ascendit quidam in arcem, ut tyrannum occideret: at ipsum quidem non inuenit, filium autem eius quum peremisset, gladium reliquit in corpore. Tyrannus ingressus, ac filium iam conspicatus mortuum, eodem gladio se transfixit: is qui ascenderat, ac tyranni filium interemerat, tanquam tyrannicida praemium petit.

DECLAMATIO.

QVVM duos tyrannos iudices uno die peremerim, alterum quidem iam aetate defectum, alterum uero florentem, eoque ad scelerum successionem idoneum, adsum tamen unicum ob utrunque praemium petiturus: idque quum solus omnium qui unquam fuere tyrannicidae, sceleratos duos uno ictu sustulerim atque mactauerim: filium quidem gladio, patrem uero nimio illo quo in filium ferebatur, affectu. Tyrannus igitur ob ea quae gessit, satis nobis supplicij dedit, quippe qui & uiuens filium spectauit occisum, & tandem (quod maxime praeter omnem spem fuit) ipse sui [A_1v] coactus est tyrannicida fieri. Filius igitur a me peremptus est, inseruiuit autem mihi, etiam mortuus, ad aliam mortem: nam qui uiuens iniurias una cum patre fecit, mortuus patrem ut potuit interfecit. Qui tyrannidem ergo sustuli, ego sum: ensisque qui peregit omnia, meus est, ordinem tantum immutaui caedium, ac perimendi sceleratos nouaui modum: illum qui fortior erat, & qui ulcisci poterat, amolitus ipse: senem uero soli relinquens gladio. Ego igitur ob ista etiam amplius aliquid a uobis expectabam, sperabamque me praemia pro peremptorum numero suscepturum, ut qui uos non praesentibus tantum malis eripuerim, sed futurorum quoque metu liberauerim, ac certam uobis libertatem praestiterim, nullo haerede scelerum relicto. At interim tot rebus a me praeclare aeditis, in periculum uenio, ne a uobis nullo

θεῖν παρ' ὑμῶν, καὶ μόνος στέρεσθαι τῆς παρὰ τῶν νόμων ἀμοιβῆς, οὓς διεφύλαξα. ὁ μὲν οὖν ἀντιλέγων, οὔ μοι δοκεῖ μοι οὐ κηδόμενος ὥς φησι τῶν κοινῶν τοῦτο ποιεῖν, ἀλλ' ἐπὶ τοῖς τετελευτηκόσι λελυπημένος, καὶ ἀμυνόμενος τὸν ἐκείνοις τοῦ θανάτου αἴτιον γεγενημένον. ὑμεῖς δὲ, ἀνάσχεσθέ μου ὦ ἄνδρες δικασταὶ πρὸς ὀλίγον τὰ ἐν τῇ τυραννίδι, καίπερ εἰδόσιν ὑμῖν ἀκριβῶς διηγουμένου. καὶ γὰρ τὸ μέγεθος οὕτω μάθοιτ' ἂν τῆς εὐεργεσίας τῆς ἐμῆς, καὶ αὐτοὶ μᾶλλον εὐφρανεῖσθε, λογιζόμενοι ὧν ἀπηλλάγητε. οὐ γὰρ ὥσπερ ἄλλοις τισὶν ἤδη συνέβη πολλάκις ἁπλῆν καὶ ἡμεῖς τυραννίδα, καὶ μίαν δουλείαν ὑπεμείναμεν, οὐδ' ἑνὸς ὑπηνέγκαμεν ἐπιθυμίαν δεσπότου, ἀλλὰ μόνοι τῶν πώποτε τὰ ὅμοια δυστυχησάντων, δύο ἀνθ' ἑνὸς τυράννους εἴχομεν, καὶ πρὸς διττὰ οἱ δυστυχεῖς ἀδικήματα διῃρούμεθα. μετριώτερος δὲ ὁ πρεσβύτης ἦν παραπολὺ, καὶ πρὸς τὰς ὀργὰς ἠπιώτερος, καὶ πρὸς τὰς κολάσεις ἀμβλύτερος, καὶ πρὸς τὰς ἐπιθυμίας βραδύτερος, ὡς ἂν ἤδη τῆς ἡλικίας τὸ μὲν σφοδρότερον τῆς ὁρμῆς ἐπεχούσης, τὰς δὲ τῶν ἡδονῶν ὀρέξεις χαλιναγωγούσης. καὶ πρός γε τὴν ἀρχὴν τῶν ἀδικημάτων ὑπὸ τοῦ παιδὸς ἄκων προσῆχθαι ἐλέγετο, οὐ πάνυ τυραννικὸς αὐτὸς ὤν, ἀλλ' εἴκων ἐκείνῳ. φιλότεκνος γὰρ ἐς ὑπερβολὴν ἐγένετο, ὡς ἔδειξε. καὶ πάντα ὁ παῖς ἦν αὐτῷ, καὶ ἐκείνῳ ἐπείθετο. καὶ ἠδίκει ὅσα κελεύοι, καὶ ἐκόλαζεν οὓς προστάττοι, καὶ πάντα ὑπηρέτει. καὶ ὅλως, ἐτυραννεῖτο ὑπ' αὐτοῦ, καὶ δορυφόρος τῶν τοῦ παιδὸς ἐπιθυμιῶν ἦν. ὁ νεανίας δὲ, τῆς μὲν τιμῆς παρεχώρει καθ' ἡλικίαν ἐκείνῳ, καὶ μόνου ἐξίστατο τοῦ τῆς ἀρχῆς ὀνόματος. τὸ δ' ἔργον τῆς τυραννίδος, καὶ τὸ κεφάλαιον, αὐτὸς ἦν. καὶ τὸ μὲν πιστὸν καὶ ἀσφαλὲς, ἀπ' αὐτοῦ παρεῖχε τῇ δυναστείᾳ. τὴν δ' ἀπόλαυσιν μόνος ἐκαρποῦτο τῶν ἀδικημάτων. ἐκεῖνος ἦν ὁ τοὺς δορυφόρους συνέχων. ὁ τὴν φρουρὰν κρατύνων. ὁ τοὺς τυραννουμένους ἐκκόπτων. ὁ τοὺς ἐπιβουλεύοντας φοβῶν. ἐκεῖνος, ὁ τοὺς ἐφήβους ἀνασπῶν. ὁ ἐνυβρίζων τοῖς γάμοις. ἐκείνῳ αἱ παρθένοι ἀνήγοντο, καὶ εἴ τινες σφαγαὶ, καὶ εἴ τινες φυγαὶ, καὶ χρημάτων ἀφαιρέσεις, καὶ βάσανοι, καὶ ὕβρεις, πάντα ταῦτα τολμήματα ἦν νεανικά. ὁ γέρων δ' ἐκεῖνος, ἠκολούθει, καὶ συνηδίκει, καὶ ἐπῄνει μόνον τὰ τοῦ παιδὸς ἀδικήματα. καὶ τὸ πρᾶγμα ἡμῖν ἀφόρητον καθειστήκει. ὅταν γὰρ αἱ τῆς γνώμης ἐπιθυμίαι τὴν ἐκ τῆς ἀρχῆς ἐξουσίαν προσλάβωσιν, οὐδένα ὅρον ποιοῦνται τῶν ἀδικημάτων. μάλιστα δὲ ἐκεῖνο ἐλύπει, τὸ εἰδέναι μακρὰν, μᾶλλον δὲ ἀΐδιον τὴν δουλείαν ἐσομένην, καὶ ἐκ διαδοχῆς παραδοθησομένην τὴν πόλιν, ἄλλοτε ἄλλῳ δεσπότῃ, καὶ πονηρῷ, κληρονόμημα γενησόμενον τὸν δῆμον. ὡς τοῖς γε ἄλλοις οὐ μικρά τις ἐλπὶς αὕτη, τὸ λογίζεσθαι, καὶ πρὸς αὐτοὺς λέγειν, ἀλλ' ἤδη παύσεται, ἀλλ' ἤδη τεθνήξεται. καὶ μετ' ὀλίγον ἐλεύθεροι γενησόμεθα. ἐπ' ἐκείνων δὲ, οὐδὲν τοιοῦτον ἠλ-

3 studio, sicut ait, istud] studio istud *1506 1514* (sicut ait *added after* studio *in margin*) *1516 1519* 6 mei] *om. 1534 1563 1566* 7 idem] *1506 1514 1517*, iidem *1516 1519*, item *1521 1528 1534 1563 1566* 22 cessit] esset *1506 1516 1519* 28–29 si qua exilia] *repeated in 1506* 35–36 successionem Rempublicam] successionem esse rempublicam *1506 1514 1516 1519*

praemio donatus abeam, solusque mercede frauder, quam leges a me seruatae statuerunt. Hic itaque meus aduersarius, nullo Reipublicae studio, sicut ait, istud agere uidetur, sed eorum caede commotus, ut in eum qui mortis eis causa fuit ulciscatur. Sed uos iudices auscultate paulisper, dum tyrannidis mala (quanquam ipsi probe sciatis) expono: nam & hoc pacto melius beneficij mei magnitudinem cognoueritis, & magis idem gaudebitis, reputantes quibus estis malis liberati. Neque enim quemadmodum alijs plerisque iam saepe accidit, ita nos quoque simplicem tyrannidem & unicam seruitutem sustinuimus: neque unius domini libidinem pertulimus, sed soli omnium quos unquam similis pressit infelicitas, duos unius loco tyrannos habuimus, & in duplices miseri iniurias distracti sumus. At moderatior admodum senex erat, & in ira mitior, & ad supplicia segnior, & ad libidines tardior: utpote aetate iam impetus eius uehementiam cohibente, & uoluptatum appetitiones refrenante. Et ad causas quidem facinorum inuitus a filio dicebatur impelli, quum ipse non admodum tyrannicus esset, nisi quod illi parebat: nam in filium (ut iam ostendit) propensus supra modum fuit. Omnia illi filius erat, illi obtemperabat: & iniuste fecit quicquid ille iubebat, & puniebat quos ille uolebat: in omnibus illi morem gerebat, ac denique sub illius tyrannide uiuebat, & ultroneus filij cupiditatum satelles erat. At iuuenis uero honore aetatis gratia patri cessit, & solo imperij nomine abstinuit: caeterum re ipsa tyrannidis caput ipse fuit. Firmitas quoque ac tutamentum principatus ab illo pendebat, quoniam & quod ex iniurijs prouenit, solus ipse fruebatur. Ille erat qui satellites ducebat, qui custodias regebat, qui subditos feriebat, qui insidiatores terrebat. Ille erat qui ephebos rapuit, qui nuptias temerauit, cui uirgines adductae sunt: & si quae caedes erant, si qua exilia, pecuniarum expilationes, tormenta, contumeliae, haec omnia [A_2] iuuenis fiebant audacia: nam senex ipse obsequebatur, & comes in malis erat, & tantum filij scelera comprobabat. Et res quidem nobis intolerabilis facta est: nam quum animi libidines ab imperio sumunt licentiam, nullum iniuriarum finem faciunt. At illud tamen nos urebat maxime, diuturnam, imo aeternam potius futuram hanc seruitutem sciebamus, & tradendam per successionem Rempublicam populumque, alij post alium domino ac scelerato haereditatem cessuram. Alijs profecto non paruam spem haec res facit, quod perpendere possunt, ac secum dicere: at iam cohibebitur, at iam morietur, ac paulo post erimus liberi. De illis uero nihil tale

πίζετο, ἀλλ' ἑωρῶμεν ἤδη ἕτοιμον τὸν τῆς ἀρχῆς διάδοχον. τοιγαροῦν οὐδ' ἐπιχειρεῖν τις ἐτόλμα τῶν γενναίων, καὶ τὰ αὐτὰ ἐμοὶ προαιρουμένων, ἀλλ' ἀπέγνωστο παντάπασιν ἡ ἐλευθερία, καὶ ἄμαχος ἡ τυραννὶς ἐδόκει, πρὸς τοσούτους ἐσομένης τῆς ἐπιχειρήσεως. ἀλλ' οὐκ ἐμὲ ταῦτ' ἐφόβησεν, οὐδὲ τὸ δυσχερὲς τῆς πράξεως λογισάμενος ἀπώκνησα, οὐδὲ πρὸς τὸν κίνδυνον ἀπεδειλίασα. μόνος δὲ μόνος πρὸς οὕτως ἰσχυρὰν καὶ πολλὴν τὴν τυραννίδα. μᾶλλον δὲ οὐδὲ μόνος, ἀλλὰ μετὰ τοῦ ξίφους ἀνῄειν τοῦ συμμεμαχημένου, καὶ τὸ μέρος συντετυραννοκτονηκότος, πρὸ ὀφθαλμῶν μὲν τὴν τελευτὴν ἔχων, ἀλλαξόμενος δὲ ὅμως τὴν κοινὴν ἐλευθερίαν τῆς σφαγῆς τῆς ἐμῆς. ἐντυχὼν δὲ τῇ πρώτῃ φρουρᾷ, καὶ τρεψάμενος οὐ ῥᾳδίως τοὺς δορυφόρους, καὶ τὸν ἐντυγχάνοντα κτείνων, καὶ τὸ ἀνθιστάμενον πᾶν διαφθείρων, ἐπ' αὐτὸ τὸ κεφάλαιον αὐτὸ τῶν ἔργων ἵεμαι, ἐπὶ τὴν μόνην τῆς τυραννίδος ἰσχύν, ἐπὶ τὴν ὑπόθεσιν τῶν ἡμετέρων συμφορῶν. καὶ ἐπιστὰς τῷ τῆς ἀκροπόλεως φρουρίῳ, καὶ ἰδὼν γενναίως ἀμυνόμενον, καὶ ἀνθιστάμενον πολλοῖς τραύμασιν, ὅμως ἀπέκτεινα. καὶ ἡ μὲν τυραννὶς ἤδη καθῄρητο, καὶ πέρας εἶχέ μοι τὸ τόλμημα. καὶ τὸ ἀπ' ἐκείνου, πάντες μὲν ἐλεύθεροι, ἐλείπετο δ' ὁ γέρων ἔτι μόνος ἄνοπλος, ἀποβεβληκὼς τοὺς φύλακας, ἀπολωλεκὼς τὸν μέγαν ἐκεῖνον αὐτοῦ δορυφόρον, ἔρημος, οὐδὲ γενναίας ἔτι χειρὸς ἄξιος. ἐνταῦθα τοίνυν πρὸς ἐμαυτόν, ὦ ἄνδρες δικασταί, τὰ τοιαῦτα ἐλογισάμην. πάντ' ἔχει μοι καλῶς. πάντα πέπρακται. πάντα κατώρθωται. τίνα δ' ὁ περίλοιπος κολασθείη τρόπον; ἐμοῦ μὲν γὰρ ἀνάξιός ἐστι, καὶ τῆς ἐμῆς δεξιᾶς, καὶ μάλιστα ἐπ' ἔργῳ λαμπρῷ, καὶ νεανικῷ, καὶ γενναίῳ ἀνῃρημένος, καταισχύνων κἀκείνην τὴν σφαγήν. ἄξιον δέ τινα δεῖ ζητῆσαι δήμιον. ἀλλὰ μετὰ τὴν συμφοράν, μὴ τὴν αὐτὴν κερδαινέτω. ἰδέτω. κολασθήτω. παρακείμενον ἐχέτω τὸ ξίφος. τούτῳ τὰ λοιπὰ ἐντέλλομαι. ταῦτα βουλευσάμενος, αὐτὸς μὲν ἐκποδὼν ἀπηλλαττόμην. ὁ δ', ὅπερ ἐγὼ προὐμαντευσάμην, διεπράξατο, καὶ ἐτυραννοκτόνησε, καὶ τέλος ἐπέθηκε τῷ ἐμῷ δράματι. πάρειμι οὖν κομίζων ὑμῖν τὴν δημοκρατίαν, καὶ θαρρεῖν ἤδη προκηρύττων ἅπασι, καὶ τὴν ἐλευθερίαν εὐαγγελιζόμενος. ἤδη οὖν ἀπολαύετε τῶν ἔργων τῶν ἐμῶν. κενὴ μὲν ὡς ὁρᾶτε πονηρῶν ἡ ἀκρόπολις. ἐπιτάττει δὲ οὐδείς, ἀλλὰ καὶ τιμᾶν ἔξεστι, καὶ δικάζειν, καὶ ἀντιλέγειν κατὰ τοὺς νόμους. καὶ πάντα ταῦτα γεγένηται δι' ἐμὲ ὑμῖν, καὶ διὰ τὴν τόλμαν τὴν ἐμὴν κἀκ τοῦ ἑνὸς ἐκείνου φόνου, μεθ' ὃν οὐκ ἔτι ζῆν πατὴρ ἐδύνατο. ἀξιῶ δ' οὖν ἐπὶ τούτοις, τὴν ὀφειλομένην δοθῆναί μοι παρ' ὑμῶν δωρεάν, οὐ φιλοκερδής, οὐδὲ μικρολόγος τις ὤν, οὐδ' ἐπὶ μισθῷ τὴν πατρίδα εὐεργετεῖν προῃ-

8–9 consorte etiam tyrannicidij] Sortem etiam tyrannicidae *1506 1514* (*changed in margin to* Consorte etiam tyrannicidij) *1516 1519* 19 adempto destitutus, nec] adempto nec *1506 1514* (destitutus *added in margin after* adempto) *1516 1519* 26 lucrifaciat; uideat] lucrifaciat uideat *1521* 27 ego] *1506 1514 1516 1519*, ergo *1517 1521 1528 1534 1563 1566* 33 tribuere] ttibuere [*sic*] *1506* 34 uobis] nobis *1506 1514* (*corrected in margin to* vobis) *1516 1519*

sperabatur, sed iam nunc paratum imperij cernebamus haeredem, quamobrem nec suscipere negocium audebat fortium quisquam, qui tamen eadem mecum cupiebant: sed desperabatur omnino libertas, & inexpugnabilis uidebatur tyrannis, cum necesse esset tam multos aggredi. At me nihil ista deterruerunt, neque perpensa negocij difficultate detractaui, neque periculum expaui. Solus quidem, solus aduersus tam fortem ac multiplicem tyrannidem, imo uero non solus, sed cum gladio auxiliari conscendi, consorte etiam tyrannicidij, mortem prae oculis habens, sed propriam tamen caedem communi libertate compensans. Cum in primam ergo custodiam incidissem, ac satellites haud facile amouissem, obuium quenque perimens, & quicquid obsisteret conficiens, in ipsum negocij caput ferebar, in ipsum unicum tyrannidis robur, in ipsam nostrarum calamitatum materiam, & in summa arcis custodia sistens, quum illum conspexissem sese generose defendentem atque resistentem, uulneribus multis tamen interfeci, ac iam quidem sublata tyrannis erat, facinus confectum erat, atque exinde protinus omnes liberi. Senex relictus est ille solus, inermis, custodibus exutus, magno illo satellite suo adempto destitutus, nec amplius ulla generosa manu dignus. Ibi ego mecum iudices talia cogitabam: totum negocium meum bene se habet: omnia peracta sunt, omnia strennue perfecta sunt. Quonam ergo iste qui superest plectetur modo? Me siquidem ac dextera mea indignus est: praecipue uero facinore tam splendido ac iuuenili & generoso confecto, cuius gloriam addita hac tam inerte caede minuerem. Dignum autem quaerere carnificem quempiam oportet, uerum post erumnam tum, ne & hanc lucrifaciat; uideat, puniatur, appositum tantum ensem habeat: huic ego reliqua committo. Haec ubi statuissem, illinc amolior. Ille uero sicut ego ante diuinaueram fecit, ac tyrannum interfecit, fabulaeque meae supremum actum addidit. Adsum ergo popularem uobis gubernationem adferens, & omnibus securitatem denuncians, ac libertatem feliciter annuncians. Nunc igitur fa[A$_2$v]ctis meis fruimini. Sceleratis enim (uti uidetis) arx uacat, imperat autem nemo, sed & honores tribuere licet, & iudicare, & ex legibus contra dicere: atque haec uobis ex me, atque hoc facinore meo profecta sunt: atque ex illa una caede, post quam pater haud amplius uiuere potuit. Dignum igitur ob ista censeo, debitum a uobis mihi praemium dari, non quod studiosus lucri sim, aut qui parua magnipendam: neque quod ob mercedem de patria benemereri in animum induxerim, sed quod mea officia

ρημένος, ἀλλὰ βεβαιωθῆναί μοι βουλόμενος τὰ κατορθώματα τῇ δωρεᾷ, καὶ μὴ διαβληθῆναι, μηδ' ἄδοξον γενέσθαι τὴν ἐπιχείρησιν τὴν ἐμήν, ὡς ἀτελῆ, καὶ γέρως ἀναξίαν κεκριμένην· οὗτος δὲ ἀντιλέγει, καί φησιν, οὐκ εὔλογον ποιεῖν με τιμᾶσθαι θέλοντα, καὶ δωρεὰν λαμβάνειν· οὐ γὰρ εἶναι τυραννοκτόνον, οὐδὲ πεπρᾶχθαί μοί τι κατὰ τὸν νόμον, ἀλλ' ἐνδεῖν τι τῷ ἔργῳ τῷ ἐμῷ, πρὸς ἀπαίτησιν τῆς δωρεᾶς. πυνθάνομαι τοίνυν αὐτοῦ, τί λοιπὸν ἀπαιτεῖς παρ' ἐμοῦ; οὐκ ἐβουλήθην; οὐκ ἀνῆλθον; οὐκ ἐφόνευσα; οὐκ ἠλευθέρωσα; μή τις ἐπιτάττει; μή τις κελεύει; μή τις ἀπειλεῖ δεσπότης; μή τίς με τῶν κακούργων διέφυγεν; οὐκ ἂν εἴποις· ἀλλὰ πάντα εἰρήνης μεστά, καὶ πάντες οἱ νόμοι, καὶ ἐλευθερία σαφής, καὶ δημοκρατία βέβαιος, καὶ γάμοι ἀνύβριστοι, καὶ παῖδες ἀδεεῖς, καὶ παρθένοι ἀσφαλεῖς, καὶ ἑορτάζουσα τὴν κοινὴν εὐτυχίαν ἡ πόλις· τίς οὖν ὁ τούτων ἁπάντων αἴτιος; τίς ὁ ἐκεῖνα μὲν παύσας, τάδε παρεσχημένος; εἰ γάρ τις ἔστι τῶν πρὸ ἐμοῦ τιμᾶσθαι δίκαιος, παραχωρῶ τοῦ γέρως. ἐξίσταμαι τῆς δωρεᾶς· εἰ δὲ μόνος ἐγὼ πάντα διεπραξάμην, τολμῶν, κινδυνεύων, ἀνιών, ἀναιρῶν, κολάζων, δι' ἀλλήλων τιμωρούμενος, τί μου διαβάλλεις τὰ κατορθώματα; τί δὲ ἀχάριστον πρός με τὸν δῆμον ποιεῖσθαι; οὐ γὰρ αὐτὸν ἐφόνευσα τὸν τύραννον· ὁ δὲ νόμος, τυραννοκτόνῳ δίδωσι τὴν δωρεάν· διαφέρει δὲ εἰπέ μοι τί ἢ αὐτὸν ἀνελεῖν, ἢ τοῦ θανάτου παρασχεῖν τὴν αἰτίαν· ἐγὼ μὲν γάρ, οὐδὲν οἶμαι, ἀλλὰ τοῦτο μόνον ὁ νομοθέτης εἶδε, τὴν ἐλευθερίαν· τὴν δημοκρατίαν· τὴν τῶν δεινῶν ἀπαλλαγήν· τοῦτ' ἐτίμησε. τοῦτ' ἄξιον ἀμοιβῆς ὑπέλαβεν, ὅπερ οὐκ ἂν εἴποις μὴ δι' ἐμὲ γεγενῆσθαι. εἰ γὰρ ἐφόνευσα δι' ὃν ἐκεῖνος ζῆν οὐκ ἐδύνατο, αὐτὸς εἴργασμαι τὴν σφαγήν· ἐμὸς ὁ φόνος, ἡ χεὶρ ἐκείνου· μὴ τοίνυν ἀκριβολογοῦ ἔτι περὶ τοῦ τρόπου τῆς τελευτῆς, μηδ' ἐξέταζε ὅπως ἀπέθανεν, ἀλλ' εἰ μηκέτ' ἔστιν, εἰ δι' ἐμὲ τὸ μηκέτ' εἶναι ἔχει· ἐπεὶ κἀκεῖνο προσεξετάσειν μοι δοκεῖς, καὶ συκοφαντήσειν τοὺς εὐεργέτας, εἴ τις μὴ ξίφει, ἀλλὰ λίθῳ, ἢ ξύλῳ, ἢ ἄλλῳ τῷ τρόπῳ ἀπέκτεινε· τί δὲ εἰ λιμῷ ἐξεπολιόρκησα τὸν τύραννον, τὴν ἀνάγκην τῆς τελευτῆς παρέχων, ἀπῄτεις ἂν καὶ τότε παρ' ἐμοῦ αὐτόχειρα τὴν σφαγήν; ἢ ἐνδεῖν ἔλεγες μοί τι πρὸς τὸν νόμον; καὶ ταῦτα, χαλεπώτερον τοῦ κακούργου πεφονευμένου; ἓν μόνον ἐξέταζε· τοῦτο ἀπαίτει· τοῦτο πολυπραγμόνει. τίς τῶν πονηρῶν λείπεται, ἢ τίς ἐλπὶς τοῦ φόβου, ἢ τί ὑπόμνημα τῶν συμφορῶν· εἰ δὲ καθαρὰ πάντα, καὶ εἰρηνικά, συκοφαντοῦντός ἐστι τῷ τρόπῳ τῶν πεπραγμένων χρώμενον, ἀποστερεῖν ἐθέλειν τὴν ἐπὶ τοῖς πεπονημένοις δωρεάν. ἐγὼ δὲ καὶ τοῦτο μέμνημαι διηγορευμένον ἐν τῷ νόμῳ, εἴ γε μὴ διὰ τὴν πολλὴν δουλείαν ἐπιλέλησμαι

8 num imperat] nun imperat *1506*, non imperat *1514 1517* 8 num iubet] non iubet *1506 1514 1517* 9 num dominus] nun dominus *1506*, non dominus *1514 1517* 9 num me] nun me *1506*, non me *1514 1517* 17 interimens] occidens *1506 1516 1519*, *om. 1514* (interimens *added in margin*)

cupiam uestro praemio esse comprobata, ne despectus sit, neue inglorius fiat meus conatus, tanquam a uobis mancus, & praemio iudicetur indignus. At iste contradicit, & me praeter aequum ait facere, qui honorari uelim, ac praemium referre: non enim esse me tyrannicidam, neque factum a me quicquam secundum legem esse, sed facto meo quiddam ad praemium petendum deesse. Rogo igitur eum, quid reliquum a me desideras? non uolui? non ascendi? non peremi? non liberaui? num imperat quisquam? num iubet quisquam? num dominus minatur quisquam? num me maleficorum effugit quisquam? non dixeris. Sed omnia pacis plena, & leges omnes redditae, & manifesta libertas, & popularis gubernatio firma, & coniugia inuiolata, & pueri extra periculum, & uirgines tutae, & festas agens ferias ob communem felicitatem ciuitas. Quis est igitur horum omnium causa? quis illa sustulit, ista praebuit? Etenim si me quisquam est hoc honore dignior, illi hac mercede cedo, ac praemio istoc abstineo. Sin uero solus ego cuncta peregi, audens, periclitans, adoriens, interimens, puniens, alterum in altero ulciscens: quid mea calumniaris officia? quid ingratum erga me populum facis? At ipsum non occidisti tyrannum: lex autem tyrannicidae praemium statuit. Interest ergo quicquam, dic mihi, an ipsum perimas, an mortis ei causam praebeas? Ego certe nihil puto, nempe hoc solum legislator spectauit, libertatem & popularem statum, ac sceleratorum amolitionem, istud honorauit, istud gratia dignum censuit, quod factum a me non esse non queas dicere. Si enim illum occidi, quo occiso iste non potuit uiuere, ipse nimirum mactaui. Caedes mea manus illius erat. Ne nimium ergo curiose de mortis modo disputes, neque examines quomodo interijt: sed an amplius non sit, an per me est, quod amplius ille non est. Quandoquidem hoc quoque mihi uideris excussurus, & sycophantam in benemerentes acturus, si quis non ense, sed lapide lignoue, aut alio quopiam modo peremisset. Quid uero si tyrannum fame obsessum, ad mortis necessitatem adegissem? etiam ne tum requireres meamet manu peractam caedem? alioqui deesse adhuc aliquid mihi ad legem implendam diceres? atque id grauiore supplicio interfecto [A_3] malefico? Vnum solum examina, istud interroga, in hoc curiosus inquire, quis facinorosorum superest? quis iniuriae metus imminet? quae uestigia calamitatum? Sin uero purgata sunt ac pacata omnia: sycophantae est, modum rerum calumniantem, uelle praemio ipsis factis debito fraudare. Ego siquidem hoc quoque in legibus declaratum memini (nisi forsan ob longam

τῶν ἐν αὐτοῖς εἰρημένων, αἰτίας θανάτου εἶναι διττάς, εἴ τις αὐτὸς ἀπέκτεινεν, ἢ εἴ τις
μὴ αὐτὸς μὲν ἀπέκτεινε, μὴ δὲ τῇ χειρὶ ἔδρασε τὸ ἔργον, ἠνάγκασε δὲ, καὶ παρέσχεν ἀφορ-
μὴν τοῦ φόνου τὰ ἴσα, καὶ τοῦτον ἀξιοῖ ὁ νόμος αὐτὸν ἀντικολάζεσθαι. μάλα δικαίως.
οὐ γὰρ ἐβούλετο τοῦ πεπραγμένου ἴσον γίγνεσθαι τὸ τῆς ἀδείας. καὶ περιττὴ ἡ λοιπὸν ἡ
ἐξέτασις τοῦ τρόπου τῆς σφαγῆς. εἶτα τὸν μὲν οὕτως ἀποκτείνοντα, κολάζειν ὡς ἀν-
δροφόνον δικαιοῖς, καὶ οὐδαμῶς ἀφεῖσθαι θέλεις. τὸν δὲ κατὰ τὸν αὐτὸν τούτῳ τρόπον
εὖ πεποιηκότα τὴν πόλιν, οὐ τῶν ὁμοίων ἀξιώσεις τοῖς εὐεργέταις. οὐδὲ γὰρ ἐκεῖνο ἂν ἔ-
χοις λέγειν, ὡς ἐγὼ μὲν ἁπλῶς αὐτὸ ἔπραξα, ἠκολούθησε δέ τι τέλος ἄλλως χρηστὸν, ἐ-
μοῦ μὴ θελήσαντος. τί γὰρ ἔτι ἐδεδίειν, τοῦ ἰσχυροτέρου πεφονευμένου; τί δὲ κατέλιπον τὸ
ξίφος ἐν τῇ σφαγῇ, εἰ μὴ πάντως τὸ ἐσόμενον αὐτὸ προεμαντευόμην; ἐκτὸς εἰ μὴ τοῦτο φῂς,
ὡς οὐ τύραννος ὁ τεθνεὼς ἦν, οὐδὲ ταύτην εἶχε τὴν προσηγορίαν, οὐδὲ δωρεὰς ἐπ' αὐτῷ
πολλὰς, εἰ ἀποθάνοι, ἡδέως ἂν ὑμεῖς ἐδώκατε. ἀλλ' οὐκ ἂν εἴποις. εἶτα τοῦ τυράννου πεφονευμένου, τῷ τὴν αἰτίαν παρασχόντι τῆς σφαγῆς, οὐκ ἀποδώσεις τὴν δωρεάν; ὢ τῆς πο-
λυπραγμοσύνης. μέλει δέ σοι πῶς ἀπέθανεν, ἀπολαύοντι τῆς ἐλευθερίας, ἢ τὸν τὴν δημοκρατίαν ἀποδεδωκότα, περιττότερόν τι προσαπαιτεῖς; καίτοι ὅ γε νόμος ὡς φῂς, τὸ κεφάλαιον ἐξετάζει τῶν πεπραγμένων. τὰ διὰ μέσου δὲ πάντα ἐᾷ, καὶ οὐκ ἔτι πολυ-
πραγμονεῖ. τί γὰρ καὶ οὐχὶ ἐξελάσας τις τύραννον, ἤδη τιμὴν ἔλαβε τυραννοκτόνου;
καὶ μάλα δικαίως. ἐλευθερίαν γὰρ κἀκεῖνος ἀντὶ δουλείας παρέσχηται. τὸ δ' ὑπ' ἐμοῦ γεγενημένον, οὐ φυγὴ, οὐδὲ δευτέρας ἐπαναστάσεως ἐλπὶς, ἀλλὰ παντελὴς καθαίρεσις, καὶ
πανωλεθρία παντὸς τοῦ γένους, καὶ ῥιζόθεν τὸ δεινὸν ἅπαν ἐκκεκομμένον. καί μοι πρὸς θεῶν
ἤδη ἀπ' ἀρχῆς ἐς τέλος, εἰ δοκεῖ, πάντα ἐξετάσατε, εἴ τι τῶν πρὸς τὸν νόμον παραλέλειπται,
καὶ εἰ ἐνδεῖ τῶν προσεῖναι ὀφειλόντων τυραννοκτόνῳ. πρῶτα μὲν δὴ γνώμην προϋπάρ-
χειν χρὴ γενναίαν, καὶ φιλόπολιν, καὶ πρὸ τῶν κοινῶν κινδυνεύειν ἐθέλουσαν, καὶ τῷ οἰ-
κείῳ θανάτῳ τὴν τῶν πολλῶν σωτηρίαν ὠνησομένην. ἆρ' οὖν πρὸς τοῦτο ἐνεδέησα, ἐμαλα-
κίσθην, ἢ προϊδόμενός τινα τῶν διὰ μέσου κινδύνων ἀπώκνησα; οὐκ ἂν εἴποις. μένε τοίνυν
ἐπὶ τούτου ἔτι μόνου, καὶ νόμιζε τὸ θελῆσαι μόνον, καὶ τὸ βουλεύσασθαι ταῦτα, εἰ καὶ μὴ χρηστὸν ἀποβεβήκει. ἐκ γε τῆς γνώμης αὐτῆς καταστάντα με, γέρας ἀξιοῦν, ὡς εὐεργέτην λαμβάνειν. ἐμοῦ μὲν οὐ δυνηθέντος, ἄλλου δὲ μετ' ἐμὲ τετυραννοκτονηκότος, ἄλογον εἰπέ μοι,

1 sim quae] sim, quae *1521* 9 benemeritis] benemeriti *1534 1563 1566* 17 necis] *1506 1514 1516 1519*, *om. 1517 1521 1528 1534 1563 1566* 19–20 aut ab eo qui democratiam restituit, amplius aliquid postulas] Ab eo vero qui rempublicam reddidit amplius quicquam desyderas *1506 1516 1519*, *om. 1514* (aut ab eo qui democratiam restituit amplius aliquid postulas *added in margin*)

seruitutem sim quae in illis dicuntur oblitus) causas mortis duas esse, siue quis ipse occiderit, seu si quis ipse quidem non occiderit, neque manu rem gesserit, coegit tamen, atque occasionem necis dedit: aequaliter hunc etiam lex plectendum censet, atque admodum quidem iuste: nam praebitam interitus causam nihilo iudicauit ipso facto minorem, ac reliqua iam de modo necis quaestio superuacua est. Illum ergo qui sic occiderit, puniendum tanquam homicidam aequum censeas, absoluique nullo pacto uelis: qui uero eodem quo ille modo ciuitati benefecerit, indignum benemeritis praemio duces? Neque enim istud possis dicere, me uidelicet id fecisse tantum: bonum autem exitum quendam temere non me id destinante, consequutum. Quid ergo pertimuissem amplius, eo qui fortior erat interempto? Quid in uulnere gladium reliquissem, nisi idipsum omnino quod erat futurum praediuinassem? Nisi hoc fortasse dixeris, quod qui peremptus est, tyrannus non erat, neque hoc nomen obtinebat, neque multa uos ob id libenter si necaretur, praemia dedissetis: sed hoc nunquam dices. Ergo interempto tyranno, illi qui necis causam praebuit non reddes praemium? o curiositatem, quomodo necatus est curas, quum libertate fruaris, aut ab eo qui democratiam restituit, amplius aliquid postulas. Atqui lex (ut dicis) ipsum rerum caput examinat, media autem omnia ualere sinit, neque ultra curiosius inquirit. Quid enim, qui in exilium tyrannum compulisset, non honorem iam tyrannicidae tulisset? Imo ac ualde quidem iuste, nam & ille libertatem pro seruitute praestitit. At quod a me factum est, non exilium, nec redintegrandae rebellionis metus, sed omnino perfecta sublatio est, & generis illius uniuersi internicio, ac totius mali radicitus excisio. Ac nunc per deos omnia mihi ab initio in finem usque (si uidetur) excutite, an praetermissum quicquam ad implendam legem fuerit, & an quicquam mihi defuit, quod adesse tyrannicidae debuit. Ante omnia igitur animum adesse generosum decet, atque Reipublicae studiosum, paratumque pericula pro communi commodo subire, ac propria morte multorum salutem redimere: ergo ad id mihi quicquam defuit? An animo fractus sum? an periculo prospiciens, per quae mihi uadendum erat detractaui? non id dixeris. Mane ergo in hoc solo, ac me finge ex eo solo quod uolui, atque isto consilio fui, [A3v] etiam si nihil inde boni prouenisset, tamen ob mentem ipsam assurgentem praemium tanquam benemerentem petere, quum tamen ego non potuerim, sed alius me sequutus tyrannum occiderit, absonum (dic mihi) aut absurdum esset tribuere,

ἢ ἄγνωμον ἦν παρασχεῖν; καὶ μάλιστα εἰ ἔλεγον, ἄνδρες, ἐβουλόμην, ἠθέλησα, ἐπεχείρησα, ἐπειράθην τῆς γνώμης, μόνος ἄξιός εἰμι τιμᾶσθαι, τί ἂν ἀπεκρίνω τότε; νῦν δὲ, οὐ τοῦτό φημι, ἀλλὰ καὶ ἀνῆλθον, καὶ ἐκινδύνευσα, καὶ μυρία πρὸ τῆς τοῦ νεανίσκου σφαγῆς ἐπόνησα· μὴ γὰρ οὕτω ῥᾷστον, μηδ᾽ εὐχερὲς ὑπολάβητε εἶναι τὸ πρᾶγμα, φρουρὰν ὑπερβῆναι, καὶ δορυφόρων κρατῆσαι, καὶ τρέψασθαι τοσούτους μόνον, ἀλλὰ σχεδὸν τὸ μέγιστον ἐν τῇ τυραννοκτονίᾳ, καὶ τὸ κεφάλαιον τῶν ἔργων, τοῦτό ἐστιν· οὐ γὰρ δὴ αὐτός γε ὁ τύραννος, μέγα, καὶ δυσάλωτον, καὶ δυσκατέργαστόν ἐστιν, ἀλλὰ τὰ φρουροῦντα, καὶ συνέχοντα τὴν τυραννίδα, ἅ τις ἂν νικήσῃ, πάντα οὗτος κατώρθωσε, καὶ τὸ λοιπὸν, ὀλίγον. τὸ δὲ δὴ ἄχρι τῶν τυράννων προσελθεῖν, οὐκ ἂν ὑπῆρξέ μοι, μὴ οὐχὶ τῶν περὶ αὐτοὺς φυλάκων, καὶ δορυφόρων ἁπάντων κεκρατηκότι, κἀκείνους ἅπαντας προνενικηκότι· οὐδὲν ἔτι προστίθημι, ἀλλ᾽ ἐπὶ τούτων αὖθις μένω· φυλάκων ἐκράτησα· δορυφόρους ἐνίκησα· τὸν τύραννον, ἀφύλακτον, ἄοπλον, γυμνὸν, ἀπέδειξα. τιμῆς ἄξιος ἐπὶ τούτοις εἶναί σοι δοκῶ, ἢ ἔτι ἀπαιτεῖς παρ᾽ ἐμοῦ τὸν φόνον; ἀλλ᾽ εἰ καὶ φόνον ζητεῖς, οὐδὲ τοῦτο ἐνδεῖ· οὐδ᾽ ἀναίμακτός εἰμι, ἀλλ᾽ εἴργασμαι μεγάλην καὶ γενναίαν σφαγὴν, νεανίσκου ἀκμάζοντος, καὶ πᾶσι φοβεροῦ· δι᾽ ὃν ἀνεπιβούλευτος κἀκεῖνος ἦν, ᾧ μόνῳ ἐθάρρει. ὃς ἀντὶ πολλῶν ἤρκει δορυφόρων· ἆρ᾽ οὖν οὐκ ἄξιος ὢ οὗτος δωρεᾶς, ἀλλ᾽ ἄτιμος ἐπὶ τηλικούτοις γένωμαι; τί γὰρ εἰ δορυφόρον ἕνα, τί δὲ εἰ ὑπηρέτην τινὰ τοῦ τυράννου ἀπέκτεινα; τί δ᾽ εἰ οἰκέτην τίμιον, οὐ μέγα ἂν ἔδοξε καὶ τοῦτο, ἀνελθόντα ἐν μέσῃ τῇ ἀκροπόλει ἐν μέσοις τοῖς ὅπλοις, φόνον τινὸς ἐργάσασθαι τῶν τοῦ τυράννου φίλων; νῦν δὲ καὶ τὸν πεφονευμένον αὐτὸν ἴδε· υἱὸς ἦν τυράννου. μᾶλλον δὲ τύραννος χαλεπώτερος, καὶ δεσπότης ἀπαραίτητος, καὶ κολαστὴς ὠμότερος, καὶ ὑβριστὴς βιαιότερος. τὸ δὲ μέγιστον, κληρονόμος τῶν ὅλων, καὶ διάδοχος, καὶ ἐπὶ πολὺ παρατεῖναι τὰς ἡμετέρας συμφορὰς δυνάμενος. βούλει τοῦτο μόνον πεπρᾶχθαί μοι; ζῆν δ᾽ ἔτι τὸν τύραννον διαπεφευγότα; γέρας δὴ ἐπὶ τούτοις αἰτῶ· τί φατέ; οὐ δώσετε; οὐχὶ κἀκεῖνον ὑφεωρᾶσθε; οὐ δεσπότης; οὐ βαρύς; οὐκ ἀφόρητος ἦν; νῦν δὲ καὶ τὸ κεφάλαιον αὐτὸ ἐννοήσατε. ὃ γὰρ οὗτος ἀπαιτεῖ παρ᾽ ἐμοῦ, τοῦτο ὡς ἐνῆν, ἄριστα διεπραξάμην, καὶ τὸν τύραννον ἀπέκτεινα ἑτέρῳ φόνῳ, οὐχ ἁπλῶς, οὐδὲ πληγῇ μιᾷ, ὅπερ εὐκταιότατον ἦν αὐτῷ, ἐπὶ τηλικούτοις ἀδικήμασιν, ἀλλὰ λύπῃ προβασανίσας πολλῇ, καὶ ἐν ὀφθαλμοῖς δείξας τὰ φίλτατα οἰκτρῶς προκείμενα, υἱὸν ἐν ἡλικίᾳ, εἰ καὶ πονηρὸν, ἀλλ᾽ οὖν καὶ ἀκμάζοντα, καὶ ὅμοιον τῷ πατρὶ, αἵματος, καὶ λύθρου ἐμπεπλησμένον· ταῦτ᾽ ἐστι πατέ-

2–3 Quid tum responsurus esses? Nunc] quid tum? Nunc *1506 1514* (responsurus esses *added in margin after* tum) *1516 1519*   4 peremeram] peremerim *1566*   11 tyrannos] tyrannum *1506 1514 1516 1517 1519 1521 1528 1534 1563 1566* (*see commentary*) 26 consydera] considera *1521*

maximeque si dicerem, o uiri, uolui, cupiui, aggressus sum, atque animi mei signa dedi: solus honore dignus sum. Quid tum responsurus esses? Nunc uero non id dico, sed & ascendi & periclitatus sum, atque innumerabilia priusquam adolescentem peremeram feci. Neque enim rem usqueadeo facilem esse suspicemini, custodiam superare, ac satellites opprimere, unumque tot uiros auertere. Sed ferme maximum in tyrannicidio, atque ipsum rei caput istud est. Nam ipse quidem tyrannus, non magnum opus est, neque magno negocio conficiendum, neque expugnatu difficile, sed ea potius quae muniunt ac tuentur tyrannidem, quae qui uicerit, is omnia peregerit: nam reliquum quidem parum est. Siquidem istud ad tyrannos usque penetrare, nequaquam licuisset mihi, nisi custodum qui eos cingunt, ac satellitum omnium uictori, ac nisi eos omnes prius deuicissem: Nihil amplius adijcio, sed ijs rursus immoror. Custodias superaui, satellites inquam, tyrannum incustoditum, inermem, nudum reddidi. Ob haec ne honore tibi dignus uideor? an adhuc a me caedem postulas? Atqui si caedem etiam quaeris, nec istud quidem deest. Neque enim incruentus sum, sed perpetraui magnam ac nobilem necem iuuenis florentis atque omnibus metuendi, per quem etiam ille tutus ab insidijs erat, quo solo confidebat, qui multorum loco satellitum suffecit. Quid tum ergo, num praemio dignus sum? num tantarum rerum honore fraudabor? Quid enim si satellitem unum, si ministrum quempiam tyranni peremissem? quid si seruum honoratiorem? an non magnum etiam hoc tibi uideretur ascendere, atque in media arce, in medijs armis aliquem ex amicis tyranni conficere? Nunc autem etiam illum qui peremptus est consydera, filius erat tyranni, imo tyrannus grauior, ac dominus inclementior, ac tortor crudelior, extortor uiolentior. Tum, quod maximum fuit, haeres omnium atque successor: postremo, qui in longum poterat nostras calamitates extendere. Vis ne hoc me solum fecisse, tyrannum autem ipsum adhuc ereptum fuga uiuere? Munus ob ista peto, quid dicitis? non dabitis? Non illum quoque suspexistis? non dominus? non grauis? non intolerandus erat? Nunc uero etiam caput ipsum intelligite. Quod enim iste a me flagitat, id quam optime fieri potuit, peregi, ac tyrannum alterius nece necaui, non uulgariter, neque uno ictu, quod illi post tot scelera maxime fuit optandum. Sed dolore multo prius exagitans, & in oculis ostendens misere prostrata, quae [A_4] illi fuerant charissima, filium quanquam malum, tamen aetate florentem, ac patri similem, sanguine ac tabo plenum. Haec sunt patrum uul-

ρων τὰ θαύματα. ταῦτα ξίφη δικαίων τυραννοκτόνων. οὗτος θάνατος ἄξιος ὠμῶν τυράννων. αὕτη τιμωρία πρέπουσα τοσούτοις ἀδικήμασι. τὸ δ' εὐθὺς ἀποθανεῖν, τὸ δ' εὐθὺς ἀγνοῆσαι, τὸ δὲ μηδὲν τοιοῦτο θέαμα ἰδεῖν, οὐδὲν ἔχει τυραννικῆς κολάσεως ἄξιον. οὐ γὰρ ἠγνόουν ὦ οὗτος, οὐκ ἠγνόουν, οὐδὲ τῶν ἄλλων οὐδείς, ὅσην ἐκεῖνος εὔνοιαν πρὸς τὸν υἱὸν εἶχε, καὶ ὡς οὐκ ἂν ἠξίωσεν ἐπιβιῶναι οὐδ' ὀλίγον αὐτῷ χρόνον. πάντες μὲν γὰρ πατέρες ἴσως πρὸς τοὺς παῖδας τοιοῦτοι. ὁ δέ, καὶ περιττότερόν τι τῶν ἄλλων εἶχεν, εἰκότως, ὁρῶν μόνον ἐκεῖνον κηδεμόνα, καὶ φύλακα τῆς τυραννίδος, καὶ μόνον προκινδυνεύοντα τοῦ πατρὸς, καὶ τὴν ἀσφάλειαν τῇ ἀρχῇ παρεχόμενον. ὥστε εἰ καὶ μὴ διὰ τὴν εὔνοιαν, ἀλλὰ διὰ τὴν ἀπόγνωσιν, εὐθὺς ἠπιστάμην τεθνηξόμενον αὐτὸν, καὶ λογιούμενον, ὡς οὐδὲν ἔτι τοῦ ζῆν ὄφελος τῆς ἐκ τοῦ παιδὸς ἀσφαλείας καθῃρημένης. ἅπαντα τοίνυν αὐτῷ ἀθρόα περιέστησα, τὴν φύσιν, τὴν λύπην, τὴν ἀπόγνωσιν, τὸν φόβον, τὰς ἤδη τῶν μελλόντων ἐλπίδας χρόνων, ἐπ' αὐτὸν ἐχρησάμην τοῖς συμμάχοις, καὶ παρὰ τὴν τελευταίαν ἐκείνην σκέψιν κατηνάγκασα. ἀπέθανεν ὑμῖν ἄτεκνος, λελυπημένος, ὀδυρόμενος, δακρύων, πεπενθηκὼς πένθος, ὀλιγοχρόνιον μὲν, ἀλλ' ἱκανὸν πατρί. καὶ τὸ δεινότατον, αὐτὸς ὑφ' αὑτοῦ, ὅσπερ θανάτων οἴκτιστος, καὶ πολλῷ χαλεπώτερος, ἢ εἰ ὑπ' ἄλλου γίγνοιτο. ποῦ μοι τὸ ξίφος; μή τις ἄλλος τοῦτο γνωρίζει; μή τινος ἄλλου ὅπλον τοῦτο ἦν; τίς αὐτὸ ἐς τὴν ἀκρόπολιν ἀνεκόμισε; πρὸ τοῦ τυράννου τίς ἐχρήσατο; τίς αὐτὸ ἐπ' ἐκεῖνον ἀπέστειλε; ὦ ξίφος κοινωνὸν, καὶ διάδοχον τῶν ἐμῶν κατορθωμάτων. μετὰ τοσούτους κινδύνους, μετὰ τοσούτους φόνους ἀμελούμεθα, καὶ ἀνάξιοι δοκοῦμεν δωρεᾶς. εἰ γοῦν ὑπὲρ μόνου τούτου τὴν τιμὴν ᾔτουν παρ' ὑμῶν, εἰ γὰρ ἔλεγον, ἄνδρες, ἀποθανεῖν ἐθελήσαντι τῷ τυράννῳ, καὶ ἀνόπλῳ ἤδη τοῦ καιροῦ κατειλημμένῳ, ξίφος τοῦτο ἐμὸν ὑπηρέτησε, καὶ πρὸς τὸ τέλος τῆς ἐλευθερίας συνήργησε πάντῃ, τοῦτο τιμῆς τε καὶ δωρεᾶς ἄξιον νομίζετε. δεσπότην οὕτω δημοτικοῦ κτήματος, οὐκ ἂν ἠμείψασθε; οὐκ ἂν ἐν τοῖς εὐεργέταις ἀνεγράψατε; οὐκ ἂν τὸ ξίφος ἐν τοῖς ἱεροῖς ἀνεθήκατε; οὐκ ἂν μετὰ τῶν θεῶν ἐκεῖνο προσεκυνήσατε; νῦν μοι ἐννοήσατε, οἷα πεποιηκέναι εἰκὸς τὸν τύραννον, οἷα δὲ εἰρηκέναι πρὸ τῆς τελευτῆς. ἐπεὶ γὰρ ὑπ' ἐμοῦ φονευόμενος, καὶ τιτρωσκόμενος πολλοῖς τραύμασιν ἐς τὰ φανερὰ τοῦ σώματος, ὡς ἂν μάλιστα λυπήσειν ἔμελλον τὸν γεγεννηκότα, ὡς ἂν ἐκ τῆς πρώτης θέας διαταράξειν, ὁ μὲν, ἀνεβόησεν οἰκτρὸν, ἐπιβοώμενος τὸν γεγεννηκότα, οὐ βοηθὸν, οὐδὲ σύμμαχον, ᾔδει γὰρ πρεσβύτην ὄντα, καὶ ἀσθενῆ, ἀλλὰ θεατὴν τῶν οἰκείων κακῶν. ἐγὼ γὰρ ἀπηλλαττόμην, ποιητὴς μὲν τῆς ὅλης τραγῳδίας γεγενημένος, καταλιπὼν δὲ τῷ ὑποκριτῇ τὸν νεκρὸν, καὶ τὴν σκηνὴν, καὶ τὸ ξίφος, καὶ

31 deos] *1506 1516 1519*, deum *1514 1517 1521 1528 1534 1563 1566*

nera, hi legitimorum tyrannicidarum gladij. Haec tyrannis crudelibus digna mors, hoc supplicium sceleribus tantis debitum. Nam illico mori, illico nescire, nullum tale spectaculum cernere, nihil habet tyrannica poena dignum. Non enim ignorabam (te appello) non inquam ignorabam, imo nec alius quisquam quantum ille erga filium gerebat affectum, & quod post illum uiuere ne paululum quidem dignaretur. Atque omnes fortasse patres sunt in filios eiusmodi. At hic certe aliquid supra caeteros habebat, idque merito, quippe qui illum solum uidebat ducem seruatoremque tyrannidis, solumque pericula patris praeoccupantem, ac firmitatem imperio praestantem. Vnde etiam quanquam non ob amorem, at ob desperationem saltem statim illum sciebam moriturum, quum cogitaret inutilem sibi uitam futuram, securitate quam illi filius praebebat ablata. Omnibus igitur illum simul circunsepsi, natura, dolore, desperatione, terrore, ac temporum etiam futurorum metu. His in illum commilitonibus usus sum, & ad ultimum illud consilium coegi. Interijt nobis orbus, afflictus, dolens, lachrymans, luctum lugens, breuem quidem, sed qui patri sufficiat, & quod grauissimum est, ipse a seipso, quod mortis genus omnium est miserrimum, multoque acerbius quam si inferatur ab alio. Vbi mihi gladius est? num quis illum agnoscat alius? num cuiusquam alterius telum est? Quis illum in arcem duxit? ante tyrannum quis usus est? quis illum tyranno misit? O ensis mecum communicans, rerum a me bene gestarum successor, post tot discrimina, post tot mortes despicimur, & indigni praemio uidemur. Si enim ob istud solum hunc a uobis honorem peterem, si dicerem, o uiri tyranno mortem cupienti, ac tum inermi forte deprehenso, meus iste subseruiuit gladius, atque operam suam ad consequendam libertatem commodauit omnibus, honore ac praemio indignum putassetis? dominum tam popularis rei non retaliassetis? non inter benefactores inscripsissetis? non inter sacra gladium ipsum reposuissetis? non secundum deos illum coluissetis? Nunc mecum cogitate, qualia tyrannum ipsum ante mortem & fecisse, & dixisse sit uerisimile, quum filium perimerem, ac uulneribus multis in parte corporis conspicua perfoderem, quo uidelicet genitor ureretur, atque aspectu primo stupesceret, miserabiliter exclamauit atque inclamauit patrem, non ut auxiliator esset aut commilito, quippe qui iam senex erat atque inualidus, sed domesticorum malorum spectator. Ego illinc digredior, totius quidem tragoediae au[A_4v]tor. Reliqui uero histrioni cadauer, & scenam, & ensem, ac caetera quae fabulae

τὰ λοιπὰ τοῦ δράματος. ἐπιστὰς δ' ἐκεῖνος, καὶ ἰδὼν υἱὸν, ὃν εἶχε μόνον, ὀλίγον ἐμπνέοντα, ᾑμαγμένον, ἐμπεπλησμένον τοῦ φόνου, καὶ τὰ τραύματα συνεχῆ, καὶ πολλὰ, καὶ καίρια, ἀνεβόησε τοῦτο, τέκνον, ἀνῃρήμεθα· πεφονεύμεθα. τετυραννοκτονήμεθα. ποῦ ὁ σφαγεύς; τίνι με τηρεῖ; τίνι με φυλάττει, διὰ σοῦ τέκνον προανῃρημένον, ἢ μή τι ὡς γέροντος ὑπερφρονεῖ; καὶ τῇ βραδυτῆτι κολάζειν δέον, καὶ παρατείνει μοι τὸν φόνον, καὶ μακροτέραν μοι τὴν σφαγὴν ποιεῖ. καὶ ταῦτα λέγων, ἐζήτει τὸ ξίφος· αὐτὸς γὰρ ἄνοπλος ἦν, διὰ τὸ πάντα τῷ παιδὶ θαρρεῖν. ἀλλ' οὐδὲ τούτου ἐνεδέησε. πάλαι δ' ἦν ὑπ' ἐμοῦ καὶ τοῦτο προπαρεσκευασμένον, καὶ πρὸς τὸ μέλλον τόλμημα καταλελειμμένον. ἀποσπάσας δὴ τῆς σφαγῆς, καὶ τοῦ τραύματος ἐξελὼν τὸ ξίφος, φησὶ, πρὸ μικροῦ μέν με ἀπέκτεινας. νῦν δ' ἀνάπαυσον ξίφος. πατρὶ πενθοῦντι παραμύθιον ἐλθὲ, καὶ πρεσβυτικῇ χειρὶ δυστυχούσῃ συναγώνισαι. ἀπόσφαξον· τυραννοκτόνησον. καὶ τοῦ πενθεῖν ἀπάλλαξον. εἴθε πρῶτός σοι ἐνέτυχον· εἴθε τὴν τάξιν προὔλαβον τοῦ φόνου· ἀπέθανον ἂν, ἀλλ' ἢ ὡς τύραννος μόνον· ἀλλ' ἔτι νομίζων ἕξειν ἔκδικον. νῦν δ' ὡς ἄτεκνος. νῦν δ' ὡς οὐδὲ φονέως εὐπορῶν. καὶ ταῦθ' ἅμα λέγων, ἐπῆγε τὴν σφαγὴν, τρέμων, οὐ δυνάμενος. ἐπιθυμῶν μὲν, ἀσθενῶν δὲ πρὸς τὴν ὑπηρεσίαν τοῦ τολμήματος. πόσαι κολάσεις ταῦτα; πόσα τραύματα; πόσοι θάνατοι; πόσαι τυραννοκτονίαι; πόσαι δωρεαί; καὶ τέλος, ἑωράκατε πάντες τὸν μὲν νεανίαν προκείμενον, οὐδὲ μικρὸν, οὐδ' εὐκαταγώνιστον ἔργον· τὸν πρεσβύτην δὲ, αὐτῷ περικεχυμένον, καὶ τὸ αἷμα ἀμφοῖν ἀνακεκραμένον. τὴν ἐλευθέριον ἐκείνην, καὶ ἐπινίκιον σπονδὴν, καὶ τὰ ἔργα τοῦ ξίφους τοῦ ἐμοῦ· αὐτὸ δὲ τὸ ξίφος ἐν μέσῳ ἀμφοτέρων ἐπιδεικνύμενον, ὡς οὐκ ἀνάξιον γεγένηται τοῦ δεσπότου, καὶ μαρτυρόμενον ὅτι μοι πιστῶς διηκονήσατο. τοῦτο ὑπ' ἐμοῦ γενόμενον, μικρότερον ἦν. νῦν δὲ λαμπρότερόν ἐστι τῇ καινότητι. καὶ ὁ μὲν καθελὼν τὴν τυραννίδα πᾶσαν, εἰμὶ ἐγώ. μεμέρισται δ' ἐς πολλοὺς τὸ ἔργον, ὥσπερ ἐν δράματι. καὶ τὰ μὲν πρῶτα, ἐγὼ ὑπεκρινάμην. τὰ δεύτερα δὲ, ὁ παῖς. τὰ τρίτα δὲ, ὁ τύραννος αὐτός. τὸ ξίφος δὲ, πᾶσιν ὑπηρέτησεν.

7 producat] producit *1534 1563 1566* 17 carnificis] carnifice *1534 1563 1566* 23 illam] *om. 1566* 26 ergo] ego *1534 1563 1566* 31–32 LVCIANI TYRANNICIDAE, THOMA MORO INTERPRETE, FINIS] FINIS Tyrannicidae Thoma Moro interprete *1506 1514*, FINIS *1528*, *om. 1516 1519 1534 1563 1566*

supererant. At ille quum adesset, ac uideret filium quem habebat unicum, uix respirantem, lacerum ac morte plenum, uulnera quoque illa densa ac multa & letalia gerentem, sic exclamauit: O nate, sublati sumus, interempti sumus, tyranni caesi sumus: ubi iste interfector est? ad quid mihi parcit? cui me reseruat malo per te iam fili praemortuum? nisi me forte utpote senem contemnit, & lente me perimere decreuit: ac mortem mihi producat, ut necem mihi faciat longiorem. Et simul ista dicens, ensem quaerebat: ipse autem erat inermis, ut qui omnem in filio spem reposuerat. At ne is quidem defuit, iamdudum enim a me ante praeparatus erat, atque ad facinus futurum relictus. Ergo ex corpore euellens, & ex uulnere gladium eximens, iamdudum me occidisti, peremisti, nunc uero mihi finem facito: O ensis, inquit, patri lugenti consolator ueni, atque infelicem senis manum adiuua, iugula tyrannum, perime, ac luctu solue. Vtinam in te prior incidissem, utinam ordinem caedis incepissem, cecidissem quidem, at ut tyrannus tantum, at ultorem sperans, nunc uero ut orbus, nunc uero ut etiam carnificis egens. Et haec simul dicens, uulnus intulit tremulus, impotens, cupiens quidem, inualidus tamen ad facinoris ministerium. Quot sunt ista supplicia? quot uulnera? quot mortes? quot tyrannicidia? quot praemia? Et tandem uidistis omnes iacentem iuuenem, opus neque paruum, neque facile, senem uero illi circunfusum, cruorem utriusque inhaerentem, atque illam libertatis & uictoriae parentem Libitinam, & nostri ensis operam: ensem uero ipsum inter utrunque monstratum, declarantem quam non indignus domino sit, testantemque quod mihi sit fideliter obsequutus. Hoc si ergo fecissem, obscurius fuisset, nunc uero redditur ipsa nouitate splendidius. Qui tyrannidem ergo omnem sustuli, ego sum: opus autem in multos distributum est, quemadmodum in fabula. Atque egi primas quidem partes ego, secundas uero filius, tertias tyrannus ipse, ensis autem subseruiuit omnibus.

LVCIANI TYRANNICIDAE,
THOMA MORO INTERPRETE, FINIS. [A_5]

DECLAMATIO
THOMAE MORI LVCIANICAE RESPONDENS.

NON putaueram iudices, ei, qui (id quod ego nunc facio) publicam causam suscepisset agendam, opus fore, ut quur id facere instituerit, rationem reddat: Neque enim ullum fore periculum, ne id malicia potius aggressus, quam pietate uideatur, quum hoc certissimum praebeat magnae integritatis argumentum, quod aliorum omnium commodis elegerit suo priuato labore consulere. Quod quanquam omnes istiusmodi causarum patronos merito posse existimem ab omni calumniae suspicione defendere, me tamen omnium meritissime, qui ut omnibus prosim, non solum hunc mihi laborem desumpsi, sed inimicicias etiam cum eo uiro contraxi, qui se tyrannos quoque iactat occidisse. Sed quoniam nihil tam recte coeptum esse uideo, quod non improborum uellicet ac deprauet iniquitas, & quosdam iam nunc mussitantes audio, qui istius oratione persuasi, hoc meum officium in peiorem partem rapiunt, statui iudices uobis huius actionis meae causas exponere, ne quis industriae meae malignus interpres eam dolori, odio, uel inuidiae conetur asscribere. Ac primum, quid est quur tyranni mortem dolere puter? nam id iste mihi nuper obiecit, probationem uero nullam attulit, dixisse tantum contentus, & credi sibi sine argumento, sine teste postulat: imo, inquit, nisi doleres, nisi tyranni mortem ulcisci cuperes, mecum non contenderes. Ergo eo solo lugere me tyranni mortem probas, quod tibi ob eius necem, praemium iniuste petenti, ego me iuste opposui? Vis uidere quam nihil dicis? Si te tyrannum occidisse probes, ego tecum litigare, nec si uelim possem, nec si possem uelim. Nunc uero quid aliud contra te dicturus sum, quam quod illum non occidisti?

2 LVCIANICAE RESPONDENS] qua superiori declamationi respondet *1506 1514 1516 1519* 6–7 certissimum] *second* s *indistinct 1521* 19 tyranni] tyrannni [*sic*] *1521;* puter] putet *1528* 22 doleres] dolores *1517*

THOMAS MORE'S DECLAMATION IN REPLY TO THE LUCIANIC ONE

I had not imagined, gentlemen of the jury, that one who undertook to plead a case in the public interest, as I now do, would need to explain why he resolved to do this. For there would be no danger of his seeming to be impelled by malice rather than by a sense of duty, since he offers as indisputable proof of his thorough integrity his willingness to exert himself, on his own initiative, for the general welfare. Though I suppose all pleaders of cases such as this can defend themselves justly from every suspicion of calumny, yet I can do this most justly of all. I have not only taken this task upon myself for the sake of the public weal but have incurred the personal enmity of this man who boasts that he killed the tyrants. But since I see that nothing is attempted, however rightly, which the malevolence of the wicked does not carp at and distort; and since even now I hear the murmurings of some who, convinced by his speech, are prejudiced against my performance of duty—I have resolved, gentlemen of the jury, to explain to you the reasons for this lawsuit of mine, lest any spiteful critic try to ascribe my zeal to grief, hatred, or envy.

First of all, why should I be thought to mourn the death of the tyrant, as my opponent has lately charged? He offered no proof, to be sure, content merely with having made the assertion; and he asks to be believed without evidence, without a witness. Nay, more than that: "Unless you were mourning," he says, "unless you desired to avenge the tyrant's death, you would not oppose me." Hence do you demonstrate that I sorrow at the tyrant's death merely by the fact that I have justly opposed you in your unjust claim to the reward for his violent end? Do you want to see how empty that retort is? If you could prove you killed the tyrant, I could not bring suit against you if I would, nor would if I could. Why indeed am I going to oppose you now, except that you did *not* kill him? If you had slain him, I

Si tu interfecisses, nihil quererer, imo laudarem, admirarer, ac praemium primus decernerem, nunc uero ideo tibi contradico, ideo tibi honorem denego, ideo aduersor, ideo queror, quia tyrannum non occidisti. Num igitur occisum, protinus dolere uideor? Ostendisse potius iudices debuit, me tyranno fuisse uel sanguine coniunctum, uel affinitate propinquum, uel beneficijs deuinctum, uel scelerum communione foederatum. At istorum quicquam ne fingere quidem potuit: ergo si neque cognatus illi, neque affinis fui, si mea opera nunquam in cuiusquam iniuriam usus est, si ab illo beneficij nihil in me collatum est, si me acerba seruitute cum caeteris simul oppressit, si me illius interitus libertati uobiscum una restituit, quid causae est ut il[A_5v]lius mortem meae salutis ac libertatis auspicium doleam? At odij certe tantundem causae est. Nam quid egit quod odium in illum prouocaret meum? Primo tyranni filium interfecit: postea uero tyranno sibi manus inferente, iste praemium tanquam tyrannicida petijt: quorum alterum, puta quod iuuenem peremit, quanquam idipsum parum consulte, parumque ex communi commodo fecerat, nisi dij nobis fuissent propitij, fecit ille tamen animo (quantum ego certe suspicor) non malo. Alterum uero, nempe quod praemium postulat quum non meruerit, ut nunc sunt hominum ingenia, non miror, & ignosco certe, modo possit auferre. Neutrum istorum odium in illum meum concitat. Extra haec nihil unquam fecit, quod ad me ullo modo pertineat: ergo tam iniquus sim, ut hominem uix tandem satis aut de facie, aut fama notum, qui me nec re offenderat, nec uerbo laeserat, gratis odio persequerer? Restat inuidiae diluenda suspicio, quae talis est, ut nullo malo carere uelim libentius. Nam quum omnia uitia sint suapte natura perniciosa, nullum tamen est liuore pestilentius: quodque pectus, cui semel insederit grauioribus tormentis exagitet. Nempe alterius fortunam, suum infortunium ducere, secundis aliorum rebus aestuare, alienis laudibus uri, aliena felicitate torqueri, an non summa miseria, non extrema dementia est? Itaque si a quoquam alio uitio iudices absum, ab hoc certe longissime

1 quererer] quaererer *1517 1519* 9 si ab] si me ab *1506 1514 1516 1517 1519*
16 petijt] periit *1517* 19 malo] male *1506 1514 1516 1517 1519*

would not complain; on the contrary I would praise and admire you, and I would be the first to vote for a reward. Now, in fact, it is for this very reason that I speak against you, for this very reason I deny the honor to you, for this very reason I appear against you, for this very reason I object: that *you did not kill the tyrant*. I do not seem on that account to be plunged into sorrow for his death, do I? My opponent ought rather to have shown, gentlemen, that I was connected with the tyrant by blood or marriage ties, or obligated to him for favors, or leagued with him in crimes! But he has been unable even to pretend anything of the sort. If therefore I was neither related to him nor connected with him, if he never employed my services to the injury of anyone, if no benefit accrued to me from him, if he oppressed me along with others by bitter slavery, if his destruction restored me as well as you to freedom, what reason is there that I should lament his death, the good omen of my safety and liberty?

Yet surely there is just as little reason for hatred on my part. What has he done to provoke my hatred? First, he killed the tyrant's son. Afterward, when the tyrant had slain himself by his own hand, this man here demanded reward as a tyrannicide. Consider, for one thing, that he did kill the youth, though with too little forethought and without benefit to the public had not the gods been gracious to us. Yet he did it, so far as I can conjecture, from no unworthy motive. The other point is that he seeks the reward. Although he has not deserved it, men's dispositions are such nowadays that I am not surprised by his seeking it, and I excuse him if he can carry it off.

Neither of these actions excites my animosity toward him. Excepting these, he never did anything that pertains to me in any way. Am I therefore so unfair that I should gratuitously prosecute, out of hatred, a man hardly known to me by looks or reputation, who had never offended me by word or deed?

There remains to be explained the suspicion of jealousy, which is such a thing that from no fault would I more earnestly wish to be free. For although all vices are of their own nature pernicious, none is more destructive than envy, which excites with exceptionally grievous torments the breast wherein it has once lodged. Surely to deem another's good fortune one's own misfortune, to rage at the success of others, to be vexed by praise of others, to be tormented by another's happiness—is not this the greatest misery, is it not the most extreme madness? And so, if I am free from any other fault,

absum. Cuius unquam fortunas impetij? Cuius res bene gestas eleuaui? Cuius laudibus unquam detraxi? Cuius famam labe respersi? Certe ab huius uitij suspicione si me mediocris ista fortuna mea non asserit, quae non tam inops est, ut aliorum opibus ac praemijs inuideam, si me anteacta uita non uindicat: quae non usqueadeo est rerum bene gestarum indiga, ut aliena debeam laude tabescere: At ipsa mehercle causa prorsus absoluit, quae talis est, ut potius omnium ueniam, quam cuiusquam mereatur inuidiam. Quaeso iudices, quod tandem odij signum, quod inuidiae documentum prae me fero? Non prouoco, non irascor, non accuso, urbem tantum in ius uocatam ab illo defendo. Sed quur sedentibus ergo caeteris, ac tacentibus uniuersis, atque in his multis & clarissimis uiris, & autoritate praestantibus, & multo ad dicendum instructioribus, ego potissimum surgo, & petenti praemia contradico? Illi ipsi profecto quin mecum sentiant non dubito: & quin ex his plerique sint, qui hoc ipsum officium, nisi ego iam suscepissem, libenter fuerint obituri: neque tamen ideo culpandus sum, quod me pro patria primus obtulerim. Quicquid est, alieni silentij causas non debeo: me certe ad dicendum cum Reipublicae causa, tum deorum immortalium respectus incitabat: nempe quum uiderem satis tenues [A6] aerarij nostri prouentus, & praesentem pecuniam nimis exiguam, tum instare multas necessarij sumptus occasiones, non ferebam uti ciuitas hoc insuper non necessario sumptu mulctaretur. Tyrannicidij praemium quantum sit non ignoratis, ac merito quidem: quod enim precium satis grande sit, quo agri, foci, fortunae, liberi, coniuges, salus, ac libertas omnium, postremo ipsae deorum arae atque templa redimuntur? Quod quo maius atque urbi onerosius est, eo magis a nobis prospiciendum est ne temere collocetur. Satis iudices, satis impensae ac sumptus imminet, satis effundendum est, ut aerarium nostrum tam profunde, non iste etiam cui nihil debemus, exhauriat. Praeterea quum hoc tyrannicidium sola deorum clementia prouenerit, qui toties inclamati calamitatum tandem nostrarum miserti, crudelissimi nos iugo tyranni soluere, ac libertati reddere uoluerunt, non ferendum putaui ut ciuitas honorem gratiamque dijs

7 tabescere: At] tabescere. At *1521*

gentlemen of the jury, I am certainly the furthest of all from this. Whose fortune have I ever attacked? Whose achievements have I disparaged? Whose praises have I ever belittled? Whose reputation have I besmirched? Assuredly if my own modest fortune—not so mean that I must envy the resources and rewards of other men—does not free me from suspicion of this fault; if I am not vindicated by the record of my life, which has not been so lacking in achievements that I should waste away with envy at another's praise, by Hercules this suit itself straightway absolves me. It is such as deserves the indulgence of everyone rather than the jealousy of anyone. I ask you, jurors, what mark of hatred, what example of envy do I exhibit? I utter no challenge, I am not angry, I make no accusation; I am only defending the city, which is summoned to the bar by him. But since there are others sitting here, all of them keeping silence, and among them many distinguished men and persons eminent in authority and much more skilled in speaking than I am, why do I of all others rise and oppose him when he seeks rewards? I doubt not that they feel the same as I do, and that there are many among them who would willingly have undertaken this duty had I not done so; yet I am not to be blamed because I was the first to offer my services to my country. I am not bound by the reasons for others' silence, whatever they are. Beyond question the public welfare and, secondly, reverence for the immortal gods, urged me to speak. When I considered the meager resources of our treasury, the present scarcity of funds, and the fact that many occasions of necessary expense confront us, I could not bear it that the state be drained of money by this extra, unnecessary expenditure. You are not unaware how large the reward for tyrannicide is—and rightly so; for what sum is large enough if it means recovery of fields, homes, fortunes, children, wives, the liberty and safety of all people and finally the very altars and temples of the gods? The more burdensome this sum is to the city, the more care we must take lest it be awarded rashly. The vast expenditures with which we are threatened, judges—quite apart from what is demanded by this man, to whom we owe nothing—are enough to empty our treasury. Besides, since this slaying of the tyrant came about only by the mercy of the gods, who, so often implored, at last took pity on our calamities and pleased to liberate us from the yoke of that cruelest of tyrants and restore us to freedom, it would in my opinion be intolerable if the city withheld homage

merentibus ablatam, homini non merenti tribueret. Totum autem hoc negocij fortunae deorumque benignitati deberi, huic nihil gratiae, apertissimis argumentis docebo: quod dum facio, quaeso iudices diligenter attendite. Tria sunt quorum iste quodlibet sufficere sibi ad hunc honorem consequendum putat, uel quod tyranni peremit filium, uel quod tyrannum tentauit occidere, uel quod pater filij nece commotus, ense quem iste reliquerat mortem sibi consciuit. Ergo illius adolescentis caedes tyrannicidium uidetur? Quid ni? nempe & ille (inquit) tyrannus erat. Quis id credat iudices, urbem unam duobus suffecisse tyrannis? duos tyrannos inuicem concordes eadem incoluisse moenia? unius urbis ambitu potuisse contineri, quorum alterutri uix uel orbis uniuersus suffecerit? Quisquis id credendum duxerit, is mihi parum uidetur tyrannicam consyderare naturam: nam legitimae quoque potestates, ac non solum legibus gubernantes, sed etiam legibus obtemperantes, & tyrannide tanto interuallo mitiores, ambitione tamen ita uincuntur, ut nec uel intimorum amicorum uitae parcant, potiusquam eos habeant imperij sui consortes. Quis tyrannum credat natura ferum ac uiolentum imperij sui, cuius ardore hominum leges protriuerit, deorum contempserit, uitam neglexerit, socium quenquam admittere? Quin brutorum quoque pleraque ferme quae (quod tyrannorum proprium est) rapto uiuunt, quibus solius pabuli cura impressit aliqua tyrannicae naturae uestigia, in proprios foetus saeuiunt, potiusquam socios illos uenationis accipiant. Et hominem tyrannum putamus, quem fastus inflat, ambitio stimulat, cupiditas urget, gloria sollicitat, suam cum quoquam posse communicare tyrannidem? At iste non solum duos tyrannos facit, uerumetiam adolescentem plusquam tyrannum uult uideri: nam ci[A_6v]uibus atroces (inquit) iniurias fecit, caede, rapina, stupro, omnibus denique scelerum formis insignis. Nomine quidem abstinuit, caeterum re ipsa tyrannidis caput erat, ac parente plus potuit, eum ut uolebat rexit. At longe contra se res habet iudices: nimirum impotens semper ac formidolosa res tyrannis est. Neque filius profecto patrem tulisset si posset, neque filio tantum

1 merentibus] benemerentibus *1506 1516 1519* 13 consyderare] considerare *1521* 15 &] ac *1534 1563 1566* 18–19 uiolentum imperij] uiolentum cum imperii *1506 1514 1516 1517 1519* 19 cuius ardore] ciuis ardore *1506 1514 1516 1517 1519* 21 pleraque ferme] plaerumque formae *1506 1514*, plerunque formae *1516 1517 1519* 22 uiuunt] uiuet *1506 1514 1516 1517 1519*, uiuut [*sic*] *1563* 26 quoquam] quoque *1506*

and gratitude owed to the gods and gave them instead to a man who does not deserve them. I shall demonstrate by the plainest proofs that this whole affair is due to fortune and divine clemency, with no thanks at all to this man. While I do this, gentlemen of the jury, I request your close attention.

There are three reasons, any one of which he thinks sufficient ground for seeking this honor: because he slew the tyrant's son, or because he attempted to kill the tyrant, or because the father, moved by the murder of his son, committed suicide with the sword this man left behind. Does the murder of that youth seem tyrannicide? "Why not? Surely he too was a tyrant." Who would believe, jurors, that one city satisfied two tyrants? That two tyrants lived in concord within the same walls? That they could be contained within the circuit of a single city, when the whole world would scarcely have been room enough for either one? Whoever asks us to believe that seems to me to have a very inadequate notion of the nature of tyranny. Even legitimate authorities, not only governing by laws but also obeying laws, and so very much milder than a tyranny, are nevertheless so dominated by the desire for power that they spare not the lives of intimate friends rather than allow them to share their rule. Is it credible that a tyrant, cruel and violent by nature, suffers any associate to share his power, which he prizes so passionately that he has trampled on the laws of men, scorned those of gods, had no respect for life? Nearly all beasts living by prey (the characteristic of tyrants), on whom hunger alone has stamped certain marks of a tyrannical nature, rage against their own offspring rather than accept them as companions of the hunt. And do we imagine that a human tyrant, puffed up by pride, driven by the lust of power, impelled by greed, provoked by thirst for fame, can share his tyranny with anyone?

Now my adversary not only supposes two tyrants but even wants to make the youth appear more than tyrant; for (it is said) he committed dreadful crimes against the citizens—murder, robbery, rape—in brief, all known forms of crime. The title he eschewed; but in reality he was the head of the tyranny and more powerful than the parent, whom he governed as he pleased.

But the truth is far otherwise, gentlemen of the jury. Certainly tyranny is always a violent and fearsome thing. If the son had had power, he would not have endured his father; nor would the father

permisisset pater ut posset. Nemo tyrannis est haerede suspectior, qui eo maiorem parenti metum incutit, quo magis ferocem eius indolem ac tyrannicos mores expresserit. Continebat ergo filij sui cupiditates, atque adolescenti stringebat potius quam laxabat habenas, ne uiribus nimium inualescens iuuenis, imperij auidus, atque opibus insolens, nec sibi iam imperans, tandem ne parenti quidem parceret, quin iam Saturno superi Iouem praeferrent. Nam si iniurias interdum fecit, quid aliud quam se parenti satellitem praebuit? ex quibus quotus quisque est, qui non grassetur, nuptias uiolet, domos compilet, phana dispoliet, obuios caedat, atque optimum quenque trucidet? Sed quoniam unus est, cuius potentia atque umbra freti, tam scelerata grassantur audacia, poenas alioqui facinorum suorum uel illi, uel publicis legibus daturi, ipsi quidem latrones, homicidae, fures, adulteri. Solus autem unus ille scelerum princeps, sub cuius nomine omnes impune delitescunt, tyrannus est. At ille adolescens si quando patrabat aliquid atrocius, patrem semper sic imperasse dicebat, neque ego quin imperarit dubito. Nam filius quanquam ea indole fuit, ut parentem aliquando uideretur (si ad tantam peruenisset aetatem) flagitijs ac sceleribus aequaturus, tamen in hac adolescentia prae illius crudelitate ac saeuitia quibus iam a puero semper assuetus insenuerat, rudis adhuc miles, ac uix tyro fuit, neque fere magnum quicquam, nisi a patre iussus atque edoctus agebat. Sed siue non nisi iussus illa faciebat, siue ipse etiam iniussus audebat, tamen quum tanquam iussus egerit, quum neque tyranni nomen usurparit, neque se pro tyranno gesserit, sed patri se parere significarit, & ausorum suorum causas in illum retulerit, quum alium se potentiorem esse confessus sit, cuius uiribus fideret, a quo omnis eius penderet impunitas: furem si uelis, aut sacrilegum, uel si quod aliud nomen mauis, appelles: at is profecto non est, in quo fieri tyrannicidium potest. Quod si illum omnia solum potuisse, ac re ipsa tyrannum fuisse contendas, & (quod paulo ante iactabas) illico eius morte liberam fuisse rempublicam, fingamus obsecro adhuc parentem uiuere, sed non fugatum tamen, quod nescio quur ipse finxisti, quippe quem nec ipse fugaueras, neque quur ei fugiendum

7 quin] quum *1566*

for his part have allowed the son to gain so much power that he could take control. No one is more suspect to tyrants than the heir, who, the more he gives vent to his savage nature and tyrannical practices, the more he terrifies his parent. Therefore he restrained his son's passions and checked rather than loosened his reins over the boy, lest the youth, growing too powerful, eager for rule and arrogant in his strength, no longer master of himself, at length would not spare even his parent; nay, the gods might prefer Jove to Saturn. If from time to time he committed outrages, what was that but proof that he was his father's accomplice? Of such persons, how few are there who would not rob, violate marriages, plunder homes, despoil temples, kill those who stand in the way, and murder the leading citizens? But since there is one man under whose power and protection they commit such outrageous crimes—else they would be punished for their deeds, either by him or by the laws, as thieves, murderers, bandits, adulterers—he alone, the sole master under whose title they all take shelter, is tyrant. And that youth, when he committed some extraordinarily outrageous deed, would always say his father had so commanded; nor do I doubt that he did command it. Though the son's temperament was such that he gave promise of some day—if he lived long enough—matching his father in shameful deeds and enormities, nevertheless in his youth, by comparison with his parent's cruelty and savagery (already thoroughly familiar to him from childhood), he was still a raw recruit, scarcely a beginner, and did scarcely anything of importance unless ordered and instructed by his father.

But whether he did not do those deeds unless commanded or whether he dared to do them himself without orders, yet, since he acted *as if* under orders; since he neither usurped the name of tyrant, nor bore himself as tyrant, but made plain that he was acting in obedience to his father and referred the reasons for his exploits to him; since he acknowledged another (in whose power he trusted) was stronger than he and the sole source of his impunity—call him robber or sacrilege if you like, or any other name you please, but assuredly he is not one against whom tyrannicide could be committed. If you contend that he alone had absolute power and was actually tyrant, and that, as you boasted a short time ago, the state became free immediately after his death, let us imagine, I beg you, the parent as still alive though not put to flight; I do not know why you feigned that, when you had neither put him to flight nor done anything to make

esset effeceras. Filio enim tantum per insidias adempto, reliquis uiribus integris, non uideo [B_1] quur patri magis desperandum, aut fugiendum fuerit, quam si aut filius ei natus non fuisset, aut peste correptus obijsset. Patrem ergo fingamus (ut dixi) uiuentem, ac filio quidem unico orbatum, sed satellitum tamen caterua cinctum, caedem filij lachrymantem: sed interfectori minantem, atque omnia suppliciorum genera destinantem, in forum uultu tristi quidem, sed tamen truci procurrere, & prolato quem tu reliquisti gladio, ingentia polliceri praemia, si quis eius ensis dominum prodiderit: hic tu foro iam ab illo, atque eius satellitibus occupato, & in caput tuum quaestione iam haberi coepta, in publicum fortis Tyrannicida procurre, & in medios globos irruens Tyrannum te occidisse proclamita, libertatem omnibus denuncia, ac Tyrannicidij praemium postula. Quid fugis? Quid latebras quaeris? Quid Tyrannicida metuis? An non libera est respublica? An non Tyrannus occisus est? Neque ergo is quem peremisti Tyrannus erat. Sed quidam potius Tyranni satelles, neque eius morte ciuitas libertati restituta est, quod solum pauloante dicebas huius legis spectasse latorem. At haeredem (inquit) occidi. Quid mihi haeredes nominat? Quid in Tyrannide leges memorat? Legum ista nomina sunt. Iuris est ista successio. An Pyratae filium si demortui patris locum impleuerit, haeredem quisquam dixerit? Intestatus semper Tyrannus moritur, quippe legibus ab illo captiuis, quae solae ratum facere testamentum possunt. Proinde qui defuncti locum Tyranni subit, haeres non est, sed nouus Tyrannus. Non enim succedit, sed inuadit. At illi nunc paruissemus. Istud qui constat? Ego contra Tyranno mortuo populum ilico liberum esse dico. Alioqui frustra lex Tyrannicidae praemium statuit, si alterius morte in alterius potestatem recidimus. Sed longe secus iudices, defuncto enim quolibet casu Tyranno, populus iam tum liber dum amici luctu occupantur, dum stupent eius morte satellites, ilico sese in libertatem asseruisset, neque plus filius aduersus populi uires tum ualuisset, quam nunc potest quisquam, uel ex amicis Tyranni potentissimus, aut genere quisquis ei fuit post filium proximus, ad quem, si suc-

2 uideo] videor *1506 1516 1519* 7 forum] suorum *1566* 8 truci] cruci *1506 1516 1519* 10 tu] tum *1506 1514 1516 1519* 20 nomina] numina *1517* 23 solae] solo *1506 1516* 30 dum] eum *1506*

him flee. For though his son had been so treacherously slain, his other forces were left intact; I fail to see what reason there would have been for the father to despair or to flee, any more than if he had not had a son or the son had died of plague. Let us therefore, as I said, imagine the father living and bereft of his only son, but nevertheless surrounded by his palace guard; bewailing the murder of his son, yet threatening the murderer and intending all kinds of punishments. Let us imagine him with mournful but grim countenance rushing into the forum and, displaying the sword you left behind, promising vast rewards if anyone makes known the owner of that sword. With the forum here already occupied by him and his retinue, and inquiry already directed towards you, rush forward, brave tyrannicide, and, dashing into the midst of the crowd, announce that you have killed the tyrant, proclaim liberty for all, and demand a tyrannicide's reward! Why do you run away? Why look for a hiding-place? Why are you, the tyrannicide, afraid? Is not the commonwealth free? Has not the tyrant been killed?—Then the one you slew was *not* the tyrant but rather some accomplice of the tyrant; nor was the city by his death restored to liberty, which, as you said a short time ago, was the sole end the proposer of this law had in view.

"But," he says, "I killed the heir." Why mention heirs to me? Why remind me of laws in a tyranny? They are laws in name only. Succession is a matter of legal right. If a pirate's son filled the place of the dead father, who would speak of the "heir"? A tyrant always dies intestate, since the laws, which alone can make a will valid, are held captive by him. In like manner, he who succeeds to the place of a deceased tyrant is not an heir but a new tyrant, for he does not succeed but usurps. "We would have been in subjection to him even now." Why assume that? I say, on the contrary, that the people are free the instant the tyrant dies. Otherwise the law decreed a reward for the tyrannicide in vain, if at the death of one tyrant we fell into the hands of another.

But the case is far different, gentlemen; for when the tyrant died, by whatever chance, then—while his friends are busy with lamentation, his accomplices stunned by his death—the people, already free, would thereupon have proclaimed their liberty. The son could no more have resisted their strength than can anyone now, either the strongest of the tyrant's cronies or whoever in his family was closest

cessionis nomen, atque haereditatis audiendum est, tam nunc Tyrannis pertinet, quam ad filium pertinuisset. Qui satellitem igitur, qui amicum, qui cognatum, qui filium Tyranni peremerit: frustra tyrannicidium iactauerit. Tyrannus ipse solus est, cuius necem tanto praemio respublica mercatur. Sed uolui (inquit), pertentaui, periclitatus sum, quod negari ne possit, filio tyranni perempto, spe futurae tyrannidis extincta, praeclarum animi mei documentum reliqui, uel hoc solum sufficere mihi ad hunc honorem puto. Hic uide obsecro quam [B_1v] nihil maliuole, quam simpliciter agam tecum omnia, quam ex re tua totum hoc negocium minime suspitiosus interpreter. Nam si alius hanc ageret causam, nec tamen ex inimicis tuis, sed ex acrioribus istis actoribus quispiam qui locos omnes excutiunt, & suspitionibus urgent, ac moleste nimium premunt, sic Hercules hunc tractaret locum, ut te nec id tentasse unquam nec destinasse contenderet. Quod si tu uociferareris mirari te quenquam tam insigni esse impudentia, ut talia dicere occiso in ipso conatu tyranni filio audeat, hic ille protinus quasi fieri non potuerit (inquiet) ut non patriam liberaturus, quod non praestitisti, non Tyrannum occisurus, quem non attigisti: sed ipsum potius iuuenem quem trucidasti perempturus, ascenderis: illatam tibi priuatim, aliquam ulturus ac retaliaturus iniuriam. Hic si instaret, urgeret, premeret, ac certas aliquas probationes illius animi tui ac propositi flagitaret, uides (ut opinor) in quantas trahereris angustias. Sed ego tecum hoc pacto non agam, quippe qui in rebus (cuiusmodi ista est) uehementer obscuris, assueui semper in meliorem partem esse procliuior. Permitto itaque tibi, ut ista fecisse animo in Rempublicam propenso uidearis. Voluisti ergo, ac tentasti prorsus auferre Tyrannidem. Hoccine tibi uidetur isto praemio compensandum? Primum quod uoluisti, quis non uidet quam sit exiguum? Nam hac ratione omnes tyrannicidij praemium peteremus. Quis enim tam frigido in Rempublicam animo fuerit, ut Tyrannum crudelissimum non libenter auferre uoluerit? Tentando uero quid aliud declarasti, quam quod esse Tyrannicida uoluisti? Quod te praeterea periculis exposuisti, an id praemium meruerit ullum, postea uidebimus: quod autem istud non meruit, spero uobis iudices esse uel sola legis recitatione per-

2 Tyrannis] Tyrannus *1517* 5 uolui (inquit),] uolui, (inquit) *1521* 9 maliuole] maleuole *1516 1519 1563*, malaeuole *1566* 17 inquiet] *1506 1514 1516 1519*, inquit *1517 1521 1528 1534 1563 1566* 20 illatam] *1506 1516 1519 1534 1563 1566*, illa tam *1514* (illa *printed as the final word in the line*, tam *as the first word in the next line*) *1517 1521 1528* 35 meruit] meruerit *1534 1563 1566*

to him after the son; to whom, if the title of inheritance and succession is to be considered, the tyranny belongs as much as it would have belonged to the son. For this reason, whoever slays an agent, a friend, a relative, a son of the tyrant, boasts of tyrannicide in vain. It is the tyrant alone whose death the state buys with so great a reward. "But I determined to do something," he says; "I made an attempt, I ventured; and you cannot deny that with the tyrant's son dead, the expectation of future tyranny eliminated, I have left behind distinguished proof of my resolution; and this alone, I think, merits the honor." Observe here, I beg you, how fairly, how frankly, I argue everything with you; how I expound your whole case with the minimum of mistrust. If another person were arguing this case, not one of your enemies either but one of the keener advocates, who scrutinize every point, and ply with doubt, and press upon you as roughly as possible, by Hercules he would so handle this point as to make it an argument that you never attempted the deed or planned to do it! If you voiced astonishment that anyone could be so surpassingly impudent as to dare to say such things when the tyrant's son was slain in that very attempt, he will reply directly to the effect that it could not fail to be the case that you climbed to the stronghold not to free your country (which you did not accomplish), not to kill the tyrant (whom you did not touch), but rather to slay the very youth whom you did murder: you did that in revenge or retaliation for some private injury done to you. If he should plead, urge, press this, and demand some certain proofs of your "resolution" and intention, you see, I am sure, into what difficult positions you would be drawn.

But I shall not deal with you in this manner, since in matters extremely obscure, like this, I am accustomed always to incline to the more lenient interpretation. So I grant that you appear to have committed the deed with patriotic motive. You wished, and forthwith attempted, to destroy the tyranny. Does this seem to you to merit this reward? That, first of all, you wished to do it: who does not see how poor a reason that is? For by this logic we should all seek reward for tyrannicide. Who was so lacking in patriotism that he did not long to destroy that cruelest of tyrants? By making an attempt what have you shown except that you wished to be a tyrannicide? Moreover, that you exposed yourself to dangers, and whether that deserved any reward, we shall consider afterward. I hope it is clear to you, gentlemen of the jury, merely from a recital of the law, that it

spicuum. Quae quum praemium nisi Tyrannicidae non statuat, qui uero Tyrannum non ceciderit, esse Tyrannicida non possit: quantumlibet quispiam tentauerit, quantiscunque sese periculis exposuerit, frustra Tyrannicidij praemium: nisi caeso Tyranno, petierit. Nam ei qui dum conatur occidere, in exilium compulerit, praemium quidem: sed neque tantum, neque tanquam Tyrannicidae decernam. Etenim si morbo quopiam laborans denunciem: quicunque me sanauerit, ei recuperata ualitudine, tria me talenta daturum, ueniat aliquis spe mercedis inductus, qui mei curam suscipiat: deinde medicamentis quibusdam adhibitis, ubi frustra se conari senserit: artem suam morbo uictam confessus, me iam deploratum relinquat: aliqua tamen molestiae parte leuatum, sanitatis illi mercedem, quia non sanauit, non debeo: rursus quia profuit, inanem prorsus a me dimittere haud aequum est. At si [B_2] post mille pharmaca, nihilo tamen melius habentem destituat: praemij nihil meretur, qui nihil iuuit: gratiae uero tantundem fere: qui quod mederi tentauit, sui gratia, non mei fecit. Quod si insigniter Medicae artis ignarus, rem tamen aggredi fuerit ausus, atque aliquantisper misere uenenis adfectum postea dimittat: quum iam non modo nihil opis tulit, sed plurimum doloris addidit: etiam si sese gratis obtulerit: utrum amore dignus est, quod me suo labore tam diu nulla praemij spe tam officiose uexauit? an summo potius odio, quod temere sese meo periculo ei negocio, cuius erat imperitus, immiscuit? Huic rei Iudices haud multum mihi uidetur praesens causa dissimilis. Lex enim Tyrannicidam conducere uehementer alicunde studet: eique praemium certum, Tyranno caeso, pollicetur. Sed Tyrannicidam quum dicit Iudices, hominem quaerit artificem: non manu tantum fortem, sed pectore quoque multo magis ualentem, consilio potius quam uiribus praestantem: qui insidias tendere, laqueos abscondere, occasiones captare nouerit. Ergo hanc prouinciam siquis huiusmodi susceperit: qui Tyrannum ipsum arte ex insidijs adoriatur, adorsum opprimat, oppressum interimat: nec re coepta semel, nisi perfecta desistat: hic Tyrannicidij praemium audacter postulet. Sin id quidem non potuerit, quod autem proximum est & confine, fecerit: Tyrannum uidelicet uel in exilium abegerit, uel ad deditionem condonata uita

4 Tyrannicidij] Tyranncidij [*sic*] *1521* 24 enim] etenim *1506 1516 1519* 31 ex] & *1528 1534 1563 1566*

did not. Since the law provides no reward *except to a tyrannicide*, and since he who has not killed a tyrant cannot be a tyrannicide, however much he has attempted, however many risks he has run, he will seek a tyrannicide's reward in vain unless the tyrant was killed. To one who in trying to kill him forced him into exile, a reward should be given; but I would not grant as big a one, or the same kind of one, as to a tyrannicide. If, struggling with some sickness, I announce that whoever heals me will receive three talents when I recover, some one led by hope of gain might come to undertake my cure. Later, when he had given me medicines, found that his efforts failed, confessed that his skill was baffled by the disease, and left me sorely afflicted but nonetheless somewhat improved, I do not owe him a fee for restoring my health, because he did not restore it; on the other hand, because he helped me, it is unfair for me to dismiss him emptyhanded. But if, after trying a thousand drugs, he leaves me no whit better, he deserves no reward who gave me no help; indeed deserves only the thanks due to one who tried to cure me for his own sake and not for mine. If, grossly ignorant of medical science, he nevertheless ventured to attack the disease, and after a time abandoned the case, with me miserably poisoned—not only having failed to help me but making me worse, even though he offered his services gratis—is he worthy of affection because, by his own exertion over so long period of time, without hope of reward, he maltreated me so obligingly? Does he not, rather, deserve the strongest condemnation for rashly meddling, to my danger, in this matter in which he was unskilled?

The present case, gentlemen, seems to me not far different from this. The law is very ready to hire a tyrannicide from somewhere, and it promises him a specific reward when the tyrant has been slain. But when it says tyrannicide, gentlemen, it seeks a resourceful man, one not only strong-handed but (much more) strong-hearted; able in strategem rather than in force; one who knows how to lay plots, hide his traps, make the most of opportunities. If one who has undertaken a business of this sort attacks the tyrant himself by means of some clever strategem, overpowers him when attacked, and slays him when overpowered, and does not desist from his work, once begun, until it is finished—this man may boldly demand the reward for tyrannicide. If he were unable to do this but instead did something approximate and related to it, for instance drove the tyrant into exile or forced him to surrender, his life being spared, or compelled him

coegerit, uel ad deponendam Tyrannidem certa conditione compulerit: hunc ego praemio dignum, neque nullo quidem, neque tamen Tyrannicidae iudico. At si quis manu potens, mentis inops, illarum penitus ignarus artium, quibus instructum esse Tyrannicidam oportet: qui rem uiribus egere tantum, ac non consilio putet, qui denique Aiaci multo sit, quam Vlyssi similior (sed Aiaci tamen iam abiudicatis armis insanienti, armenta hominum loco trucidanti); si huiusmodi, inquam, quispiam rem tantam conficiendam sibi desumpserit: tum nec insidias collocans, nec tempus eligens, nec occasionem expectans: impetu quodam proruat, nec ab ipso tamen Tyranno incipiat, sed in satellites eius insiliat, dato interim illi sibi cauendi loco; tum subducto Tyranno: re temere coepta, stulte gesta, per ignauiam relicta, ac penitus infecta: sola sibi fuga, abiecto etiam gladio, consulat; postea uero uel defuncto, uel interfecto Tyranno, in publicum prodeat: praemium tanquam Tyrannicida postulet, atque huiusmodi utatur oratione. Volui Iudices, ausus sum, tentaui, periclitatus sum. Vtrum Iudices illi Tyrannicidij praemium decerneretis, quia Tyrannum tentauit occidere? an malam potius gratiam haberetis, ac dignum [B_2v] etiam supplicio duceretis, quod sua temeritate non se solum frustra periculis obiecerat, sed urbem etiam uniuersam in summum discrimen una praecipitauerat: utpote qui Tyrannum stulte irritando fecerit, & ciuibus infestiorem, & aduersus insidias cautiorem? Videtis ergo Iudices quemadmodum id quod iste uel solum satis esse confidebat, usque adeo nihil adiuuat, ut etiam nonnihil officiat. Quamobrem si neque is, quem peremit, Tyrannus fuit: nec satis Tyranni filium occidisse fuit: tentasse uero temere, plus quam frustra fuit, reliquum est, ut ultimum illud, Tyranni uidelicet ipsius mortem, excutiamus: quam iste sibi nos debere disputat. Hoc totius negocij caput est, hoc si uobis iste persuaserit, causae nihil est quin uicerit. Contraque si ego hanc partem euicero, atque sacram hanc, quod aiunt, anchoram illi praecidero, nonne ilico necesse est fluctuet, ac naufragio pereat? Idcirco Iudices hic etiam atque etiam obsecro: ut quam maxime sitis attenti, dum Tyranni caedem doceo, ex qua tota ista pendet con-

6 similior (sed] similior. Sed *1521* 7 trucidanti); si] trucidanti. Si *1521* 12 loco; tum] loco. Tum *1521* 14 consulat; postea] consulat. Postea *1521* 23 infestiorem] *1506 1514 1516 1517 1519 1534 1563 1566*, inuestiorem *1521 1528* 31 euicero] uicero *1563 1566*

to relinquish his tyranny on a certain condition—this man I deem worthy of some reward, yet not the reward for tyrannicide. If a person physically powerful but slow-witted, and utterly unfamiliar with the skill a tyrannicide must possess, who supposed the job could be done by force alone and not with careful planning; who, finally, would be much more like Ajax than Ulysses but like Ajax running mad when the arms have been awarded and slashing at cattle instead of men; if, I say, such a person took upon himself the execution of so great a business and then, failing to devise a strategem or choose the proper time for awaiting his chance, rushed forward in his attack but instead of beginning with the tyrant himself sprang at his guards, the tyrant meanwhile having opportunity to look out for himself; and after that, the tyrant having escaped, the affair rashly attempted, stupidly managed, abandoned through cowardice, and wholly unfinished, he thinks only of his own flight, even throwing his sword away; and later, when the tyrant has died or has been killed, he should appear in public and claim the reward as if he were the tyrannicide, and make a speech of this kind: "I resolved, jurors, I made an attempt, I tried, I essayed it"—would you give him the reward for tyrannicide, gentlemen of the jury, because he *tried* to kill the tyrant? Or would you, rather, bear him ill will and esteem him deserving of punishment because, by his recklessness, he had not only exposed himself alone, uselessly, to dangers, but at the same time had thrown the entire city into extreme peril, since by foolishly inciting him he made the tyrant more menacing to the citizens and more wary of plots?

You see, therefore, gentlemen, how that which he relied on to be sufficient in itself is so far from helping him that it damages his case considerably. Accordingly, if the man he killed was *not* the tyrant, and it was *not* enough to have killed the tyrant's son, but to have made the attempt recklessly was more than vain, it remains for us to examine the last point, the death of the tyrant himself, which this man contends we owe to him. This is the crux of the whole matter. If he persuades you of his view on this, there is nothing to prevent his winning; and if on the contrary I win this point and, as they say, cut away his sheet anchor, must he not at once, of necessity, be tossed about and perish in the shipwreck? For this reason, gentlemen of the jury, I hereby request you again and again to be as attentive as possible while I demonstrate that the death of the tyrant, on which this entire controversy hangs, has no connection at all with my opponent. You

trouersia, nihil ad istum quicquam pertinere. Totum ergo hunc locum Iudices sic ab isto tractatum esse meministis, ut qui uobis persuadere cuperet, uti crederetis eum iam tum quum filium perimeret, parentem quod postea fecit, praescisse facturum. Sciebam, inquit, satis esse filium occidere, sciebam patrem ilico sese post mortem filij perempturum. Imo sciebas certe, quum sic hanc causam ageres, opus esse tibi ut illa praescisse uidereris. Alioqui frustra te praemium Tyrannicidij petiturum: si neque ipse Tyrannum peremisses, neque id saltem fecisses, unde illi scires exitium imminere. Eam ob rem Iudices exitum eius facti tam certum uideri uoluit, ut uobis etiam audientibus dixerit, ob idipsum sese a Tyranno manum abstinuisse, eumque sibijpsi pariter & istius gladio reliquisse: quem alioqui, ut ait, facile potuisset occidere, fecissetque, nisi de exitu securus scilicet, tunc de industria pepercisset, ut paulo post miserius interiret. Hic igitur quid faciam? quo me potissimum uertam? unde argumenta conquiram, quibus hunc probem non esse rerum futurarum praescium? Quin illum percontemur potius, ac rationes aliquas exigamus, quibus ille nobis fidem rei tam longe supra fidem faciat, unde hanc tam mirabilem diuinandi peritiam nactus sit, utrum ne homine quopiam docente didicerit, an numine potius inspirante conceperit. Dic igitur nobis Tiresia, quonam probamento facies, uti constet comprehensam esse tibi rerum futurarum scientiam? defossum alicubi thesaurum effode, cogitationes nostras euolue, abstrusum aliquid atque occultatum erue, quod miremur omnes: nempe eiusdem artis esse puto, [B3] & quae praesentia latent edicere, & quae sunt futura praedicere. Aut si tu futuris duntaxat uales, aliqua nunc edissere aliquot post hoc annis: aut si libet, saeculis potius euentura: quae quum ex tuo praescripto ceciderint omnia, tum demum redito, & futura te praescisse dicito. Interim profecto aegre, quantum suspicor, obtinebis: ut quod te nesciente fiebat, id praescisse credaris antequam fieret. Quod si tum, quum filium interimeres, ignorabas patrem sese, quod postea fecit, occisurum: quur tu nunc eius caedis praemium postulas, quam nisi uelis impudenter esse

19 hanc tam] tam hanc *1506 1514 1516 1519* 29 aegre] aegrae *1506* 30 fiebat] sciebat *1517*

recall that this whole ground was covered by him in the manner of one who wanted to persuade you to believe that even at the time he slew the son he knew in advance the parent would do what afterward he did. "I knew it was enough to kill the son," he says. "I knew the father would take his own life instantly after the death of his son." Nay, rather you knew quite well that when you thus argued this case it was incumbent on you to appear to have foreknown those facts! Else you would seek the reward for tyrannicide in vain if you had not yourself killed the tyrant, or at least done that as a result of which you knew his destruction was close at hand. This is why, gentlemen of the jury, he wanted the result of his act to seem so certain: that he might tell you, his listeners, it was for that very reason he withheld his hand from the tyrant and left him to himself—and to this man's sword as well. Otherwise he could easily have killed him—so he says—and would have done so except that, sure of his death, he purposely refrained in order that the tyrant shortly after would die the more wretched death.

So then, what am I to do with this story? Where can I possibly turn? Where find arguments to show that this man is not able to foretell future events? Rather let us question him and demand some of the reasons for which he would have us believe a thing so far beyond credibility; whence he got such marvelous skill in prophecy; whether he learned it from a teacher or grasped it rather by divine inspiration. Tell us, then, Tiresias, how will you demonstrate that you have achieved this knowledge of future events? Dig up buried treasure somewhere, disclose our thoughts, bring forth something mysterious and secret, which we may all wonder at; for to declare what present events lie hidden and to predict what future ones will be is, I suppose, the function of this art. Or, if you can only foretell future happenings, inform us now of some events that will occur some years hence; or, if it please you, events of future ages. When all these will have come to pass in accordance with your promise, then return and declare that you had foreknown the future. Meantime you will have difficulty, I suspect, in persuading us that you knew before it happened what occurred without your knowledge. If, then, when you killed the son you did *not* know that the father would slay himself, as afterward he did, why do you now demand the reward for his murder—which, unless you are willing to be a brazen liar, you

mendax, fateare necesse est, te ignorante, atque adeo ne cogitante quidem, perpetratam esse? Sed ideo se fortasse putat huius etiam necis autorem: quoniam illa caedes quam fecit, istius quoque, tametsi praeter spem, causa tamen aliquo modo fuit. Qua in re uos longe alia Iudices opinor esse sententia. Neque enim si Tyrannum casu quisquam aut mente captus occidisset, ei Tyrannicidij praemium decerneretis. Quid ita? Nempe quod inscius uterque atque imprudens occidisset, quanquam istius causa est aliquanto, ut mihi uidetur, inferior. Nam si alteruter illorum praemium peteret, tametsi peteret qui peremisset ignarus: atque ideo frustra peteret, peteret tamen qui peremisset: nunc uero & isto nesciente, & non ab ipso peremptus est. At nihil ego, inquit, neque casu, neque imprudens feci: sed filium consulto trucidaui, atque ita patri uolens ac prudens mortis causam praebui: qui, ni ego filium occidissem, adhuc Tyrannus uiueret. Age accedam etiam propius. Si tu Tyrannum aggressus ut perimeres: deinde uictus ab eo, proiecto etiam gladio, fugeres, atque is equo te persequutus, equo collapso, praeceps in gladium tuum tam opportune caderet, ut eodem transfigeretur, an non hic posses eadem omnia dicere, uoluisse te uidelicet, ac uolentem aggressum esse: uolentem igitur prudentemque causas ei mortis attulisse? nam nisi tu illum fuisses adortus, ille non fuisset occisus. Sed nonne uides: ut eadem opera, uel magis fuga tua gloriari liceat, & ignauiae tuae praemium petere? Nam nisi tu fugisses, ille non cecidisset: nisi tu gladium turpiter abiecisses, nec transfixus ille fuisset. Postremo hac ratione ignauos etiam Tyrannicidas esse liceat. Quemadmodum licet uolens adortus esses ut interimeres, tamen postquam re infecta fugisses, quod postea factum esset, tuum non iudicaretur: licet id factum non fuisset, nisi tu aliquid ante fecisses, ita etiamsi Tyrannum perempturus ascendisti, filiumque, dum patrem quaeris, occidisti: tamen cum pergere ac perficere quod incoeperas, uel timore non ausus sis, uel negligentia nolueris, uel casu non potueris: sed re prorsus infecta

26 interimeres, tamen] interimeres: tamen *1521*

must confess was committed without your being aware of it or even thinking of it?

But perhaps this is the very reason he considers himself the one responsible for the tyrant's death, since the murder he *did* commit was in some manner (though beyond expectation) the cause of it. On this subject I dare say you, gentlemen of the jury, are of a very different opinion. If someone had killed the tyrant by chance, or in a fit of madness, you would not have given the reward for tyrannicide to him. Why? Surely because in either case the killer had killed without knowing it and without intending it. *This* man's plea, it seems to me, is somewhat weaker. For if either of those others claimed the reward, though the one who had killed unwittingly would therefore demand it in vain, nevertheless that claimant had, after all, killed him. But in the present circumstances the tyrant was slain without this man's knowing about it at all and by no act of his. "But," he says, "I did nothing by accident or without knowing it. I murdered the son deliberately, and thus designedly and knowingly provided the father with a reason to die—who, had I not killed his son, would still be living as tyrant." Permit me to examine this more closely. If you attacked the tyrant in order to kill him and then, overcome by him and throwing your sword away, you fled; and if when he was pursuing you on horseback his horse stumbled and he very opportunely fell headlong on your sword, so that he was pierced through by it; could you not say all these same things here, namely that you had intended it and that intending it you attacked him, hence by intending and planning it you caused his death—since unless you had attacked him he would not have been killed? But do you not see that in the same manner you could, rather, boast of your flight and seek reward for your cowardice? For unless you had fled, he would not have fallen; unless you had disgracefully thrown your sword away, he would not have been transfixed. Finally, by this reasoning cowards also may be tyrannicides! Just as in that case, what followed after would not be deemed your doing, though you would have attacked to kill (but ran away with the deed unperformed), and though it would not have followed unless you had done something earlier:—so, even though you did climb to the citadel to kill the tyrant, and while searching for the father slew the son, yet since what you had undertaken to perform you either dared not do because of fear, would not do because of negligence, or could not do because of chance, but

redieris, quicquid inde postea te inscio atque in[B3v]sperante prouenerit, id a te profectum esse ne dixeris. Siquidem quicquid tuum dici potest, ibi desijt, ubi tu destitisti. At nec istud fortassis ei quod ipse fecit simile esse concedet. Sed mihi hoc pacto rursus opponet. Is quem tu proponis, non ea mente Tyrannum aggressus est: ut se postea uicto ac fugiente, ille uictor dum persequeretur, occumberet. Ideoque quod non proposuit, merito suum uocare non potest. At ego eo proposito peremi filium: ut pater sese dolore commotus occideret: atque id facturum animo meo percepi. Videtis Iudices, ut nobis illa diuinatione sua rursus occurrit? Quaeremus igitur ab eo, quonam pacto praesenserit? praesciuerit ne? an coniecerit? Si se praesciuisse respondeat, neminem credo ei crediturum: sin coniecisse, interim nescisse se fatetur: sed opinatum esse tantum, hoc est, dubitasse, incertum fuisse: postremo quid aliud quam ignorasse? Sed uideamus tamen quibus signis, quam perspicuis argumentis, rem tam inopinabilem ita collegerit euenturam, ut quod alius nemo sperare potuisset, id ille sibi tanquam certum atque ineuitabile proposuerit. Noueram inquit, quam misere deperibat filium. Ita ne id tandem adeo te certum ac securum reddidit: ut necem eius non tanquam forte secuturam, sed necessario futuram destinares? Scio iudices, haud mediocres illos affectus esse, quos erga liberos parentum pectoribus inseuit natura, neque tamen aut tantos, aut cuiquam tam exploratos crediderim: ut promittere sibi ac spondere audeat, id quod iste se fecisse narrat, interempto filio patrem ultroneum ei comitem futurum. Nam quotusquisque ex his, quorum filij & unici, & charissimi quotidie uel morbo cadunt, uel dolo pereunt, uel bello occumbunt, uel casu intereunt, usqueadeo moerore consternatur, ut sibi mortem sua sponte consciscat? Sed amori, inquit, etiam desperatio non minor occasio desiderandae mortis accessit. Quamobrem obsecro, an tu quum filium perimeres, reliquos una satellites omnes occidisti? non dices, opinor, stragem te tantam fecisse. Caeteros igitur

9 percepi] praecepi *1506 1514 1516 1519* 17 ineuitabile] *1506 1516 1519*, inopinabile *1514 1517 1521 1528 1534 1563 1566* (*see commentary*)

straightway returned with the deed unachieved, and then afterward something occurred unknown to you and unexpected by you, you cannot say it was effected by you. Even if any of it could be called yours, it ceased to be so then and there when you abandoned your enterprise.

Now it may be that he will not concede that this is a fair representation of what he did but will contradict me again, in this fashion: "This man you imagine did not attack the tyrant with the thought that afterward the victorious tyrant, in pursuit of his defeated and fugitive foe, would fall to his death. Hence what he did not intend he cannot justly call his. But as for me, I *did* slay the son with the intention that the father, overwhelmed by grief, would kill himself; and in my mind's eye I foresaw this would happen." Do you see, gentlemen of the jury, that once more he confronts us with that divination of his? We ought, therefore, to demand of him how he perceived it would happen. Did he have foreknowledge of it? Or did he surmise it? If he replies that he foreknew it, I am confident no one will believe him. If he says he surmised it, he confesses meanwhile that he did not *know* it but only supposed it; confesses, that is, that he was doubtful, uncertain—what else, finally, but that he did not know it at all? Yet let us consider by what signs, what clear evidence, he thus inferred the eventuality of a thing so conjectural that what nobody else could have hoped, this man imagined to himself as sure and inevitable. "I had known how desperately he loved his son," he says. So that made you certain and confident, did it, that you could determine his death would follow, not so much through chance but of necessity? I am aware, gentlemen, of the extraordinary affection for their children that nature has planted in the hearts of parents. But I would not have believed it to be either so great, or so thoroughly tested, that one would dare promise himself what this man says *he* did: that a father would be the voluntary companion of his son in death. How many of those whose sons—their only, dearly loved sons—die every day from disease or perish by reason of treachery or fall in battle or die by accident are so overwhelmed by grief that they commit suicide? "But," he says, "besides love, desperation was equally a reason for his desiring death." So then, I ask you, when you slew the son, did you kill all his surviving followers too? You will not affirm, I dare say, that you made so big a slaughter! So he still had the others; he

adhuc retinebat: opum satis, uirium satis habebat. Quapropter uno adempto, quum tot adhuc essent incolumes: quorum omnium intererat maxime hunc incolumem esse, quur ei usqueadeo desperandum fuit, ut non ab urbe, sed ex orbe festinandum fuit. An usquam gentium uiuere quenquam hodie suspicemur, qui id fecisset, quod Tyrannus iste fecit. Quid de alijs quaerimus? quin te potius interrogemus, quem uerisimile est de te coniecturam hanc fecisse, & Tyrannum ex animo tuo spectasse. Si tibi ergo filius perimeretur, atque insuper imminere uideretur nonnullum & fortunae simul & uitae periculum: num potius eligeres te comitem filio [B_4] dare, quam mortem illius ulcisci. An temet ipse ne ab alijs occidereris, occideres? Certe, ut pro te quoque respondeamus, non faceres. Quomodo ergo in mentem tibi uenire potuit: ut quod nec alij fecerunt, nec quisquam fecisset, nec tute facturus esses, id Tyrannum cogitares facturum? At plane, inquit, cogitabam: alioqui cur ibi gladium meum reliquissem. Recte nimirum ignauiae tuae nos admones. Nam cum hoc dicit Iudices: nonne id uobis uidetur dicere, praesensi certe: alioqui cur inde fugissem? quid enim aliud est: alioqui cur gladium ibi reliquissem, quam alioqui cur inde abiecto gladio turpiter me in pedes dedissem. Nam quid opus fuit gladium Tyranno relinquere: Ne deesset ei scilicet, quo periret? Itane qui omnium gladios timet, ipse gladio caret. Qui quicquid habet, gladio peperit, gladio possidet, gladio tuetur, ei gladius unquam abfuerit? O nouum prodigium Iudices, Tyrannus sine gladio. Neque illi gladius defuit, nec iste gladium ei reliquit, sed abiecit: nec futurum quod euenit, uel leuissima coniectura praeuidit. Sed posteaquam in arcem temere (nescio quomodo) perrepsisset, atque ibi adolescentem (ut est iuuenta semper incautior) solum, securum, ac nihil minus expectantem, de improuiso adortus oppresisset: ac potuisset fortasse progressus, ulterius eadem opera Tyrannum sustulisse: ilico hominem timor inuasit, metuentem ne uoce uel gemitu morientis audito, iam tum proditus concurrentibus Tyranni satellitibus, caperetur. Iam ante oculos eius obuersabantur uincula, carcer, tormenta, ac mortes mille, mille supplicia: quorum imaginatione uana perterritus, iam strepitum omnem, omnem sonitum, ac

4 festinandum fuit] festinaret effugere *1506 1516 1519*, festinandum fuerit *1563 1566* 24 abfuerit?] abfuerit. *1521* 30 ulterius] altius *1566* 31 metuentem] intuentem *1506 1514 1516 1517 1519*

had plenty of wealth, plenty of resources. And therefore, when a single person was slain and so many were safe, including—most important of all—this man, the tyrant, why was it so great a grief to him that he should flee in haste, not from the city but from the earth? Are we to believe that there is anyone in the world today who would have done what that tyrant did? Why ask about others? Let us question you instead, for probably you had made this supposition about yourself and viewed the tyrant by the light of your own character. If your son perished, and your fortune and your life seemed threatened, you would not choose to join your son rather than avenge his death, would you? Or would you kill yourself to avoid being killed by others? Of course not. (I will answer for you.) Then how could you have imagined that the tyrant would do what others have not done, what nobody would have done, and what you yourself would not do?

"But clearly I was thinking of it," he retorts, "else why would I have left my sword there?" You do well, surely, to remind us of your cowardice! For when he says this, gentlemen of the jury, does he not seem to you to be saying, "Of course I knew what would happen, else why had I fled from that place?" For what difference is there between "Else why would I have left my sword there?" and "Else why did I basely throw my sword aside and run away?" Now of what use was it to leave the sword for the tyrant? To make certain he would not lack means of dying? So the man who feared everybody's sword lacked a sword himself, did he? Was he ever without a sword—he who got by the sword, held by the sword, and guarded by the sword whatever he possessed? A wondrous prodigy, jurors: a tyrant without a sword! No: he did not lack a sword; nor did this man here leave a sword behind for him. He threw it away; and he did *not* foresee what was going to happen in the future, even by the slightest guess. But after he had rashly broken into the citadel—I know not how—and there suddenly attacked and overpowered the young man, who (with the carelessness of youth) was alone, off guard, not in the least suspicious; and, advancing farther, might perhaps have been able to deal with the tyrant in the same manner—at that instant fright took hold of him, fearful as he was lest, already betrayed to the tyrant's retinue by the cry and groans of the dying youth, he would be captured. Already before his eyes were the chains, dungeon, tortures, and a thousand deaths, a thousand punishments. Terrified by this empty fancy, fearful now of every noise, every sound, and at last

postremo suam ipsius umbram expauescens: tam nunc repente timidus, quam ante temerarius, ex arce se proripuit: nec secum gladium saltem tollere ausus est: seu ne esset fuga tardior, seu ne cum ense deprehensus, insidiatus fuisse Tyranno diceretur: quo nunc perempto recurrit insolens, & tanquam ipse occiderit, Tyrannicidij praemium postulat. Age ergo Tyrannum ipsum non quaero an peremeris: hoc tantum quaero, an peremisse potueris. Si non potueris: ergo occasionem non expectasti, locum idoneum non elegisti, tempus opportunum non captasti: sed temere, sine consilio, sine ratione, praeceps incepisti, quod perficere non ualuisti. Nec illum ergo te iactes occidisse, quem te fateris nec potuisse. Sin potueris: magnae profecto uel inertiae, uel ignauiae fuit, quod non feceris. Imo, inquit, potui: sed de industria supersedi. Satis iam feceram, filium occideram: patrem dolori suo, & gladio meo reliqui, quo eum [B_4v] sese perempturum praeuidi. O inuerecundum, si ista mentiris. O insanum, si non mentiris, si tam incredibilia finxisti, miramur impudentiam, si tam absurda cogitasti, miramur amentiam. Tu ne adeo eras insanus, ut quum uno ictu potueris, & uitam tuam, & Reipublicae salutem in tuto collocare, malueris omnia dubijs fortunae casibus exponere, & tibi futurum promittere, quod sanus auderet nemo sperare? Quod si Tyrannus id uoluisset, quod tute haud dubie fecisses, & quod illum quoque facturum longe uerisimilius quam quod fecit fuit: conclamasset satellites, coegisset sicarios, armasset carnifices, ac prolato filij cadauere, & natura crudelis, & tam atroci spectaculo irritatus, iram ac furorem illum effudisset, primum in te, per quem filius occisus, deinde in urbem uniuersam, propter quam occisus est, quae si contigissent (ut tua dementia propemodum contigerant) neque tu miser hodie uiueres, qui hoc praemium peteres, neque nos Rempublicam ullam a qua peti posset haberemus. Sed dij immortales, Iudices, uota precesque nostras recordati sunt: Dij seruitutis nostrae mala miserati sunt: Dij nobis in summis atque extremis periculis auxiliati sunt. Qui quum semper huic urbi succurrere statuissent, id potissimum tempus elegerunt, quo maxime nobis beneficium suum commendare possent. Nam Tyrannus quan-

17 absurda] absurde *1563 1566*

afraid of his own shadow, suddenly as timid as before he was rash, he rushed from the citadel; he did not even dare to carry his sword with him, for fear his flight would be slowed or, arrested with a sword in his possession, he would be accused of having plotted against the tyrant—at whose death he now returns arrogantly and demands the reward for tyrannicide, as if he had killed him!

Bear in mind, then, that I am not asking whether you killed the tyrant himself. I ask only this: *could* you have killed him? If not, then you did not await opportunity, you did not choose a suitable place, you did not seize the proper moment; but recklessly, rashly, without plan, without thought, you undertook what you were unable to carry through to completion. Do not boast, therefore, of having killed him whom you confess you were not able to kill. But if you *were* able, it was due to great want of skill, or cowardice, that you did not do so. "Not at all," he says. "I could have done it but refrained deliberately. I had already done enough; I had killed the son. The father I left to his grief and to my sword, with which—I foresaw—he would kill himself." Shameless man, if you are lying! Insane, if you are not! If you invented things so incredible we marvel at your impudence; if you reasoned so absurdly we marvel at your stupidity. Were you so mad that when able at a single stroke to ensure your own life and the safety of the republic, you preferred to leave everything exposed to mere chance and to promise yourself as a future occurrence what no sane man would dare to hope? What if the tyrant had been disposed to do what you yourself would doubtless have done, and what it is far more likely he would have done than what he actually did—summon his guard, call his ruffians together, arm his scoundrels; and, when the body of his son was brought before him, his cruel nature and his rage at so horrid a sight would have caused him to vent his wrath and fury first of all on you, by whom his son was slain, and then on the entire city for which he was slain? Had these things happened (as, thanks to your folly, they came close to happening), you would not be alive today, you miserable wretch, to seek this reward, nor would we have any commonwealth of which it could be sought.

But the immortal gods, jurors, remembered our prayers and entreaties; the gods took pity on the miseries of our enslavement; the gods came to our aid in our worst, most extreme perils. Though they had always intended to rescue this city, they chose the most opportune occasion especially to bestow their blessing on us. For though the ty-

quam semper erat molestus uiuente filio, tamen eo nomine minus grauis incumbebat ciuibus, ne miseram penitus atque exhaustam urbem filio relinqueret. At eo trucidato propter quod ante pepercerat, cui dubium esse potest, quin funditus omnia direpturus fuerit? Postquam ergo Respublica istius primum temeritate, deinde ignauia in extremum illud periculum corruisset, superi tempus iam uenisse rati, quo perpetuam nobis insculperent fauoris sui memoriam, omnia mala quae tam prope ceruicibus nostris imminebant, subito in ipsum Tyranni caput auerterunt, idque tam celeriter, ut citius nos periculo liberatos esse, quam in periculo fuisse cognouerimus, ne nos interim saltem potuisset discriminis tanti metus urgere. Quis Tyrannum putasset, Iudices, reperto filij sui cadauere, in sese potius quam in hanc urbem gladium fuisse uersurum, nisi nostri studio superi in propriam illum perniciem immissis ei Furijs, agitassent? Itaque iam nunc uidere mihi uideor micantes latronis oculos, obducta supercilia, contractam frontem, genas pallentes, dentes stridentes, labra tumentia. Denique qualem Pentheum describunt Poetae, toto ore, toto uultu, suae prodentem mentis insaniam. Quum primum ingressus filium reperiret occisum, quid illum fecisse, quid clamasse suspicemur? [B5] quid aliud quam ut impium atque dementem spurcissimo rictu insana in superos euomuisse conuicia? O Deorum iram, o numinum inuidiam. Video caelites odij uestri signa: uideo liuoris atri uestigia. Nihil uobis uiuit iniquius, nihil ambitiosius, nihil inuidentius. Soli imperare, soli regnare uultis, nec satis propria felicitate contenti, semper aliena tabescitis. Quur non mecum in certamen descenditis? Quur ignauum insidiatorem filio summisistis? Ille quisquis erat, cum Tyranno in certamen etiam ingredi non ausus est: hoc certe saltem gaudeo, quod nemo se poterit Tyrannicidam dicere, nemo Tyrannicidij praemium petere. Nemo enim Tyrannum occidet hodie, nisi Tyrannus. Tyrannus ego hodie uel Dijs inuitis moriar. Huiusmodi ergo deliria quum blaterasset, in gladium tandem amens ac furiosus incubuit. Tyrannus igitur Iudices istius gladio, imo nec istius, quippe quem ante abiecerat, manu quidem suapte,

3 quod] quem *1534 1563 1566* 11 urgere] vrgente *1506 1516 1519 1563* 22 numinum] numirium [*sic*] *1506* 30 occidet] occid et *1521*

rant was always oppressive when the son was alive, yet he was less burdensome to citizens for that very reason; he did not want to bequeath to his son a city internally miserable and exhausted. But with the murder of him on whose account he had forborne previously, who can doubt that he would have totally destroyed everything? After the state had fallen into the gravest danger, first because of this man's rashness, then by his cowardice, the gods, thinking the time had come to fashion for us an everlasting memorial of their favor, suddenly diverted all the calamities pressing so closely on us to the head of the tyrant himself, and so swiftly that we knew we were freed from danger before we realized we had been in danger—before dread of so great a crisis could even move us. Who would have thought, gentlemen of the jury, that after the body of his son had been found the tyrant would have turned his sword on himself rather than on this city, unless the gods, through concern for us, had driven him to his own destruction by loosing the Furies upon him? Even now I seem to see the glittering eyes of the brigand, the knitted brows, the contracted forehead, the pale cheeks, the gnashing teeth, the swelling lips; in short, as the poets describe Pentheus, showing his madness with his whole face, his whole countenance. When he first came in and found his son slain, what might we suppose he did, what exclaimed? What else, accursed and frenzied as he was, but to have vomited from his filthy mouth insane abuse against the gods? "O wrath of the gods, O hatred of the divine powers! I see the manifestations of your ill-will, you denizens of heaven. I see the signs of your dark malice. Nothing exists more wicked, more vainglorious and malevolent than you. You wish to rule alone, to govern alone; yet, not sufficiently contented with your own happiness, you are always consumed by envy of others' happiness. Why did you not come down to earth to oppose me? Why did you send instead a cowardly plotter against my son? Whoever he was, he did not even dare to match his strength with the tyrant's. This at any rate I rejoice in, that no one will be able to call himself a tyrannicide, no one seek the reward for tyrannicide, because no one will kill the tyrant today—except the tyrant. I shall die today as tyrant, despite the displeasure of the gods." When he had babbled frantic words of this sort, at length, frenzied and distraught, he fell upon the sword.

The tyrant, then, lies dead, transfixed by this man's sword—no, no, not by *his*, since he had previously thrown it away; by his own

sed sola Deorum opera perfossus iacet. At nunc iste sibi cuius ibi nullae partes erant, primas uendicat. Itaque qui me sycophantam uocabas: uide obsecro, uter nostrum huic uitio propior est, ego ne, qui tecum hodie pro Republica superisque dimicans, praemium tamen nec uictor postulo: an tu potius, qui desertor ac fugitiuus, contendis tamen alijs, atque his quidem Dijs uincentibus ipse triumphare? Desine, desine aliena uirtute partam tibi arrogare uictoriam. Desine Deorum in hanc urbem tam clarum obscurare beneficium. Desine Deorum laudibus obsistere, & ab hac temeraria petitione desiste. Quod si iste Iudices molestus esse perrexerit, uos tamen ipsam rem aequis lancibus expendite: Nam iste quid aliud, quam Tyrannum ut sibi caueret admonuit? Dij ne cauere sibi posset, ne insidijs amplius opus esset, effecerunt. Iste quid aliud quam gladio suo Tyrannum in nos omnes armauit? Dij gladium illum a nobis in Tyranni iugulum retorserunt. Iste quid aliud denique, quam uniuersam urbem in summum periculum dementia sua coniecit? Dij corrigentes istius insaniam, discrimen illud subito in prosperrimam securitatem conuerterunt. Vos ergo Iudices per deos immortales obtestor: per deos huius charissimae libertatis, huius insperatae felicitatis autores, ne quod nobis deorum omnium consilio ac uirtute successit, id uos unius hominis amentiae referri sinatis acceptum: neue hanc urbem unquam in deos liberatores tam ingratam esse, neue patiamini ut salutem suam debere se potius humanae temeritati quam deorum benignitati fateatur, quos ita demum sperare licet futuros semper huic urbi propitios, si nos eorum quae contulere memores, eos (uti aequum est) beneficiorum suorum recognoscamus autores. Alioqui si nos (quod absit) ingrati, quae ab illis [B5v] profecta sunt, in alios referamus, gratiamque superis debitam impendamus hominibus: uicissim hercle metuendum est: ne dij quoque suum erga nos fauorem imminuant: ac Reipublicae nostrae curam, ut indignae quae ab illis curetur, abijciant. Quamobrem ut aliquando finem dicendi faciam: quandoquidem iste peccauit officio: & bono animo male fecit: dij uero eius peccatum in commoda nostra uerterunt: ac dij quidem coegerunt: sed se tamen Tyrannus interfecit: tum praemium qui coegere non petunt, petere autem qui peremit

2 sycophantam] sycophantem *1521* 19 charissimae] *1506 1516 1519*, clarissimae *1514 1517 1521 1528 1534 1563 1566* 24 quos ita demum] quos demum *1563* 31 indignae] indigne *1506 1516 1519*

hand, in truth, but through the act of the gods alone. Yet now this man, who played no part at all there, claims the leading role. And so I ask you who called me cheat to consider which of us is closer to this fault, I who today clash with you on behalf of the state and the gods—yet without demanding a victor's reward—or you, a deserter and fugitive, who strive for a triumph when others—and those the gods—are the real victors? Cease, cease to arrogate to yourself the victory produced by another power than yours. Cease to becloud so signal a favor of the gods upon this city. Cease to obstruct our praises of the gods, and refrain from this presumptuous claim.

But if he continues to be troublesome, gentlemen of the jury, weigh the fact in even scales. What else did he do but warn the tyrant to be on his guard? The gods brought it about that the tyrant could not guard himself, and that there should be no further need of plots. What else did he do than arm the tyrant with his own sword against us all? The gods diverted that sword from us to the throat of the tyrant. Finally, what else did he do than plunge the whole city into the greatest danger by his folly? The gods, amending his madness, suddenly turned that danger into the most fortunate safety. I entreat you, then, jurors, by the immortal gods, the gods who are the sources of this most precious freedom, this unlooked-for happiness, not to allow what came to us through the design and power of all the gods to be ascribed to the madness of one man; nor to allow this city ever to be so ungrateful to the gods their liberators; nor to suffer it to confess that its safety is owed to the temerity of a human being rather than to the benevolence of the gods, who we may now hope will always be propitious toward this city if we, mindful of what they have bestowed, acknowledge them (as is right) the authors of their blessings. But if—may it never come about!—we prove ungrateful, ascribing their deeds to others, and giving to men the gratitude owed to gods, we must fear in turn, by Hercules, lest the gods curtail their favor toward us and leave off the protection of our commonwealth as unworthy of their guardianship.

To conclude, at last, what I have to say: since this man erred in a dutiful act, and blundered with good intentions, but the gods turned his misdeed to our benefit; and since it was the gods who caused the tyrant's death, though the tyrant actually killed himself; and moreover, since they who brought it about do not seek a reward, and the man who committed the murder cannot seek one—in your decision,

non potest: uos sententijs uestris Iudices & huic ueniam, & superis gratiam decernite: & urbem ab huius praemij debito, quo eam liberam esse dij uoluerunt, absoluite. Dixi.

DECLAMATIONIS THOMAE MORI ADVERSVS TYRANNICIDAM FINIS.

4–5 DECLAMATIONIS . . . FINIS] *om. 1516 1534 1563 1566*, Finis *1519*

gentlemen of the jury, give pardon to this man and thanks to the gods; and absolve the city of the obligation of this reward, from which the gods wanted it to be free.

I have finished.

THE END OF THOMAS MORE'S DECLAMATION AGAINST THE *TYRANNICIDA*

COMMENTARY

COMMENTARY

IN THE COMMENTARY, head words are cited from the Latin text in boldface type. The following bibliography and list of abbreviations includes the titles of all works cited frequently in the Introduction and notes. The titles of works referred to only once or occurring only in a brief cluster of references are given in full as they occur. Abbreviations used to designate classical texts are those employed in *The Oxford Classical Dictionary* (Oxford, 1949).

BIBLIOGRAPHY AND SHORT TITLES

Adams, Robert P., *The Better Part of Valor*, Seattle, 1962.

Allen, J. W., *A History of Political Thought in the Sixteenth Century*, 2d ed., London, 1941.

Allen, P. S., *Erasmus*, Oxford, 1934.

———, "Linacre and Latimer in Italy," *English Historical Review, 18* (1903), 514–17.

Allinson, Francis G., *Lucian Satirist and Artist*, New York, 1927.

Althusius, Johannes, *The Politics*, trans. Frederick S. Carney, London, 1965.

Altrocchi, Rudolph, "The Calumny of Apelles in the Literature of the Quattrocento," *PMLA, 36* (1921), 454–91.

Armstrong, C. A. J., "An Italian Astrologer at the Court of Henry VII," *Italian Renaissance Studies*, ed. E. F. Jacob, London, 1960, pp. 433–54.

Augustine, *De civitate Dei*, ed. Juan Luis Vives, Frankfort and Hamburg, 1661.

Baldwin, C. S., *Ancient Rhetoric and Poetic*, New York, 1924.

Barker, Arthur E., "Clavis Moreana: The Yale Edition of Thomas More," *Journal of English and Germanic Philology, 65* (1966), 318–30.

Bauer, Albert, "Der Einfluss Lukians von Samosata auf Ulrich von Hutten," *Philologus, 75* (1919), 437–62.

Baxter, J. H., and Johnson, Charles, *Medieval Latin Word-List*, London, 1950.

Bodin, Jean, *The Six Bookes of a Commonweale*, ed. Kenneth Douglas McRae, Cambridge, Mass., 1962.

Bolgar, R. R., *The Classical Heritage and Its Beneficiaries*, Cambridge, 1954.

Bompaire, J., *Lucien écrivain*, Paris, 1958. Cited as "Bompaire, *Lucien écrivain*."
Bonner, S. F., *Roman Declamation in the Late Republic and Early Empire*, Liverpool, 1949.
Bornecque, H., *Les déclamations et les déclamateurs d'après Sénèque le père*, Lille, 1902.
Bouck, Constance W., "On the Identity of Papyrius Geminus Eleates," *Transactions of the Cambridge Bibliographical Society*, *2* (1958), 352–58.
Bradner and Lynch. *See* More.
Bridgett, T. E., *Life and Writings of Sir Thomas More*, London, 1891.
Brown, Rawdon, *Four Years at the Court of Henry VIII*, 2 vols., London, 1854.
Browne, Sir Thomas, *Religio Medici*, ed. J.-J. Denonain, Cambridge, 1955.
Burckhardt, Jacob, *The Civilization of the Renaissance in Italy*, trans. S. G. C. Middlemore, 3d ed. rev., New York, 1950.
Caccia, Natale, *Note su la fortuna di Luciano nel rinascimento*, Milan, s.a.
Carlyle, R. W., and Carlyle, A. J., *A History of Mediaeval Political Theory in the West*, 6 vols., Edinburgh and London, 1905–36.
Caster, M., *Lucien et la pensée religieuse de son temps*, Paris, 1937.
A Catalogue of the Harleian Manuscripts, 4 vols., London, 1808–12.
Chambers, R. W., *The Place of St. Thomas More in English Literature and History*, London, 1937.
———, *Thomas More* (reprint), London, 1948.
Christ, W. von, et al., *Geschichte der griechischen Litteratur*, 6th ed., 3 vols., Munich, 1912–24.
Clark, D. L., *Rhetoric in Greco-Roman Education*, New York, 1957.
Clarke, M. L., *Rhetoric at Rome*, London, 1953.
Coville, Alfred, *Jean Petit: La Question du tyrannicide au commencement du xve siècle*, Paris, 1932.
Craig, Hardin, "Dryden's Lucian," *Classical Philology*, *16* (1921), 141–63.
Croiset, M., *Essai sur la vie et les oeuvres de Lucien*, Paris, 1882.
Curtius, E. R., *European Literature and the Latin Middle Ages*, trans. Willard R. Trask, New York, 1965.
CW 2, *CW 4*, *CW 5*, and *CW 8*. *See* More.
Daly, L. J., *The Political Theory of John Wyclif*, Chicago, 1962.
Dean, Leonard F., "Literary Problems in More's *Richard III*," *PMLA*, *58* (1943), 22–41.
Delcourt, Joseph, *Essai sur la langue de Sir Thomas More*, Paris, 1914.
DNB. *Dictionary of National Biography* (reprint), Oxford, 1959–60.
Dictionnaire de théologie catholique, ed. A. Vacant et al., Paris, 1903–50.
Dodds, E. R., *Pagan and Christian in an Age of Anxiety*, Cambridge, 1965.
Dorsch, T. S., "Sir Thomas More and Lucian: An Interpretation of *Utopia*," *Archiv für das Studium der neueren Sprachen und Literaturen*, *203* (1966–67), 345–63. Cited as "Dorsch, 'Sir Thomas More and Lucian'."
Du Cange, Charles Du Fresne, *Glossarium mediae et infimae Latinitatis*, ed. L. Favre, 10 vols., Paris, 1937–38.

Duff, J. Wight, *A Literary History of Rome in the Silver Age*, ed. A. M. Duff, 3d ed., New York, 1960.
Elyot, Thomas, *The Governour*, ed. H. H. S. Croft, 2 vols., London, 1883.
Erasmus, Desiderius, *Desiderii Erasmi Roterodami opera omnia*, ed. J. Clericus, 10 vols., Leiden, 1703–06. Cited as "*LB*."
———, *Opera omnia Desiderii Erasmi Roterodami*, Amsterdam, 1969–.
———, *Erasmi opuscula*, ed. Wallace K. Ferguson, The Hague, 1933. Cited as "Ferguson, *Erasmi Opuscula*."
———, *Opus epistolarum Des. Erasmi Roterodami*, ed. P. S. Allen et al., 12 vols., London, 1906–58. Cited as "*EE*."
———, *The Adages of Erasmus*, trans. Margaret Mann Phillips, Cambridge, 1964.
———, *The Colloquies of Erasmus*, trans. Craig R. Thompson, Chicago and London, 1965. Cited as "*Colloquies of Erasmus*."
———, *The Education of a Christian Prince*, trans. Lester K. Born, New York, 1936.
EW, 1557 and *EW*, 1931. *See* More.
Ferguson, Wallace K., *The Renaissance in Historical Thought*, Cambridge, Mass., 1948.
Fletcher, Harris, "The Earliest (?) Printing of Sir Thomas More's Two Epigrams to John Holt," *Studies in Honor of T. W. Baldwin*, ed. Don Cameron Allen, Urbana, 1958, pp. 53–65.
Förster, Richard, "Lucian in der Renaissance," *Archiv für Litteraturgeschichte*, *14* (1886), 337–63.
Frith, John, *A Mirror or Glass to Know Thyself. The Works of the English Reformers: William Tyndale and John Frith*, ed. Thomas Russell, 3 vols., London, 1831.
Gewerstock, Olga, *Lucian und Hutten*, Berlin, 1924.
Gibson, R. W., and Patrick, J. M., *St. Thomas More: A Preliminary Bibliography*, New Haven and London, 1961. Cited as "Gibson and Patrick."
Goldschmidt, E. P., "The First Edition of Lucian of Samosata," *Journal of the Warburg and Courtauld Institutes*, *14* (1951), 7–20.
———, *The First Cambridge Press in Its European Setting*, Cambridge, 1955.
———, "Lucian's *Calumnia*," *Fritz Saxl*, ed. D. J. Gordon, London, 1957, pp. 228–44.
Hall, Edward, *Henry VIII*, ed. Charles Whibley, 2 vols., London, 1904.
Hamilton, Bernice, *Political Thought in Sixteenth-Century Spain*, Oxford, 1963.
Hauffen, Adolf, "Zur Litteratur der ironischen Enkomien," *Vierteljahrschrift für Litteraturgeschichte*, *6* (1893), 161–85.
Hay, Denys, "The Early Renaissance in England," *From the Renaissance to the Counter-Reformation*, ed. Charles H. Carter, New York, 1965, pp. 95–112.
Heep, Martha, *Die Colloquia Familiaria des Erasmus und Lucian*, Halle, 1927.
Hume, David, *The Life of David Hume, Esq. Written by Himself*, London, 1777.

Husner, Fritz, "Die Bibliothek des Erasmus," *Gedenkschrift zum 400. Todestage des Erasmus von Rotterdam*, Basel, 1936, pp. 228–59. Cited as "Husner."

John of Salisbury, *Policraticus*, ed. C. C. J. Webb, 2 vols., Oxford, 1909.

———, *The Statesman's Book of John of Salisbury*, trans. John Dickinson, New York, 1927.

Kaiser, Walter, *Praisers of Folly*, Cambridge, Mass., 1963.

Knowles, David, *The Historian and Character*, Cambridge, 1963.

Kristeller, P. O., *Iter Italicum*, 2 vols., London and Leiden, 1963–67.

Lamson, Roy, and Smith, Hallett, *Renaissance England*, New York, 1956.

Lathrop, H. B., *Translations from the Classics into English from Caxton to Chapman, 1477–1620*, Madison, 1933. Cited as "Lathrop."

Lewis, C. S., *English Literature in the Sixteenth Century*, Oxford, 1954.

Lewy, Guenter, *A Study of the Political Philosophy of Juan de Mariana, S. J.*, Geneva, 1960.

Liechtenhan, R., "Die politische Hoffnung des Erasmus und ihr Zusammenbruch," *Gedenkschrift zum 400. Todestage des Erasmus von Rotterdam*, Basel, 1936, pp. 144–65.

Lucian, *Luciani Samosatensis opera*, ed. Gilbertus Cognatus and Ioannes Sambucus, 4 vols., Basel, 1563.

———, *Luciani Samosatensis opera omnia*, ed. J. Benedictus, 2 vols., Saumur, 1619; Amsterdam, 1687.

———, *The Works of Lucian of Samosata*, trans. H. W. Fowler and F. G. Fowler, 4 vols., Oxford, 1905. Cited as "Fowler Lucian."

———, ed. and trans. A. M. Harmon, K. Kilburn, and M. D. Macleod, 8 vols., London and Cambridge, Mass., 1913–67. Cited as "Loeb Lucian."

———, *A dialogue betwene Lucian and Diogenes of the life harde and sharpe, and of the lyfe tendre and delicate*, London, ca. 1530.

———, *Necromantia, A dialog of the Poete Lucyan . . .*, London, ca. 1522.

———, *Satirical Sketches*, trans. Paul Turner, London, 1961.

Lupton, J. H., *A Life of John Colet, D.D.*, 2d edition (1909), reprinted. Hamden, Conn., 1961.

Luther, Martin, *D. Martin Luthers Werke*, kritische Gesammtausgabe, Weimar, 1883–.

McCarthy, Barbara P., "Lucian and Menippus," *Yale Classical Studies*, *4* (1934), 1–55.

McConica, James Kelsey, *English Humanists and Reformation Politics*, Oxford, 1965.

McCutcheon, Elizabeth, "More's Use of Litotes in *Utopia*," *Moreana*, *31–32* (1971), 107–21.

Machiavelli, Niccolo, *The Chief Works and Others*, trans. Allan Gilbert, 3 vols., Durham, N.C., 1965.

———, *Discourses*, trans. Leslie J. Walker, 2 vols., London, 1950.

Mariana, Juan de, *De rege et regis institutione*, Toledo, 1599.

Marrou, H. I., *A History of Education in Antiquity*, trans. G. Lamb, London, 1956.
Mason, H. A., *Humanism and Poetry in the Early Tudor Period*, London, 1959.
Mesnard, Pierre, *L'essor de la philosophie politique au xvie siècle*, Paris, 1936.
Mitchell, R. J., "Thomas Linacre in Italy," *English Historical Review*, *50* (1935), 696–98.
More, Thomas, *The Complete Works of St. Thomas More:* Vol. 2, *The History of King Richard III*, ed. R. S. Sylvester; Vol. 4, *Utopia*, ed. Edward Surtz, S.J., and J. H. Hexter; Vol. 5, *Responsio ad Lutherum*, ed. John M. Headley, trans. Sr. S. Mandeville; Vol. 8, *The Confutation of Tyndale's Answer*, ed. Louis A. Schuster, Richard C. Marius, James P. Lusardi, and Richard J. Schoeck, New Haven, 1963–. Cited as "*CW 2*," "*CW 4*," "*CW 5*," and "*CW 8*."
———, *The Workes . . . in the Englysh Tonge*, London, 1557. Cited as "*EW*, 1557."
———, *Opera omnia Latina*, Frankfort and Leipzig, 1689.
———, *The English Works of Sir Thomas More*, ed. W. E. Campbell and A. W. Reed, et al., 2 vols., London and New York, 1931. Cited as "*EW*, 1931."
———, *The Correspondence of Sir Thomas More*, ed. Elizabeth Frances Rogers, Princeton, 1947. Cited as "Rogers."
———, *The Latin Epigrams of Thomas More*, ed. L. Bradner and C. A. Lynch, Chicago, 1953. Cited as "Bradner and Lynch."
———, *Utopia*, ed. J. H. Lupton, Oxford, 1895.
New Catholic Encyclopedia, New York, 1967.
Niemann, Gottfried, *Die Dialogliteratur der Reformationszeit nach ihrer Entstehung und Entwicklung*, Leipzig, 1905.
Nifo, Agostino, *De rege et tyranno*, Naples, 1526.
Pace, Richard, *De fructu qui ex doctrina percipitur*, ed. and trans. Frank Manley and Richard S. Sylvester, New York, 1967. Cited as "Pace, *De fructu*."
Palmer, Henrietta R., *List of English Editions and Translations of Greek and Latin Classics Printed before 1641*, London, 1911.
Pauly, A., Wissowa, G., and Kroll, W., *Real-Encyclopädie d. classischen Altertumswissenschaft*, Stuttgart, 1894–.
Pizzi, Clemente, *L'umanista Andrea Ammonio*, Florence, 1956.
Plattard, Jean, *L'oeuvre de Rabelais*, Paris, 1910.
Ponet, John, "Short Treatise of Politic Power," in Hudson, Winthrop S., *John Ponet*, Chicago, 1942.
Rayment, Charles S., "The *Tyrannicida* of Erasmus: Translated Excerpts with Introduction and Commentary," *Speech Monographs*, *26* (1959), 233–47. Cited as "Rayment, '*Tyrannicida*'."
Reed, A. W., *Early Tudor Drama*, London, 1926.
———, "Sir Thomas More," *The Social and Political Ideas of Some Great Thinkers of the Renaissance and Reformation*, ed. F. J. C. Hearnshaw, London, 1925.

Renouard, Ph., *Bibliographie des impressions et des oeuvres de Josse Badius Ascensius*, 3 vols., Paris, 1908.
Rentsch, J., *Lucienstudien*, Plauen, 1895.
Reynolds, E. E., *Thomas More and Erasmus*, London, 1965.
Rogers. *See* More.
Roper, William, *Lyfe of Sir Thomas Moore, Knighte*, ed. E. V. Hitchcock, London, 1935.
Ruysschaert, José, "A Note on the 'First' Edition of the Latin Translations of Some of Lucian of Samosata's Dialogues," *Journal of the Warburg and Courtauld Institutes*, *16* (1953), 161–62.
Salutati, Coluccio, *De tyranno*, ed. Francesco Ercole, Bologna, 1942.
Schoenstedt, Friedrich, *Der Tyrannenmord im Spätmittelalter*, Berlin, 1938.
Schroeder, H. J., ed. and trans., *Disciplinary Degrees of the General Councils*, St. Louis and London, 1937.
Schulze, P., *Lucian in der Literatur und Kunst der Renaissance*, Dessau, 1906.
Schwartz, Jacques, *Biographie de Lucian de Samosate*, Brussels, 1965.
Seneca Rhetor, *L. Annaei Senecae patris scripta quae manserunt*, ed. H. J. Müller, Vienna, 1887.
———, *Controverses et suasoires*, ed. H. Bornecque, Paris, 1932.
———, *The Suasoriae of Seneca the Elder*, ed. and trans. William A. Edward, Cambridge, 1928.
Stapleton, Thomas, *Tres Thomae*, Douai, 1588.
STC. A Short-Title Catalogue of Books Printed in England, Scotland, and Ireland, 1475–1640, London, 1926.
Surtz, Edward, "Aspects of More's Style in *Utopia*," *Studies in the Renaissance*, *14* (1967), 93–109.
———, *The Praise of Pleasure*, Cambridge, Mass., 1957.
———, *The Praise of Wisdom*, Chicago, 1957.
Sylvester, R. S., "Si Hythlodaeo credimus: Vision and Revision in Thomas More's *Utopia*," *Soundings* (New Haven, Conn.), *51* (1968), 272–89.
Thomas Aquinas, *Opera omnia*, Rome, 1882–.
———, *On the Governance of Rulers* (*De regimine principum*), trans. Gerald B. Phelan, Toronto, 1935.
Thompson, Craig R., "Better Teachers than Scotus or Aquinas," *Medieval and Renaissance Studies* No. 2, ed. John L. Lievsay, Durham, N.C., 1968, pp. 114–45.
———, *The Translations of Lucian by Erasmus and St. Thomas More*, Ithaca, N.Y., 1940.
———, "Erasmus' Translation of Lucian's *Longaevi*," *Classical Philology*, *35* (1940), 397–415.
———, "Erasmus, More, and the Conjuration of Spirits," *Moreana*, *24* (1969), 45–50.
Thomson, J. A. K., "Erasmus in England," *England und die Antike*, Leipzig, 1932, pp. 64–82. Cited as "Thomson, 'Erasmus in England.'"

Tyndale, William, *The Practice of Prelates*, ed. Henry Walter, Cambridge, 1849.

———, *The Supper of the Lord*, ed. Henry Walter, Cambridge, 1850.

Ure, P. N., *The Origin of Tyranny*, Cambridge, 1922.

Wagstaffe, John, *The Question of Witchcraft Debated*, London, 1669.

Weiss, R., *Humanism in England During the Fifteenth Century*, 2d ed., Oxford, 1957.

Woolf, Cecil N. Sidney, *Bartolus of Sassoferrato*, Cambridge, 1913.

Wortham, James, "Sir Thomas Elyot and the Translation of Prose," *Huntington Library Quarterly*, *11* (1948), 219–40.

Letter to Ruthall. Thomas Ruthall, whom Erasmus addresses as "humanissime Ruthalle" (*EE*, *1*, 423.2), was an outstanding Tudor example of the successful ecclesiastic and royal servant. He became Dean of Salisbury in 1502, Chancellor of Cambridge University and Archdeacon of Gloucester in 1503, and from 1509 until his death (1523) was Bishop of Durham. He had been in the service of the Crown as early as 1497, and in 1499 was sent on an embassy to Louis XII of France; this may have been the diplomatic errand to which More refers near the end of his letter, although he implies that there had been other missions as well. In the same year, 1499, Ruthall was made Royal Secretary. He went on another embassy to France in 1513 and was present at the Field of the Cloth of Gold in 1520. He became Privy Councillor in 1516, and in his later years was an agent or associate of Wolsey. Giustinian, the Venetian ambassador, remarked that Ruthall sang treble to Wolsey's bass (Rawdon Brown, *Four Years at the Court of Henry VIII* [London, 1854], *1*, 260). How closely More and Ruthall were acquainted we can only surmise. The present letter seems the sole surviving evidence of correspondence between them, but More's respect for this churchman, a rising man at Court, is unmistakable.

Ruthall has been termed the first Secretary to be the subject of a dedication (Denys Hay, "The Early Renaissance in England," *From the Renaissance to the Counter-Reformation*, ed. Charles H. Carter [New York, 1965], p. 102), because the Italian nuncio, Petro Griffo, inscribed an oration to him in 1509. More's dedication of Lucian appeared three years earlier.

Erasmus' translation of Lucian's *Timon*, printed in the 1506 volume, is also inscribed to Ruthall (*EE*, *1*, 423–24). In 1515, Erasmus dedicated an edition of Seneca's *Lucubrationes* to him (ibid., *2*, 51–54).

2/6 **praeceptum.** *Ars P.*, 333–34, 343. Cf. *EE*, *1*, 425.26–36.

2/7 **hoc . . . praestitisse.** "Nulla comoedia, nulla satyra cum huius dialogis conferri debeat, seu voluptatem spectes, seu spectes vtilitatem" (*EE*, *1*, 426.48–50); and compare the rest of the letter with More's judgment.

2/22 **Horatius.** The reference is uncertain; perhaps *Epist.*, I, xvii, 40 or I, xx, 19–24.

2/27 **doctissimus.** Erasmus says Chrysostom is "vtilissimus magister ad Christianam facundiam" (*EE*, *6*, 50.248).

2/28 **Homiliam.** I do not know if this claim originated with More or if he borrowed it, but I have not found an earlier example of it. In the *Elogia Luciani* prefaced to an edition and translation of Lucian's writings (Basel, 1563), Erasmus' one-time secretary, Gilbert Cousin (Cognatus; see *EE*, *9*, 42–45 and my *Colloquies of Erasmus*, p. 16), quotes from More without acknowledgment this statement about Chrysostom's use of

Lucian's *Cynicus* (*1*, a6 verso; repeated in *3*, 759). Much else that Cousin writes on Lucian may have been borrowed from Erasmus.

The notion that Chrysostom introduced a portion of Lucian's *Cynicus* into his homilies on St. John's Gospel is puzzling. More's assertion to this effect is accepted by more than one scholar, but neither he nor they have divulged precisely where in the text of Chrysostom the supposedly borrowed passage or passages are to be found. Cousin simply repeats what More says. In the seventeenth century, it is true, we meet the statement that Chrysostom borrows from *Cynicus* in his eightieth homily on St. John's Gospel—which Cousin does *not* specify—but that assertion will not bear examination. (Cf. Hardin Craig, "Dryden's Lucian," *Classical Philology*, *16* [1921], 145.) In the eightieth homily on John, Chrysostom deplores men's excessive solicitude for food, property, and the things of this world instead of the soul's welfare. These statements are commonplaces; we could easily find many more sources—and far more likely ones—than *Cynicus*. I find nothing of Lucian in any of Chrysostom's homilies.

Many years later (1523) Erasmus wrote that Chrysostom "habet facilitatem, perspicuitatem, suauitatem, copiam cum Luciano communem" (*EE*, *6*, 50.251–52). Was some such observation as this made by Erasmus when he and More were translating Lucian, and if so did it mislead More? Not impossible but improbable, since there is no satisfactory evidence that Erasmus knew Chrysostom as early as 1505–06. The earliest mention of him appears in a letter of 1511 (*EE*, *1*, 467.1).

4/5 **angusta uia.** All editions until the one issued by Giunta, Florence, 1519, print *uita* for *uia*, but *uia* is surely right. More is merely quoting the familiar passage in Matthew 7:14.

4/15 **Plinius.** The elder Pliny, *HN*, VII, lv, 188–90.

4/15 **alij.** In his *Question of Witchcraft Debated* (1669), John Wagstaffe included (pp. 81–128) an English version of Lucian's *Philopseudes* and wrote of it: ". . . this dialogue is not atheistical. Otherwise Sir Thomas Moore would not have taken the trouble to translate it out of Greek into Latin, and so to make it more communicable to the Christian world." That this English translation as well as a Tudor one of *Menippus* "may be" by More has been asserted (*DNB*, *13*, 893), but there is no evidence that he ever made an English version of Lucian's *Philopseudes*. On *Menippus* see below, pp. 142–43.

4/22–28 **ut beatissimo . . . irrisit.** The first of two passages softened by the editors of *1566*. For the other see textual note to 4/33–6/1.

4/23–28 **Augustino . . . irrisit.** Lucian's story is in *Philopseudes*, xxv, p. 65/26–37 of this edition. This seems the only incident corresponding to More's words, though Lucian does not say the men are Spurinnae or soothsayers (Spurinna was the name of the soothsayer who warned Julius Caesar to beware of the Ides of March). More's passage has troubled some

commentators. H. B. Lathrop even suggested that it might be a reference to Augustine's youthful Manichaeism (*Translations from the Classics into English*, p. 37). Another suggestion (my own) was that More may have had Gregory the Great in mind, since Gregory has in his *Dialogues* (iv, 37) a similar tale, "with only the names changed": the judge of the underworld says, "Not this man but Stephen the smith is the one I wanted." Miss Rogers has pointed out, however (*Correspondence*, p. 12 n.), that the story is indeed in Augustine, *De cura pro mortuis gerenda*, xii, 15. The two men involved in the case of mistaken identity are named Curma. By textual corruption this name finally became Curina, as for example in a 1483 edition of Augustine's *Opuscula* (Venice, Octavianus Scotus). In a 1491 edition (Venice, Dionysius Bertochus) the passage is further corrupted to "de turma Curina." Which of the numerous printed editions of Augustine was used by More we do not know, but apparently he emended *Curina* to *Spurina*. At least he was correct in stating that the story is found in Augustine's pages.

4/31 **fabulam.** Saints' lives, says Erasmus when refusing a request to write some, "partim habentur fabulis anilibus simillimae, partim eo proditae stilo vt nemo doctus aut grauis absque nausea possit legere" (to Albert of Brandenburg, Cardinal Archbishop of Mainz, 1517; *EE*, *3*, 177.53–54; and see his life of Jerome in Ferguson, *Erasmi opuscula*, 136.65–78).

6/2–3 **ne ueritas . . . mendacijs.** Erasmus says much the same thing in *Adagia*, *LB*, *2*, 658A–B.

6/7–8 **ubi . . . autoritas.** "Fracta enim vel leviter diminuta auctoritate veritatis, omnia dubia remanebunt: quae nisi vera credantur, teneri certa non possunt" (Augustine, *De mendacio*, x, 17). See an apposite passage in Erasmus' life of Jerome; Ferguson, *Erasmi opuscula*, 134.12–135.22.

6/18 **regulam.** The "rule" is that goods of the soul, if placed in the scales with corporeal and external goods, will easily outweigh them. See Cicero, *Tusc.*, V, xvii, 51.

6/27 **grauitasque.** But Erasmus praises Ruthall's *singularis ingenii morumque facilitas* (*EE*, *1*, 423.1–2).

6/28 **prudentissimus princeps.** More's term *prudentissimus* must be taken, obviously, as laudatory, yet there may be a slight degree of irony in it too. We recall that after the king's death More did not refrain from writing some harsh lines about Henry VII's governance. See the verses from his poem on the king (below, n. to 100/14).

Cynicus

An English version of *Cynicus* (*STC* 16894), believed to have been made from More's Latin translation, survives in two printed copies, one in the Bodleian, the other in the Huntington Library. This is entitled *A dialogue*

betwene Lucian and Diogenes of the life harde and sharpe, and of the lyfe tendre and delicate. (The Greek texts and More's Latin have "Cynicus," not "Diogenes.") The Bodleian copy gives Thomas Berthelet as printer and London as the place of printing, but no translator's name and no date; the Huntington copy, which seems to lack one leaf, has no information at all about the printing. In Henrietta R. Palmer's *List of English Editions and Translations of Greek and Latin Classics Printed before 1641* (London, 1911), p. 71, the translation is attributed to Sir Thomas Elyot, whose authorship appears now to be generally accepted. Berthelet printed most of Elyot's other works.

The plausible suggestion that Elyot translated from More's Latin was first made, so far as I am aware, by Lathrop, p. 38. James Wortham's study of Elyot as translator, "Sir Thomas Elyot and the Translation of Prose" (*Huntington Library Quarterly, 11* [1948], 219–40), assumes Elyot's authorship of the translation and says it "is, in fact, translated from More's Latin" (p. 234), but does not discuss the evidence.

This translation of Lucian, ca. 1530, is the earliest English one in prose to appear in print.

On an original dialogue, *Hermathena*, imitating Lucian and possibly from Elyot's pen, see Constance W. Bouck, "On the Identity of Papyrius Geminus Eleates," *Transactions of the Cambridge Bibliographical Society, 2* (1958), 352–58.

More changes the name of the Cynic's questioner from "Lycinus" (so the 1496 and 1503 Greek texts) to "Lucianus." In *1503* the opening speech is erroneously attributed to the Cynic.

11/17 **LVCIANVS.** The name of the speaker is correct in most editions, wrong only in *1521*, *1528*.

11/22 **copia.** Antithesis of *copia* and *inopia* seems to have pleased More (cf. *Utopia*, *CW 4*, 68/18–19); but *copia* is perhaps too strong a word for Lucian's *ἱκανόν*, which is closer to *satis*.

13/22 **LVCIANVS.** In *1503*, this speech is erroneously given to the Cynic.

15/12 **diutius . . . immoretur.** More's rendering misses the point: "is likely to be ruined by too much."

17/10 **aurei.** More takes *χρυσῶν* to be in apposition with *ἐλεφαντίνων* but it belongs rather with *ἀργυρῶν*, "silver and gold" cups, not "gold and ivory" beds.

17/26 **piscium.** Added by More.

17/31 **cratere.** Object of *uti*. In *1506*, *craterae*; and dative in the Greek text. Possibly More wrote *craterae*, but if so this form was changed in *1514*.

17/34 **nolo.** More's version in *1506* has *volo*, but both the sense and the Greek demand *nolo*, as in *1514*.

23/1 **consuetudine cupiditatis.** The Greek means custom and appetite, not custom of appetite.

23/24 **homines.** That is, rich or proud men.

Menippus

A translation of *Menippus* in English verse, accompanied by More's Latin version, was printed by John Rastell, More's brother-in-law, probably between 1520 and 1525: *Necromantia, A dialog of the Poete Lucyan, for his fantesye faynyd for a mery pastyme. And furst by hym compylyd in the greke tonge. And after translated owt of greke in to latyn and now latly translatyd owt of laten in to englyssh for the erudicion of them which be disposyd to lerne the tongis. Interlocutores. Menippus et Philonides.* The colophon has: "Iohannes Rastell me fieri fecit. Cum priuilegio regali." No date is given.

On John Rastell and the connections between his family and More, see A. W. Reed, *Early Tudor Drama* (London, 1926), and a summary in *EW*, 1931, *1*, 2–4.

This printed translation survives in a copy in the Macclesfield collection at Shirburn Castle and a fragment in the Bodleian Library (Douce frag. f. 13; cf. *STC* 16895). The fragment consists of sixty-six lines from two parts of the dialogue, Aii, Aii verso, Av, Avi (corresponding to 25/17–24, 27/2–11, 31/30–39, 33/15–25 of the present edition). Some lines from the Shirburn Castle copy, without More's Latin, are printed in *EW*, 1931, *1*, 208–10; some from the Douce fragment in Lathrop, pp. 37–38.

Joseph Delcourt speaks more than once of a *manuscript* at Shirburn Castle containing a Latin prose translation and an English verse translation of *Menippus*, and adds that an edition of this manuscript was to be published by l'abbé Colle (*Essai sur la langue de Sir Thomas More* [Paris, 1914], pp. 376, 377). If a manuscript from which Rastell printed does exist, it must have considerable textual authority. But I can find no trace of it, nor have I learned anything about l'abbé Colle or the intended publication. I strongly suspect that Delcourt was misinformed about the manuscript and that what was reported to him was the printed copy. He makes no mention of a printed copy at Shirburn Castle.

Reed thought this verse translation was "possibly More's" (*EW*, 1931, *1*, 209). Fortunately for More's poetical reputation, it is not his. Not only is the verse too crude (cf. Lathrop, p. 38), but the translation has at least one blunder More could not have made: More's "Tiresiam Boeotium" (29/37) is rendered (Aiv verso) "Boyce of Tyre." We meet Boyce of Tyre for "Tiresiam" again near the end of the dialogue (B3 verso, corresponding to 41/25). Reed argues that in another work printed by Rastell the colophon "Iohannes Rastell me fieri fecit" implies authorship as well as printing (*Early Tudor Drama*, pp. 106, 112). If that is so, the same may be true of this translation.

The Latin text of the Shirburn Castle copy differs from *1506*, *1516*, *1517*, *1519*, *1521* too often to allow us to assume it was set from one of those

editions. I have noticed only one difference from *1514*, at 37/31: *incedentem* for *incidentem*. We must conclude that it was probably set from *1514*. If not, it must have been taken from some unrecorded copy.

In the *editio princeps* of 1496, the name of the second speaker is usually abbreviated as *Φι*, but *Φιλω* and *Φιλωνίδης* occur near the end of the dialogue. In *1503* the name is printed first as *Φιλωνίδης*, afterwards as *Φιλω*. Some modern editions print *Φιλωνίδης*, others *Φίλος*.

25/5–6 **SALVE . . . redditus.** Euripides, *HF.*, 523–24.

25/9 **claua.** The word means "club" or "cudgel," but the word in More's source is πῖλος, "a felt cap" (*pilleus*, *pilleum*). He translates πῖλος by *claua* in 31/24 also.

25/12–14 **Adsum . . . procul.** Euripides, *Hec.*, 1–2. In Erasmus' translation of this play, made a few years earlier than the translation of Lucian, these lines are rendered:

> Adsum profectus e profundis manibus,
> Noctisque portis, caeca qua silentium
> Ab arce porro coelitum sita est domus.

25/21 **iuuenta.** More's *iuuenta* in the second line of verse is due to the reading νέου in *1503*; the usual reading in this fragment, which is possibly from the lost *Andromeda* of Euripides, is νοῦ.

25/25–26 **Res . . . Tiresiai.** Adapted slightly from *Od.*, xi, 164–65.

27/19–20 **amico? . . . Ego.** Between *amico* and *Ego* the Greek text has a sentence omitted in *1506* but restored in the marginal corrections to *1514*: "and first I'll tell you the reasons for my decision, why I longed to go down."

27/24 **hercle.** Added by More.

29/5 **Hesiodi.** *Op.*, 287–92.

31/5 **Mithrobarzanes.** "Barzanes" is a name for "governor" in the old Utopian language (*Utopia*, *CW 4*, 132/8).

31/22 **noctis parte.** This addition in *1521* clarifies the sentence but is not in More's Greek source and is therefore suspect.

31/24 **claua.** See note to 25/9.

31/31–32 **utpote . . . emissus.** In *The Frogs* of Aristophanes, Dionysus goes to the underworld disguised.

31/37 **Ingredimur . . . obortis.** From *Od.*, xi, 5. The passage is printed as prose in More's Greek source and probably he failed to recognize it as a line of verse. But the editor or corrector of *1521* did recognize it, and accordingly changed More's rendering to a Latin hexameter. None of the

snatches of Homer or other quotations from the poets, except the lines from Euripides at the opening of *Menippus*, is printed as verse in *1506*.

33/6 **daemones.** One of Erasmus' colloquies, *Exorcismus*, describes how More and his father-in-law, John Colt, played a practical joke on a credulous priest by pretending to invoke spirits. Cf. Craig R. Thompson, "Erasmus, More, and the Conjuration of Spirits," *Moreana*, *24* (1969), 45–50.

33/7 **Hecaten . . . Proserpinam.** In the Greek a hexameter, source unknown.

33/10 **fuit.** Between this word and *Ac* is a verse (*Il.*, xx, 61) omitted in *1506*. See textual notes.

33/16 **celerrime.** Greek *ταχὺ*. *Celeberrime* in all editions until *1534*, but *celerrime* is surely correct.

33/30 **Tortores.** Tormentors, torturers. Cf. *Richard III*, *CW 2*, 259.

33/31–32 **adulteri . . . sycophantae.** More alters Lucian's list slightly by adding murderers and omitting tax collectors.

33/33 **patrantium.** A weak word for Lucian's *κυκώντων*, "those who stir things up."

35/24 **Stoicorum.** More's source has *στοᾶς*; other textual traditions have *σκιᾶς*, "shade," which is the sense required in this passage.

35/35 **discesserant.** *Decedo* for *discedo* occurs in *Utopia* (*CW 4*, 222/30) and in the *1506* text of More's Lucian, but the latter form prevails in most editions, including *1514*.

37/21 **hominum uita.** The reflections of Menippus on "All the world's a stage" are one of the most famous, and most elaborate, expressions of this topos in classical literature. For the metaphor in antiquity see E. R. Curtius, *European Literature and the Latin Middle Ages*, trans. Willard R. Trask (New York, 1953), pp. 138–44; E. R. Dodds, *Pagan and Christian in an Age of Anxiety* (Cambridge, 1965), pp. 8–12; Minos Kokolakis, *The Dramatic Simile of Life* (Athens, 1960). At least two passages in More's later writings are clearly indebted to this passage in *Menippus*. One is in *Richard III* (*CW 2*, 81/6–10; cf. p. 258), the other and less familiar in *The Four Last Things*: "If thou sholdest perceue that one wer ernestly proud of the wering of a gay golden gown, while the lorel playth the lord in a stage playe, woldest thou not laugh at his foly, considering that thou art very sure, that whan the play is done, he shal go walke a knaue in his old cote? Now thou thinkest thy selfe wyse ynough whyle thou art proude in thy players garment, & forgettest that whan thy play is done, thou shalt go forth as pore as he. Nor thou remembrest not that thy pageant may happen to be done as sone as hys" (*EW*, 1557, sig. fg_2v). Further on we read: "For thou woldest not for shame, that men should think thee

so mad, to enuy a poore soule, for playing the lord one night in an enterlude" (ibid., sig. fg3–fg3v). In *Utopia* also (*CW 4*, 98/10–14) are a few lines that may have been suggested by the passage in *Menippus*. The conclusion of Erasmus' colloquy *Abbatis et eruditae* likewise uses this metaphor. For other examples of Lucian's use of it see *Tyrannicida*, 91/38–93/1, 93/27–30.

39/15 **despectim.** If this reading is correct, the word seems intended as an adverb, to render ταπεινῶς in *1503*. Later texts read ταπεινὸς.

41/20 **Aridello.** Σκελετός means "withered," "dried up." *Aridellus* is More's adaptation of the Latin equivalent, *aridus*.

41/21 **Manicensis.** Apparently More's invention, from *Manes*.

41/22 **Proserpina.** More changes Βριμώ to "Proserpina," another and more common name for the goddess, but thereby misses the word-play in his source's ἐνεβριμήσατο ἡ Βριμώ.

41/34 **priuatorumque.** Added by More to explain *idiotarum*.

41/36 **principia semper ac fines.** More reverses the order of τέλη καὶ ἀρχάς.

43/1–2 **Haec . . . corripuit.** Cf. *Od.*, xi, 539.

43/8 **Trophonij templum.** The cave at Lebadeia in Boeotia, where he was worshipped as a hero, was regarded as an entrance to the underworld and was visited by persons seeking oracles. It had a depressing effect on the visitors, for whoever went into Trophonius' cave never laughed again. See Erasmus' *Adagia*, *LB*, *2*, 292F–294B.

Philopseudes

45/23 **optimae.** This correction was not made until *1534* but is clearly needed.

47/1 **coeli.** Uranus.

47/4 **quispiam . . . mutatus.** We should expect *quaepiam* and *mutata*.

47/13 **satiuos.** The "sown men" of Thebes, warriors who sprang from the dragon's teeth sown by Cadmus.

47/34 **referrent.** More's Greek text (and *1496* agrees) has a singular, διεξιόντος; better texts read διεξιόντες. In the translation *referrent* must be preferred, but this word is changed marginally to *referret* in *1514*.

51/35 **clauumque . . . extrudis.** One of Erasmus' favorite proverbs. Cf. *Adagia*, *LB*, *2*, 70B–E.

53/13 **circa plenum . . . forum.** When the market-place was full of people, i.e. the forenoon.

53/22 **inquit.** See textual notes. More apparently overlooked *τῶν φίλων τις* or the compositor failed to set his translation of these words. Even the correction, made in the margin of *1514*, does not go far enough, for the words *παρών, θάρρει* are left untranslated. Completed first in *1521*.

53/35–36 **phrynique, ac physali.** Kinds of toads. Cf. Pliny, *HN*, XXXII, xviii, 50.

55/2 **insibulauit.** A mediaeval form. Cf. Du Cange, *Glossarium mediae et infimae Latinitatis*, s.v. *sibulare*.

55/10 **ferebant.** Singular in the Greek.

55/21 **Alexiclis.** If the text is what More wrote, he tripped over a Greek idiom here. The meaning of the Greek is: "in the house of Glaucias, son of Alexicles." Moreover the name is wrong in the translation. It should be, as in More's source, *Ἀλεξικλέους*, Latin *Alexiclis*. Perhaps this is what More wrote, but *cl* in manuscript is easily mistaken for *d*. The name appears as *Alexidis* in all editions of More's translations that I have collated.

55/23 **Demaeneti filiam.** So More's source. Some texts say she is the "wife of Demeas."

55/23 **disciplinas.** *τοὺς λόγους*.

55/26 **absoluerat.** *ἀνέλυε*. He "reduced" imperfect figures in syllogisms; a technical term in Aristotelian logic.

55/35 **Alexiclem.** Here too the name is wrong in editions of More's translations. It is surprising if More followed the *Ἀναξικλέα* of *1503* (also *1496*) instead of emending this obvious error to *Ἀλεξικλέα*, as the sense of the passage requires.

57/27 **terroribus.** The Greek, *δειμάτων*, proves that *terroribus* in *1566*, not *erroribus* as in other editions, is correct.

57/37 **abigitque.** Ending two successive verbs with *-que*, as *1506* does, seems questionable Latinity. If the reading in *1506* is accurate, the explanation may be that More followed δὲ . . . δὲ in his Greek source; or the typesetter misread More's manuscript.

59/8 **cruce.** Plural in the Greek.

59/24 **formosam illam.** Masculine in the Greek.

59/25 **ingredientibus.** Although all editions consulted, except *1566*, agree on *egredientibus*, the Greek *εἰσιόντων* demands *ingredientibus*.

59/28 **uulsis.** "Plucked"; a questionable rendering of *ἠνεμωμένον*, "blown by the wind."

61/6 **qui apud Minoem.** The Greek is *ὁ τοῦ Μίνωος*, "son of Minos."

61/8–9 **nisi . . . quin.** If *quin* is read, *nisi* can be kept and the sentence is intelligible, though awkward. Apparently the corrector of *1521* who substituted *si non* as well as *quin* intended to recast the entire sentence, omitting *non autem*, but did not do so. (I owe this suggestion to Professor James Hutton.)

61/35 **Antigonus.** *Antiochus*, in *1506* and other editions of More's translations earlier than *1534*, is wrong. Other passages in More's translation (49/22, 51/14, 65/19, 65/22, 65/38) print the name correctly.

61/39 **ostia circumuertens.** More's literal rendering of *θύραν περιτρέπων* (*1503*) can only mean something like "upsetting" or "overturning" (opening and closing?) the door. The phrase is worse than obscure because his Greek text is questionable; undoubtedly *θύραν* should be, as in the Loeb edition, *θυίαν* (*θυείαν*), "mortar," and the meaning is "upsetting the mortar."

63/25 **Mormolycium.** *μορμολυκεῖον*, "hobgoblin," "bugbear."

63/34 **pedibus.** Singular in the Greek.

65/33 **colum.** "Thread," i.e. he is living beyond his allotted time.

67/27 **caniculus.** A Maltese, in the Greek text; More omits this fact.

67/36 **quod prouerbio dici solet.** Added by More.

73/14 **pureque . . . loquentem.** In some texts (including *1496*) this phrase is preceded by a negative particle: Pancrates spoke not pure but imperfect Greek. The negative is omitted in *1503* and hence in More's translation.

73/19 **uersantem.** I.e. swimming.

73/25 **scobinaue.** The Greek has *κόρηθρον*, "broom." More's *scobina* is "rasp," a rough file, in classical usage, but *scoba* for "broom" (1504) is recorded in J. H. Baxter and Charles Johnson, *Medieval Latin Word-List* (London, 1950), p. 377.

73/31 **pessulum, pessulum.** The Greek text has *ὕπερον*, "pestle" (*pistillum*). More's *pessulum* ("bolt") is wrong, though perhaps the printer is more to blame than the translator. Elsewhere in this anecdote the correct word, *pistillum*, occurs.

77/16 **PHILO.** Names of speakers are not attached to the final comments of Philocles and (77/23) Tychiades in *1503*.

Tyrannicida

In Lucian's declamation the claimant's case turns upon the *status* or basis of definition. Quintilian teaches that in every judicial case three questions must be asked: Whether a thing is, what it is, and of what kind it is: *an sit, quid sit, quale sit* (*Inst.*, III, vi, 80, following Cicero, *De Or.*, II,

xxiv, 104 and II, xxvi, 113; *Part. orat.*, ix, 33; *Orator*, xiv, 45; *Top.*, xxi, 82 and xxiv, 92; cf. Rayment, "*Tyrannicida*," pp. 234–36; D. L. Clark, *Rhetoric in Greco-Roman Education*, pp. 72–73, 240–41). Is there a question of fact, e.g. was the man killed? Secondly, was the killing premeditated or not, intentional or accidental, and so on? For killing in self-defense or by accident cannot be defined as murder. Third, what sort of action was the killing—good or bad, favorable or unfavorable, useful or harmful to the state? Nature herself prescribes these questions, says Quintilian, and if they are settled no further question need be asked (III, vi, 80–82). In Lucian's *Tyrannicida*, as in some Roman examples (Seneca, *Controv.*, VII, iv; Quintilian, V, x, 36, where he points out that questions of definition may be intimately connected with motive and asks whether, for example, a man is a tyrannicide if he kills a tyrant by whom he was caught in the act of adultery; and see Rayment, "Tyrannicida," as cited above), we must know the definition of tyrannicide before we can decide the merits of the argument. There is no difference of opinion as to whether the tyrant in Lucian is dead or whether the man who now claims the reward killed the tyrant's son. The question is whether the claimant's being, as he asserts, the "cause" of the tyrant's death is the same, before the law, as actually killing the tyrant; in short, what is the nature of, and consequently the definition of, tyrannicide? If the claimant's argument is accepted, he must win his case. His opponent, later joined by Erasmus and More, denies that his claim to have been the "cause" of the tyrant's death meets the requirements of tyrannicide. They define tyrannicide as the actual killing of the tyrant himself, not the doing of something that is later described, with the advantages of *vaticinatio ex eventu*, as having brought about that death. Even if the claimant's act had been the indirect cause, that is not enough.

In declamations on such topics it is possible (as Rayment points out, p. 234) to make tyrannicide incidental to other issues, a fact underlining the artificial character of declamations. In one of Seneca's *controversiae*, on ingratitude (II, v), a tyrannicide divorced his wife because of her barrenness, although she was so devoted a wife that when tortured by the tyrant she did not divulge her husband's intention of assassinating him. The husband is now accused of ingratitude. In another case (III, vi), a man who chased a tyrant into a house and then set fire to the house in order to kill him accomplished this deed and received a tyrannicide's reward—but now is sued for damages by the owner of the house. In such violations of logic or probability a show of legality or of legalism may exist, but the rules of the rhetorical game as understood and accepted by practitioners and auditors did not demand strict logic at the expense of eloquence.

79/18 **filium . . . occisum.** Lucian says the man was killed "before his time," παρὰ τὴν τελευτήν, a point omitted by More, who has merely *occisum*.

81/3 **sicut ait.** Omitted in *1506* but added in the margin of *1514*. ὥς φησι is in More's source.

83/26 **uerum . . . tum.** More's Greek text is corrupt here. See Harmon's note in the Loeb edition of Lucian, *5*, 452–53.

83/34 **haec.** More omits πάντα.

85/2 **a uobis.** Added by More.

89/11 **tyrannos.** More has *tyrannum*, but a plural is needed. Not only is the word plural in his source, but *eos* in 89/12 refers to *tyrannos*.

89/15 **inquam.** More substitutes this for Lucian's ἐνίκησα.

89/27–28 **grauior . . . uiolentior.** Repetition of *-or* in this lurid passage recalls 77/19.

91/31 **deos.** Plural in the Greek and in *1506*.

93/5 **malo.** Added by More.

93/12 **occidisti, peremisti.** Two words for Lucian's ἀπέκτεινας.

More's Reply to Lucian's *Tyrannicida*

No review or even outline of the literature of tyranny and tyrannicide from ancient times to the sixteenth century can be attempted in this note, but a few references may be useful. These should be supplemented by accounts and bibliographies in such standard works as A. Pauly, G. Wissowa, and W. Kroll, *Real-Encyclopädie d. classischen Altertumswissenschaft* (Stuttgart, 1894–); W. von Christ, W. Schmidt, O. Stählin, *Geschichte der griechischen Litteratur* (Munich, 1912–24); A. Vacant et al., *Dictionnaire de théologie catholique* (Paris, 1903–50); *New Catholic Encyclopedia* (New York, 1967); R. W. and A. J. Carlyle, *A History of Mediaeval Political Theory in the West* (Edinburgh and London, 1905–36); J. W. Allen, *A History of Political Thought in the Sixteenth Century* (London, 1941). The point to be emphasized here is the antiquity and complexity of the questions "What is a tyrant?" and "Is tyrannicide permissible?" Questions of this kind were bound to assume different forms from time to time. In the sixteenth century, to take only one example, they received much attention as a result of the conflicts between the French monarchy and its enemies.

As a rhetorician Lucian writes on tyrants in *Tyrannicida*, *Phalaris* I and II, and *Cataplus*. Greek political experience with tyrants dated from the seventh century B.C. Not all early tyrants were oppressive, but by the late sixth century the word τύραννος was becoming synonymous with "oppressor." By contrast with the *polis* of the fifth century, tyranny seemed mere virtueless despotism; in the fourth century Plato describes it vividly, in *Republic* viii–ix, as the worst of all forms of government. Simonides eulogized Harmodius and Aristogeiton, who slew Hipparchus, brother of

the tyrant Hippias, at Athens in 514 B.C. From Xenophon's imagined conversation between Hieron of Syracuse and Simonides, from Plato, and from Aristotle's *Politics* (especially 1309^a–1315^b) to Lucian and Libanius (who, like Lucian, was a Syrian devoted to Hellenism), tyranny provided a topic for educators, rhetoricians, and moral philosophers. In Roman imperial times, when Lucian and Libanius lived, rhetorical interest in tyranny is much more evident than political discussion of it. As government becomes more oligarchic or despotic, the topic of tyrannicide becomes more artificial. It may be firmly established in the schools or the theater, but treatment of it becomes more remote from political realities and from daily life.

Christianity did not at first change, fundamentally, the aims or curricula of schools, but if we traced the history of tyranny and tyrannicide as topics through the centuries we would find them treated, it is scarcely necessary to say, from new perspectives and on changed assumptions. We would find Judith the "type" of tyrannicide, and efforts made to reconcile the Christian duty of obedience to legitimate rulers with the Christian precept of "We must obey God rather than men." We may safely assume More's familiarity with the main Christian conceptions of tyranny and tyrannicide. Of these the opinions of John of Salisbury and St. Thomas Aquinas might be instanced as representative of mediaeval Christian learning on the subject. John of Salisbury, who is commonly regarded as the first mediaeval writer with a reasoned doctrine on tyrannicide, concludes that an oppressive tyrant may lawfully and justly be killed "and the people liberated for the service of God" ("iustum esse publicos occidi tirannos et populum ad Dei obsequium liberari"; *Policraticus*, VIII, xx, ed. C. C. J. Webb [Oxford, 1909], *2*, 376; and see *The Statesman's Book of John of Salisbury*, trans. John Dickinson [New York, 1927], pp. lxvi–lxxvi). According to St. Thomas, sedition is a mortal sin, since it is opposed to justice and the common good; yet resistance to a tyrannical and unjust authority has not the nature of sedition, for such an authority is not directed to the common good but only to the convenience of the ruler (*S.T.*, 2, 2, q. 42, art. 2). In one brief passage Thomas considers the lawfulness of killing a tyrant if he has obtained power by violence and against the will of his subjects (*Comm. in P. Lombard.*, ii, D. 44, q. 2, art. 2, 5). In *De regimine principum*, however, he rejects tyrannicide. Tyranny is the worst form of government, yet we are not to think that killing an intolerable tyrant is an act of virtue. For such a deed would not accord with the apostolic admonition of passive obedience to rulers. Any action against tyrants must be taken by public authority, not through private presumption. If none is taken effectively, then the only recourse is appeal to God (I, iii and vi).

The judgments of John of Salisbury and St. Thomas Aquinas are only two of many which could be extracted from mediaeval writings, but they are fairly typical of opinions expressed by Christian writers. Wyclif could be cited also; he does not go so far as John of Salisbury in his *De civili*

dominio and *De officio regis* (cf. L. J. Daly, *The Political Theory of John Wyclif* [Chicago, 1962], pp. 123–27). Bartolus of Sassoferrato must be mentioned because of his *De regimine civitatis* and *De tyrannia* (cf. Cecil N. Sidney Woolf, *Bartolus of Sassoferrato* [Cambridge, 1913], pp. 162–74), and Salutati because of his *De tyranno* (ed. Francesco Ercole [Bologna, 1942]). The murder in 1407 of Louis of Orleans, brother of King Charles VI of France, at the instigation of John the Fearless, Duke of Burgundy, produced a notorious defense of "tyrannicide" by a theologian, Jean Petit (see Alfred Coville, *Jean Petit: La question du tyrannicide au commencement du xve siècle* [Paris, 1932]; Friedrich Schoenstedt, *Der Tyrannenmord im Spätmittelalter* [Berlin, 1938]). In 1415 the Council of Constance condemned the proposition that any vassal or subject may, and ought, to kill any tyrant regardless of oaths of fealty and without any judicial decree or command (*Disciplinary Decrees of the General Councils*, ed. and trans. H. J. Schroeder [St. Louis and London, 1937], p. 451).

Writers *de regimine principum* had plenty of examples to cite from ancient history when they wished to warn of the dangers to kingdoms and subjects from tyrannical rulers. They could appeal to Cicero's defense of Milo (or to his letters to Atticus, IX, iv, and *De Officiis*, III, iv, 19). But Christian writers had, as Christians, special difficulties, as our references to Thomas Aquinas indicate, and these difficulties do not diminish as we come closer to the sixteenth and seventeenth centuries. In *De rege et tyranno* (1526), Agostino Nifo includes a section (xliii) on "An liceat impune occidere tyrannum" in which he follows both Cicero, *Ad Atticum*, and Aquinas.

On tyranny in the Italian Renaissance Jacob Burckhardt's essay on "The State as a Work of Art" in his *Civilization of the Renaissance in Italy* is illuminating. The greatest Italian analyst of statecraft, Machiavelli, was of course unknown to Erasmus and More in their Lucianic years, but because of Thomas Cromwell's regard for his writings, and because of his later reputation in England, "the murderous Machiavel" is always of interest to students of Tudor political writing. The prince depicted by Machiavelli is not a tyrant in the usual classical sense of the term, because he rules for the good of the state, not solely for his private profit. He may from time to time seem to act, or in fact have to act, tyrannically, for reasons of state; but he is not a tyrant in the sense intended by most writers on tyrannicide. Machiavelli does not approve of tyranny or tyrants as such. If a tyrant becomes incorrigibly oppressive, the only remedy may be assassination (*Discourses*, I, lviii, 9). John Ponet's *Short Treatise of Politic Power* (1556) seems to be the first English work that clearly allows tyrannicide (see the facsimile reprint, with full introduction, in Winthrop S. Hudson, *John Ponet* [Chicago, 1942], and pp. 157–61 of the introduction). Of Continental contributions the most significant were Bodin's *La république* (1576) and the *Vindiciae contra tyrannos* (1579); La Boétie's *Servitude volontaire* (1576) should be mentioned too. See also Juan de Mariana, *De rege et regis institutione* (1599) and Johannes Althusius' *Politica*

(1603). A recent translation of Althusius by Frederick S. Carney (Boston, 1964) is available. Cf. Pierre Mesnard, *L'essor de la philosophie politique au xvie siècle* (Paris, 1936), pp. 388–406, 500–04, 552–59); Bernice Hamilton, *Political Thought in Sixteenth-Century Spain* (Oxford, 1963).

Among literary treatments of tyrants and tyranny, those in Erasmus' *Adagia*, that great treasury of ancient wisdom and moral experience—a favorite book throughout the sixteenth century—express both fervently and wittily the sensitive, civilized scholar's hatred of the violence to which unbridled power so often leads (e.g. "Aut regem aut fatuum nasci oportere," *LB*, *2*, 106C–111F; "Ut fici oculis incumbunt," ibid., *2*, 653F–655C; "Scarabeus aquilam quaerit," ibid., *2*, 869A–883F). His *Institutio principis Christiani* stresses, like so many handbooks for princes, the urgency of careful education if the future ruler is to avoid the temptations of tyranny. (Lester K. Born's translation, *The Education of a Christian Prince* [New York, 1936], has a good historical introduction. See also R. Liechtenhan, "Die politische Hoffnung des Erasmus und ihr Zusammenbruch," *Gedenkschrift*, pp. 144–65; and Adams, *The Better Part of Valor*, passim.) Erasmus translated Xenophon's *Hieron* (*LB*, *4*, 643A–654A; cf. 531A–C). He notes that tyrannicide is a common topic for μελέται (ibid., *9*, 108B).

Having glanced at the background of More's subject, we may turn next to the speech itself.

When More sent his children directions for writing Latin letters (Rogers, pp. 256–57), he advised them to write out their compositions in English first, and he required them to scrutinize their drafts before making fair copies. This sensible procedure must have been common enough with young pupils, but did it remain More's own practice? He seems to have written an English and a Latin version of *Richard III* almost simultaneously (see Sylvester, *CW 2*, liv–lix); but the composition of *Richard III* is a special and very puzzling case. More was a careful writer who took pains with revisions (ibid., pp. xli–xliii), unlike his collaborator Erasmus, who wrote *stans pede in uno* and hated to rewrite (*EE*, *1*, 3.5–7; *11*, 207.36–38). We have no means of deciding whether More made a draft of his declamation in English before writing it out in Latin. Considering his advice to others on such topics, the pains he customarily took with his own writing, and his legal experience, we are justified in surmising that he would have at least outlined his speech before composing it; but whether he would have outlined it in English is another question. As for Erasmus, it is most improbable that he ever used any language but Latin, even in drafting or outlining. So far as we know, he seldom made any outlines. He always composed *currente calamo*. To revise went against his nature, he says, and "You know how hard it is to oppose nature" (*EE*, *11*, 207.37–38).

According to the consensus of rhetorical wisdom, "embalmed and treasured up on purpose to a life beyond life," every speech must have a beginning, a middle, and an end. The speaker must labor to discover what he ought to say in order to convince or persuade (*inventio*), a requirement

entailing thorough investigation of all relevant circumstances and their relationships; he must arrange his arguments suitably (*dispositio*); use appropriate, effectual language (*elocutio*, embracing everything meant by "style"); memorize the speech (*memoria*); and deliver it impressively (*actio*; "Actio, inquam, in dicendo una dominatur," says Cicero in *De Or.*, III, lvi, 213).

The first three of these resources or requirements embrace most of what we may term the logical and literary aspects of declamation. The other two, *memoria* and *actio*, belong to the actor's art—but the skilled speaker is always an actor. The usual judicial questions (see above, pp. 147–48) of (1) *an sit*, (2) *quid sit*, and (3) *quale sit*, for example, are subsumed under *inventio*. (1) The tyrant's death occurred; no dispute about that. (2) But what sort of death was it? Accidental, premeditated, deliberate, unpremeditated but deliberate? Who or what was responsible for the killing? These are crucial questions for More's imagined speaker to answer. He argues that although the claimant's killing of the son did in a manner cause the father to commit suicide, the slaying of the son had not been premeditated; the claimant encountered him unexpectedly and could not have foreseen that the son's death would impel the tyrant to suicide. Therefore that suicide cannot be defined as tyrannicide. In a legal sense a tyrant cannot, by killing himself, commit tyrannicide. (At least this would be against the rules in declamation.) Furthermore, a man's being, in some sense or other, the indirect cause of a tyrant's death is not in itself sufficient excuse for claiming reward. As for (3), the quality of the act—was it good or bad?—More holds that killing the son was an exceedingly rash deed. It might have prompted the tyrant to take terrible vengeance on the city. Mercifully, the gods prevented this. The claimant may now be pardoned, but how preposterous for him to have claimed a reward for tyrannicide!

The speech itself has, of course, various parts, and in classical rhetoric there are various acceptable ways of dividing and arranging these, depending on the complexity of the case and the strategy adopted by the speaker. Rhetoricians usually listed five or six main parts. We may enumerate these and indicate the divisions of More's declamation.

1. *Exordium* or introduction, to win attention, gain the good will of judges or jurors, and give them preliminary information. More, as the pretended speaker, assures the jurors of the correctness of his motives in appearing against the claimant. He does so only as a public duty; it is absurd to allege, as the claimant has done, that he (More) had any sympathy with the tyranny (94/3–96/12) or that he is jealous of the defendant 96/25–100/1).

2. *Narratio*, a statement of the facts of the case (as the speaker wants the jurors to see them). More merely reminds his hearers of the main facts (96/14–25). He has no need to narrate these at length here, since both sides agree that the claimant slew the son and that the tyrant killed himself after finding the son's body; but often he returns to the theme of "what actually happened."

3. After a brief *divisio* stating what he intends to prove (100/1–4), More proceeds to his principal business, *confirmatio* and *refutatio*.

4. *Confirmatio* or affirmative proof, and

5. *Refutatio* or refutation of the opponent's claims.

He begins by enumerating the claimant's reasons for demanding the reward (100/4–7): (a) because he killed the son, or (b) because he made an honorable and daring attempt to kill the father, or (c) because the father committed suicide with the sword left behind by the claimant. He then takes up the divisions of each of these claims, refutes their specious logic, and demonstrates their failure to satisfy the definition of tyrannicide. (a) He rejects the assertion that the son "was in fact" tyrant (100/26–104/18). He forces the jury to imagine what suffering the city would have experienced if the tyrant had not slain himself. Killing the "heir" is not the same as killing the tyrant (104/18–106/5). (b) Nor are good intentions enough (106/25–108/23). If they were, many citizens could claim reward. No: the reward belongs only to the person who actually kills the tyrant (108/24–26). (c) The tyrant's death was not something for which the city is indebted to this claimant, who had not and could not have arranged or foreseen what would happen after the son's death. More devotes nearly half his speech to this argument, on which his case depends (112/15–120/29). The law does not reward a person for having been, in one way or another, the indirect cause of a tyrant's death. The claimant shamelessly demands reward for something brought about by divine Providence. What he adduces as convincing "proof"—that his action in leaving his sword in the body of the slain son is evidence of his intention and foresight—is turned against him, for More insists that mere fright made him discard his sword (118/15–120/6). The tyrant's destruction was the work of the gods (120/29–122/32).

6. *Peroratio* or conclusion. The summing up takes only a few minutes (122/32–126/3). The jury is asked to pardon the foolish claimant and give due thanks to the gods.

More's declamation likewise exemplifies the application of *prosopopoeia* or impersonation to a judicial speech. Lucian himself reminds us that an orator or declaimer is an actor as well as a speaker (*De saltatione*, lxv), and Quintilian has some interesting passages on the important though difficult art of so assuming the character of the person described, accused, or defended, that the audience will be swayed as the orator desires (*Inst.*, III, viii, 49–54; VI, ii, 36. Quintilian refers specifically to *suasoriae*, and his treatment is cited for this reason by D. L. Clark, *Rhetoric in Greco-Roman Education*, pp. 222–24; but Rayment rightly points out ("Tyrannicida," p. 234, n. 4) that impersonation is no less applicable to *controversiae*. An orator, like an actor, must force his soul so to his own conceit that he will seem to embody the character who "speaks." Thus More as a speaker impersonates his opponent briefly at times, making his proffered explanations sound unconvincing and naive (e.g. 94/21–23, 104/18, 106/5–8, 110/16–17, 112/4–6, 114/12–14, 116/4–9, 116/18, 116/28–29, 118/15–20,

120/13–15). For such purposes, tone of voice, gesture, bearing—the actor's arts—must be well understood and confidently used. After a purple passage describing the tyrant's grief and wrath on discovering the body of his son, the speaker assumes the role, bursting into imprecations against the malevolent gods (122/21–31). This is the only heightened dramatic utterance in the speech. We find many examples of rhetorical mannerisms and devices; but More is a lawyer as well as a rhetorician, and he never loses sight of the sharp quillets of the law. He analyzes the claimant's case and demonstrates, with sarcasm as well as legal citation and moral argument, the failure of that case to meet the conditions of reward for tyrannicide.

96/19 **malo.** Earlier editions read *male* but we should prefer *malo* (modifying *animo*), with *1521*. To say the claimant killed the son *non male* would be obscure at best, and might imply an argument More is at pains to refute. For, whatever the claimant's motive in killing the son, the sole question for the court to decide is whether he killed the father, who was tyrant. More insists he should have killed the tyrant or nobody.

98/27–31 **Quod . . . exhauriat.** We recall More's concern about governmental expenditures when, in the Parliament of 1504, he helped to defeat a proposal for a grant to the king. The Macarians, neighbors of the Utopians, limit their royal treasury to a thousand pounds (*CW 4*, 96/12–29).

100/14 **legitimae . . . potestates.** This is a point More emphasized, as the reader of *Richard III* and *Utopia* is aware. In his congratulatory poem on the coronation of Henry VIII, 1509, he wrote that

Eneruare bonas immensa licentia mentes
  Idque etiam in magnis assolet ingeniis.

(Text in Bradner and Lynch, p. 18.) In this poem he speaks with surprising bluntness about oppressions by Henry VII. He says the accession of the son marks "the end of our slavery, the beginning of our freedom" (p. 16). Laws have regained their authority, property is now safe, people no longer dread informers, tyranny is gone. Yet More did not regard Henry VII as anything but a legitimate monarch.

Another of his Latin poems affirms that although neither a monarchy nor a senate is necessarily a good form of government, a senate is less of a risk:

Difficile est numerum forsan reperire bonorum,
  Sic facile est unum saepius esse malum.
Et fuerit medius saepe inter utrunque senatus,
  Sed tibi uix unquam rex mediocris erit. (p. 83)

"The desire of a kingdome knoweth no kindred" (*Richard III*, *CW 2*, 41/24–25; and cf. the marginal summary on p. 84: "Authority loueth no partners").

102/1 **Nemo tyrannis.** "Infelices esse tyrannos in filiis" is the title of a brief section (xxxiii) in Agostino Nifo's *De rege et tyranno*, 1526.

102/7 **Saturno.** Saturn was identified by the Romans with Cronus, one of the Titans. Cronus revolted against his father Uranus but was later overthrown by his own son, Zeus.

104/5 **satellitum.** This word, which occurs half a dozen times in the speech, is used also in *Richard III* (*CW 2*, 40/23, and see p. 207). More has an epigram on the theme *Regem non satellitium sed virtus reddit tutum* (Bradner and Lynch, p. 51).

104/30–31 **in libertatem asseruisset.** A technical phrase in Roman law.

114/9 **illorum.** Referring to "si . . . occidisset" in lines 5–6.

116/17 **ineuitabile.** The reading *inopinabile*, which contradicts the sense of this crucial passage, appears in *1514* (followed by *1517*, *1521*, *1528*, *1534*, *1563*, *1566*); undoubtedly because the compositor's eye fell upon *inopinabilem* in the corresponding position in *1506*, directly above *ineuitabile*.

118/24–25 **Neque . . . abiecit.** The Argument to Lucian's speech states clearly that the claimant left his sword in the son's body (79/6–7, and see 87/13, 93/11–12). More's scornful denial of this, and his insistence that the sword was thrown away in panic (118/15–120/6, 122/32–124/1) are important points in his attack on the claimant's assertions. For the purposes of his own declamation, More takes the Argument to be less than a neutral statement of the facts, regarding it instead as merely a summary of the claimant's specious case.

120/30 **dij immortales.** Both Erasmus and More in their declamations introduce this important point—that deliverance is due to the clemency of the gods—early in their arguments but emphasize it most in their perorations. On this point, see G. Marc'hadour, *The Bible in the Works of Thomas More* (Nieuwkoop, 1969–72), *5*, 115–16.

122/15–18 **Itaque . . . insaniam.** With this passage compare one in *Richard III* (*CW 2*, 47/16–18, and see 87/13–21) on "the out & inward troubles of tyrauntes."

122/17 **Pentheum.** Pentheus, as many poets relate, was torn in pieces by his mother and other women for his impiety. See Euripides, *Bacchae*.

124/32–33 **bono animo male fecit.** Cf. note on 96/19.

APPENDIX

Modern Translations of Lucian's Dialogues

THE CYNIC

LYCINUS

You there, why in heaven's name have you the beard and the long hair, but no shirt? Why do you expose your body to view, and go barefooted, adopting by choice this nomadic antisocial and bestial life? Why unlike all others do you abuse your body by ever inflicting on it what it likes least, wandering around and prepared to sleep anywhere at all on the hard ground, so that your old cloak carries about a plentiful supply of filth, though it was never fine or soft or gay?

CYNIC

I need no such cloak. Mine is the kind that can be provided most easily and affords least trouble to its owner. Such a cloak is all I need. But *you* tell *me* something, I beg you. Don't you think that there's vice in extravagance?

LYCINUS

Yes indeed.

CYNIC

And virtue in economy?

LYCINUS

Yes indeed.

CYNIC

Why, then, when you see me living a more economical life than the average man, and them living a more extravagant life, do you find fault with me rather than with them?

LYCINUS

Because, upon my troth, I do not think your manner of life more economical than that of the average man, but more wanting—or rather completely wanting and ill-provided. For you're no better than the paupers who beg for their daily bread.

CYNIC

Well then, since the argument has reached this point, would you like us to examine just what is want and what sufficiency?

LYCINUS

Yes, if you wish it.

CYNIC

Then is sufficiency for each man that which meets his needs? Or would you call it something else?

LYCINUS

That's good enough.

CYNIC

And want that which comes short of his requirements and fails to meet his needs?

LYCINUS

Yes.

CYNIC

Then there's nothing wanting in my way of life. No part of it fails to fulfil my needs.

LYCINUS

How do you mean?

CYNIC

Suppose you consider the purpose of anything which we need. For example doesn't a house aim at giving protection?

LYCINUS

Yes.

CYNIC

Well, what is the purpose of clothes? Do not they too aim at giving protection?

LYCINUS

Yes.

CYNIC

But why, tell me, have we ever found need for protection itself? Isn't it for the better condition of the person protected?

LYCINUS

I think so.

CYNIC

Well, do you think that my feet are in worse condition?

LYCINUS

I don't know.

CYNIC

Well, this is how you can find out. What is the function of feet?

LYCINUS

To walk.

CYNIC

Then, do you think my feet walk worse than the feet of the average man?

LYCINUS

In this case perhaps the answer is no.

CYNIC

Then neither are they in worse condition, if they fulfil their function no worse.

LYCINUS

Perhaps so.

CYNIC

Then, as far as feet are concerned, I seem to be in no worse condition than the average man?

LYCINUS

So it seems.

CYNIC

Well, take the rest of my body. Is it in any worse state? For if it's

worse, it's weaker, since the virtue of the body is strength. Is my body weaker?

LYCINUS

It doesn't seem to be.

CYNIC

Then neither my feet nor the rest of my body would appear to be wanting in respect of protection. For, if they were wanting, they would be in bad condition; for want is everywhere an evil and detracts from the condition of the things in which it occurs. Another point. My body seems to be no worse nourished from finding its nourishment in the food that comes first to hand.

LYCINUS

That's quite easy to see.

CYNIC

It wouldn't be healthy if it were wrongly nourished, for bad food harms the body.

LYCINUS

That's so.

CYNIC

How then, tell me, when all this is so, can you denounce and pour scorn on my way of life, and call it miserable?

LYCINUS

Because, in heaven's name, although Nature, whom you hold in such honour, and the gods have given the earth for all to enjoy, and from it have provided us with many good things, so that we have abundance of everything to meet not only our needs but also our pleasures, nevertheless you share in few if any of all these things, and enjoy none of them any more than do the beasts. You drink water just as they do, you eat anything you find, as do the dogs, and your bed is no better than theirs. For straw is good enough for you just as it is for them. Moreover the coat you wear is no more respectable than that of a pauper. However, if you who are quite content with all this turn out to be of sound mind, god was wrong in the first place in making sheep to have fleeces, in the second place in making the vines to produce the sweetness of wine, and yet again in giving such wonderful variety to all else with which we are provided,

our olive-oil, honey and the rest, so that we have foods of all sorts, and pleasant wine, money, a soft bed, beautiful houses, and everything else admirably set in order. For the products of the arts too are gifts of the gods, and to live deprived of all these is miserable, even if one has lost them at the hands of another, as have men in prison; but it is much more miserable if a man deprives himself of all the finer things of life. That is no less than palpable madness.

CYNIC

Well, perhaps you're right. But tell me one thing. Suppose a rich man proves a zealous and generous host and invites to dinner at one and the same time many men of all kinds, some of them ailing, others men in perfect health, and suppose he has gone on to spread before them a profusion of foods of all sorts. Suppose a man were to snatch up all these and eat them all and not merely the dishes near him, but also those at a distance provided for the sick men, he himself being in good health, in spite of the fact that he has but a single stomach, needs little to nourish him, and is likely to destroy himself by the surfeit. What is your opinion of such a man? Is he sensible?

LYCINUS

Not in my opinion.

CYNIC

Well, is he temperate?

LYCINUS

He's not that either.

CYNIC

Well, suppose that a man sharing this same table pays no heed to the great variety of dishes, but chooses one of those closest to him sufficient to his need, and eats of this in moderation, confining himself to this one dish, and not so much as looking at the others; don't you consider this man to be more temperate and a better man than the other?

LYCINUS

I do.

CYNIC

Well, do you understand or must I tell you?

LYCINUS

What?

CYNIC

That god is like that good host and puts before men many varied dishes of all sorts, that they may have what suits them, some of the dishes being for the healthy, others for the sick, some for the strong, others for the weak, not for all of us to make use of all of them, but that each may use the things in his reach, and only such of them as he needs most.

But you resemble very closely that man who snatches up everything in his uncontrolled greed. You wish to use everything and not merely what you have at home but what comes from every corner of the earth, you don't think your own land and sea adequate, but import your pleasures from the ends of the earth, you always prefer the exotic to the home-produced, the costly to the inexpensive, what is hard to obtain to what is easy, and in short you choose to have worries and troubles rather than to live a carefree life. For those many costly provisions for happiness, in which you take such pride, come to you only at the cost of great misery and hardship. For consider, if you will, the gold for which you pray, the silver, the expensive houses, the elaborate dresses, all that goes along with these; consider how much they cost in trouble, in toil, in danger, or rather in blood, death and destruction for mankind, not only because many men are lost at sea for the sake of these things, and suffer terribly in searching for them abroad or manufacturing them at home, but also because they are bitterly fought for, and for them you lay plots against one another, friends against friends, children against fathers, and wives against husbands. Thus too it was, I imagine, that Eriphyle betrayed her husband for gold.

And yet all these things happen, although the many-coloured robes can afford no more warmth, and the gilded houses no more shelter, though neither the silver nor the golden goblets improve the drink, nor do the ivory beds provide sweeter sleep, but you will often see the prosperous unable to sleep in their ivory beds and expensive blankets. And need I tell you that the many foods so elaborately prepared afford no more nourishment, but harm the body and produce diseases in it? And need I mention all the inconvenient things that men do and suffer to gratify their sexual passions? Yet this is a desire which is easy to allay, unless one aims at licentious indulgence. And in gratifying this desire men do not even seem to be content with madness and corruption, but now they pervert the use of things, using everything for unnatural purposes, just as if in preference to a carriage a man chose to use a couch as if it were a carriage.

LYCINUS

And who does that?

CYNIC

You do so, when you use human beings as beasts of burden, bidding them carry your couches on their shoulders as though they were carriages, and you yourself lie up there in state, and from there steer your men as though they were donkeys, bidding them take this turning rather than that. And the more any of you does this, the luckier he is thought. And, as for those who not only use flesh for food, but also conjure forth dyes with it, as for example the purple-dyers, don't you think that they too are making an unnatural use of the handiworks of god?

LYCINUS

By Zeus, that I do not; for the flesh of the purple-fish can produce dye as well as food.

CYNIC

But it doesn't exist for that purpose. For in the same way too a man could force a mixing-bowl into service as a pitcher; but that's not why it came into being. But how could anyone describe in full the misery of people like these? For it's so very great. Yet you reproach *me* for not wishing to share it with them. But I live like that moderate man, making a feast of what is in my reach, and using what is least expensive, with no desire for dainties from the ends of the earth.

Furthermore, if you think I live the life of a beast, because the things I need and use are small and few, it may be that the gods are inferior even to the beasts—if we use your argument. For the gods need nothing. But, so that you may learn more exactly what is involved in having few needs, and what in having many, reflect that children have more needs than adults, women than men, invalids than healthy people, and, in general, the inferior everywhere has more needs than the superior. Therefore the gods have need of nothing, and those nearest to them have the fewest needs.

Do you think that Heracles, the best of all mankind, a godlike man and rightly considered a god, was compelled by an evil star to go around naked, wearing only a skin and needing none of the same things as you do? No, *he* was not ill-starred, he who brought the rest of men relief from their banes, nor was *he* destitute who was the master of both land and sea; for no matter what he essayed, he prevailed over all everywhere, and never encountered his equal or superior, till he left the realm of man. Do you think that *he* couldn't provide blankets and shoes, and that was why he went around in the state he did? No one could say that; no, he had self-

control and hardness; he wished to be powerful, not to enjoy luxury. And what of his disciple, Theseus? Was he not king of all the Athenians, son of Poseidon, as they say, and best man of his day? Yet he too chose to wear no shoes, and to walk about naked; he was pleased to have a beard and long hair, and not only he but all the other men of old too. For they were better men than you, and not a single one of them would have submitted to the razor any more than would a lion. For they thought that soft smooth flesh became a woman, but, just as they themselves were men, so too they wished to appear men, thinking the beard an ornament of men, as is the mane an ornament of horses and lions, to whom god has given additional gifts to grace and adorn them. So too has he given men the addition of a beard. These men of old therefore are the ones that *I* admire and should like to emulate, but the men of to-day I do not admire for the "wonderful" prosperity they enjoy in the matter of food and clothing, and when they smooth and depilate every part of their bodies, not even allowing any of their private parts to remain in its natural condition.

I pray that I may have feet no different from horses' hooves, as they say were those of Chiron, and that I myself may not need bedclothes any more than do the lions, nor expensive fare any more than do the dogs. But may I have for bed to meet my needs the whole earth, may I consider the universe my house, and choose for food that which is easiest to procure. Gold and silver may I not need, neither I nor any of my friends. For from the desire for these grow up all men's ills—civic strife, wars, conspiracies and murders. All these have as their fountainhead the desire for more. But may this desire be far from us, and never may I reach out for more than my share, but be able to put up with less than my share.

Such, you see, are our wishes, wishes assuredly far different from those of most men. Nor is it any wonder that we differ from them in dress when we differ so much from them in principles too. But you surprise me by the way that you think that a lyre-player has a particular uniform and garb, and, by heavens, that a piper has his uniform, and a tragic actor his garb, but, when it comes to a good man, you don't think that he has his own dress and garb, but should wear the same as the average man, and that too although the average man is depraved. If good men need one particular dress of their own, what one would be more suitable than this dress which seems quite shameless to debauched men and which they would most deprecate for themselves?

Therefore my dress is, as you see, a dirty shaggy skin, a worn cloak, long hair and bare feet, but yours is just like that of the sodomites and no one could tell yours from theirs either by the colour of your cloaks, or by the softness and number of your tunics, or by your wraps, shoes, elaborate hair-styles, or your scent. For nowadays you reek of scent just

like them—you, who are the most fortunate of men! Yet of what value can one think a man who smells the same as a sodomite? So it is that you are no more able to endure hardships than they are, and no less amenable to pleasures than they. Moreover, your food is the same as theirs, you sleep like them and walk like them—or rather just like them prefer not to walk but are carried like baggage, some of you by men, others by beasts. But *I* am carried by my feet wherever I need to go, and *I* am able to put up with cold, endure heat and show no resentment at the works of the gods, because I am unfortunate, whereas you, because of your good fortune, are pleased with nothing that happens, and always find fault, unwilling to put up with what you have, but eager for what you have not, in winter praying for summer, and in summer for winter, in hot weather for cold, and in cold weather for hot, showing yourselves as hard to please and as querulous as invalids. But whereas the cause of *their* behaviour is illness, the cause of *yours* is your character.

Again you would have us change and you reform our manner of life for us because we often are ill-advised in what we do, though you yourselves bestow no thought on your own actions, basing none of them on rational judgment, but upon habit and appetite. Therefore you are exactly the same as men carried along by a torrent; for they are carried along wherever the current takes them, and you wherever your appetites take you. Your situation is just like what they say happened to the man who mounted a mad horse. For it rushed off, carrying him with it; and he couldn't dismount again because the horse kept running. Then someone who met them asked him where he was off to, and he replied, "Wherever this fellow decides," indicating the horse. Now if anyone asks you where you're heading for, if you wish to tell the truth, you will simply say that it's where your appetites choose, or more specifically where pleasure chooses, or now where ambition, or now again where avarice chooses; and sometimes temper, sometimes fear, or sometimes something else of the sort seems to carry you off. For you are carried along on the back not of one but of many horses, and different ones at different times—but all of them mad. As a result they carry you away towards cliffs and chasms. But before you fall you are quite unaware of what is going to happen to you.

But this worn cloak which you mock, and my long hair and my dress are so effective that they enable me to live a quiet life doing what I want to do and keeping the company of my choice. For no ignorant or uneducated person would wish to associate with one that dresses as I do, while the fops turn away while they're still a long way off. But my associates are the most intelligent and decent of men, and those with an appetite for virtue. These men are my particular associates, for I rejoice in

the company of men like them. But I dance no attendance at the doors of the so-called fortunate, but consider their golden crowns and their purple robes mere pride, and I laugh at the fellows who wear them.

And I'd have you know that my style of dress becomes not only good men but also gods, though you go on to mock it; and so consider the statues of the gods. Do you think they are like you or like me? And don't confine your attentions to the statues of the Greeks, but go round examining foreigners' temples too, to see whether the gods themselves have long hair and beards as I do, or whether their statues and paintings show them close-shaven like you. What's more, you will see they are just like me not only in these respects but also in having no shirt. How then can you still have the effrontery to describe my style of dress as contemptible, when it's obvious that it's good enough even for gods?

MENIPPUS
OR THE DESCENT INTO HADES

MENIPPUS

All hail, ye halls and portals of my home!
What joy you give mine eyes, to light returned!

A FRIEND

Isn't this Menippus the Cynic? Assuredly nobody else, unless I cannot see straight; Menippus all over. Then what is the meaning of that strange costume—a felt cap, a lyre, and a lion's skin? Anyhow, I must go up to him. Good day, Menippus; where under the sun have you come from? It is a long time since you have shown yourself in the city.

MENIPPUS

I come from Dead Men's Lair and Darkness Gate
Where Hades dwells, remote from other gods.

FRIEND

Heracles! Did Menippus die without our knowing it, and has he now come to life all over again?

MENIPPUS

Nay, I was living when I went to Hell.

FRIEND

What reason had you for this novel and surprising trip?

MENIPPUS

Youth spurred me, and I had more pluck than sense.

FRIEND

My dear fellow, do stop your play-acting; come off your blank-verse, and tell me in plain language like mine what your costume is, and why you had to go down below. Certainly it is not a pleasant and attractive journey!

MENIPPUS

Friend, 'twas necessity drew me below to the kingdom of Hades,
There to obtain, from the spirit of Theban Teiresias, counsel.

FRIEND

Man, you are surely out of your mind, or you would not recite verse in that way to your friends!

MENIPPUS

Don't be surprised, my dear fellow. I have just been in the company of Euripides and Homer, so that somehow or other I have become filled with poetry, and verses come unbidden to my lips. But tell me, how are things going on earth, and what are they doing in the city?

FRIEND

Nothing new; just what they did before—stealing, lying under oath, extorting usury, and weighing pennies.

MENIPPUS

Poor wretches! They do not know what decisions have been made of late in the lower world, and what ordinances have been enacted against the rich; by Cerberus, they cannot possibly evade them!

FRIEND

What is that? Has any radical legislation been passed in the lower world affecting the upper?

MENIPPUS

Yes, by Zeus, a great deal; but it is not right to publish it broadcast and expose their secrets. Someone might indict me for impiety in the court of Rhadamanthus.

FRIEND

Oh, no, Menippus! In Heaven's name don't withhold your story from a friend! You will be telling a man who knows how to keep his mouth shut, and who, moreover, has been initiated into the mysteries.

MENIPPUS

It is a perilous demand that you are imposing upon me, and one not wholly consistent with piety. However, for your sake I must be bold. The

motion, then, was passed that these rich men with great fortunes who keep their gold locked up as closely as Danae——

FRIEND

Don't quote the motion, my dear fellow, before telling me what I should be especially glad to hear from you; that is to say, what was the purpose of your going down, who was your guide for the journey, and then, in due order, what you saw and heard there; for it is to be expected, of course, that as a man of taste you did not overlook anything worth seeing or hearing.

MENIPPUS

I must meet your wishes in that, too, for what is a man to do when a friend constrains him? First, then, I shall tell you about my decision—what impelled me to go down. While I was a boy, when I read in Homer and Hesiod about wars and quarrels, not only of the demigods but of the gods themselves, and besides about their amours and assaults and abductions and lawsuits and banishing fathers and marrying sisters, I thought that all these things were right, and I felt an uncommon impulsion toward them. But when I came of age, I found that the laws contradicted the poets and forbade adultery, quarrelling, and theft. So I was plunged into great uncertainty, not knowing how to deal with my own case; for the gods would never have committed adultery and quarrelled with each other, I thought, unless they deemed these actions right, and the lawgivers would not recommend the opposite course unless they supposed it to be advantageous. Since I was in a dilemma, I resolved to go to the men whom they call philosophers and put myself into their hands, begging them to deal with me as they would, and to show me a plain, solid path in life.

That was what I had in mind when I went to them, but I was unconsciously struggling out of the smoke, as the proverb goes, right into the fire! For I found in the course of my investigation that among these men in particular the ignorance and the perplexity was greater than elsewhere, so that they speedily convinced me that the ordinary man's way of living is as good as gold.

For instance, one of them would recommend me to take my pleasure always and to pursue that under all circumstances, because that was happiness; but another, on the contrary, would recommend me to toil and moil always and to subdue my body, going dirty and unkempt, irritating everybody and calling names; and to clinch his argument he was perpetually reciting those trite lines of Hesiod's about virtue, and talking of "sweat," and the "climb to the summit." Another would

urge me to despise money and think it a matter of indifference whether one has it or not, while someone else, on the contrary, would demonstrate that even wealth was good. As to the universe, what is the use of talking about that? "Ideas," "incorporealities," "atoms," "voids," and a multitude of such terms were dinned into my ears by them every day until it made me queasy. And the strangest thing was that when they expressed the most contradictory of opinions, each of them would produce very effective and plausible arguments, so that when the selfsame thing was called hot by one and cold by another, it was impossible for me to controvert either of them, though I knew right well that nothing could ever be hot and cold at the same time. So in good earnest I acted like a drowsy man, nodding now this way and now that.

But there was something else, far more unreasonable than that. I found, upon observing these same people, that their practice directly opposed their preaching. For instance, I perceived that those who recommended scorning money clove to it tooth and nail, bickered about interest, taught for pay, and underwent everything for the sake of money; and that those who were for rejecting public opinion aimed at that very thing not only in all that they did, but in all that they said. Also that while almost all of them inveighed against pleasure, they privately devoted themselves to that alone.

Disappointed, therefore, in this expectation, I was still more uncomfortable than before, although I consoled myself somewhat with the thought that if I was still foolish and went about in ignorance of the truth, at all events I had the company of many wise men, widely renowned for intelligence. So one time, while I lay awake over these problems, I resolved to go to Babylon and address myself to one of the Magi, the disciples and successors of Zoroaster, as I had heard that with certain charms and ceremonials they could open the gates of Hades, taking down in safety anyone they would and guiding him back again. Consequently I thought best to arrange with one of these men for my going down, and then to call upon Teiresias of Boeotia and find out from him in his capacity of prophet and sage what the best life was, the life that a man of sense would choose.

Well, springing to my feet, I made straight for Babylon as fast as I could go. On my arrival I conversed with one of the Chaldeans, a wise man of miraculous skill, with grey hair and a very majestic beard; his name was Mithrobarzanes. By dint of supplications and entreaties, I secured his reluctant consent to be my guide on the journey at whatever price he would. So the man took me in charge, and first of all, for twenty-nine days, beginning with the new moon, he took me down to the Euphrates in the early morning, toward sunrise, and bathed me; after which he

would make a long address which I could not follow very well, for like an incompetent announcer at the games, he spoke rapidly and indistinctly. It is likely, however, that he was invoking certain spirits. Anyhow, after the incantation he would spit in my face thrice and then go back again without looking at anyone whom he met. We ate nuts, drank milk, mead, and the water of the Choaspes, and slept out of doors on the grass.

When he considered the preliminary course of dieting satisfactory, taking me to the Tigris river at midnight he purged me, cleansed me, and consecrated me with torches and squills and many other things, murmuring his incantation as he did so. Then after he had becharmed me from head to foot and walked all about me, that I might not be harmed by the phantoms, he took me home again, just as I was, walking backward. After that, we made ready for the journey. He himself put on a magician's gown very like the Median dress, and speedily costumed me in these things which you see—the cap, the lion's skin, and the lyre besides; and he urged me, if anyone should ask my name, not to say Menippus, but Heracles or Odysseus or Orpheus.

FRIEND

What was his object in that, Menippus? I do not understand the reason either for the costume or for the names.

MENIPPUS

Why, that, at any rate, is obvious and not at all shrouded in mystery. Since they had been before us in going down to Hades alive, he thought that if he should make me look like them, I might easily slip by the frontier-guard of Aeacus and go in unhindered as something of an old acquaintance; for thanks to my costume they would speed me along on my journey just as they do in the plays.

Well, day was just beginning to break when we went down to the river and set about getting under way. He had provided a boat, victims, mead, and everything else that we should need for the ritual. So we shipped all the stores, and at length ourselves

"Gloomily hied us aboard, with great tears falling profusely."

For a space we drifted along in the river, and then we sailed into the marsh and the lake in which the Euphrates loses itself. After crossing this, we came to a deserted, woody, sunless place. There at last we landed with Mithrobarzanes leading the way; we dug a pit, we slaughtered the sheep, and we sprinkled their blood about it. Meanwhile the magician held a burning torch and no longer muttered in a low tone but shouted as loudly as he could, invoking the spirits, one and all, at the top of his lungs; also the Tormentors, the Furies,

"Hecate, queen of the night, and eery Persephoneia."

With these names he intermingled a number of foreign-sounding, meaningless words of many syllables.

In a trice the whole region began to quake, the ground was rent asunder by the incantation, barking of Cerberus was audible afar off, and things took on a monstrously gloomy and sullen look.

"Aye, deep down it affrighted the king of the dead, Aïdoneus"—

for by that time we could see almost everything—the Lake, and the River of Burning Fire, and the palace of Pluto. But in spite of it all, we went down through the chasm, finding Rhadamanthus almost dead of fright. Cerberus barked a bit, to be sure, and stirred slightly, but when I hastily touched my lyre he was at once bewitched by the music. When we reached the lake, however, we came near not getting across, for the ferry was already crowded and full of groaning. Only wounded men were aboard, one injured in the leg, another in the head, and so on. They were there, in my opinion, through some war or other.

However, when good old Charon saw the lion-skin he thought that I was Heracles, so he took me in, and not only ferried me across gladly but pointed out the path for us when we went ashore. Since we were in the dark, Mithrobarzanes led the way and I followed after, keeping hold of him, until we reached a very large meadow overgrown with asphodel, where the shades of the dead flitted squeaking about us. Going ahead little by little, we came to the court of Minos. As it chanced, he himself was sitting on a lofty throne, while beside him stood the Tormentors, the Furies, and the Avengers. From one side a great number of men were being led up in line, bound together with a long chain; they were said to be adulterers, procurers, tax-collectors, toadies, informers, and all that crowd of people who create such confusion in life. In a separate company the millionaires and the money-lenders came up, pale, pot-bellied, and gouty, each of them with a neck-iron and a hundred-pound "crow" upon him. Standing by, we looked at what was going on, and listened to the pleas of the defendants, who were prosecuted by speakers of a novel and surprising sort.

FRIEND

Who were they, in Heaven's name? Don't hesitate to tell me that also.

MENIPPUS

You know these shadows that our bodies cast in the sunshine?

FRIEND

Why, to be sure!

MENIPPUS

Well, when we die, they prefer charges and give evidence against us, exposing whatever we have done in our lives; and they are considered very trustworthy because they always keep us company and never leave our bodies.

But to resume, Minos would examine each man carefully and send him away to the Place of the Wicked, to be punished in proportion to his crimes; and he dealt most harshly with those who were swollen with pride of wealth and place, and almost expected men to bow down and worship them; for he resented their short-lived vainglory and superciliousness, and their failure to remember that they themselves were mortal and had become possessed of mortal goods. So, after stripping off all their quondam splendour—wealth, I mean, and lineage and sovereignty—they stood there naked, with hanging heads, reviewing, point by point, their happy life among us as if it had been a dream. For my part I was highly delighted to see that, and whenever I recognized one of them, I would go up and quietly remind him what he used to be in life and how puffed up he had been then, when many men stood at his portals in the early morning awaiting his advent, hustled about and locked out by his servants, while he himself, bursting upon their vision at last in garments of purple or gold or gaudy stripes, thought that he was conferring happiness and bliss upon those who greeted him if he proffered his right hand or his breast, to be covered with kisses. They chafed, I assure you, as they listened!

But to return to Minos, he gave one decision by favour; for Dionysius of Sicily had been charged with many dreadful and impious crimes by Dion as prosecutor and the shadow as witness, but Aristippus of Cyrene appeared—they hold him in honour, and he has very great influence among the people of the lower world—and when Dionysius was within an ace of being chained up to the Chimera, he got him let off from the punishment by saying that many men of letters had found him obliging in the matter of money.

Leaving the court reluctantly, we came to the place of punishment, where in all truth, my friend, there were many pitiful things to hear and to see. The sound of scourges could be heard, and therewithal the wails of those roasting on the fire; there were racks and pillories and wheels; Chimera tore and Cerberus ravened. They were being punished all together, kings, slaves, satraps, poor, rich, and beggars, and all were sorry for their excesses. Some of them we even recognized when we saw them, all that were recently dead. But they covered their faces and turned away,

and if they so much as cast a glance at us, it was thoroughly servile and obsequious, even though they had been unimaginably oppressive and haughty in life. Poor people, however, were getting only half as much torture and resting at intervals before being punished again. Moreover, I saw all that is told of in the legends—Ixion, Sisyphus, Tantalus the Phrygian, who was certainly in a bad way, and earthborn Tityus—Heracles, how big he was! Indeed, he took up land enough for a farm as he lay there!

After making our way past these people also, we entered the Acherusian Plain, where we found the demigods and the fair women and the whole crowd of the dead, living by nations and by clans, some of them ancient and mouldy, and, as Homer says, "impalpable," while others were still well preserved and substantial, particularly the Egyptians, thanks to the durability of their embalming process. It was not at all easy, though, to tell them apart, for all, without exception, become precisely alike when their bones are bare. However, with some difficulty and by dint of long study we made them out. But they were lying one atop of another, ill-defined, unidentified, retaining no longer any trace of earthly beauty. So, with many skeletons lying together, all alike staring horridly and vacuously and baring their teeth, I questioned myself how I could distinguish Thersites from handsome Nireus, or the mendicant Irus from the King of the Phaeacians, or the cook Pyrrhias from Agamemnon; for none of their former means of identification abode with them, but their bones were all alike, undefined, unlabelled, and unable ever again to be distinguished by anyone.

So as I looked at them it seemed to me that human life is like a long pageant, and that all its trappings are supplied and distributed by Fortune, who arrays the participants in various costumes of many colours. Taking one person, it may be, she attires him royally, placing a tiara upon his head, giving him body-guards, and encircling his brow with the diadem; but upon another she puts the costume of a slave. Again, she makes up one person so that he is handsome, but causes another to be ugly and ridiculous. I suppose that the show must needs be diversified. And often, in the very middle of the pageant, she exchanges the costumes of several players; instead of allowing them to finish the pageant in the parts that had been assigned to them, she re-apparels them, forcing Croesus to assume the dress of a slave and a captive, and shifting Maeandrius, who formerly paraded among the servants, into the imperial habit of Polycrates. For a brief space she lets them use their costumes, but when the time of the pageant is over, each gives back the properties and lays off the costume along with his body, becoming what he was before his birth, no different from his neighbour. Some, however, are so ungrateful that when Fortune

appears to them and asks her trappings back, they are vexed and indignant, as if they were being robbed of their own property, instead of giving back what they had borrowed for a little time.

I suppose you have often seen these stage-folk who act in tragedies, and according to the demands of the plays become at one moment Creons, and again Priams or Agamemnons; the very one, it may be, who a short time ago assumed with great dignity the part of Cecrops or of Erectheus soon appears as a servant at the bidding of the poet. And when at length the play comes to an end, each of them strips off his gold-bespangled robe, lays aside his mask, steps out of his buskins, and goes about in poverty and humility, no longer styled Agamemnon, son of Atreus, or Creon, son of Menoeceus, but Polus, son of Charicles, of Sunium, or Satyrus, son of Theogiton, of Marathon. That is what human affairs are like, it seemed to me as I looked.

FRIEND

But tell me, Menippus; those who have such expensive, high monuments on earth, and tombstones and statues and inscriptions—are they no more highly honoured there than the common dead?

MENIPPUS

Nonsense, man! If you had seen Mausolus himself—I mean the Carian, so famous for his monument—I know right well that you would never have stopped laughing, so humbly did he lie where he was flung, in a cubby-hole, inconspicuous among the rest of the plebeian dead, deriving, in my opinion, only this much satisfaction from his monument, that he was heavy laden with such a great weight resting upon him. When Aeacus measures off the space for each, my friend—and he gives at most not over a foot—one must be content to lie in it, huddled together to fit its compass. But you would have laughed much more heartily, I think, if you had seen our kings and satraps reduced to poverty there, and either selling salt fish on account of their neediness or teaching the alphabet, and getting abused and hit over the head by all comers, like the meanest of slaves. In fact, when I saw Philip of Macedon, I could not control my laughter. He was pointed out to me in a corner, cobbling worn-out sandals for pay! Many others, too, could be seen begging at the cross-roads—your Xerxeses, I mean, and Dariuses and Polycrateses.

FRIEND

What you say about the kings is extraordinary and almost incredible. But what was Socrates doing, and Diogenes, and the rest of the wise men?

MENIPPUS

As to Socrates, there too he goes about cross-questioning everyone. His associates are Palamedes, Odysseus, Nestor, and other talkative corpses. His legs, I may say, were still puffed up and swollen from his draught of poison. And good old Diogenes lives with Sardanapalus the Assyrian, Midas the Phrygian, and several other wealthy men. As he hears them lamenting and reviewing their former good-fortune, he laughs and rejoices; and often he lies on his back and sings in a very harsh and unpleasant voice, drowning out their lamentations, so that the gentlemen are annoyed and think of changing their lodgings because they cannot stand Diogenes.

FRIEND

Well, enough of this, but what was the motion that in the beginning you said had been passed against the rich?

MENIPPUS

Thanks for reminding me. Somehow or other, in spite of my intention to speak about that, I went very much astray in my talk.

During my stay there, the city fathers called a public meeting to discuss matters of general interest; so when I saw many people running in the same direction, I mingled with the dead and speedily became one of the electors myself. Well, various business was transacted, and at last that about the rich. After many dreadful charges of violence and mendacity and superciliousness and injustice had been brought against them, at length one of the demagogues rose and read the following motion.

(MOTION)

"Whereas many lawless deeds are done in life by the rich, who plunder and oppress and in every way humiliate the poor,

"Be it resolved by the senate and people, that when they die their bodies be punished like those of the other malefactors, but their souls be sent back up into life and enter into donkeys until they shall have passed two hundred and fifty thousand years in the said condition, transmigrating from donkey to donkey, bearing burdens, and being driven by the poor; and that thereafter it be permitted them to die.

"On motion of Scully Fitzbones of Corpsebury, Cadavershire."

After this motion had been read, the officials put it to the vote, the majority indicated assent by the usual sign, Brimo brayed and Cerberus howled. That is the way in which their motions are enacted and ratified.

Well, there you have what took place at the meeting. For my part, I did what I came to do. Going to Teiresias, I told him the whole story and

besought him to tell me what sort of life he considered the best. He laughed (he is a blind little old gentleman, pale, with a piping voice) and said: "My son, I know the reason for your perplexity; it came from the wise men, who are not consistent with themselves. But it is not permissible to tell you, for Rhadamanthus has forbidden it." "Don't say that, gaffer," said I. "Tell me, and don't allow me to go about in life blinder than you are." So he took me aside, and after he had led me a good way apart from the others, he bent his head slightly toward my ear and said: "The life of the common sort is best, and you will act more wisely if you stop speculating about heavenly bodies and discussing final causes and first causes, spit your scorn at those clever syllogisms, and counting all that sort of thing nonsense, make it always your sole object to put the present to good use and to hasten on your way, laughing a great deal and taking nothing seriously."

> "So he spoke, and betook him again through the asphodel
> meadow."

As it was late by then, I said: "Come, Mithrobarzanes, why do we delay? Why not go back to life again?" To this he replied: "Never fear, Menippus; I will show you a quick and easy short cut." And then, taking me to a place murkier than the rest of the region and pointing with his finger to a dim and slender ray of light coming in as if through a keyhole, a long way off, he said: "That is the sanctuary of Trophonius, where the people from Boeotia come down. So go up by that route and you will be in Greece directly." Delighted with his words, I embraced the sorcerer, very laboriously crawled up through the hole somehow, and found myself in Lebadeia.

THE LOVER OF LIES, OR THE DOUBTER

TYCHIADES

Can you tell me, Philocles, what in the world it is that makes many men so fond of lying that they delight in telling preposterous tales themselves and listen with especial attention to those who spin yarns of that sort?

PHILOCLES

There are many reasons, Tychiades, which constrain men occasionally to tell falsehoods with an eye to the usefulness of it.

TYCHIADES

That has nothing to do with the case, as the phrase is, for I did not ask about men who lie for advantage. They are pardonable—yes, even praiseworthy, some of them, who have deceived national enemies or for safety's sake have used this kind of expedient in extremities, as Odysseus often did in seeking to win his own life and the return of his comrades. No, my dear sir, I am speaking of those men who put sheer useless lying far ahead of truth, liking the thing and whiling away their time at it without any valid excuse. I want to know about these men, to what end they do this.

PHILOCLES

Have you really noted any such men anywhere in whom this passion for lying is ingrained?

TYCHIADES

Yes, there are many such men.

PHILOCLES

What other reason, then, than folly may they be said to have for telling untruths, since they choose the worst course instead of the best?

TYCHIADES

That too has nothing to do with the case, Philocles, for I could show you many men otherwise sensible and remarkable for their intelligence who have somehow become infected with this plague and are lovers of lying, so that it irks me when such men, excellent in every way, yet delight in deceiving themselves and their associates. Those of olden time should be known to you before I mention them—Herodotus, and Ctesias of Cnidus, and before them the poets, including Homer himself—men of renown, who made use of the written lie, so that they not only deceived those who listened to them then, but transmitted the falsehood from generation to generation even down to us, conserved in the choicest of diction and rhythm. For my part it often occurs to me to blush for them when they tell of the castration of Uranus, and the fetters of Prometheus, and the revolt of the Giants, and the whole sorry show in Hades, and how Zeus turned into a bull or a swan on account of a love-affair, and how some woman changed into a bird or a bear; yes, and of Pegasi, Chimaerae, Gorgons, Cyclopes, and so forth—very strange and wonderful fables, fit to enthrall the souls of children who still dread Mormo and Lamia.

Yet as far as the poets are concerned, perhaps the case is not so bad; but is it not ridiculous that even cities and whole peoples tell lies unanimously and officially? The Cretans exhibit the tomb of Zeus and are not ashamed of it, and the Athenians assert that Erichthonius sprang from the earth and that the first men came up out of the soil of Attica like vegetables; but at that their story is much more dignified than that of the Thebans, who relate that "Sown Men" grew up from serpents' teeth. If any man, however, does not think that these silly stories are true, but sanely puts them to the proof and holds that only a Coroebus or a Margites can believe either that Triptolemus drove through the air behind winged serpents, or that Pan came from Arcadia to Marathon to take a hand in the battle, or that Oreithyia was carried off by Boreas, they consider that man a sacrilegious fool for doubting facts so evident and genuine; to such an extent does falsehood prevail.

PHILOCLES

Well, as far as the poets are concerned, Tychiades, and the cities too, they may properly be pardoned. The poets flavour their writings with the delectability that the fable yields, a most seductive thing, which they need above all else for the benefit of their readers; and the Athenians, Thebans and others, if any there be, make their countries more impressive by such means. In fact, if these fabulous tales should be taken away from Greece, there would be nothing to prevent the guides there from starving to death, as the foreigners would not care to hear the truth, even gratis!

On the other hand, those who have no such motive and yet delight in lying may properly be thought utterly ridiculous.

TYCHIADES

You are quite right in what you say. For example, I come to you from Eucrates the magnificent, having listened to a great lot of incredible yarns; to put it more accurately, I took myself off in the midst of the conversation because I could not stand the exaggeration of the thing: they drove me out as if they had been the Furies by telling quantities of extraordinary miracles.

PHILOCLES

But, Tychiades, Eucrates is a trustworthy person, and nobody could ever believe that he, with such a long beard, a man of sixty, and a great devotee of philosophy too, would abide even to hear someone else tell a lie in his presence, let alone venturing to do anything of that sort himself.

TYCHIADES

Why, my dear fellow, you do not know what sort of statements he made, and how he confirmed them, and how he actually swore to most of them, taking oath upon his children, so that as I gazed at him all sorts of ideas came into my head, now that he was insane and out of his right mind, now that he was only a fraud, after all, and I had failed, in all these years, to notice that his lion's skin covered a silly ape; so extravagant were the stories that he told.

PHILOCLES

What were they, Tychiades, in the name of Hestia? I should like to know what sort of quackery he has been screening behind that great beard.

TYCHIADES

I used to visit him previously, Philocles, whenever I had a good deal of leisure; and to-day, when I wanted to find Leontichus, a close friend of mine, as you know, and was told by his boy that he had gone off to the house of Eucrates in the early morning to pay him a call because he was ill, I went there for two reasons, both to find Leontichus and to see Eucrates, for I had not known that he was ill.

I did not find Leontichus there, for he had just gone out a little while before, they said; but I found plenty of others, among whom there was Cleodemus the Peripatetic, and Deinomachus the Stoic, and Ion—you know the one that thinks he ought to be admired for his mastery of Plato's doctrines as the only person who has accurately sensed the man's meaning

and can expound it to the rest of the world. You see what sort of men I am naming to you, all-wise and all-virtuous, the very fore-front of each school, every one venerable, almost terrible, to look at. In addition, the physician Antigonus was there, called in, I suppose, by reason of the illness. Eucrates seemed to be feeling better already, and the ailment was of a chronic character; he had had another attack of rheumatism in his feet.

He bade me sit by him on the couch, letting his voice drop a little to the tone of an invalid when he saw me, although as I was coming in I heard him shouting and vigorously pressing some point or other. I took very good care not to touch his feet, and after making the customary excuses that I did not know he was ill and that when I learned of it I came in hot haste, sat down beside him.

It so happened that the company had already, I think, talked at some length about his ailment and were then discussing it further; they were each suggesting certain remedies, moreover. At any rate Cleodemus said: "Well then, if you take up from the ground in your left hand the tooth of the weasel which has been killed in the way I have already described and wrap it up in the skin of a lion just flayed, and then bind it about your legs, the pain ceases instantly."

"Not in a lion's skin, I was told," said Deinomachus, "but that of a hind still immature and unmated; and the thing is more plausible that way, for the hind is fleet and her strength lies especially in her legs. The lion is brave, of course, and his fat and his right fore-paw and the stiff bristles of his whiskers are very potent if one knew how to use them with the incantation appropriate to each; but for curing the feet he is not at all promising."

"I myself," said Cleodemus, "was of that opinion formerly, that it ought to be the skin of a hind because the hind is fleet; but recently a man from Libya, well informed in such things, taught me better, saying that lions were fleeter than deer. 'No fear!' said he: 'They even chase and catch them.'"

The company applauded, in the belief that the Libyan was right in what he said. But I said, "Do you really think that certain incantations put a stop to this sort of thing, or external applications, when the trouble has its seat within?" They laughed at my remark and clearly held me convicted of great stupidity if I did not know the most obvious things, of which nobody in his right mind would maintain that they were not so. The doctor Antigonus, however, seemed to me to be pleased with my question, for he had been overlooked a long time, I suppose, when he wanted to aid Eucrates in a professional way by advising him to abstain from wine, adopt a vegetarian diet, and in general to "lower his pitch."

But Cleodemus, with a faint smile, said: "What is that, Tychiades? Do you consider it incredible that any alleviations of ailments are effected by such means?" "I do," said I, "not being altogether full of drivel, so as to believe that external remedies which have nothing to do with the internal causes of the ailments, applied as you say in combination with set phrases and hocus-pocus of some sort, are efficacious and bring on the cure. That could never happen, not even if you should wrap sixteen entire weasels in the skin of the Nemean lion; in fact I have often seen the lion himself limping in pain with his skin intact upon him!"

"You are a mere layman, you see," said Deinomachus, "and you have not made it a point to learn how such things agree with ailments when they are applied. I do not suppose you would accept even the most obvious instances—periodic fevers driven off, snakes charmed, swellings cured, and whatever else even old wives do. But if all that takes place, why in the world will you not believe that this takes place by similar means?"

"You are reasoning from false premises, Deinomachus," I replied, "and, as the saying goes, driving out one nail with another; for it is not clear that precisely what you are speaking of takes place by the aid of any such power. If, then, you do not first convince me by logical proof that it takes place in this way naturally, because the fever or the inflammation is afraid of a holy name or a foreign phrase and so takes flight from the swelling, your stories still remain old wives' fables."

"It seems to me," said Deinomachus, "that when you talk like that you do not believe in the gods, either, since you do not think that cures can be effected through holy names." "Don't say that, my dear sir!" I replied. "Even though the gods exist, there is nothing to prevent that sort of thing from being false just the same. For my part, I revere the gods and I see their cures and all the good that they do by restoring the sick to health with drugs and doctoring. In fact, Asclepius himself and his sons ministered to the sick by laying on healing drugs, not by fastening on lions' skins and weasels."

"Never mind him," said Ion, "and I will tell you a wonderful story. I was still a young lad, about fourteen years old, when someone came and told my father that Midas the vine-dresser, ordinarily a strong and industrious servant, had been bitten by a viper toward midday and was lying down, with his leg already in a state of mortification. While he was tying up the runners and twining them about the poles, the creature had crawled up and bitten him on the great toe; then it had quickly gone down again into its hole, and he was groaning in mortal anguish.

"As this report was being made, we saw Midas himself being brought up on a litter by his fellow-slaves, all swollen and livid, with a clammy skin and but little breath left in him. Naturally my father was distressed,

but a friend who was there said to him: 'Cheer up: I will at once go and get you a Babylonian, one of the so-called Chaldeans, who will cure the fellow.' Not to make a long story of it, the Babylonian came and brought Midas back to life, driving the poison out of his body by a spell, and also binding upon his foot a fragment which he broke from the tombstone of a dead maiden.

"Perhaps this is nothing out of the common: although Midas himself picked up the litter on which he had been carried and went off to the farm, so potent was the spell and the fragment of the tombstone. But the Babylonian did other things that were truly miraculous. Going to the farm in the early morning, he repeated seven sacred names out of an old book, purified the place with sulphur and torches, going about it three times, and called out all the reptiles that there were inside the boundaries. They came as if they were being drawn in response to the spell, snakes in great numbers, asps, vipers, horned snakes, darters, common toads, and puff-toads; one old python, however, was missing, who on account of his age, I suppose, could not creep out and so failed to comply with the command. The magician said that not all were there, and electing one of the snakes messenger, the youngest, sent him after the python, who presently came too. When they were assembled, the Babylonian blew on them and they were all instantly burned up by the blast, and we were amazed."

"Tell me, Ion," said I, "did the messenger snake, the young one, give his arm to the python, who you say was aged, or did the python have a stick and lean on it?"

"You are joking," said Cleodemus: "I myself was formerly more incredulous than you in regard to such things, for I thought it in no way possible that they could happen; but when first I saw the foreign stranger fly—he came from the land of the Hyperboreans, he said—, I believed and was conquered after long resistance. What was I to do when I saw him soar through the air in broad daylight and walk on the water and go through fire slowly on foot?" "Did you see that?" said I—"the Hyperborean flying, or stepping on the water?" "Certainly," said he, "with brogues on his feet such as people of that country commonly wear. As for the trivial feats, what is the use of telling all that he performed, sending Cupids after people, bringing up supernatural beings, calling mouldy corpses to life, making Hecate herself appear in plain sight, and pulling down the moon? But after all, I will tell you what I saw him do in the house of Glaucias, son of Alexicles.

"Immediately after Glaucias' father died and he acquired the property, he fell in love with Chrysis, the wife of Demeas. I was in his employ as his tutor in philosophy, and if that love-affair had not kept him too busy,

he would have known all the teachings of the Peripatetic school, for even at eighteen he was solving fallacies and had completed the course of lectures on natural philosophy. At his wit's end, however, with his love-affair, he told me the whole story; and as was natural, since I was his tutor, I brought him that Hyperborean magician at a fee of four minas down (it was necessary to pay something in advance towards the cost of the victims) and sixteen if he should obtain Chrysis. The man waited for the moon to wax, as it is then, for the most part, that such rites are performed; and after digging a pit in an open court of the house, at about midnight he first summoned up for us Alexicles, Glaucias' father, who had died seven months before. The old gentleman was indignant over the love-affair and flew into a passion, but at length he permitted him to go on with it after all. Next he brought up Hecate, who fetched Cerberus with her, and he drew down the moon, a many-shaped spectacle, appearing differently at different times; for at first she exhibited the form of a woman, then she turned into a handsome bull, and then she looked like a puppy. Finally, the Hyperborean made a little Cupid out of clay and said: 'Go and fetch Chrysis.' The clay took wing, and before long Chrysis stood on the threshold knocking at the door, came in and embraced Glaucias as if she loved him furiously, and remained with him until we heard the cocks crowing. Then the moon flew up to the sky, Hecate plunged beneath the earth, the other phantasms disappeared, and we sent Chrysis home at just about dawn. If you had seen that, Tychiades, you would no longer have doubted that there is much good in spells."

"Quite so," said I, "I should have believed if I had seen it, but as things are I may perhaps be pardoned if I am not able to see as clearly as you. However, I know the Chrysis whom you speak of, an amorous dame and an accessible one, and I do not see why you needed the clay messenger and the Hyperborean magician and the moon in person to fetch her, when for twenty drachmas she could have been brought to the Hyperboreans! The woman is very susceptible to that spell, and her case is the opposite to that of ghosts; if they hear a chink of bronze or iron, they take flight, so you say, but as for her, if silver chinks anywhere, she goes toward the sound. Besides, I am surprised at the magician himself, if he was able to have the love of the richest women and get whole talents from them, and yet made Glaucias fascinating, penny-wise that he is, for four minas."

"You act ridiculously," said Ion, "to doubt everything. For my part, I should like to ask you what you say to those who free possessed men from their terrors by exorcising the spirits so manifestly. I need not discuss this: everyone knows about the Syrian from Palestine, the adept in it, how many he takes in hand who fall down in the light of the moon

and roll their eyes and fill their mouths with foam; nevertheless, he restores them to health and sends them away normal in mind, delivering them from their straits for a large fee. When he stands beside them as they lie there and asks: 'Whence came you into his body?' the patient himself is silent, but the spirit answers in Greek or in the language of whatever foreign country he comes from, telling how and whence he entered into the man; whereupon, by adjuring the spirit and if he does not obey, threatening him, he drives him out. Indeed, I actually saw one coming out, black and smoky in colour." "It is nothing much," I remarked, "for you, Ion, to see that kind of sight, when even the 'forms' that the father of your school, Plato, points out are plain to you, a hazy object of vision to the rest of us, whose eyes are weak."

"Why, is Ion the only one who has seen that kind of sight?" said Eucrates. "Have not many others encountered spirits, some at night and some by day? For myself, I have seen such things, not merely once but almost hundreds of times. At first I was disturbed by them, but now, of course, because of their familiarity, I do not consider that I am seeing anything out of the way, especially since the Arab gave me the ring made of iron from crosses and taught me the spell of many names. But perhaps you will doubt me also, Tychiades." "How could I doubt Eucrates, the son of Deinon," said I, "a learned and an uncommonly independent gentleman, expressing his opinions in his own home, with complete liberty?" "Anyhow," said Eucrates, "the affair of the statue was observed every night by everybody in the house, boys, young men and old men, and you could hear about it not only from me but from all our people." "Statue!" said I, "what do you mean?"

"Have you not observed on coming in," said he, "a very fine statue set up in the hall, the work of Demetrius, the maker of portrait-statues?" "Do you mean the discus-thrower," said I, "the one bent over in the position of the throw, with his head turned back toward the hand that holds the discus, with one leg slightly bent, looking as if he would spring up all at once with the cast?" "Not that one," said he, "for that is one of Myron's works, the discus-thrower you speak of. Neither do I mean the one beside it, the one binding his head with the fillet, the handsome lad, for that is Polycleitus' work. Never mind those to the right as you come in, among which stand the tyrant-slayers, modelled by Critius and Nesiotes; but if you noticed one beside the fountain, pot-bellied, bald on the forehead, half bared by the hang of his cloak, with some of the hairs of his beard wind-blown and his veins prominent, the image of a real man, that is the one I mean; he is thought to be Pellichus, the Corinthian general."

"Yes," I said, "I saw one to the right of the spout, wearing fillets and

withered wreaths, his breast covered with gilt leaves." "I myself put on the gilt leaves," said Eucrates, "when he cured me of the ague that was torturing me to death every other day." "Really, is our excellent Pellichus a doctor also?" said I. "Do not mock," Eucrates replied, "or before long the man will punish you. I know what virtue there is in this statue that you make fun of. Don't you suppose that he can send fevers upon whomsoever he will, since it is possible for him to send them away?" "May the manikin be gracious and kindly," said I, "since he is so manful. But what else does everyone in the house see him doing?"

"As soon as night comes," he said, "he gets down from the pedestal on which he stands and goes all about the house; we all encounter him, sometimes singing, and he has never harmed anybody. One has but to turn aside, and he passes without molesting in any way those who saw him. Upon my word, he often takes baths and disports himself all night, so that the water can be heard splashing." "See here, then," said I, "perhaps the statue is not Pellichus but Talos the Cretan, the son of Minos; he was a bronze man, you know, and made the rounds in Crete. If he were made of wood instead of bronze, there would be nothing to hinder his being one of the devices of Daedalus instead of a work of Demetrius; anyhow, he is like them in playing truant from his pedestal, by what you say." "See here, Tychiades," said he, "perhaps you will be sorry for your joke later on. I know what happened to the man who stole the obols that we offer him on the first of each month." "It ought to have been something very dreadful," said Ion, "since he committed a sacrilege. How was he punished, Eucrates? I should like to hear about it, no matter how much Tychiades here is going to doubt it."

"A number of obols," he said, "were lying at his feet, and some other small coins of silver had been stuck to his thigh with wax, and leaves of silver, votive offerings or payment for a cure from one or another of those who through him had ceased to be subject to fever. We had a plaguy Libyan servant, a groom; the fellow undertook to steal and did steal everything that was there, at night, after waiting until the statue had descended. But as soon as Pellichus came back and discovered that he had been robbed, mark how he punished and exposed the Libyan! The unhappy man ran about the hall the whole night long unable to get out, just as if he had been thrown into a labyrinth, until finally he was caught in possession of the stolen property when day came. He got a sound thrashing then, on being caught, and he did not long survive the incident, dying a rogue's death from being flogged, he said, every night, so that welts showed on his body the next day. In view of this, Tychiades, mock Pellichus and think me as senile as if I were a contemporary of Minos!" "Well, Eucrates," I said, "as long as bronze is bronze and the work a

product of Demetrius of Alopece, who makes men, not gods, I shall never be afraid of the statue of Pellichus, whom I should not have feared very much even when he was alive if he threatened me."

Thereupon Antigonus, the physician, said, "I myself, Eucrates, have a bronze Hippocrates about eighteen inches high. As soon as the light is out, he goes all about the house making noises, turning out the vials, mixing up the medicines, and overturning the mortar, particularly when we are behindhand with the sacrifice which we make to him every year." "Has it gone so far," said I, "that even Hippocrates the physician demands sacrifice in his honour and gets angry if he is not feasted on unblemished victims at the proper season? He ought to be well content if anyone should bring food to his tomb or pour him a libation of milk and honey or put a wreath about his gravestone!"

"Let me tell you," said Eucrates, "—this, I assure you, is supported by witnesses—what I saw five years ago. It happened to be the vintage season of the year; passing through the farm at midday, I left the labourers gathering the grapes and went off by myself into the wood, thinking about something in the meantime and turning it over in my mind. When I was under cover, there came first a barking of dogs, and I supposed that my son Mnason was at his usual sport of following the hounds, and had entered the thicket with his companions. This was not the case, however; but after a short time there came an earthquake and with it a noise as of thunder, and then I saw a terrible woman coming toward me, quite half a furlong in height. She had a torch in her left hand and a sword in her right, ten yards long; below, she had snake-feet, and above she resembled the Gorgon, in her stare, I mean, and the frightfulness of her appearance; moreover, instead of hair she had the snakes falling down in ringlets, twining about her neck, and some of them coiled upon her shoulders.—See," said he, "how my flesh creeps, friends, as I tell the story!" And as he spoke he showed the hairs on his forearm standing on end (would you believe it?) because of his terror!

Ion, Deinomachus, Cleodemus, and the rest of them, open-mouthed, were giving him unwavering attention, old men led by the nose, all but doing obeisance to so unconvincing a colossus, a woman half a furlong in height, a gigantic bugaboo! For my part I was thinking in the meantime: "They associate with young men to make them wise and are admired by many, but what are they themselves? Only their grey hair and their beard distinguishes them from infants, and for the rest of it, even infants are not so amenable to falsehood." Deinomachus, for instance, said: "Tell me, Eucrates, the dogs of the goddess—how big were they?"

"Taller than Indian elephants," he replied; "black, like them, with a shaggy coat of filthy, tangled hair.—Well, at sight of her I stopped, at

the same time turning the gem that the Arab gave me to the inside of my finger, and Hecate, stamping on the ground with her serpent foot, made a tremendous chasm, as deep as Tartarus; then after a little she leaped into it and was gone. I plucked up courage and looked over, taking hold of a tree that grew close by, in order that I might not get a dizzy turn and fall into it headlong. Then I saw everything in Hades, the River of Blazing Fire, and the Lake, and Cerberus, and the dead, well enough to recognise some of them. My father, for instance, I saw distinctly, still wearing the same clothes in which we buried him."

"What were the souls doing, Eucrates?" said Ion. "What else would they be doing," he said, "except lying upon the asphodel to while away the time, along with their friends and kinsmen by tribes and clans?" "Now let the Epicureans go on contradicting holy Plato," said Ion, "and his doctrine about the souls! But you did not see Socrates himself and Plato among the dead?" "Socrates I saw," he replied, "and even him not for certain but by guess, because he was bald and pot-bellied; Plato I could not recognise, for one must tell the truth to friends, I take it.

"No sooner had I seen everything sufficiently well than the chasm came together and closed up; and some of the servants who were seeking me, Pyrrhias here among them, came upon the scene before the chasm had completely closed. Tell them, Pyrrhias, whether I am speaking the truth or not." "Yes, by Heaven," said Pyrrhias, "and I heard barking, too, through the chasm and a gleam of fire was shining, from the torch, I suppose." I had to laugh when the witness, to give good measure, threw in the barking and the fire!

Cleodemus, however, said, "These sights that you saw are not novel and unseen by anyone else, for I myself when I was taken sick not long ago witnessed something similar. Antigonus here visited and attended me. It was the seventh day, and the fever was like a calenture of the most raging type. Leaving me by myself and shutting the door, they all were waiting outside; for you had given orders to that effect, Antigonus, on the chance that I might fall asleep. Well, at that time there appeared at my side while I lay awake a very handsome young man, wearing a white cloak; then, raising me to my feet, he led me through a chasm to Hades, as I realised at once when I saw Tantalus and Ixion and Tityus and Sisyphus. Why should I tell you all the details? But when I came to the court—Aeacus and Charon and the Fates and the Furies were there—a person resembling a king (Pluto, I suppose) sat reading off the names of those about to die because their lease of life chanced to have already expired. The young man speedily set me before him; but Pluto was angry and said to my guide: 'His thread is not yet fully spun, so let him be off, and bring me the blacksmith Demylus, for he is living beyond the

spindle.' I hastened back with a joyful heart, and from that time was free from fever; but I told everyone that Demylus would die. He lived next door to us, and himself had some illness, according to report. And after a little while we heard the wailing of his mourners."

"What is there surprising in that?" said Antigonus: "I know a man who came to life more than twenty days after his burial, having attended the fellow both before his death and after he came to life." "How was it," said I, "that in twenty days the body neither corrupted nor simply wasted away from inanition? Unless it was an Epimenides whom you attended."

While we were exchanging these words the sons of Eucrates came in upon us from the palaestra, one already of age, the other about fifteen years old, and after greeting us sat down upon the couch beside their father; a chair was brought in for me. Then, as if reminded by the sight of his sons, Eucrates said: "As surely as I hope that these boys will be a joy to me"—and he laid his hand upon them—"what I am about to tell you, Tychiades, is true. Everyone knows how I loved their mother, my wife of blessed memory; I made it plain by what I did for her not only while she was alive but even when she died, for I burned on the pyre with her all the ornaments and the clothing that she liked while she lived. On the seventh day after her death I was lying here on the couch, just as I am now, consoling my grief; for I was peacefully reading Plato's book about the soul. While I was thus engaged, Demaenete herself in person came in upon me and sat down beside me, just as Eucratides here is sitting now"—with a gesture toward the younger of his sons, who at once shuddered in a very boyish way; he had already been pale for some time over the story. "When I saw her," Eucrates continued, "I caught her in my arms with a cry of grief and began to weep. She would not permit me to cry, however, but began to find fault with me because, although I had given her everything else, I had not burned one of her gilt sandals, which, she said, was under the chest, where it had been thrown aside. That was why we did not find it and burned only the one. We were continuing our conversation when a cursed toy dog that was under the couch, a Maltese, barked, and she vanished at his barking. The sandal, however, was found under the chest and was burned afterwards.

"Is it right, Tychiades, to doubt these apparitions any longer, when they are distinctly seen and a matter of daily occurrence?" "No, by Heaven," I said: "those who doubt and are so disrespectful toward truth deserve to be spanked like children, with a gilt sandal!"

At this juncture Arignotus the Pythagorean came in, the man with the long hair and the majestic face—you know the one who is renowned for wisdom, whom they call holy. As I caught sight of him, I drew a breath of relief, thinking: "There now, a broadaxe has come to hand to use

against their lies. The wise man will stop their mouths when they tell such prodigious yarns." I thought that Fortune had trundled him in to me like a *deus ex machina*, as the phrase is. But when Cleodemus had made room for him and he was seated, he first asked about the illness, and when Eucrates told him that it was already less troublesome, said: "What were you debating among yourselves? As I came in, I overheard you, and it seemed to me that you were on the point of giving a fine turn to the conversation!"

"We are only trying to persuade this man of adamant," said Eucrates, pointing to me, "to believe that spirits and phantoms exist, and that souls of dead men go about above ground and appear to whomsoever they will." I flushed and lowered my eyes out of reverence for Arignotus. "Perhaps, Eucrates," he said, "Tychiades means that only the ghosts of those who died by violence walk, for example, if a man hanged himself, or had his head cut off, or was crucified, or departed life in some similar way; and that those of men who died a natural death do not. If that is what he means, we cannot altogether reject what he says." "No, by Heaven," replied Deinomachus, "he thinks that such things do not exist at all and are not seen in bodily form."

"What is that you say?" said Arignotus, with a sour look at me. "Do you think that none of these things happen, although everybody, I may say, sees them?" "Plead in my defence," said I, "if I do not believe in them, that I am the only one of all who does not see them; if I saw them, I should believe in them, of course, just as you do." "Come," said he, "if ever you go to Corinth, ask where the house of Eubatides is, and when it is pointed out to you beside Cornel Grove, enter it and say to the doorman Tibius that you should like to see where the Pythagorean Arignotus exhumed the spirit and drove it away, making the house habitable from that time on."

"What was that, Arignotus?" asked Eucrates. "It was uninhabitable," he replied, "for a long time because of terrors; whenever anyone took up his abode in it, he fled in panic at once, chased out by a fearful, terrifying phantom. So it was falling in and the roof was tumbling down, and there was nobody at all who had the courage to enter it.

"When I heard all this, I took my books—I have a great number of Egyptian works about such matters—and went into the house at bed-time, although my host tried to dissuade me and all but held me when he learned where I was going—into misfortune with my eyes open, he thought. But taking a lamp I went in alone; in the largest room I put down the light and was reading peacefully, seated on the ground, when the spirit appeared, thinking that he was setting upon a man of the common sort and expecting to affright me as he had the others; he was squalid and long-haired and blacker than the dark. Standing over me,

he made attempts upon me, attacking me from all sides to see if he could get the best of me anywhere, and turning now into a dog, now into a bull or a lion. But I brought into play my most frightful imprecation, speaking the Egyptian language, pent him up in a certain corner of a dark room, and laid him. Then, having observed where he went down, I slept for the rest of the night.

"In the morning, when everybody had given up hope and expected to find me dead like the others, I came forth to the surprise of all and went to Eubatides with the good tidings that he could now inhabit his house, which was purged and free from terrors. So, taking him along and many of the others too—they went with us because the thing was so amazing—I led them to the place where I had seen that the spirit had gone down and told them to take picks and shovels and dig. When they did so, there was found buried about six feet deep a mouldering body of which only the bones lay together in order. We exhumed and buried it; and the house from that time ceased to be troubled by the phantoms."

When Arignotus, a man of superhuman wisdom, revered by all, told this story, there was no longer any of those present who did not hold me convicted of gross folly if I doubted such things, especially as the narrator was Arignotus. Nevertheless I did not blench either at his long hair or at the reputation which encompassed him, but said: "What is this, Arignotus? Were you, Truth's only hope, just like the rest—full of moonshine and vain imaginings? Indeed the saying has come true: our pot of gold has turned out to be nothing but coals."

"Come now," said Arignotus, "if you put no trust either in me or in Deinomachus or Cleodemus here or in Eucrates himself, tell whom you consider more trustworthy in such matters that maintains the opposite view to ours." "A very wonderful man," said I, "that Democritus who came from Abdera, who surely was thoroughly convinced that nothing of this kind can exist. He shut himself up in a tomb outside the gates, and constantly wrote and composed there by night and by day. Some of the young fellows, wishing to annoy and alarm him, dressed themselves up like dead men in black robes and masks patterned after skulls, encircled him and danced round and round, in quick time, leaping into the air. Yet he neither feared their travesty nor looked up at them at all, but as he wrote said: 'Stop your foolery!' So firmly did he believe that souls are nothing after they have gone out of their bodies."

"That," said Eucrates, "amounts to your saying that Democritus, too, was a foolish man, if he really thought so. But I will tell you another incident derived from my own experience, not from hearsay. Perhaps even you, Tychiades, when you have heard it, may be convinced of the truth of the story.

"When I was living in Egypt during my youth (my father had sent me

travelling for the purpose of completing my education), I took it into my head to sail up to Koptos and go from there to the statue of Memnon in order to hear it sound that marvellous salutation to the rising sun. Well, what I heard from it was not a meaningless voice, as in the general experience of common people; Memnon himself actually opened his mouth and delivered me an oracle in seven verses, and if it were not too much of a digression, I would have repeated the very verses for you. But on the voyage up, there chanced to be sailing with us a man from Memphis, one of the scribes of the temple, wonderfully learned, familiar with all the culture of the Egyptians. He was said to have lived underground for twenty-three years in their sanctuaries, learning magic from Isis."

"You mean Pancrates," said Arignotus, "my own teacher, a holy man, clean shaven, in white linen, always deep in thought, speaking imperfect Greek, tall, flat-nosed, with protruding lips and thinnish legs." "That self-same Pancrates," he replied: "and at first I did not know who he was, but when I saw him working all sorts of wonders whenever we anchored the boat, particularly riding on crocodiles and swimming in company with the beasts, while they fawned and wagged their tails, I recognised that he was a holy man, and by degrees, through my friendly behaviour, I became his companion and associate, so that he shared all his secret knowledge with me.

"At last he persuaded me to leave all my servants behind in Memphis and to go with him quite alone, for we should not lack people to wait upon us; and thereafter we got on in that way. But whenever we came to a stopping-place, the man would take either the bar of the door or the broom or even the pestle, put clothes upon it, say a certain spell over it, and make it walk, appearing to everyone else to be a man. It would go off and draw water and buy provisions and prepare meals and in every way deftly serve and wait upon us. Then, when he was through with its services, he would again make the broom a broom or the pestle a pestle by saying another spell over it.

"Though I was very keen to learn this from him, I could not do so, for he was jealous, although most ready to oblige in everything else. But one day I secretly overheard the spell—it was just three syllables—by taking my stand in a dark place. He went off to the square after telling the pestle what it had to do, and on the next day, while he was transacting some business in the square, I took the pestle, dressed it up in the same way, said the syllables over it, and told it to carry water. When it had filled and brought in the jar, I said, 'Stop! don't carry any more water: be a pestle again!' But it would not obey me now: it kept straight on carrying until it filled the house with water for us by pouring it in! At

my wit's end over the thing, for I feared that Pancrates might come back and be angry, as was indeed the case, I took an axe and cut the pestle in two; but each part took a jar and began to carry water, with the result that instead of one servant I had now two. Meanwhile Pancrates appeared on the scene, and comprehending what had happened, turned them into wood again, just as they were before the spell, and then for his own part left me to my own devices without warning, taking himself off out of sight somewhere."

"Then you still know how to turn the pestle into a man?" said Deinomachus. "Yes," said he: "only half way, however, for I cannot bring it back to its original form if it once becomes a water-carrier, but we shall be obliged to let the house be flooded with the water that is poured in!"

"Will you never stop telling such buncombe, old men as you are?" said I. "If you will not, at least for the sake of these lads put your amazing and fearful tales off to some other time, so that they may not be filled up with terrors and strange figments before we realise it. You ought to be easy with them and not accustom them to hear things like this which will abide with them and annoy them their lives long and will make them afraid of every sound by filling them with all sorts of superstition."

"Thank you," said Eucrates, "for putting me in mind of superstition by mentioning it. What is your opinion, Tychiades, about that sort of thing—I mean oracles, prophecies, outcries of men under divine possession, voices heard from inner shrines, or verses uttered by a maiden who foretells the future? Of course you doubt that sort of thing also? For my own part, I say nothing of the fact that I have a holy ring with an image of Apollo Pythius engraved on the seal, and that this Apollo speaks to me: you might think that I was bragging about myself beyond belief. I should like, however, to tell you all what I heard from Amphilochus in Mallus, when the hero conversed with me in broad day and advised me about my affairs, and what I myself saw, and then in due order what I saw at Pergamon and what I heard at Patara.

"When I was on my way home from Egypt I heard that this shrine in Mallus was very famous and very truthful, and that it responded clearly, answering word for word whatever one wrote in his tablet and turned over to the prophet. So I thought that it would be well to give the oracle a trial in passing and ask the god for some advice about the future—"

While Eucrates was still saying these words, since I could see how the business would turn out and that the cock-and-bull story about oracles upon which he was embarking would not be short, I left him sailing from Egypt to Mallus, not choosing to oppose everyone all alone: I was aware, too, that they were put out at my being there to criticise their lies. "I am going away," I said, "to look up Leontichus, for I want to speak to him

about something. As for you, since you do not think that human experiences afford you a sufficient field, go ahead and call in the gods themselves to help you out in your romancing." With that I went out. They were glad to have a free hand, and continued, of course, to feast and to gorge themselves with lies.

There you have it, Philocles! After hearing all that at the house of Eucrates I am going about like a man who has drunk sweet must, with a swollen belly, craving an emetic. I should be glad if I could anywhere buy at a high price a dose of forgetfulness, so that the memory of what I heard may not stay with me and work me some harm. In fact, I think I see apparitions and spirits and Hecates!

PHILOCLES

Your story has had the same enjoyable effect upon me, Tychiades. They say, you know, that not only those who are bitten by mad dogs go mad and fear water, but if a man who has been bitten bites anyone else, his bite has the same effect as the dog's, and the other man has the same fears. It is likely, therefore, that having been bitten yourself by a multitude of lies in the house of Eucrates, you have passed the bite on to me; you have filled my soul so full of spirits!

TYCHIADES

Well, never mind, my dear fellow; we have a powerful antidote to such poisons in truth and in sound reason brought to bear everywhere. As long as we make use of this, none of these empty, foolish lies will disturb our peace.

THE TYRANNICIDE

A man went to the Acropolis to slay the tyrant. He did not find him, but slew his son and left his sword in the body. When the tyrant came and saw his son already dead, he slew himself with the same sword. The man who went up and slew the tyrant's son claims the reward for slaying the tyrant.

Two tyrants, gentlemen of the jury, have been done to death by me in a single day, one already past his prime, the other in the ripeness of his years and in better case to take up wrongdoing in his turn. Yet I have come to claim but one reward for both, as the only tyrant-slayer of all time who has done away with two malefactors at a single blow, killing the son with the sword and the father by means of his affection for his son. The tyrant has paid us a sufficient penalty for what he did, for while he still lived he saw his son, prematurely slain, in the toils of death, and at last (a thing incomparably strange) he himself was constrained to become his own executioner. And his son not only met death at my hands, but even after death assisted me to slay another; for though while he still lived he shared his father's crimes, after his death he slew his father as best he might.

It was I, then, who put an end to the tyranny, and the sword that accomplished everything was mine. But I inverted the order of executions, and made an innovation in the method of putting criminals to death, for I myself destroyed the stronger, the one capable of self-defence, and resigned the old man to my unaided sword.

It was my thought, therefore, that I should get for this a still more generous gift from you, and should receive rewards to match the number of the slain, because I had freed you not only from your present ills, but from your expectation of those that were to come, and had accorded you established liberty, since no successor in wrongdoing had been left alive. But now there is danger that after all these achievements I may come away from you unrewarded and may be the only one to be excluded from the recompense afforded by those laws which I maintained.

My adversary here seems to me to be taking this course, not, as he says, because of his concern for the interests of the state, but because of his grief over the dead men, and in the endeavour to avenge them upon the man who caused their death. On your part, however, gentlemen of

the jury, bear with me for a moment while I recount the history of their tyranny, although you know it well; for then you can appreciate the greatness of my benefaction and you yourselves will be more exultant, thinking of all that you have escaped.

It is not as it has often before been with others; it is not a simple tyranny and a single slavery that we have endured, nor a single master's caprice that we have borne. Nay, of all those who have ever experienced such adversity we alone had two masters instead of one and were torn asunder, unlucky folk! between two sets of wrongs. The elder man was more moderate by far, less acrimonious in his fits of anger, less hasty in his punishments, and less headlong in his desires, because by now his age was staying the excessive violence of his impulses and curbing his appetite for pleasures. It was said, indeed, that he was reluctantly impelled to begin his wrongdoings by his son, since he himself was not at all tyrannical but yielded to the other. For he was excessively devoted to his children, as he has shown, and his son was all the world to him; so he gave way to him, did the wrongs that he bade, punished the men whom he designated, served him in all things, and in a word was tyrannised by him, and was mere minister to his son's desires.

The young man conceded the honour to him by right of age and abstained from the name of sovereignty, but only from that; he was the substance and the mainspring of the tyranny. He gave the government its assurance and security, and he alone reaped the profit of its crimes. It was he who kept their guardsmen together, who maintained their defences in strength, who terrorised their subjects and extirpated conspirators; it was he who plucked lads from their homes, who made a mockery of marriages; it was for him that maids were carried off; and whatever deeds of blood there were, whatever banishments, confiscations of property, applications of torture, and outrages—all these were a young man's emprises. The old man followed him and shared his wrongdoing, and had but praise for his son's misdeeds. So the thing became unendurable to us; for when the desires of the will acquire the licence of sovereignty, they recognise no limit to wrongdoing.

What hurt us most was to know that our slavery would be long, nay unending, that our city would be handed down by succession from despot to despot, and that our folk would be the heritage of villains. To other peoples it is no slight comfort to think, and to tell one another, "But it will stop soon," "But he will die soon, and in a little while we shall be free." In their case, however, there was no such comfort; we saw the successor to the sovereignty already at hand. Therefore not one of the brave men who entertained the same purpose as myself even ventured to make an attempt. Liberty was wholly despaired of, and the tyranny was

thought invincible, because any attempt would be directed against so many.

This, however, did not frighten me; I did not draw back when I estimated the difficulty of the achievement, nor play the coward in the face of danger. Alone, alone, I climbed the hill to front the tyranny that was so strong and many-headed—yet, not alone but with my sword that shared the fray with me and in its turn was tyrant-slayer too. I had my death in prospect, but sought to purchase our common liberty with the shedding of my own blood. I met the first guard-post, routed the guardsmen with no little difficulty, slew whomsoever I encountered, destroyed whatsoever blocked my path. Then I assailed the very forefront of my tasks, the sole strength of the tyranny, the cause of our calamities. I came upon the warden of the citadel, I saw him offer a brave defence and hold out against many wounds; and yet I slew him.

The tyranny, therefore, had at last been overthrown, my undertaking had attained fulfilment, and from that moment we all were free. Only an old man still remained, unarmed, his guards lost, that mighty henchman of his gone, deserted, no longer even worthy of a valiant arm.

Thereupon, gentlemen of the jury, I thus reasoned with myself: "All has gone well for me, everything is accomplished, my success is complete. How shall the survivor be punished? Of me and my right hand he is unworthy, particularly if his slaying were to follow a glorious, daring, valiant deed, dishonouring that other mortal thrust. He must seek a fitting executioner, a change of fate, and not profit by having the same one. Let him behold, suffer his punishment, have the sword lying at hand; I commit the rest to him." This plan formed, I myself withdrew, and he, as I had presaged, carried through with it, slew the tyrant, supplied the ending to my play.

I am here, then, to bring you democracy, to notify all that they may now take heart, and to herald the glad tidings of liberty. Even now you are enjoying the results of my achievements. The acropolis, as you see, is empty of malefactors, and nobody issues orders; you may bestow honours, sit in judgement, and plead your cases in accordance with the laws. All this has come about for you through me and my bold deed, and in consequence of slaying that one man, after which his father could no longer continue in life. Therefore I request that you give me the reward which is my due, not because I am greedy or avaricious, or because it was my purpose to benefit my native land for hire, but because I wish that my achievements should be confirmed by the donative and that my undertaking should escape misrepresentation and loss of glory on the ground that it was not fully executed and has been pronounced unworthy of a reward.

This man, however, opposes my plea, and says that I am acting unreasonably in desiring to be honoured and to receive the gift, since I am not a tyrant-slayer, and have not accomplished anything in the eyes of the law; that my achievement is in some respect insufficient for claiming the reward. I ask him, therefore: "What more do you demand of me? Did I not form the purpose? Did I not climb the hill? Did I not slay? Did I not bring liberty? Does anyone issue orders? Does anyone give commands? Does any lord and master utter threats? Did any of the malefactors escape me? You cannot say so. No, everything is full of peace, we have all our laws, liberty is manifest, democracy is made safe, marriages are free from outrage, boys are free from fear, maidens are secure, and the city is celebrating its common good fortune. Who, then, is responsible for it all? Who stopped all that and caused all this? If there is anyone who deserves to be honoured in preference to me, I yield the guerdon, I resign the gift. But if I alone accomplished it all, making the venture, incurring the risks, going up to the citadel, taking life, inflicting punishment, wreaking vengeance upon them through one another, why do you misrepresent my achievements? Why, pray, do you make the people ungrateful towards me?"

"Because you did not slay the tyrant himself; and the law bestows the reward upon the slayer of a tyrant!" Is there any difference, tell me, between slaying him and causing his death? For my part I think there is none. All that the lawgiver had in view was simply liberty, democracy, freedom from dire ills. He bestowed honour upon this, he considered this worthy of compensation, and you cannot say that it has come about otherwise than through me. For if I caused a death which made it impossible for that man to live, I myself accomplished his slaying. The deed was mine, the hand was his. Then quibble no longer about the manner of his end; do not enquire how he died, but whether he no longer lives, whether his no longer living is due to me. Otherwise, it seems to me that you will be likely to carry your enquiry still further, to the point of carping at your benefactors if one of them should do the killing with a stone or a staff or in some other way, and not with a sword.

What if I had starved the tyrant out of his hold and thus occasioned the necessity of his death? Would you in that case require me to have killed him with my own hand, or say that I failed in any respect of satisfying the law, even though the malefactor had been done to death more cruelly? Enquire into one thing only, demand this alone, disturb yourself about this alone, whether any one of the villains is left, any expectation of fearfulness, any reminder of our woes. If everything is uncontaminated and peaceful, only a cheat would wish to utilise the manner of accomplishing what has been done in order to take away the gratuity for the hard-won results.

I remember, moreover, this statement in the laws (unless, by reason of our protracted slavery, I have forgotten what is said in them), that there are two sorts of responsibility for manslaughter, and if, without taking life himself or doing the deed with his own hand, a man has necessitated and given rise to the killing, the law requires that in this case too he himself receive the same punishment—quite justly, for it was unwilling to be worsted by his deed through his immunity. It would be irrelevant, therefore, to enquire into the manner of the killing.

Can it, then, be that you think fit to punish as a murderer one who has taken life in this manner, and are not willing under any circumstances to acquit him, yet when a man has conferred a boon upon the city in the same way, you do not propose to hold him worthy of the same treatment as your benefactors? For you cannot even say that I did it at haphazard, and that a result followed which chanced to be beneficial, without my having intended it. What else did I fear after the stronger was slain, and why did I leave the sword in my victim if I did not absolutely prefigure exactly what would come to pass! You have no answer, unless you maintain that the dead man was not a tyrant and did not have that name; and that the city would not have been glad to make many presents on his account if he should lose his life. But you cannot say so.

Can it be that, now the tyrant has been slain, you are going to refuse the reward to the man who caused his death? What pettiness! Does it concern you how he died, as long as you enjoy your liberty? Do you demand any greater boon of the man who gave back your democracy? "But the law," you say, "scrutinises only the main point in the facts of the case, ignoring all the incidentals and raising no further question!" What! was there not once a man who obtained the guerdon of a tyrannicide by just driving a tyrant into exile? Quite rightly, too; for he bestowed liberty in exchange for slavery. But what I have wrought is not exile, or expectation of a second uprising, but complete abolition, extinction of the entire line, extirpation, root and branch, of the whole menace.

Do, in the name of the gods, make a full enquiry, if you like, from beginning to end, and see whether anything that affects the law has been left undone, and whether any qualification is wanting that a tyrant-slayer ought to have. In the first place, one must have at the outset a will that is valiant, patriotic, disposed to run risks for the common weal, and ready to purchase by its own extinction the deliverance of the people. Then did I fall short of that, play the weakling, or, my purpose formed, shrink from any of the risks that lay ahead? You cannot say so. Then confine your attention for a moment to this point, and imagine that simply on account of my willing and planning all this, even if the result had not been favourable, I presented myself and demanded that in

consequence of the intention itself I should receive a guerdon as a benefactor. Because I myself had not the power and someone else, coming after me, had slain the tyrant, would it be unreasonable, tell me, or absurd to give it me? Above all, if I said: "Gentlemen, I wanted it, willed it, undertook it, essayed it; simply for my intention I deserve to be honoured," what answer would you have made in that case?

But as things are, that is not what I say; no, I climbed the acropolis, I put myself in peril, I accomplished untold labours before I slew the young man. For you must not suppose that the affair was so easy and simple—to pass a guard, to overpower men-at-arms, to rout so many by myself; no, this is quite the mightiest obstacle in the slaying of a tyrant, and the principal of its achievements. For of course it is not the tyrant himself that is mighty and impregnable and indomitable, but what guards and maintains his tyranny; if anyone conquers all this, he has attained complete success, and what remains is trivial. Of course the approach to the tyrants would not have been open to me if I had not overpowered all the guards and henchmen about them, conquering all these to begin with. I add nothing further, but once more confine myself to this point: I overpowered the outposts, conquered the bodyguards, rendered the tyrant unprotected, unarmed, defenceless. Does it seem to you that I deserve honour for that, or do you further demand of me the shedding of his blood?

But even if you require bloodshed, that is not wanting either, and I am not unstained with blood; on the contrary, I have done a great and valiant deed in that I slew a young man in the fullness of his strength, terrible to all, through whom that other was unassailed by plots, on whom alone he relied, who sufficed him instead of many guardsmen. Then am I not deserving of a reward, man? Am I to be devoid of honours for such deeds? What if I had killed a bodyguard, or some henchman of the tyrant, or a valued slave? Would not even this have seemed a great thing, to go up and slay one of the tyrant's friends in the midst of the citadel, in the midst of arms? But as it is, look at the slain man himself! He was a tyrant's son, nay more, a harsher tyrant, an inexorable despot, a more cruel chastiser, a more violent oppressor; what is most important, he was heir and successor to everything, and capable of prolonging vastly the duration of our misery.

Suppose, if you will, that this was my sole achievement—that the tyrant has made his escape and is still alive. Well and good, I demand a guerdon for this. What do you all say? Will you not vouchsafe it? Did you not view the son, too, with concern? Was he not a despot? Was he not cruel, unendurable?

As it is, however, think of the crowning feat itself. What this man requires of me I accomplished in the best possible way. I killed the tyrant

by killing someone else, not directly nor at a single blow, which would have been his fondest prayer after misdeeds so monstrous. No, first I tortured him with profound grief, displayed full in his view all that was dearest to him lying exposed in pitiable case, a son in his youth, wicked, to be sure, but in the fullness of his strength and the image of his sire, befouled with blood and gore. Those are the wounds of fathers, those the swords of tyrannicides who deal justly, that is the death deserved by savage tyrants, that the requital befitting misdeeds so great. To die forthwith, to know nothing, to see no such spectacle has in it nothing worthy of a tyrant's punishment.

For I was not unaware, man—I was not unaware, nor was anyone else, how much love he had for his son, and that he would not have wanted to outlive him even a little while. To be sure, all fathers no doubt have such feelings toward their children; but in his case there was something more than in the case of others; naturally, for he discerned that it was his son who alone cherished and guarded the tyranny, who alone faced danger in his father's stead, and gave security to his rule. Consequently I knew that he would lay down his life at once, if not through his love, then at all events through his despair, considering that there was no profit in life now that the security derived from his son had been abolished. I encompassed him, therefore, with all manner of toils at once—his nature, his grief, his despair, his misgivings about the future; I used these allies against him, and forced him to that final decision. He has gone to his death childless, grief-stricken, in sorrow and in tears, after mourning but a little while, it is true, yet long enough for a father; gone (and that is most horrible) by his own hand, the most pitiable of deaths, far more bitter than as if it should come about at the hand of another.

Where is my sword? Does anyone else recognise this? Was this any other man's weapon? Who carried it up to the citadel? Who preceded the tyrant in its use? Who commissioned it against him? Good sword, partner and promoter of my successes, after so many perils, after so many slayings, we are disregarded and thought unworthy of a reward! If it were for the sword alone that I sought the meed of honour from you—if I were pleading: "Gentlemen, when the tyrant wished to die and at the moment found himself unarmed, this sword of mine served him and did its part in every way towards the attainment of liberty—account it worthy of honour and reward," would you not have requited the owner of a possession so valuable to the state? Would you not have recorded him among your benefactors? Would you not have enshrined the sword among your hallowed treasures? Would you not have worshipped it along with the gods?

Now then, imagine, I beg you, what the tyrant no doubt did and what

he said before his end. When I sought to slay the son and wounded him again and again in those parts of his body which could be seen, that so I might grieve the parent most, that so I might rend his heart through the first sight, he raised a doleful cry, calling his parent to him, not to aid him or share the conflict—for he knew him to be old and weak—but to behold his own calamities. Before I slipped away, I had myself composed the whole plot of the tragedy, but had left to the actor the body, the stage-setting, the sword, and the remainder of the play. When the other made his appearance and saw his only son with but little breath in him, bloodied, covered with gore, his wounds close together, numerous, and vital, he raised this cry: "My child, we are destroyed, assassinated, fallen victims to the tyrant-slayer! Where is the executioner? For what purpose is he keeping me, for what purpose reserving me, now that I am already destroyed through you, my child? Or is it perhaps that he contemns me as an old man, and also by his dilatoriness (since I must be punished) protracts my death and makes my execution longer?"

With these words he sought a sword; for he was unarmed on account of his complete reliance upon his son. But that too was not wanting; long beforehand, that too had been provided by me and left behind for the bold deed that was to come. So, withdrawing the sword from the victim, plucking it from the wound, he said: "A little while ago you gave me death; now give me repose, O sword. Come to console a mourning father; lighten the task of an aged hand beset by adversity; let my blood; be tyrant-slayer to me; quit me of my woe. Had I but encountered you first! had I but inverted the order of deaths! I should have perished; but simply as tyrant—but thinking still that I should have an avenger, while now I die as one who is childless, as one who can hardly so much as find a man to take his life!" Thereupon he hastened his despatch, trembling, incapable, craving it, to be sure, but lacking the strength to serve his bold purpose.

How many punishments were there in all this? How many wounds? How many deaths? How many tyrant-slayings? How many rewards? And at the end you have all seen not only the young man exposed in death (no slight accomplishment or easy to achieve), but the old man prostrate upon him, you have seen the blood of both intermingled (that thank-offering for liberty and for victory), and the havoc of my sword; aye, the sword itself between them both, evincing that it has not been unworthy of its owner and testifying that it served me faithfully. Had this been done by me, it would be less of an achievement; but now it is more splendid by reason of its novelty. It is I, to be sure, who overthrew the entire tyranny; but the performance has been distributed among many people as in a play; the leading part was played by me, the second by the son, the third by the tyrant himself, and the sword served all.

INDEX

INDEX